DANCE A WHILE

Handbook of
FOLK, SQUARE, and
SOCIAL DANCE

FOURTH EDITION

by

JANE A. HARRIS
Department of Physical Education
Washington State University
Pullman, Washington

ANNE PITTMAN
Department of Health, Physical Education
and Recreation
Arizona State University
Tempe, Arizona

MARLYS S. WALLER
Formerly of School of
Physical and Health Education
University of Washington
Seattle, Washington

Burgess Publishing Company

426 South Sixth Street • Minneapolis, Minn. 55415

FOREWORD

In 1947, I met three exuberant young teachers at the University of Texas. I was impressed by their enthusiasm and the interest they generated in the University community and throughout Texas in dance focus they taught. Three years later the first edition of *Dance A While* was published. It was a good book: it was helpful to teachers, it was clear, and it reflected the exuberance of the young people who had written it.

Now, some 18 years later, *Dance A While* appears in a new size and format, updated in bibliography and record list, and extended in the social dance area. It is even more attractive and more usable than in previous editions. The growth of this text in breadth and depth in successive editions has reflected the continuing interest and increasing maturity of the authors.

These three authors have made a contribution over and beyond the immediate circle of their own teaching. Through this teaching aid, they have been able to provide for the rest of us, not only the *how* of dance form, but also the understanding of the background and the variations of individual dances as well as a warm and humanistic approach to the nature of learning.

It is my hope that many new teachers will find in this fourth edition, the quality of enthusiasm and the expressive-communicative aspects of the folk and social dances of our time.

RUTH ABERNATHY

University of Washington
Seattle, Washington

May 3, 1968

i

PREFACE

The overall purpose behind *Dance A While* has been to provide under one cover a comprehensive coverage of dance forms as represented by the areas culturally designated in the United States as square dance, folk dance, and social dance. The continuous purpose which prompts each new edition is the desire to include the best of contemporary materials, yet preserve those dance forms which have become traditional.

Specifically, *Dance A While* provides the teacher and recreation leader with a practical basis for evaluating each teacher-learning situation for effective selection of dance materials to meet the needs which exist within and among groups. In addition, *Dance A While* provides creative suggestions for enriching the dance experience through the use of costumes, music, community resources, and planned integration with other subjects.

In each edition we have selected additional dances because the elements contained in each, e.g. basic step, formation, and nationality background, provide better balance of coverage for that particular section. Dance selection has never depended upon *fads* as a criteria for inclusion.

The dance materials appearing in *Dance A While* depend upon the use of available recordings. One of the chief purposes of this addition was to update record sources and to indicate those records which are out of print. We feel it is important to include the out of print records in the listing for each dance because a majority of schools and colleges still have these records in their collections.

The majority of dances presented are also available in other references. Bibliographical references noted with each dance or the extensive bibliographical listing in the back of the book will increase the reader's familiarity with dance literature of any one or all sections. The bibliography includes books, magazines, record references and other source materials. In addition, a comprehensive glossary serves to define and clarify the terminology of dance.

We hope that *Dance A While* will continue to be a happy, handy source of usable materials for all who wish to dance and to sustain the joy of participation in dance.

JANE HARRIS ERICSON
ANNE PITTMAN
MARLYS SWENSON WALLER

ACKNOWLEDGMENTS

The authors wish to express their sincere appreciation to the Departments of Physical Education at Arizona State University, Washington State University and the University of Washington, for their encouragement and enthusiastic support of the third edition of *Dance A While*. We are especially grateful to Miss Ruth Wilson, Chairman of the Department of Physical Education for Women, University of Washington, for the sharing of her research in background materials on foreign countries; to Lawton Harris, Stockton, California, for his assistance with details; the teachers and leaders who have generously consented to the use of their material (those names appear on the page where the material is used); the anonymous teachers and leaders who have passed their material along and made it available to all; and the friends that have assisted in the production of *Dance A While*. The Aqua Record Company, Seattle, Washington; The Record Center, Chicago, Illinois; and The Folk Dance Record Service, New York City, New York, gave considerable assistance in bringing the records listed up to date.

The authors wish to thank Ralph Page for contributing the chapter on Contra Dance. His historical description of the Contra Dance is informative and pleasant reading as well as a thorough coverage of Contra Dance history. The Contra Dance chapter enables *Dance A While* to reflect more truly the current American folk dance scene. Grateful appreciation is expressed to Keith Hoffnogle for his cooperation and creative efforts in the art work for the entire book.

Appreciation is expressed to many of the country's leading Folk and Square Dance teachers with whom the authors have been privileged to work and study. The opportunity and experience afforded by such leaders as Herb and Pauline Greggerson, Ranch Dance School, Ruidoso, New Mexico; the late Dr. Lloyd Shaw, Cheyenne Mountain School, Colorado Springs, Colorado; Jane Farwell Hinrichs, Germany; Mary Ann and Michael Herman, Folk Dance House, New York City, New York; Ralph Page, Keene, New Hampshire; Dvora Lapson, Director of Jewish Dance Education, New York City, New York; Gretal and Paul Dunsing, Chicago, Illinois; Gordon E. Tracie, Seattle, Washington; Henry "Buzz" Glass, Oakland, California; and Bob Osgood, Los Angeles, California, has been an invaluable aid to the authors.

The authors wish to thank the Folk Dance Federation of California for permission to use the copyrighted dance annotation form popularized in their books, *Folk Dances From Near and Far*, and in their monthly magazine, *Let's Dance!*

A special thanks is due to the families of the authors who have made it possible to be creative and productive in the writing of the third edition. The warm smiles, the helping hands, the re-arrangement of schedules, and blessings have sped the authors merrily on their way.

Jane Harris Ericson
Anne Pittman
Marlys Swenson Waller

TABLE OF CONTENTS

NOTES ON THE DANCE

THE BEGINNING

Rhythm, both external and internal, is the well spring from which dance and its twin sister, music, arise. Externally, nature and man's daily activities provide us with innumerable examples of the rhythm patterns to which we all respond. The ebb and flow of the tide, the revolving seasons, and the seemingly inevitability of day and night are never ceasing reminders of this rhythm. Daily pursuits requiring motor skills in work and play, when performed efficiently, are rhythmic. Swinging a tennis racquet, wielding a hammer, or pitching a curved ball require a rhythm response.

Man's physical and mental processes — the heart beat, pulmonary action, and the rhythmic patterns of things seen and heard stored in the mind — are constant internal rhythmic sources. Thus sheer physical exuberance in response to the environment and the physiological rhythms essential to life, perhaps, provide enough evidence to establish man as a rhythmic being. When these inner rhythms are overtly synchronized in movement and gesture with the thousands of patterned sounds of nature, man — the mimic — begins to dance.

Precise knowledge about how and why man first danced will never be known. However, through the study of primitive dance forms which still exist, we have learned that man, both ancient and contemporary, employed dance ritual for all major events of life; chief among these were courtship, communication, and religion.

Dance as a mode of communication served man in two ways; first, as a means of evoking the blessings and appeasing the anger of the supernatural, and, second, as a way of formulating and exchanging feelings and thoughts on a non-verbal level, man to man. In discussing the communication between man and the supernatural evident in the mimetic dances of the Australian aborigines, Waterman reports:

> Commonly, the dances are re-enactments of episodes in the sacred myths — those narratives that serve as a supernatural charter and guidebook for religious belief, social organization, and most aspects of life in nonliterate societies. The sacred dances illustrated the myth, making it seem more comprehensible, in much the same way that graphic illustrations are sometimes used to make Bible stories seem more real. And if, as the proverb claims, "a good picture is worth five thousand words," a good ritual dance must be worth a hundred thousand.[1]

Prior to the development of a faculty for verbal expression, it is quite possible that man used dance ritual to communicate feelings, thoughts, and meanings to his fellow man. Waterman states:

> The humor, pathos, fear, and many other effective "messages" are transmitted by patterned bodily movement and received emphatically by the beholder. This process, particularly as it applies to the "social dances," is extremely important both in stirring up group emotions, as in the case of a war dance, and in maintaining group morale by supporting with recreational dances what might be called the "euphoria level" of the society. Such as the nature and the efficacy of the sublinguistic communication system afforded by the dance that it has been seriously postulated that dance may have been the first method of communication used in and

[1] Waterman, Richard A. "Role of Dance In Human Society", *Focus on Dance II*: An Interdisciplinary Search for Meaning in Movement. Edited by Bettie Jean Wooten. Washington, D.C.: National Section on Dance, American Association for Health, Physical Education and Recreation. 1962. p. 47.

among human groups, prior and ancestral to spoken language. Be this as it may, the importance of dance as communication in all human societies, at the present day, can hardly be denied.[2]

Perhaps it is the universality of these major life events that gives rise to the similarity in dance movements found in practically every culture throughout the world.

As civilization developed, the rhythmic movements and gestures representing man's early dance expressions became more complex and specialized. Dance in the Western world evolved along two rather distinct levels. Dances which concerned the mysteries and magic of life and death were developed for mass instructional purposes and

became more complex in movement and meaning, thus requiring special performers for execution. Dances on this level were largely religious in nature and purpose and were generally performed as public spectacles or ceremonies.

The second level of dance belonged to the people and was made up of folk or communal dances. These dances, social by the very fact that they arose from the sheer joy and eternal desire to move rhythmically, survived even the widespread disapproval of the early Christian Church. Despite disapproval in one form or another throughout history, folk dance, the dance of the people, has continued to play an important part in the lives of all men in every era.

INFLUENCES ON DANCE

There are ample records in literature, history, and in general descriptions of the day to indicate the sources, development, and contribution of folk arts from the sixteenth century to the present day.[3] Due to what may be termed the "folk process" it is not always easy or possible to trace the evolution or to determine the original purpose of a given dance.

As this term indicates, folk dance is dynamic, not static. This dynamic quality gives rise to ever recurring arguments centering around authenticity and change. Richard Kraus of Columbia University points out that:

Obviously, since there often are different versions of the same dance (as performed in different regions or by different groups), the word "authentic" has only relative meaning. To use it to describe a dance may mean that the dance was once done in a given time and place in this way, and was so recorded for posterity. It may mean that, in the judgment of an expert, the dance is clearly typical in form and style of a given nationality, or that the version presented has been widely observed in the present day. It

may also imply that this is the version taught by a respected national authority, or shown by an exhibition group with a good reputation for traditional performance.[4]

Despite the increase, since the sixteenth century, in descriptive recording of folk forms, the "folk process" continues to be highly non-verbal and this dynamic quality continues to move these forms up the scale to enrich all dance and to keep a relationship to folk dance constantly renewed. The many influences inflected upon dance by the folk process are mirrored by the dance itself. Chief among these influences, as reflected in the style and pattern of the dances are: climate, geography, costume, nature and character of the people, music, and any characteristic of the period.

The purpose of a dance may reflect a people's likeness in the areas of religion, occupation, celebration of seasons, war, courtship, weddings, and funerals. The English Maypole dance, for example, had its beginnings as a pagan dance of fertility. Further, the gyrations of the Italian Tarantella were intended as curative measures against the bites of a large hair spider.

---

2 Waterman. *Op. cit.,* p. 48.

3 Ashton, Dudley. "Contributions of Dance to Physical Education." *Journal of Health, Physical Education and Recreation.* Vol. 27, No. 4, April, 1956. p. 19.

4 Kraus, Richard G. *Folk Dancing: A Guide for Schools, Colleges, and Recreation Groups.* New York: The Macmillan Company, 1962. p. 7.

Claudia Chapline writes of a religious dance which purposed to protect the Church from the outer world:

> The ancient Hebrews danced their prayer and praise and were instructed in the Old Testament to "Praise Him with the timbrel and dance" (Psalm 150). The earliest Christian ritual, the "Hymn of Jesus," as described in the apocryphal Acts of John, written about A.D. 120, was a sacred dance in which the Apostles, joining hands, circled slowly around Christ singing a hymn. This mystic circle was used as a symbol for the protection of the Church from the outer world. Ecclesiastical dancing survived in modified form as late as the 17th century in France and to the present day in Spain.[5]

The original purpose of many dances was to transmit to the youth occupational skill, attitude, or custom that could not be expressed in speech or writing. Many of these traditional mimetic occupational dances remain in the literature today and are used primarily in the elementary grades. Ashton writes:

> The guilds (during the middle ages) wielded control over both the work and the recreation of their members. Traditional mimetic occupational dances belonging to specific trades were jealously guarded and taught only to their members. The Sword Dance of both Sweden and Norway, ... has been accredited to the Guild of Metalworkers. Clothmakers had elaborate dances depicting the processes involved in their trade. The shoemakers, butchers, tailors, bakers, fishermen, coopers, coppersmiths, and furriers each had dances identified with the members but varying slightly from country to country.... At the great guild festivals, these dances were performed. Passed from guild member to guild member, they were one means of preserving folk customs.[6]

The climate of a country or an area affects the quality of the dance movement. The movements in countries with colder climates tend to be very vigorous and involve a great deal of stamping; in the hot, humid climates the movements tend to flow and appear effortless. The tempo of a dance, however, is not necessarily influenced by the climate since climates vary; more often, it is the purpose of the dance which determines the tempo.

The role which geography plays in influencing dance is both interesting and significant. People who live in the mountains, by necessity, dance in a very small space. The style of movement is influenced by the actual ground upon which they dance. Mountains, as physical features, have served to preserve folk dances in their original form; plains, rivers, and valleys, as physical features, are more favorable to interchange of dances. The following quote from Ashton serves to illustrate the influence of the character of the people and the geography:

> The location of the Mediterranean population on the three great southern peninsulas — the Italian, the Iberian, and the Balkan — is an important factor in their early dance forms. The sea acted both as a barrier for exchange of ideas and as a means of contact.... The peasant culture is static and so are the dance forms; they have changed very little through hundreds of years.[7]

Costume is determined by two basic factors, climate and geography. A costume is utilitarian in purpose; essentially it serves to protect the body from the elements and to suit the life and work of the owner. Furthermore, as individuals and groups become more sophisticated, costumes serve to indicate status, prestige, and wealth. Costumes have an interesting and often unique effect upon the characteristic dance movements exhibited by the wearers.

The style and range of dance movement may be unlimited or highly restricted depending upon the material and cut of the foot wear, skirt, trousers, coat, jacket, or head gear worn by the dancer. Contrast, for example, the unlimited freedom and balance exhibited by the barefoot dancer of Southeastern Asia with the flat, plodding, foot

---

[5] Chapline, Claudia. "Dance and Religion." *Journal of Health, Physical Education, and Recreation.* Vol. 28, No. 8, November 1957. p. 39.
[6] Ashton. *Op. Cit.,* p. 20.
[7] Ashton. *Op. Cit.,* p. 19.

action produced by the inflexibility of the heavy nailed boot used in the Austrian laendler. The role articles of attire play in forming dance movement is an important element in studying the style and background of the dance.[8]

Music, the twin sister of dance, is intimately related to movement in dance. Although the step pattern for a German, Danish, or Russian waltz or polka can be the same, in reality, there are marked differences as performed by these as well as other national groups. These differences are largely due to the characteristic features of the music of a particular group of people. It is predominantly music which reveals the often subtle differences in the performance of an otherwise commonly shared step pattern. Further, it is music which gives to a common step pattern the unique characteristics inherent in a group's cultural background.

Lawson writes:

Folk dances begin when movements performed together are co-ordinated by common rhythms and sounds. From these rhythms and sounds develop a people's music and language. Therefore wherever the intimate relationship of movement, music, and language has been retained, the dance represents a national style.[9]

There is ample evidence of mutual exchange of ideas and influence between the dancing masters in the courts of the aristocracy and the peasants. The primary effect upon folk dance was to refine it and make it more polite in terms of court customs and behavior, and, depending upon the era and prestige of a peculiar court, to spread dancing which incorporated folk forms to other European Courts. Joan Lawson points out in *European Folk Dance*, "As each court took turn in outshining the others, so its particular fashions dominated the world."[10]

DEFINITION OF TERMS

The term *social dance* has been variously used to mean all dances designed to bring people together for group participation and enjoyment and in the twentieth century to refer to a specific type, namely, ballroom dance. Under the broader use of the term, all dance when carried on for purposes of group participation and sociability may be referred to as social dance.

Folk Dance, as its name implies, is the traditional dance of a people within a specific culture, evolved by them and embodying a national or regional flavor characteristic of them. Folk dance is communal in purpose and unique in that it is predicated upon the principle of group participation. The movements used and skill required in a specific folk dance, although often complex, are well within the grasp of the average layman.

All of the dance areas presented in *Dance A While* are communal by nature and by purpose intended to facilitate group participation; thus all of these dances may rightfully be termed social dance. However, a more definitive analysis of the term social dance reveals that it identifies the nature and purpose of these dances while the term folk dance identifies the source of the dances. Neither term is wholly desirable since each contributes only fragments to the whole concept of the dance forms which represent this area. However, by vent of tradition and use, a choice can and has been made between the two terms. The term folk dance is most preferred since it more clearly distinguishes the total area of dance forms, belonging to and springing from the people, from ancient and contemporary dance forms which are cloistered by highly skilled groups who create, choreograph, and direct dances chiefly for performance purposes; ballet and modern dance are two examples of the latter. Therefore, all dance areas presented may be traditionally and rightfully classified as folk dance, including modern ballroom

[8] For a more comprehensive discussion of the Development and Influence on dance read *European Folk Dance* by Joan Lawson, p. 35-46, reference in bibliography, 70 (p. 379).

[9] Reference in bibliography: 70 (p. 52).

[10] Lawson. *Op. Cit.,* p. 15.

dance which is an outgrowth of folk dance. Again, where logic and precision cease, tradition and common usage come to the rescue! Common usage has been that the terms Social Dance and Ballroom Dance are acceptably synonymous. In view of this, and because of the current preference for the term, *Social Dance* will be used to designate this member of the folk dance family.

The material in *Dance A While* represents six of the principal subtypes within the overall family of folk dance; they are: Western Square Dance, Contra Dance, Round Dance, International Folk Dance, Social Dance, and Mixers and Icebreakers. The general term *Folk and Square Dance* is used quite widely in America since in our idiom *Folk Dance* commonly refers to American Round and European or International Dance while the term *Square Dance* is, happily, seldom misappropriated to represent any other dance form. *American Folk Dance*, as a term, is appropriate and quite proper in referring to square and round dance in America; however, at the present time, at least, the term *Folk and Square Dance* is far more widely used and understood.

FOLK DANCE IN AMERICA

Roots . . . Folk dance along with other elements of culture brought to America by people from many nations has been diffused into our great democratic melting pot and become a colorful thread in our national life. For this reason it would be rather difficult to isolate any dance and identify its origin as purely American. The Fox Trot and dances of the American Indian are perhaps two exceptions. In addition to the diversity which characterized its inception, folk dance in America remains noticeably provincial. Folk dance, as a cultural heritage and expression, is fashioned and influenced by many and diverse forces. Speech, dress, manners, religion, locale, and characteristics of the people in various parts of America give it identifiable regional preference and flavor. Thus certain forms are associated with or considered to be typical of particular regions. Regional differences are reflected perhaps more widely in square dance than in any other type. Play party games illustrate regional preference where religious beliefs frown upon dance generally.

Types . . . The American folk dance scene is characterized by active and enthusiastic interest in five major types of dance: Play Party Games, Round Dances, Square Dances, Contra and Circle Dances, and Social Dance. The primary sources from which these types developed are dances brought by immigrants, that is, ethnic dances which are performed by nationality groups, especially in urban areas; composed dances which have been set to the traditional pattern, style, and music of a particular country, such as the Weggis Dance and Blue Pacific; and dances that originate in America but have roots which may be traced to other countries, such as the square and round dance.

Purpose . . . The communal nature coupled with the fact that folk dance is uniquely predicated upon group participation makes it the most social form of dance. Folk dance in America serves as one of the most popular leisure pursuits. As a culturally rich interest area, it offers its many enthusiastic adherents the very rare opportunity to combine joy in rhythmic movement, fun, and group fellowship with the need, in the twentieth century, to engender appreciation of the national and racial backgrounds of fellow citizens in the local and world community. However, it is well to remember that joy in rhythmic movement, fun, and fellowship are and have been the primary purposes. That knowledge and understanding accrue in such a pleasant setting is not a happy accident but rather a rare and invaluable reality. The exploitation of either purpose at the expense of the other would be unfortunate. In reference to the study of international and intercultural understanding through folk dance, Sauthoff cautions:

Rather careless thinking is evident. It has already been shown that without similar culture backgrounds, the dance cannot possibly convey the meaning it

*was meant to have, either to the perform-
er or to the spectator.[11]*

Despite this cultural gap it is possible to
become empathic through the media of
music, rhythm, and movement. Folk dance
best serves human relations and increases
awareness of likes not differences.

Growth . . . The status presently enjoyed by
the folk dance movement in America may
well be credited to one individual in particular and one group primarily. The individual, Elizabeth Burchenal, introduced folk
dance into the physical education programs
of New York in 1905. The group, physical
educators in New York and throughout the
land, who recognized its educational value,
persisted, often regardless of current carry-
over value, in keeping it in the curriculum.

The folk dance movement has literally
exploded from this modest beginning under
academic stewardship into a leisure activity of nation-wide interest and import. Indices of growth and national importance as
a leisure pursuit include: 1. establishment
of local, state, regional, and national organizations solely devoted to the promotion of a
particular dance form; 2. publication of periodicals and related literature such as books,
instructional pamphlets devoted to dissemi-
nation of materials and information of common interest; 3. production of a visible variety of commercial products specifically
directed at this market, such as musical
recordings, articles of clothing, novelties
and gadgets of all kinds; 4. mass participa-
tion-spectator events, such as festivals,
jamborees, workshops, and conventions;
5. specialization in terms of instructors,
classes, and institutes requiring the full-
time attention of professional specialists.
The two most evident results of the growth
and maturation of this movement are the
acceptance of folk dance as an adult form
of recreation and the recognition of it as a
living form of folk art.

In addition to the role public education
has played in preserving folk dance, due
notice should also be given to the contributions made by the many ethnic groups who
have retained active interest in their particular dance forms and customs. These
groups, found in urban and rural sections
of America, have generously shared their
dance heritage with their fellow Americans
and thus added immeasurably to the diversity and color so typical of American life.
The diverse cultural background in America
affords students of the dance a rare opportunity to study folk dance in groups in
which they are indigenous.

Sauthoff notes the need for urgency by
cautioning:

*Inevitably these folk dances will be lost
as the second and third generation de-
scendants become more concerned with
the cultural forms they make for themselves out of new experiences and the
country in which they have their rightful
birth.[12]*

So far the roles and unique contributions
made to the folk dance movement by key
individuals and groups and the important
indices of growth have been noted. Although
these are interesting and important considerations, two basic questions concerning
growth remain to be answered. Why should
this relatively quiet and predominantly rural
form of recreation be suddenly caught up in
the mass mania of urban living? Why should
an activity traditionally used to celebrate
an occasional wedding, holiday, or seasonal
event explode into such popularity that it
should require special clothes, training and
be avidly pursued four or five evenings a
week. In the absence of answers provided
by specifically designed research, we must
rely upon empirically derived explanations.
Thus, two explanations, one the result of
social forces and one the result of techno-
logical progress, seem plausible.

The population shift from rural to urban
areas resulted in the restriction of acquaint-
ances to the smaller primary group, the
family. Thus people began to seek extended
friendships by affiliating with community
social agencies, such as Y.M.C.A., Y.W.C.A.,
churches, etc. Leadership in these agencies,
in turn, was pressed to seek techniques and
devices for promoting greater socialization
among its membership. This search led to

---

11 Sauthoff, Hermine. "Folk Dance: An Expression of Culture." *Journal of Health, Physical Education,
and Recreation.* Vol. 10, No. 7, September 1939, p. 390.
12 Sauthoff. *Op. Cit.,* p. 390.

assigning high priority to activities which required group action and frequent change of partners. Folk dance, widely considered to be the most social form of dance, provided a logical solution.

A similar shift of population occurs during national crises. Perhaps more properly described as population displacement, the shift, for example, during World War II, gave rise to a great need for social devices and techniques which provided means by which groups and individuals suddenly removed from their normal social setting could find companionship and good fellowship. Folk dance, again, proved to be a unique medium for engendering a friendly, wholesome, and mutually interesting group climate for socialization.

By vent of these social forces, thousands were introduced, charmed, and intrigued by folk dance in one form or another. In addition, widespread use of folk dance provided the training ground for leadership. Thus emerged the public and the leadership necessary to provide the impetus for the rapid growth of the folk dance movement.

It is quite common in the twentieth century to find advances in science and technology to be causal factors in the growth and development of most endeavors. So it is in dance and particularly so in folk dance. The improvement in technical quality of recording sound, increased durability of records, and the widespread availability of records closely parallels the general growth, widespread interest, and participation in folk dance. Czarnowski[13] declares that, "the greatest single factor in expansion of folk dance is availability of excellent recordings of traditional music played on native instruments." Recorded music, vocal instructions, single flip side recordings have enormously increased the participation in folk dance. The availability of records makes it possible to carry on extensive programs in the public schools. Family rec room parties, regular club programs, church, camps, and youth agencies depend upon records as a primary source of leadership in program-

ming. Thus technology has contributed immeasurably to the growth and development of folk dance.

Without a doubt, this formerly gentle and occasionally enjoyed form of dance has become an avidly pursued hobby to thousands of Americans, and, as a consequence, has become highly specialized. Specializing in a hobby is not a phenomenon unique to folk dance. There is a rather obvious evidence in American culture to support the generalization that it is relatively typical for Americans to succumb to the latest fad and to literally ride their favorite hobby to death. As a result the question arises, can the movement continue to expand if the dancer with average skill needs to acquire special training in order to participate even occasionally? Armstrong[14] asks an equally important question, "Is it progress to limit a natural mass participation activity by the necessity for extensive and continual training?"

Although these consequences resulting from specialization in a hobby are of concern to the movement in general, hobbyists have contributed greatly to the popularity of folk dance through public performances and exhibitions, thus introducing the non-participating public to the dance. In addition, it has been the avid interest of the hobbyist which has been instrumental in raising the general level of dance skill.

Trends . . . Even a cursory view of the folk dance movement reveals a number of *trends* holding great promise as well as a number which are of a more heuristic nature. For a more coherent consideration, trends will be arranged topically according to their relevance. The three topics are: the folk dance movement inclusively, folk dance in the community, and folk dance in formal education.

The *folk dance movement* has progressed from a mass activity to a more exclusive and casual small group activity. This is chiefly an environmental trend. The disappearance of mass group dancing typical of the early 1940's and 50's, in all dance areas, has often

[13] Czarnowski, Lucile. "Folk Dance in Education" *Focus on Dance — I 1960.* Gertrude Lippincott, Editor, National Section on Dance. American Association for Health, Physical Education and Recreation, Washington 6, D.C. p. 6-7.

[14] *Ibid.,* Armstrong, Don. "Square Dance Today." p. 19.

been taken as an indication of a decline in interest. On the contrary, in social dance the "big band, big ballroom," era has merely changed environment. We now find increased interest in professional studio dancing, exclusive clubs, and informal game room gatherings in the home dancing to recorded music. In like manner square and round dancing is centered in the more exclusive, highly skilled club groups, and has become the "focus for fun" of many game room gatherings in the home.

The use of the term "exclusive" perhaps refers more to the necessity for a higher skill level as a prerequisite for club membership rather than to selection in terms of social preference. There is empirical if not actual research evidence, however, that the more recent small group setting is, in fact, highly selective in terms of social preference. The heuristic possibilities inherent in this observed trend should provide a rather fruitful area of investigation for the student of dance.

The mass-to-small group activity trend has been perhaps less typical of International Folk Dance. Somewhat in reverse direction, it has moved from the village green to the civic auditorium. International Folk Dance, by its very nature, has always required a higher degree of skill. Increased mass participation has not decreased the emphasis upon the small group club activity. On the contrary, the mass activity in this form of dance is actually an outgrowth of a highly developed club network which through local, state, and regional federation has combined to produce mass spectacles. These spectacles have served to increase public spectator interest, to raise the general level of skill, to increase the dancer's and the public's knowledge of the background of dances, and to increase the common repertory of dances known in a given geographical area.

The practice of sharing both the work and reward of *leadership* from within a group has practically ceased. Program planning, direction, and teaching are largely conducted by either local full time professionals engaged to conduct each meeting or by individuals or couples who have specialized in a particular form of dance as a hobby and

have given of their time generously and enthusiastically. Traditionally, instruction in Social Dance has been of a specialized professional character and dispensed on a commercial basis through dance studios. This has not been the pattern, especially in the early stages, of Square and Round dance. Leadership in Square and Round dance has come largely from the enthusiastic amateur, volunteer, or, in some instances, a professionally trained physical education teacher specially trained and interested in this area. International Folk Dance leadership has generally been developed from within the dance area. Early leadership came from ethnic groups whose knowledge and skill were traditionally, if not formally, developed. This area of dance, as compared to Square and Round, has always required a higher minimal skill for performance and most certainly for teaching.

All dance areas have profited from the enormous increase in leadership training opportunities. The variety and type of training offered ranges from college and university credit courses, to organizationally sponsored workshops and institutes, to commercially combined vacation-training sessions. The latter have notably increased, particularly in Square and Round dance. One need only check the increased advertisements in dance periodicals to affirm this observation. Certification of leadership other than that which is already relevant to preparation for positions in physical education and recreation in education, public, and private agencies has not been attempted on any grand scale. Leadership in the Social Dance area approaches a form of certification via affiliation with the Dancing Masters' Association of America, and/or equivalent training through some high prestige nation-wide dance school. Certification of leadership is another heuristic notion which could prove fruitful to students of the dance.

The focus in *organizational* structure has moved from the local to the regional and national level. Organizational strength at the national level continues to gain momentum and support from participants and leaders alike. Square dance, the most recent dance form to emerge at the national level, flourishes despite rather wide differences in technique and style. In all areas, and particularly in square dance, there is a definite and continuous movement toward standardization of terms and movements aimed primarily at increased communication among dancers. The overall trend in all areas is toward increased participation, need for skill training, and a decrease in spectator interest resulting from increased opportunity to become participants.

In the community in general, the participation trend is away from the occasional dance party toward participation on a regular club basis meeting regularly once a week or twice a month. Average dance skill will no longer suffice, one must have specialized skill. The rapid increase in the number of calls, terms, and techniques demands continuous attendance in order to keep up.

In formal education the dance picture has been rather slow and at all times definitely behind progress in the community. However, many changes have taken place in the past twenty years. Notable among these are: (a) folk dance is no longer considered to be an activity exclusively for girls, (b) similarly it is no longer considered to be exclusively for elementary school children, and (c) classes at all school levels are increasingly being conducted on a co-educational basis. Although the dance program in education has lagged behind that in the community, there is no reason why it should continue to do so. As an integral part of community life the school should be looked to to produce the skills and leadership so vitally needed in this leisure age.

FACILITIES AND EQUIPMENT FOR DANCE

FACILITIES

Community facilities such as those operated by recreation centers, schools, churches, and civic agencies provide the choice meeting place for a dance group. Military clubs, USO buildings, barns, recreation rooms, and basements have been found satisfactory. During the summer months, many groups take advantage of outdoor facilities such as parks, tennis courts, pavilions, patios, porches, and streets. A well ventilated room with good acoustics, adequate lighting, heating, and sufficient floor space is essential. An area too small may limit the freedom of movement and the type of dance. An area too large may generate acoustical problems which can distort the music and verbal instructions, interrupt the concentration of the dancer, and thus break up the spirit of the occasion. A square dance set requires approximately ten to twelve square feet of space.

Floor . . . The condition of the floor is of vital concern. The various dance forms require varying degrees of "slickness." The basic essential, for all forms, is cleanliness. The following should be considered in conditioning the floor for comfortable dancing.

1. Clean the floor with an oiled mop prior to use.
2. Use dance crystals with discretion. Unfinished or worn floors may require crystals. Crystals are seldom necessary on highly polished floors or smooth cement. It is dangerous and uncomfortable to dance on a floor that is too slick.
3. Corn meal is a satisfactory substitute for dance crystals, but should be used with the same precaution. (Mix 5 pounds of meal with ½ cup of light oil for mops. Put in a little at a time and stir until meal is moist.)
4. A slick floor may be improved by swabbing with a wet mop or wetting the soles of the dancers' feet. Chalk on the shoe soles will also add in reducing slickness. Common household cleansers are abrasive and will damage wax surfaces and are therefore not recommended.
5. Paraffin produces a beautiful floor finish. It has been used successfully on finished and unfinished floors. This effect may be produced by: (a) sprinkling finely ground ordinary paraffin sparingly upon floor, (b) allowing dancers' movements to spread and work materials in (although sticky at first, after a short while the floor will become beautifully smooth), (c) keeping a container of finely grated paraffin handy and encouraging dancers to use it when needed. Thus, a near perfect floor condition may be maintained and the cleaning problem made remarkably easier.
6. There is considerable difference between the construction of a floor specifically for dance use and an ordinary gymnasium floor. An expert should be consulted to take advantage of the needs particular to dance.

Acoustics . . . Since permanent acoustical treatment is a very expensive process, it is seldom found except in a newer type of building. Many groups have to conduct their dances in a hall where the acoustics are poor. This is a handicap to the teacher or caller, and to the dancers. However, poor conditions have never hampered the determination of a group that is enthusiastic for dancing. When challenged by such conditions, collective ingenuity will come forth with some solution if the group is given a chance to contribute ideas or suggestions or even time and effort. Following are practical suggestions which have been found to improve the sound in a gymnasium or hall where acoustics are inadequate.

1. Drapes of any material (burlap, flannelette, etc.) hung against the walls, all around the room, are successful in improving the sound in a gymnasium or high ceiling room. They may be hung from a wire at about 30 feet high and caught every 15 feet along the wall. Drapes are a practical investment for a school when the gymnasium is used also as an auditorium and a dance place.
2. Blankets or rugs hung against the walls or suspended from the ceiling are a successful temporary treatment. These may be designed to complement the decorations.
3. Acoustics in the ordinary gymnasium may be notably improved by allowing mats to be hung around the walls. These aid the acoustics as well as providing for an efficient and effective means of mat storage.
4. Ceilings may be lowered by decorating with crepe paper streamers or similar decorative materials.
5. Human bodies absorb sound. The sound system adjusted to an empty room is not always adequate when the room is filled with dancers. In setting up for a large dance, it is wise to work with assistance and to be prepared to make last-minute adjustments relevant to crowd and space.

Facility Check List . . . In addition to concern for the floor and acoustics when selecting an adequate space for a dance, inquire about the availability of certain other essential facilities. The following items will serve as a valuable check list for accurate appraisal of an appropriate dance facility.

1. adequate drinking water and rest rooms
2. kitchen
3. chairs for spectators and dancers
4. cloakrooms or racks for coats, hats, etc.
5. electrical control switches, outlets, extension cords
6. tables for information desk or serving
7. piano
8. telephone
9. directional signs in a large building
10. fire exits and regulations
11. janitorial services and regulations
12. parking area
13. stage or platform
14. cost in relation to number of participants

EQUIPMENT

The tremendous advance in quality, precision, and design of equipment constitutes the major contributions made by science and technology to folk dance. The excellence of recording has played a singularly important factor in this growth. Equally important is the advance in precision instruments for the reproduction of sound. All of the essential items for dancing, the public address system, record player, records, and live music in the form of the accompanist and the band, have benefited from these achievements.

Public Address System . . . It is absolutely essential to have a public address system when working with groups larger than twenty to thirty. The success of any dance is directly related to the ability of the participants to hear the music, caller, master of ceremonies, teacher or leader. In addition, the adequate reception of sound permits more efficient active crowd control and minimum voice strain.

The adequacy of a public address system is determined by the space in which it is to be used and the size of the group. The acoustical reaction of any system to be used is dependent upon the size, shape, and materials used in the construction of the space. It is not necessarily correct to assume that a system which operates adequately in one space will likewise be adequate for any other space. Human bodies absorb sound; therefore, large groups require systems with greater and more precision in amplification.

The minimum essentials for a system include: a turntable, speaker, microphone, tone control which operates for both microphone and speaker, and a volume control. Additional features which are highly desirable if economically feasible are: variable speed turntable, separate tone control for microphone and phonograph, separate volume control for each, outlets for more than two speakers and two microphones, and a monitor speaker for the caller or teacher.

The turntable should be chosen to accommodate all record speeds commercially available.

A record player is often adequate for dance situations. The essential factors needed are a manual arm control, variable speed, and volume control. The type of record player designed for continuous play, the juke box, is not practical for instruction or live direction of a program of dancing.

Equipment cost varies in relation to the number and complexity of features included in a wide range of models offered by various manufacturers. Since cost is an important determinant of selection, durability of equipment becomes a major consideration especially in the average public recreation and school situation where often rough and continuous use is the rule. The following suggestions may prove helpful to the prospective buyer: (a) try a variety of systems in the particular location or space in which it is to be used, and (b) consult owners of various kinds of equipment to get their reactions both pro and con. Teachers and callers who own systems and use them under a variety of conditions are in excellent position to give unbiased opinions concerning the worth and effectiveness of the equipment.

Use of Public Address System . . . *Speakers* should be placed in front of and away from the microphone to avoid possible feed-back. Place speakers above the level of the group so that the sound will carry to all parts of the room, thus avoid sound absorption by the group. A monitor or small speaker can be attached to the set and placed behind the teacher or caller, enabling better coordination of voice and music.

The *microphone* is a very delicate instrument and should be handled with great care. There are three ways of using the microphone: (a) attach it to a stand which supports it independently of the leader, (b)

connect it to a length of cord and use as a hand microphone, or (c) attach it to an adjustable frame which fits, like a collar, around the neck of the teacher or caller.

Proper *tone and volume control* can be invaluable to the speaker in assisting him or her to acquire a more distinct and pleasing voice quality. Generally, the man's voice requires an increase of treble in the tone, a woman's voice needs base tones added. A speaker should adjust these controls in advance and at the same time find the proper distance to stand from the microphone for best results. The distance is approximately eight inches.

When working with live music, it is best to have a separate microphone and speaker for the music. If this is not possible, then the leader should locate himself and his mike in front of and close to the musicians, preferably closer to the bass fiddle or other instrument which carries the beat.

The *turntable* location is a matter of convenience. It should be at the proper height and on the preferred side of the teacher or caller which makes for the easiest and most effective control of the entire system. Electrical cords should be fastened out of the way so as not to interfere with safe and easy passage of the leader and group about the room. Records should be placed within easy reach. If the turntable is not constructed to absorb the vibrations from the dancers' movement, a mat of sponge rubber, or even a blanket may be placed underneath to prevent displacement of the needle arm.

Public address equipment requires careful handling. When not in use, equipment should be covered, locked, and placed where it will not be in the way of other activities. When the player does not work, check all electric connections first. Extra tubes, fuses, and cords should be kept handy in case of emergency.

MUSIC

Records . . . Modern methods of mechanically and electrically reproducing sound in the form of discs, tapes, and wire recordings provide the primary source of musical accompaniment for all forms of dance. Recorded music of superior quality and its

mass availability at a modest cost makes it possible to bring colorful and authentic music for dance accompaniment to even the most remote sections of our country. It is, therefore, not incongruous to hear modern jazz emitting from a Papago Indian wickiup or a Navajo hogan in remote reservations in the great Southwest.

Selecting Records . . . The modern demand for and cost of producing dance recordings is at such a level that it is commercially feasible for several companies to record musical accompaniment for a single dance routine. With this variety to choose from, it becomes increasingly necessary for a teacher or leader to learn how to select the best and most appropriate musical accompaniment. The following suggestions may serve to guide the novice teacher or leader in becoming more discriminating in the selection of musical accompaniment for a single dance or a particular form of dance.

1. The music should include an introductory passage so that the dancers may begin in unison.
2. A steady tempo is desirable unless a change is appropriate to a particular dance.
3. The music should be authentic, that is, if a dance is traditionally done to a specific tune, and the recording is available it should take preference in selection.
4. The phrasing should be clear and definite.
5. Albums are not always preferable to single records since the records included may not all be usable.
6. The non-breakable recording is preferable.
7. Records are available in a variety of speeds. One should select the speeds appropriate to machine and storage space.
8. Problems of storage and care should be carefully considered before buying.

The various types of dance or dance forms, by their very nature, require special consideration when selecting recorded accompaniment. The following suggestions are grouped according to their relevance to the following four types of dance.

FOLK AND ROUND: There are often several recordings available for the same dance. The record which corresponds in sequence to the direction for the dance should be selected. It is generally advisable to use the record recommended by the dance reference. Remember, however, that no list of suggested recordings will remain current. When re-ordering it is advisable and reasonably reliable to request the record shop to recommend and/or make substitution where requested records are no longer available.

SQUARE DANCE: Problems of selection in this area center around finding recordings suitable to the caller's voice, and to the desired tempo and rhythm pattern which the caller can follow. Callers should make selections only after intensive listening and practice calling to a variety of records. The availability of excellent callers on records offers the following advantages: it makes it possible to use them as a model in learning to supplement the calling of the teacher in musical keys not within his vocal range, and it provides an opportunity for a group to hear a greater variety in calling. One of the easiest and most enjoyable means of keeping "current" on recordings is involvement in community dance activities. Refer to page 382 for a recommended list of square dance records.

SOCIAL DANCE: There is an encouraging increase in the number, quality, and appropriateness of recordings for this type of dance. The teacher should select records which are definite in beat, regular in tempo, and appropriate for listening. Listening carefully before buying, with these points in mind, is not only advisable but economical. Long play records which provide a complete album of one type of dance music, such as Cha Cha or Waltz, are advisable for those who teach several classes or specialize in this type of dance. Albums featuring a variety of dance on one record, perhaps two Cha Chas, two Rumbas, etc., are recommended and appropriate for those who teach few and/or occasional classes. For the specialized teacher, more music per dance is needed, for the non-specialists, variety is more appropriate. The radio is a constant source of current music. Jotting down the title and name of the recording artist facilitates securing the record through local shops and aids in keeping a current collection for teaching.

Use of Records for Teaching . . . One must develop the art of effective teaching by use of records. A wide range of experience provides the teacher with some of the more reliable methods applicable to a variety of learning situations. Some of the techniques involved in the process are:

1. Know the records and be familiar with the sequence of the music and with the way the dance fits the music before using it in class. It is an advantage to be able to hum or whistle the tune.
2. Have all of the records which are to be used during any one class period laid out and arranged in order.
3. Develop a technique of setting and picking up the needle-arm so that the record will begin at the beginning and can be stopped at the end of a phrase.
4. Play the music for the group to hear before each part of the dance is presented.
5. Verbal cues should be in time with the music.
6. Give the starting signal at the appropriate time according to the introduction on the record. Warn the group if there is no introduction on the record.
7. If there is an adjustable speed control on the record player, turn the speed down so the steps can be done slowly. Then, gradually move the speed up until the dance is done at normal tempo. When there is no speed control, a part of the dance should be practiced without music, gradually speeding up the tempo via verbal cues, until it can be done at the tempo of the record.

Care of Records . . . Records are damaged by dirt, lint, and fingerprints from everyday use. Careful handling, proper storage, and a quick washing once or twice a year will extend the life of records for years.

To wash records dip them in warm soapy water, wipe dry with a soft cloth. Dip immediately into clear rinse water, wipe again. Dry thoroughly with towel. Do not let record sit in water. Do not stack records if wet.

To store records place them in a vertical position in a case with a divider between each record. The better cases have a soft cushion-like material in the bottom to protect the rim, and a tight cover to keep dirt and dust out. Albums should likewise be stored in a vertical position. The 45 rpm discs should be stored flat and preferably in albums. Clear marking and systematic storing facilitates use and prevents unnecessary handling.

Handling records carefully in order not to mark them with fingerprints is important. A soft record duster or chamois should be used to clean records before using. A brush attached to the needle arm will sweep away lint. When in active use, it is best to stand records vertically in an insulated holder. Stacking records increases daily damage. Records should be stored immediately after use.

Checking records out to students for *extra practice* is desirable and essential to learning. However, it can be a costly procedure and may handicap class progress due to loss and breakage. A suggested solution is for the teacher to replace old scratchy records with new ones and retire old records to a special check-out file for student practice. Over a period of time a reasonably good practice file may be accumulated, thus accommodating and encouraging students' desire to indulge in extra practice.

Piano Accompaniment . . . Some teachers prefer to have piano accompaniment for teaching dance. The advantages are numerous and attractive in a variety of ways. Chief among them is the saving in time afforded by not having to attend to and adjust mechanical devices during the presentation of a lesson. The accompanist can introduce music with the movement very early and make the rhythm clear and definite. The beginner is able to hear the beats of the music better. The introduction of accompaniment in the early stages trains the dancers from the beginning to let the music help cue them in pattern or step changes, thus counting is avoided. The pianist can play the music at any tempo, can repeat the music, or can isolate any part of it for practice. As the teacher and the accompanist work together, the accompanist will sense when to start playing while the group is practicing. She can pick up a particular sequence without having the class stop. In every group there are some people who have rhythm problems and do not hear the underlying beat. The accompanist can help these people with special sessions on fundamental beat and foot patterns. The teacher who is fortunate to have the assistance of a talented accompanist is more fully able to concentrate on the group. The problem of finding a competent accompanist and the expense involved can seriously limit the expansion of a dance program. These are the chief limitations to having piano accompaniment for dance.

It is important for the teacher or leader to plan for dancers to move gradually from response to piano accompaniment to response to recorded music. Recordings represent the primary source of music for leisure time use of dance skills.

A bored pianist and accompaniment which lacks proper rhythm and spirit are handicaps to teaching. Therefore, great care should be exercised in the selection of an accompanist. The following are suggested as highly *desirable* and may serve as guides in determining the competence of an accompanist.

1. Have a thorough background in musical training.
2. Play in a steady rhythm, accenting certain parts to help the dancers while learning.
3. Know the music well enough to be able to give attention to the group and the teacher during performance.
4. Rehearse all new music prior to the class.
5. Adjust the tempo to the dancers' ability or change the rhythm to accompany the teacher's analysis, gradually making it correct when new material is presented. For example, sometimes a polka is taught from a two-step.
6. Knowing how to dance increases sensitivity to ways in which cooperation between teacher, dancer, and accompanist may be enhanced.
7. Develop and vary the music to make it interesting for the dancers since most folk music is noted simply.

WORKING WITH ACCOMPANIST: The teacher and accompanist should agree on certain signals. "Ready and" or "ready begin" are usually used by the teacher for starting. Lowering of the hand with the palm down indicates a slow tempo; raising the hand with the palm up indicates a faster tempo. A nod of the head or a hand raised above the dancers' heads means to stop the music at the end of the dance. Waving the hand back and forth above the dancers' heads, or vocal "stop" means to stop the music immediately. The teacher should stand at all times in the view of the accompanist, so that all signals are readily seen. Her instructions should be loud enough so that all can hear, including the accompanist.

The teacher can do a great deal to make the accompanist an integral part of the group. When the accompanist becomes a real part of the group, and not just a tool, everyone benefits because the involvement stimulates greater interest in what is happening. The music complements the activity, it does not dominate it.

Live Music . . . While records or simple accompaniment is more practical for regular class use, a live band or orchestra adds much color, flavor, and a festive spirit needed for the special occasion or party dance. It is sometimes difficult to find musicians who specialize in playing for folk, square, and round dancing. The dance program should be sent to the musicians in advance so that they will know what is expected of them. For social dancing, a good "up-to-date" repertoire of musical selections is essential. The musicians should play easily and readily and be interested in the dance, ready to start or stop at the leader's command. They are part of the group. The best musicians, colorful as they may be, should, like the leader, blend with the group. The dancers are the focal point of the dance. If the musicians enter into the spirit of the occasion, everyone is much happier.

The instruments commonly used for *square dance* are the following: "fiddle," piano, banjo, bass violin, and guitar. The "fiddle" is sufficient for small groups if the fiddler is good. A piano is also adequate, yet a combination of three to five instruments is most desirable.

The instruments used for *international folk dance* vary. The accordion, horns, and reed instruments are used with other combinations, as well as foreign musical instruments native to a particular country. The musicians of foreign instruments are adept in playing folk pieces with a genuine folk quality.

For *social dance* a three to seven piece orchestra is adequate, depending upon the talent of the group. An audition is usually advisable when considering an unknown band. Small bands or combos may sometimes be assembled from the talent in the community or school. In all cases the band should be notified of the specific type of music desired. This will vary with the age of the group to be entertained. Some suggestions are: (1) a good variety of foxtrots, swing, waltz, and Latin American dances for adult groups; (2) a selection of old time favorites for senior citizens; and (3) fast and slow swing and jazz, foxtrots, and a few Latin numbers for teen-agers. Often, latent talent in a group may be discovered by making instruments available to dancers so that anyone can pick them up and join in with the accompaniment. For example, a banjo, guitar, or violin in the room or on top of the piano may attract attention and be the focal point for starting a band within the group.

ORGANIZATION FOR EFFECTIVE TEACHING OF DANCE

CLASSIFICATION OF GROUPS

Dance groups may be classified according to their primary purpose. Based on this criterion, four classifications may be distinguished: instructional, recreational, exhibition, and professional. However, the term used to indicate the primary function is not meant to be exclusively indicative of the entire purpose and function of a group. In addition to its primary purpose or function, a group may have one or several objectives, such as instruction and recreation, or instruction and exhibition. The *instructional group* may be sponsored by a school, recreation agency, individual, or church with a designated leader or instructor responsible for all planning and teaching. The *recreational group* is characterized by a common desire and interest, void of compulsion to participate in an activity for the inherent satisfaction gained from the activity itself. The purpose of the *exhibition group* is to prepare for precision work, performance and demonstrations of advanced dances. A shared common interest is perhaps the most accurate definition of purpose for the *professional group* made up of active teachers, leaders, callers, and highly skilled performers. The professional group sets the standards for teaching and performance in the dance, furnishes leadership for workshops, and provides a recreational outlet for themselves.

PROCEDURE FOR GROUP ORGANIZATION

A dance club, class, or exhibition group seldom comes into being spontaneously. Upon careful examination, the apparent spontaneity is more often the result of careful advanced planning by an individual or small nucleus of individuals who have an intense common interest which they desire to share with a larger group. Successful group organization is largely dependent upon two factors: (a) a common interest around which a group may rally, and (b) systematic planning based upon the democratic principle of group participation in plans and deliberations. Once an individual or nucleus group becomes committed to a particular common dance interest, systematic planning will center around the following concerns.

Promotion . . . Promotion is chiefly the task of selling an idea to others. In the community friends, neighbors, business associates, community centers, churches, or fraternal organizations are logical groups to tap for membership. In school, promotion is generally more successful when headed by student leaders. Boys and girls who are already looked to for leadership in student government, athletics, social activities, or clubs can set the machinery in motion and stimulate tremendous interest in a newly formed dance class or club. Student leaders backed by the enthusiastic support of such influential members of the faculty as the principal, coach, physical education staff, class advisors, counselors, and club sponsors more certainly assures the success of any such undertaking.

Organization . . . The degree of formality or informality of a class or club is largely governed by the aspirations of the members and the objectives of the group. The informal group is more apt to discuss an impending problem, volunteer for the necessary work involved, and thus share the responsibility for achieving goals as the necessity arises. Formal organization, with specifically designated responsibilities, perhaps best serves large groups and long term objectives. Regardless of the type of organization adopted by a group, it should be functional in terms of member aspirations and group objectives.

Leadership . . . The problem of leadership may be solved in a number of ways. The basic choice is between volunteer and professional leadership. Groups may choose either type from outside their own membership or, as in the case of volunteer leadership, it may come from within the group. Professional dance specialists are generally always from outside the group. The rapidity with which new material is introduced and consumed has made the full time professional a necessity. However, the widespread popularity of dance and the increased opportunity for specialized training has increased the number of "highly competent" volunteers. Many groups still prefer to share leadership within the group and where the competence is high this remains the practice. In the final analysis, however, the choice of leadership rests with member aspirations and group objectives.

All phases of instruction are to a large extent only as effective as the skill of the leader or teacher. Among the more important factors upon which effective leadership skill depends are:

1. *Preparation:* Knowledge of and skill in dance, maturity of judgment, self-control, poise, sense of humor, friendly manner, enthusiasm, and personal attractiveness.

2. *Skill in planning:* Well defined objectives, logical progressions, sequential ordering of materials, and evaluations related to stated objectives.

3. *Presentation:* Ability to control the group, give accurate demonstrations, clear verbal explanations, and make smooth transitions from one phase of the activity to another in a well modulated voice.

4. *Sensitivity to group need:* Keen awareness of group's need for sociable, pleasant, fun filled relationships, alertness and adjustment to changes in learning situations, skill in analyzing individual difficulties and in giving assistance.

Finances . . . Income for the support and continuance of a group comes primarily from dues, assessment, or admission charges. It is common practice to levy dues by the month or year. If assessments are the chief source of income, they are generally levied as the need arises, perhaps for a Christmas party, guest teacher or caller, or to meet incidental expenses incurred by the group. Expenditures made by a dance group generally go for space rental, musicians, instruction, refreshments, decorations, or for equipment rental.

PROGRAM PLANNING

General Comments . . . The content of a program will vary according to the interests of the group, level of ability, type of dancing, number of sessions, and the occasion. *The regular club* program will show a certain amount of progression over a period of time, inasmuch as there is new material being presented at intervals. *The special party program* for any group will be an attractive arrangement of material the members already know, combined with a reasonable number of mixers and novelty activities. The *one night session* program will need to be simple, fun, and adjustable to suit the mood of the crowd. The following are general suggestions on program planning for these types of programs.

1. Begin with a few well known dances. Play music prior to regular session to provide atmosphere and to give early arrivals an opportunity to dance informally if they desire.

2. Begin the session officially with several mass activity type mixers which do not require partners for participation, such as a grand march or a circle mixer.

3. Dance several familiar and popular numbers early in the program to keep the group interested and active while the remainder of the group gathers.

4. Review the dances that have been learned recently.

5. Not more than one or two new dances

should be taught during any regular session.

6. Vary the content of the material (patterns, figures, steps, number of people involved, etc.). Give dancers opportunity to request dances.
7. Start and finish the evening with dances with a slow tempo. Fast, medium, and slow tempo dances should be alternated throughout the evening. Plan a specific dance for closing, a goodnight waltz or a group dance, in which everyone can participate.
8. Intermissions should be spaced for greater psychological effect — after a vigorous number, halfway through the program, or for the benefit of the musicians.
   Note: Use recorded music during the intermissions and at the close of the regular program if enthusiasm warrants.
9. A three to four hour program will generally require 20 to 40 dances. It is wise to plan approximately 10 extra dances in case they are needed.
10. A social break for refreshments is usually desirable either during or at the close of the evening's activities. It offers an opportunity for members to become better acquainted and strengthens group cohesiveness.

Specific Comments . . . *FOR SQUARE AND ROUND DANCE SESSIONS:* The common practice in programming consists of "two tips and two rounds." The caller calls two square dances (two tips), and these are followed by two round dances (a schottische and the varsouvianna). One of the two rounds may be a mixer. This sequence is repeated through the entire program. This is common but not standard program practice. Variations include programming two tips and one round, and where round dances are not favored, a break is inserted after two tips.

FOR FOLK DANCE SESSIONS: The folk dance program should include variety in nationality, basic steps, number of dancers involved in a pattern, and frequent changes in tempo. If a program is to represent only one nationality, perhaps Sweden, variety may be achieved by planning for variation in basic steps, numbers involved in patterns, and style.

FOR SOCIAL DANCE SESSIONS: An evening's program of general dancing for adults may include fourteen foxtrots, five swing numbers, three waltzes, two cha chas, two rumbas, two sambas, and perhaps one tango. A program for the high school teenager may include six foxtrots, twelve swing numbers, two twists, four cha chas, two rumbas, two sambas, one tango, and one waltz. Waltz and Latin American groups require special planning. The content of any program will vary according to age level, interest, skill, and current popularity of certain dances.

The Special Party . . . The special party program for members of a regular dance group should include familiar dance favorites. It is not an appropriate time to "teach" new dances or techniques. The general fun and enthusiasm may be enhanced by skits, novelty mixers, and exhibition numbers by special guest performers. The following specific suggestions may be helpful to the inexperienced group or leader.

1. The leader should work with the group in planning the party. Helping with the arrangements may heighten anticipation and is often as enjoyable as the occasion itself.
2. The program sequence should be planned well in advance of the occasion and circulated to the membership via a printed program. A program board may be used to inform members of program content before and during the party.
3. The height of festivity may be achieved by planning the program, decorations, and refreshments around a theme.
4. Dances should be selected to range in difficulty from simple, or more familiar, to complex, or more difficult.
5. Visitors and special guests should be introduced and included in all or, at least, in an appropriate part of the program.
6. Special guest artists, exhibitions, or other forms of entertainment may add to the festivity of the occasion but should not detract from lively participation in the session by the group as a whole.

7. Mixers, novelty activities, and games should be planned to highlight the party program.

A THEME PARTY

Occasion: Square dance party.

Theme: Chinese.

Promotion: Appropriate posters stimulate interest, such as "Confucius say, Big wheels not only go around in circles, but make squares — July 7, at 8:30 p.m., Lynn Recreation Center."

Costumes and decorations: Provide construction paper or scraps of wallpaper cut to size and ready to assemble on a table with all necessary equipment, such as string, scotch tape, and scissors. Guest may construct a coolie hat, lantern or fan. The coolie hats are to be worn throughout the evening. Lanterns and fans should be strung quickly for decorations.

Name tags: The guest's first name plus the last name of a Chinese family, such as . Wong or Chan, is printed on the name tag. This procedure is related to the organization of the last dance of the evening.

Master of ceremonies: The caller, in special costume, is carried in by coolies in a sedan chair (stretcher). Appropriate music is supplied by a record run backwards on a recording machine.

Program: Rename dances to fit the theme. For example:

1. Shanghai Two-Step by Sum Fun
2. Chopsticks Stomp by Smilee Gus
3. Canton Square by Tealeaf Kid
4. Wan Ham Bo by Chink O Pen
5. Fan Tan Go by One Sung Low

Last dance of evening: All dancers gather in square dance sets according to family name on name tag and, after last dance, sit down on the floor in their family groups.

Refreshments: A parade of coolies, some carrying pails of punch on a pole across their shoulder, others carrying imitation torch sticks piled high with doughnuts, dance into the room led by a 9 to 10 man Chinese dragon. After parading around the room, the dragon continues to dance, while the coolies quickly distribute punch, doughnuts, paper cups, and napkins to each group. The entire group can be served in ten minutes.

Note: The imaginative and creative leader will be able to develop and enlarge upon this brief theme outline in many clever and interesting ways.[1]

One Night Sessions... The "one night stand" is often the dance party of the year for some groups such as a class barn party or a church dance mixer. A trained leader is often brought in from outside the group to conduct party games and run the program. There are many unknown factors which make planning difficult. The number may often be indefinite; the range of ability may vary; and the balance of sexes, more often than not, may be uneven. The one thing the group has in common is a desire to have a good time. An effective leader will be guided by these principles:

1. People enjoy group participation if they are allowed to join in willingly and are not forced to take part.
2. One should plan a simple flexible program which can be quickly adjusted to the mood and caprices of the situation.
3. Non-partner dances, novelty activities, and mixers that are learned quickly are more effective in these unpredictable groups.
4. Dances for threes or odd numbers are especially suitable where there are more of one sex than another.
5. A high level of performance is not necessary. The group needs to do the dances sufficiently well to feel comfortable and have fun.
6. Careful planning includes getting the group active as soon as possible and moving from one activity to the next in well planned transitions.
7. A dance or mixer that has been particularly satisfying may be worth repeating. The group may even request a repeat. The leader may work "request dances" into the program if they are appropriate for the majority.
8. A sensitive leader will know when to stop. Any single dance or mixer should

---

not last more than five minutes. An hour of organized mixers and dances is generally sufficient. Square or ballroom dancing may be used to vary or extend the time. Other forms of social recreation such as games, skits, stunts, and refreshments may supplement the party.

Ballroom dance is an all time favorite dance activity for single sessions. An evening of ballroom dancing requires a minimum of pre-planning. Leadership for program direction is not necessary. The primary objective is to create an evening of easy, pleasant activity where old and new friends may meet and dance. A few mixers are appropriate and useful. Mixers should be of an informal partner-exchange type carried out when couples are arranged informally around the floor. This is preferable to the circle patterned step mixers associated with square and round dance. The inclusion of a currently popular novelty dance serves to provide a change of pace and adds to the fun of the evening. The planning committee should be cautioned to resist the temptation to turn this type of session into a "grand mixer."

SOCIAL RESPONSIBILITY

Orientation ... The leader attacks the problem of planning in much the same manner whether the dance activity is chosen by or required of a group. In either case there is a selling job to be done. The degree of persuasion is perhaps more acute in the non-choice situation. In either case, the leader will need to find out as much as possible about the group in order to plan the first session. The following questions will aid in eliciting the information needed for planning.

1. What kind of people, age, type, etc., constitute the group?
2. How many are there in the group?
3. Where does the group meet? What facilities are available?
4. What time do they meet? How long?
5. How many lessons are scheduled?
6. What do they wish to dance? What dances are popular in the locale?

An advance meeting with a few members of the group affords a convenient opportunity to elicit needed planning information. This representative group could help touch off the spark of enthusiasm needed to quickly establish an atmosphere of ease, friendliness, mutual respect, and unity in the group. By making learning automatically a fun and not a work experience, by asking for suggestions and questions, and by providing ample opportunities for members to become acquainted, the first session becomes a valuable experimental and information gathering period for the leader. In addition to revealing the general level of group interest, the first session may also be used to determine (a) the ability level of the group, and (b) the reaction of the group to the activity, to the leader, and to each other. The advance planning meeting and the first session combine to give the leader the basic information needed to determine the type of material to be covered, the probable rate of progression, and the kinds of techniques and devices necessary to work with the group and make the dance experience informative, satisfying, and enjoyable.

Social Aids ... The use of an *attractive name tag* is an aid in the process of getting acquainted and helping people feel at ease. Square and folk dance clubs have used them with tremendous success. They are equally welcome among students in a class.

Still another successful idea has been the appointment of a *host and hostess* for each session. These two have the responsibility of seeing that everyone has a chance to dance, that name tags are out and ready, that visitors are included in the activities, and that guests are met and made to feel welcome. It is a great help to the leader to have the group take over this responsibility. In a large group, hostessing turns should be rotated among members. Thus turns would not occur often enough to interfere with enjoyment and participation.

A group may need help in learning to accept responsibilities for taking turns, making introductions, and showing others mannerly considerations. A leader may assist by casually providing opportunities which gradually develop into pleasant habits. For example:

1. "Thank your partner for the dance and take the next lady for your new partner."
2. "Get together with the couple nearest you, introduce your lady and exchange partners."
3. "Escort your lady to the side and introduce her to someone who is sitting out."
4. "Ladies, please take your partner to the side and introduce him to a new partner."
5. "There are a few extra ladies. Between each dance will the ladies who are dancing take turns trading out so that everyone will get a chance to dance." This can work the same for the men.

Fun With Cutting In . . . In almost every mixer there is a break where an extra person could step in and "steal" a partner, which automatically puts someone out. This can be good fun if everyone gets into the spirit of it. If the leader will show the group how, and will encourage "stealing a partner" during the mixers, the problem of extra men or women in a group is reduced. For example, in the Hitch Hiker Mixer, as the men turn back to pick up the next lady, it is easy for an extra man to move in ahead and take the new lady. Several extra men may "cut in," each trying to secure a partner quickly to avoid being left out. This lends a game-like element to the dance.[2]

"Cutting-in" is a fun technique also used in square dancing. It should be stressed, however, that the skill of cutting in lies in the ability to cut the other person out and yourself in without breaking the continuity or the rhythm of the figure.

"Cutting-in" in social dance may also be made into a fun-like situation. For example: use one or two couples; give the girls a peach, the boys a lemon; they cut in by passing the peach or lemon to another boy or girl.

Uneven Numbers . . . In the club situation, the leader will find that neither adults nor teenagers like the session where the proportion of men to women is uneven. Drop outs are numerous as a result. When the situation is generally even in numbers with only few extras, the leader can rather skillfully handle partner changes so that no one person is left out more than one dance at a time. In the school situation, experience has shown that students do not object strenuously, in folk and square dance classes, to girls taking the man's part in order to enable all to participate. In this situation special attention should be given to periodic rotation of the girls taking the man's part, and use of rooters' caps, scarves, pennies, or hats to distinguish girls taking the man's part. Uneven numbers is a rather common occurrence and, therefore, a problem in all dance situations, except perhaps in clubs that restrict membership to couples. Leaders, therefore, need to be particularly alert and unusually resourceful. An extensive repertoire of non-partner dances, dances for three's, and simple partner exchange mixers are imperative to the instructional or recreational success in any group.

Culminating Activities . . . Interest and enthusiasm generated by a series of lessons or a season of dancing may often culminate in the desire for a special event appropriately celebrating the achievements in skills and fellowship gained by a group. The following suggestions may serve to stimulate the leader, teacher, or the group in planning for such an event.

1. Combine several beginner classes for a late afternoon or evening dance party.
2. A caller or guest may be invited to make it a special occasion.
3. Attend a festival or jamboree as a group.
4. School groups may culminate their work by giving a demonstration for the school assembly.
5. Take pictures of the group in costume.
6. Invite an exhibition team to put on a performance for the class or group.
7. The leader may post a list of community dance opportunities, such as classes, clubs, summer camps, workshops, and festivals, for the information of the group.

---

[2] For additional mixer suggestion refer to p. 338-339.

Social Etiquette . . . Many of the psychological aspects which influence dancing are directly related to one's being at ease socially. Fear of not knowing what to do or say, of being embarrassed, or of making a mistake creates an insecurity which detracts from enjoyment of the activity and is a strong detriment to learning. At the classroom level, a respected teacher can do much to overcome these fears and set an easy social atmosphere by conducting early discussions with the group in order to establish a mental attitude conducive to good learning.

Etiquette is everybody's responsibility. It is part of helping everyone to have a good time. Each individual should contribute by being a good partner. Class discussions might include:

1. Careful thought to personal grooming in advance, including appropriate dress for the occasion, makes it possible for an individual to feel secure and confident in appearance.
2. Giving proper attention to a partner makes that person feel good. Security develops from a friendly smile, a cheery word, or an alertness to partner rather than boredom or looking around at others.
3. Encouragement builds confidence. Good partners cover up each other's difficulties and overlook each other's weaknesses. They do not apologize for their dancing, but they can enjoy a laugh together over an obvious error. A word of praise or an expression of enjoyment from a partner is all too rare a gift.
4. Cooperation creates a feeling of working together. It helps a partner relax and have more courage to try new ideas and to be creative. The ability to talk over a problem and to work out the solution can be stimulating. Partners should encourage each other to try a difficult part again or ask for help from the instructor.

In addition to discussion, a teacher can contribute to the easy social adjustment of the group by direct teaching and application of correct social procedures. Some aspects of etiquette may be set with a class at the first meeting when establishing what is expected of the group. These are suggested:

5. A lady always accepts graciously a gentleman's request to dance unless she has a very good excuse, in which case she should not accept an invitation from another gentleman.
6. A gentleman does not stand on the sidelines or "cut in" when there is a lady waiting to dance.
7. A gentleman and lady always accept graciously any partner with whom he or she may be paired in a mixer. If they do not wish to cooperate, they should sit out during a mixer.
8. It is poor taste to sing or show off in any way.
9. It is not in good taste to smoke or chew gum while dancing.

Some aspects of social etiquette may be more meaningfully taught as they apply to the social situation. These are suggested:

10. The gentleman should take the lady's hand, arm, or hold his arm for her to take, and in this manner guide her onto the floor. If there is a crowd at the edge of the dance floor, the gentleman should precede the lady and make way through the crowd.
11. Couples dance freely around the floor in a counter-clockwise direction and do not cut across or move in an opposite direction against traffic. Couples who dance a faster pattern should dance nearer the outside edge of the floor so they can proceed comfortably. In round dancing, couples often dance in a circle formation counter-clockwise around the floor.
12. It is not acceptable to dance open or fast patterns which require extra space when on a crowded dance floor.
13. A gentleman always thanks a lady after dancing with her, and she acknowledges the courtesy.
14. When couples are talking together, it is customary to introduce one's partner and see that he or she meets one's friends.
15. It is not good taste to teach, or to ask a partner to teach, new steps on the floor at a ballroom dance. Sitting out is preferable if the lady or gentleman is not familiar with the dance being played.

16. In square dancing, couples should introduce themselves and be cordial to the others in the set. It is customary to thank the other couples when the dance is over.

17. It is not good taste to leave or change to another set after the sets have been formed. The same procedure should be observed also between tips. If it is necessary to leave, ask a couple from the sidelines to fill in.

18. It is proper to help beginners in a set if it can be done with a few simple cues or a careful steer in the right direction. It is not good taste to take over the situation and proceed to teach them.

Other aspects of social etiquette may best be taught by setting up a particular situation for practice of acceptable social procedures. The teacher may announce a period for cutting in and at this time discuss procedures as well as provide actual practice. Discussion and practice may center around these aspects of etiquette:

19. A gentleman does not "cut in" on the gentleman who has taken his partner until another gentleman has "cut in." "Tag" is a synonymous term in some sections of the country.

20. A lady does not refuse to change partners when a gentleman "cuts in" if stags are permitted at the dance.

21. When "cutting in," a gentleman touches the left shoulder of the lady's partner. If he is not acquainted with the couple, he introduces himself to the gentleman who in turn introduces him to the lady.

Greater learning through role playing may be provided by setting up a party period with members of the group taking the parts of the host, hostess, patrons, guests, etc. Time may be allowed for discussing such considerations as:

22. It is customary that one speak to the patrons and guests at a dance. Arrangements should be made for them to take part in the affair and to be made to feel welcome.

23. It is customary to thank the caller, the host and hostess, and the chaperones before leaving.

24. A gentleman never leaves a lady unaccompanied on the dance floor. He should introduce her to another gentleman with whom he is acquainted, take her to a group of her friends, to the hostess, or to the place where she was sitting when he asked her to dance, then excuse himself.

25. When couples are talking together, it is customary to introduce one's partner and see that he or she meets one's friends.

COSTUMES FOR DANCING

Dance is a hobby to most people who participate regularly. Hobbyists the world over indulge in the purely recreational pleasure of "riding a hobby." Just as the skier, golfer, or fisherman takes pride in his gear and expresses sparkling enthusiasm over each newly acquired piece, so the dancer goes in for costumes, record collections, and keeping up with the latest in his favorite dance medium. Because of this, a folk or square dance festival is a very interesting and colorful event, for the spectator and the participant. Costuming adds to the full appreciation of the activity.

Costuming, however, is not essential for dancing. Emphasis should be given to the appropriateness of the dress. Many people find folk and square dancing an activity they enjoy occasionally and therefore feel no need to acquire atmospheric dress. Appropriate dress for the lady may consist of a crisp cotton blouse and a dirndl skirt. The man may choose lightweight slacks and a sport shirt with long sleeves. Shoes should be low heeled, lightweight and comfortable. This casual costume allows freedom of movement and maximum comfort. It is suitable for class or club groups at any time.

Groups and individuals who specialize in square dance costumes may dress in styles reminiscent of the pioneer days or in those styled from present day vogues. The lady may wear the costume of the Southern belle with full hoop skirt, billowy petticoats, and ruffled pantalettes, or she may wear the shorter squaw dress and flat slippers. The Western touch is popular for the man. He may wear blue jeans and a cowboy shirt, open at the neck, and a colorful silk tie; or he may be more elaborately dressed in frontier pants, an embroidered shirt, gambler's tie, and fancy cowboy boots.

Groups specializing in international folk dance may choose to dress individually to represent some nationality for their more formally planned programs. This means that a member of such a group may eventually acquire a wardrobe representing many different nationalities. Costumes are not always authentic but generally do represent the distinctive elements found in costumes for that particular country.

The social dance occasion may be as informal as a jam session or as formal as a prom, the costume being left to the good taste of the individual, and the demand of the occasion.

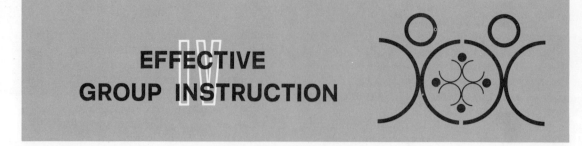

EFFECTIVE
GROUP INSTRUCTION

Effective group instruction and the ultimate achievement of a group is dependent upon the instructor's ability to select and plan appropriate materials to meet the group's needs. The manner in which material is selected and organized depends upon the purpose of the group, the objectives to be accomplished, and the over-all plan for teaching.

PURPOSE AND OBJECTIVES

Objectives are developed out of an analysis of the interest and desires of individuals in a group and the knowledge, skill, and aspiration of a qualified teacher. Joining a group signals the initial interest and desire of an individual. The purpose in joining may range from a desire to learn how to dance, to learn to dance better, to learn more about dance. Once the initial interest has been demonstrated it is the unique responsibility of the teacher to maintain and develop it in two ways: (a) for the leisure time benefit of the individual, and if possible, (b) for a contribution to the general skill and knowledge level of a particular dance form. Objectives are goals to be accomplished. Providing a sense of accomplishment and achieving objectives, therefore, requires astute selection and presentation of dance material. Experience has demonstrated that in general, dancers share a common desire for:

1. The ability to perform skills satisfactorily.
   a. To learn current dances in order to take advantage of opportunities to dance in community groups.
   b. To perform well enough to be at ease and enjoy dancing as a recreational activity.
2. Knowledge which contributes to better understanding of specific relationships involved in dance.
   a. To develop ability to follow the beat of the music.
   b. To develop security and understanding of basic steps, positions, etc.
   c. To develop confidence in leading and following.
3. Satisfying social relationships within a group.
   a. To get acquainted and share a common interest with others.
   b. To have a good time.

SELECTIVE PLANNING

Selecting materials is in essence a *problem solving* procedure. The problems of a particular group shape the criteria by which material is selected. This approach affords the teacher an opportunity and a challenge to work with a group in a democratic and cooperative atmosphere in which the group is assisted in discovering, setting, and accomplishing its objectives in relation to self-determined needs. Although admittedly its chief disadvantage is that it is more time consuming than the traditional method of teaching, perhaps this disadvantage is more than offset by the quality of accomplish-ment and interest engendered. Common problems which affect material selection center around:

1. *Range of skill and motor ability.* Skill is seldom distributed evenly in a group. Although it may be clustered at one end or the other of a continuum, it will still represent a range. In an advance group the range is as apparent, although not as formidable, in relation to the skills to be achieved as in a beginner group. Material, therefore, must accommodate all skill levels and at the same time provide for sequential progression toward a mini-

mum standard of accomplishment for all. Dances involving locomotor skills can keep the level of participation and incentive high until the skill range of a group is narrowed to a manageable commonality.

2. *Range of experience and association.* Prior experience infers formal learning which bears upon the interest and attitude of the individual. Association refers to the informal experiences such as imitating dance movements without formal instruction and participation in rhythmic activities not normally termed dancing, such as marching in a band or drill team, twirling a baton, or informal response to television or radio music. Selection of familiar or currently popular dances may assist in maintaining interest and enhancing progress of both types of individuals.

3. *Range of intellectual capacity.* This is an ever present problem in interpersonal communication. However, in dance verbal instructions can be greatly enhanced by active demonstration and practice with verbal cues. Material should be selected which lends itself to rather clear demonstration where intellectual capacity or lack of verbal sophistication is apparent.

4. *Range in purposes.* Individuals, more often than not, have two purposes for joining a group. One, a conscious purpose, "to learn to square dance," the other, an unconscious one, "to find fellowship and companionship." The reverse is as often true. Awareness of the dual nature of purposes may alert a teacher who might otherwise press a group to accomplish perfection and range of information not consciously desired by members of the group.

5. *Group structure.* Groups seldom appear in even numbers and alphabetical order! Orderliness in number and balance in sex representation are the exceptional characteristics of groups. Dances for threes, mixers, and non-partner circle dances help solve these ever present problems. The size of a group can be a problem in presentation of materials; however, with the aid of the modern amplification systems and clear verbal analysis large groups can be accommodated rather well.

In addition to selecting materials to solve group and individual problems, materials must be chosen in relation to the total dance program. The dance program in elementary school may be sequentially planned to cover six years, in junior high to cover three years, and in senior high to cover three to four years. The year's program, at any school level, is further subdivided into units of instruction and daily lesson plans. Each subdivision is organized systematically, having specific objectives, progression, and procedures. Each part relates to the other, and all fit together to form one sequentially related plan. Materials selected for a specific unit should be related to the over-all plan. Any over-all program should be flexible enough to allow for adaptation of materials in a unit to meet the specific needs of a particular group preferably in the direction of regular progression toward specifically planned goals for an entire school system. Systematic evaluations in terms of stated objectives will indicate necessary revision of sequential programing in relation to changing needs of the students. The following basic planning guides are applicable to the total dance program, unit plan, lesson plan, and are generally relevant to school or community recreation programs.

Planning Guides . . . The following guides may also be used as criteria for evaluating as well as for planning a dance program. In planning these guides serve to provide opportunity for experience with dance activities and material which represents:

1. Basic steps, positions, and formations.
2. Variation in numbers within a group. For example: dances for two, three, four, etc.
3. Dance terminology.
4. A representative number of countries or figures which constitute the range of a particular type of dance.
5. Dances and styles popular in or peculiar to the specific locale. It is important to note that styles, techniques, and dance

sequences differ throughout the country.

6. Variation in musical accompaniment, style, and tempo.

7. Orientation to socially acceptable practices.

Total Dance Program . . . The total dance program is not an isolated experience to be used at any one specific level but should be a planned progressive sequence throughout the entire school curriculum. In much the same manner, community dance programs should offer similar opportunities. These basic guides are as important in planning the total dance program as in planning the unit or lesson plan.

Unit Plan . . . The unit plan is an essential segment of the total dance program and concerns itself with specific dance experiences. Units should be planned and linked together to offer adequate progressive experience in each dance area in the total program. The unit should not be an end in itself but rather one of many stepping stones leading to the culmination of an effective total dance program. The following factors need to be carefully considered in planning a unit:

1. Number of people.
2. Age, sex, skill, and dance experience.
3. Time allotment, that is, class periods per week, successive or divided, and number of weeks per unit.
4. Facilities and equipment.
5. Leadership experience.
6. Relationship of unit to school curriculum.
7. Relationship of unit to community recreation program.

Lesson Plan . . . The lesson plan is a progressive outline of specific materials and procedures to be presented in a given period of time. It assures smooth transition within the lesson from one part to another and orderly progression in the unit from the first to the final lesson. Such pre-planning should not establish inflexible barriers which limit the adaptability of the lesson to the group or to the situation as it may arise in class. The extent of detail to be included in a lesson plan will vary depending upon the experience of the teacher. The beginning teacher will perhaps need more detail than the more experienced teacher. The following outline suggests some of the major parts to be included in a lesson plan. Some lessons may include all, some may include only a selected part, depending upon the location of the lesson in the series in a unit and the purpose of the lesson. For example: the first lesson in a series will perhaps omit review of old materials, while another lesson may be entirely devoted to review.

GENERAL OBJECTIVES in a dance lesson should be related to the objectives of the entire unit in terms of skill, understanding, and attitude. For example: (a) to learn six basic dance steps, or (b) to learn five different national dances.

SPECIFIC OBJECTIVES are objectives to be accomplished within a daily lesson. For example: (a) to learn the two step, or (b) to learn a singing square.

When a group, after a series of lessons, has learned all six basic dance steps then they have accomplished one of the general objectives of the unit, that is, "to learn the six basic dance steps." Thus the specific objective "to learn the two step," which appears on a daily lesson plan is related to the general objective of the unit. Any one general objective may require one, several, or the entire unit to accomplish. General objectives in the area of attitudes and understanding are usually designed to be evaluated at the end of the unit to measure accomplishment. Objectives are statements of desired behavior changes that can be systematically evaluated to determine if, in fact, change has occurred.

PROCEDURE AND ORGANIZATION: This is the portion of the lesson in which the order of presentation is outlined. There are approximately five essential parts to be outlined and three to be integrated. The integrated parts are: class organization, progression, and method. Any one of the integrated parts must blend into and accommodate the material and essential purpose of any outlined part. For example: the review section may require a very different type of class organization from that needed in any other part of the lesson. The same may be true of the method of teaching used in review. A brief demonstration without detailed analysis may suffice in review while the reverse may be needed for presentation of new materials. Progression may occur in cumulative fashion from the beginning to the end of the lesson, or in any one part of the lesson. Progression is practiced when any one part of the lesson or the whole lesson moves from the familiar to the unfamiliar, simple to complex, or from the part to whole. The five parts to be outlined are:

1. *Roll Call and Announcements:* This is the business portion of the lesson. Although a part of the lesson plan, the activities included need not be so formalized that they detract from the friendly, informal nature of the dance activities. Class bulletin boards may carry announcements and name tags for roll purposes thus making the opening of class a time for informal examination of display materials, questions and answers, and individual assistance. This portion of the lesson should be so cleverly planned that it is hardly noticeable as a "business session" but will, in fact, serve the same purpose. In large classes calling roll can reduce teaching and learning time. Teachers should make every effort to devise clever, speedy procedures for calling roll without taking vital class time from the activity.

2. *Review and/or Warm Up:* Review suggests a formal run through of previously learned materials directed by the teacher for the purpose of refreshing the students' memory or as a "catch up" for those who may have been absent when certain materials were presented. Warm up suggests the informal participation by students prior to formal presentation by the teacher. The warm up session may demonstrate keen interest by the students in the activity, and equipment should be available for students so that they may carry on self-directed activities prior to the formal presentation of the lesson. Formal review does not necessarily have to be a part of every lesson. On the other hand, it is often wise to devote one or several entire lessons to review.

3. *New Materials:* As the title implies this is the portion of the lesson in which materials not presented before are intro-duced. New material may be in the form of a new step, such as the mazurka, the magic step, or a new square dance figure, round dance, or international folk dance. Since it may take several lessons to learn a fundamental or dance figure, not every lesson will contain new material. New material may also appear in the form of an adaptation of a dance, such as the conversion of a routine into a mixer by altering the last figure, etc.

4. *The Activity:* This is the portion of the lesson in which the dance, which has been presented as new material, is done in its entirety and repeated for fun and enjoyment. Short dances may be taught and danced in the same lesson. Completing the instructional portion of the lesson as efficiently as possible allows for a greater portion of the lesson time to be spent on dancing and enjoying what has been taught. This should be a major objective in teaching and learning.

5. *Evaluation:* If the objectives predict the behavior changes to be accomplished, then it is the task of the teacher, in this section of the lesson, to determine if, in fact, the predicted behavior changes have occurred. Certainly if specific objectives of a lesson are meant to be accomplished in that lesson, it is important that the teacher devise clever means of evaluating that lesson to determine the degree of change. The bulletin board when used as an instructional aid can be of great value in daily evaluation. For example: if "to learn the two step" is the specific objective of a lesson, several days prior to the lesson the teacher may put up a diagram of the foot pattern, accompanied by a written analysis of the movement; during the evaluation portion of the lesson three by five cards may be passed out containing one or two questions concerning the execution, etc., of the two step. Students may answer questions from class or bulletin board information and return cards by placing them in an envelope provided on the bulletin board. This evaluation takes teacher preparation time outside of class but costs little in teaching time in class. It provides an easy means of evaluating the

students' understanding of the moves to be made in the two step even if the skill was not acquired in the class period. In this manner understanding of skills can be evaluated prior to acquisition. Later the skill of execution may be evaluated by means of a performance or skill test. Evaluations of this type keep the student informed on progress in skill and understanding as well as provide information upon which the teacher may base revisions of the lesson procedures, content, and progressions, thus increasing the possible behavior changes projected by knowing the daily degree of change and the direction of that change. Learning experiences based on facts gathered from systematic evaluation of the actual learning experience are more apt to produce desired behavior changes than experiences revised on any other basis.

In addition to evaluation aimed at recording pupil progress and gathering information for revision of future lessons, the teacher should check over a lesson and note: (a) omitted content to be used in the next lesson; (b) difficult portions to be reviewed, and (c) number of students needing extra help. This habit of checking each lesson after it has been presented not only helps in planning effectively for the next lesson but contributes to the professional growth of the teacher.

ORIENTATION TO DANCE CLASS

Setting the Stage . . . The need for setting the stage for sociability is often great, particularly in the school situation where boys' and girls' physical education classes are combined for dance activities. The procedure is difficult because there must be a delicate balance between forcing an issue and ignoring it. Enthusiastic participation and promotion by both men's and women's staffs is needed to bring about an acceptance of the idea by the group.

A frank discussion with each group, concerning enjoyment and skills gained from co-educational play, creates interest in combined classes. Some schools have been successful in promoting co-educational dance activities after social relationships have already had a start in co-educational sports such as volleyball, badminton, or games.

Group Planning . . . Allowing the group to participate in the plan will go a long way in developing a better understanding. A steering committee of class leaders from each group can serve as valuable instigating and promoting forces for co-educational classes. With enthusiastic support from students in each class, initial problems may be easily solved.

The First Meeting . . . In preparation for the first meeting of the class, the physical education teachers should meet separately with the boys and girls to discuss and clarify their responsibilities in careful grooming, in helpfulness, and in the encouragement of respect for the feelings of others as well as the need for a comfortable atmosphere in order to promote the best possible learning situation. In addition, the first class meeting should be carefully thought out and planned to provide an enjoyable time and to convince the group that the idea is a sound one. Significant factors to consider are:

1. A short talk with the entire group defining the general rules of behavior so students will know exactly what is expected of them. These rules should cover: (a) cooperation by dancing with anyone in class who asks, (b) expecting and cooperating in frequent partner changes, (c) freedom to ask questions and request help, and (d) providing every personal effort to make the learning experience pleasant and enjoyable for all members of the class.

2. Use of name tags in order to help students get acquainted with each other.

3. Devices for getting and changing partners are essential to the general morale of a co-education class. It is wise to work out several automatic partner getting devices for the early lessons until students can choose their own partners and mix with greater ease. In the first lesson it is unwise: (a) to ask boys to choose

partners, (b) to line students up in rows to secure partners, or (c) to allow them to sit down, boys on one side, girls on the other.

4. Devices for forming sets of three, four, six, or eight.[1]
5. Mixers and non-partner dances.[2]
6. Early instruction in social etiquette can make the situation more easy for all. Assist students in learning: (a) how to introduce partner to others, (b) how to ask partner for a dance, and (c) how to thank partner for a dance.

7. Appropriate material for the age level. Use lively, catchy music along with many novelty mixers. Current tunes may be used for mixer routines formerly done to music now out of fashion!
8. Active group participation keeps the interest of the group. Long waits or lectures concerning what is going to happen usually results in loss of interest. Keep activity high, talk low!
9. End the lesson with an exciting "hint" of something special for the next lesson.

CLASS PROCEDURE

General Procedure . . . The suggestions that follow constitute rather specific guide lines for class procedures relevant to selection of materials, achieving variety within a class period, and use of enrichment materials to make the class period a warm, friendly, and informative experience.

1. Materials should correspond to the skill level of the group.
2. Beginning activities should include the entire group. Non-partner circle dances are useful for this purpose.
3. The first dances should be simple and short.
4. Materials should be planned in progressive sequences so that each succeeding part learned is relevant to and dependent upon the preceding part.
5. Plan activities which make use of uneven numbers of men and women.
6. Plans should include frequent partner changes.
7. Plans should allow time and opportunity to practice social responsibilities.
8. New steps should be practiced in the normal dance situation as soon as possible. For example: a ballroom dance step taught in a line or circle formation for method reasons should be adapted as soon as possible to the setting in which it is to be traditionally executed.
9. New and review material should be included in each lesson.

10. Arrangement of dances in a lesson should provide for periods of activity and rest; contrast in style, step and pattern, variety in formation, such as circles, lines, sets, couples, etc.
11. Presentation of material should include stimulating interest through cultural information about the dances. This gives some meaning to the dance and greater appreciation of the style.
12. Unique features of a dance should be discussed to assist dancers in distinguishing one dance from another.
13. Ample time should be allowed for practice, questions, requests and suggestions. This is a time when the teacher can give valuable individual assistance.
14. Original work should be encouraged. The social dancer is particularly anxious to be free from set routines. However, in other dance forms dancers enjoy putting together their own routines for the schottische, polka, and waltz.
15. Visual aids supplement teaching. Pictures, diagrams, maps, cartoons, articles, movies, and special demonstrations stimulate interest. Costumes, dolls, and other types of folk lore add to the cultural understanding of the dance. Learning is often more accurate when a list of dances is posted so that dancers may check the spelling, pronunciation, meaning, style and basic steps.

---

[1] Refer to pages 359 and 360.
[2] Refer to pages 354 and 355.

Teaching a Specific Dance ... A successful learning experience, in any activity, is dependent to a large extent upon the preparation of the teacher. Teachers are generally trained in the over-all methods of presenting materials in a given area; however, the variety of material within a given subject area is so great that it is often necessary to give particular attention to specific procedures for preparing to teach a particular kind of material within an area. Dance is an activity within a larger program of activities to which teachers need to give attention to some rather specific suggestions for preparation. The teacher must be thoroughly familiar with the basic steps, music, and dance sequence before attempting to teach any dance. Preparation may be guided by observing the following notations.

TEACHER PREPARATION

1. Knowledge of the basic steps.
2. Understanding of sequence of the step patterns and their relation to the music.
3. Familiarity with music, its introduction, sequence, and tempo.
4. Ability to demonstrate the steps accurately, with or without music.
5. Readiness of all materials in order to make the best possible use of class time.

PRESENTATION OF THE DANCE

The procedure for analysis of a dance for teaching will vary according to the dance. However, many of the steps in the procedure are similar and therefore applicable to all types of dance.

1. Give the name of the dance. Write it on the board. If it is unusual and uncommon, have the class pronounce the name.
2. Give the nationality of the dance and any background which will add interest and make the dance more meaningful. Such information need not be given all at once, but may be interspersed here and there between steps when the dancers need a chance to catch their breath.
3. Play a short part of the record, enough to give the class an idea of the character, quality, and speed of the music.
4. Arrange the group in the desired formation. It may be practical to do this first.

5. Teach the difficult steps or figures separately. Refer to Suggestions for Teaching of Basic Steps, page 43.
   a. Teach basic step patterns, such as the waltz or polka, independently of the dance. They should be mastered before being used in a dance.
   b. If the dance has steps which can be learned better from a line or circle formation, isolate these and teach them before starting to teach the dance.
   c. If a specific step and pattern are involved, teach the isolated step first, then the figure. Talk the step through while demonstrating it, then direct the entire class in the pattern at the same time. In square dance, a skillful teacher can have everyone walk through one portion together rather than have one group do it first while the others watch, then all walk through it. If they are confused, go back and have one group do it.
6. Dances with *short* sequences: demonstrate the entire dance and cue the class as they do it.

   Dances with *long* sequences: analyze the part, try it without music first, and then with music. This process continues for the entire dance.

   This procedure is particularly usable for pattern or routine dances, such as folk or round dances. Specific adaptations are necessary for square and social dancing. Suggestions for these forms of dance follow:

   SQUARE DANCE. Teach and practice in advance any new techniques to be used. Walk the group through the new figure. Be sure to use the same terminology as the "call." Then let the group dance it to the music and the call. When the call is on the record, let the group hear a portion of the record to become adjusted to the caller's voice before dancing. For additional help refer to Square Dance Section, page 54.

   SOCIAL DANCE. Walk the group through the new step first without a partner, then with a partner, giving the lead reminder to the man. Direct the group to practice it once or twice in unison, synchronizing the step with the music. Then let the class scatter about the floor and practice the step, dancing around the room in normal ballroom style. For additional help refer to Social Dance Section, page 264.

7. Give a starting signal. *"Ready — and"* is a helpful signal in getting everyone to start together. The teacher should practice this so it can be given at the correct time. The timing is usually: *Ready*, (pause) *and*. Accent the word *and*. The first step of the dance comes on the next accented beat after the word *and*.

8. Demonstrate with a partner as each part is explained to the group. It is not necessary to have a special partner. For many dances, the teacher can select an alert member of the class and tell her with what foot the step should begin. As the teacher explains the step, and at the same time illustrates and leads the action, the partner should be able to follow easily. For a more difficult pattern, the teacher should practice with the student a few minutes before class begins. Do not use the same student all the time.

9. Correct errors in the whole group first, and give individual help as it is needed later.

10. Start slowly and gradually speed up the music to normal tempo. When working with a record player, if a speed control mechanism is not available, the teacher should gradually speed up the dance, doing it without music until it is the same tempo as the record. For additional help in teaching with piano refer to page 14, with records to page 13.

11. Use the blackboard to help explain and clarify rhythm patterns. Have the group clap difficult tempos and rhythms.

12. Teach first the part which repeats. For example: teach the chorus and then the first verse. If the dance is long, it is not necessary to teach all the verses the same day.

13. Give lead reminders which are necessary to help the man guide his partner into the figure or pattern of steps.

14. Demonstrate and practice *style* right along with the step pattern. For example: the manner in which the foot is placed on the floor, the resultant body action, and the position of the arms is a total relationship which should be learned altogether. If it requires unusual coordination, style can be taught separately. For specific styling comments, refer to the directions given for each dance in the book.

15. Cue the dance steps by the use of the microphone, until the dancers have had sufficient practice to remember the routine. Cueing by the use of descriptive words *in time to the* music is very helpful. Example: step, point, step, point, slide, slide, slide.

16. Change plans if a dance is too difficult or a poor choice for the group. Select another dance rather than spend time on a poor choice.

17. Be confident in correcting your own errors in teaching. All teachers make errors now and then. It is wise to correct them immediately. This can be done with a sense of humor or a light touch.

18. Be generous with praise and encouragement to the group.

19. Show personal enthusiasm and enjoyment for the dance. A teacher's enthusiasm and genuine interest in her teaching does much to help others enjoy it.

REVIEW

1. Review verbally, having the class tell the sequence of the dance. Then try the dance with the music, cueing the important changes.

2. Pick out the spots that need review and practice them. Point out the details of style and leading. Repeat the dance.

3. Announce the dance several days later, play the record, and see how far the dancers can progress without a cue.

4. Avoid letting the class form the habit of depending on a cue to prompt them. Cueing is only a teaching device.

5. If possible make records available before and after class for those who wish to practice. Refer to page 13 for suggestions on practice records.

Evaluation . . . In the school situation where a final grade is required for each student in a dance class, some consideration must be given to a fair means of evaluating the student. While some feel that it destroys the recreational value of a class to conduct tests, most students are anxious to be graded if they feel that they have had a reasonable opportunity to show what they know.

Occasional tests serve to stimulate better learning, to show progression, accomplishment, and serve as a booster to those who are slow or disinterested. From the teacher's point of view they focus attention on the students who need special help or encouragement and on the material that needs review. There are two kinds of tests: the practical or skill test and the written test.

PRACTICAL TEST: This is a test of ability to perform a dance skill. For example: a test on the waltz, schottische, or polka; a test on the fundamentals of square dance; or a test on basic steps in social dance. The following are types of practical tests that have been used for dance with reasonable efficiency and success.

1. *Subjective Rating* — determined from comments checked on a prepared check sheet. Five students at a time may be checked as they perform a skill individually or with partners. The sheet is given to the student so that he may benefit from comments; afterwards he signs it and turns it in.

2. *Systematic use of an achievement chart.* Each student may be checked off as a few at a time are observed during the last ten minutes of a series of class periods.

3. *An accumulative grade system* through use of name tags or numbers. The teacher circulates and writes down a grade for each as they dance. This should be done several times so that an average grade can be taken. If the students wear name tags throughout the

course, the teacher can jot down grades at frequent intervals and thereby keep a progress chart on each student. Improvement may be quite clearly evident with this system of checking.

4. *Colored tags may be used for grading.* The teacher circulates and gives each student a colored tag representing her opinion of the student's ability: blue — excellent, red — good, yellow — fair, green — poor, and white — does not know. At the end of the period, each student writes his name upon the tags given him and turns it in. This method is effective in grading ballroom dance and can be used for each type of dance, such as the rumba, tango, waltz, etc.

5. *Student Check List.*[3] Students check each other on a prepared check sheet. For example: good rhythm, poor lead, inconsistent step, etc. They can check five persons with whom they dance. The student should sign the check sheet. The teacher can then draw up a summary of the opinions. This is very helpful in grading and also in knowing which students need extra help.

Written Test . . . The *knowledge test* gives every student a chance to show what he has learned, although he may perform the skill poorly. Two kinds of written tests have proved most satisfactory in grading.

1. The *pop quiz* is a five minute test in which the student is asked to identify a fundamental step, a rhythm pattern, a specific style, position, or lead. It should require only a few words to write and should have a specific positive answer. These can be corrected in class.

2. The *objective test* is usually given as a final test. It should be given far enough in advance to get the papers corrected, returned, and discussed in class, with time allowed for questions and corrections. The objective test in dance should be set up to include material on etiquette, fundamental steps, rhythm, position, style, and history. There should be several types of questions: true and false, multiple choice, identification, etc. Directions should be written clearly on

---

[3] Refer to p. 36 for sample circulation check sheet.

the test so that students will not need to ask questions on procedures. The method of scoring should be indicated on the test paper.

Grading in class should be handled efficiently in order to avoid long periods of inactivity and subsequent loss of interest. All cards, tags, pencils, numbers, and other materials must be ready for use. The class that is prepared for the testing period in advance is usually cooperative and helpful. With proper motivation, the dancers should feel that they can have as much fun as usual even though they are aware of being graded.

Grading should not take up an entire period. Each class period should include some dancing just for fun, free from grading. This will restore the spirit and relieve the tension which is sometimes present during the grading time. Grading should be scheduled throughout the semester and not left until the end. All final grading should be finished before the last week so that the last two periods may be devoted to perfecting the dances and to enjoyment of the activity as pure recreation.

Use of Resource Materials . . . As in any other field of interest, one of the teacher's greatest jobs today is that of keeping abreast of the new materials. Such things as books, magazines, films, maps, costumes, and records are in constant turn over. They may be directly or indirectly related to a unit on folk, square, or social dance. The teacher must bridge the gap between pure activity and related knowledges if he is to offer enrichment in the cultural aspects of dance.

Folk dance has represented part of the culture of people as far back as primitive times. How can folk dances be meaningful today in the lives of people unless they relate directly to the people themselves? There are many ways in which the teacher can bring meaning into teaching. Relating to the community is perhaps one of the most direct methods. The teacher must explore the possibilities of the community as a resource. Ethnic groups in many communities contribute tremendous color in carrying out their family traditions. Students from other countries in the high schools and universities all over the land bring us rich materials in costume, folk song, records, and dances. What they tell us of their countries today brings their dances closer to a real experience.

Local clubs, parents, and even students in class may show a dance, tell about a costume, teach a dance, or assist with a program. Exchange invitations between the local club group and the school not only creates better public relations between the school or recreation center and the community, but draws the young people into seeing the place of the dance activity in the life of the community.

A teacher can call attention to and encourage young people to see concerts, foreign films, festivals, art shows, exhibitions, plays, and television performances as cultural opportunities which may be associated with the dance unit. A teacher who participates in some of these activities enriches his own background. The teacher who belongs to a dance group in the community knows what is going on, has a chance to strengthen his own skills and keep up on new materials so closely available.

Summer camps and workshops are offered in every field of dance for teachers who wish to obtain new or refresher material and combine it with a week's summer vacation.

A teacher who maintains an informative attractive bulletin board and brings interesting bits of information, pictures, clippings, articles, and questions to the classroom is the teacher who breaks the shell of non-verbal communication and opens a whole new world of meaning and understanding.

Name:_____

DANCE: Fox, Swing, Waltz, Rumba, Samba, Tango,
Cha Cha Cha

RHYTHM: (G F P)
Smooth
Beat (on/off...)
Definite (in-...)
Jerky
Late or delayed
With partner (not...)

BASIC STEP: (G F P)
Clear (not...)
Correct (in-...)
Certain (un-...)
Sideward motion

USE OF BASIC STEP:
Transitions (clear, not,
  late, jerky)
Combinations (smooth,
  awkward)
Variations — few, good
Contrast — clear, none

FOOTWORK: (G F P)
Glide
Steps (too short/long)
Straddles, feet apart
Toes in/out
Lacks hip reach

BODY POSITION:
Posture (G F P)
Slumps, pulls away
On angle, shoulder hunch
Too close/far apart
Too relaxed/tense

LEAD & FOLLOW (G F P)
Hand high, low, good
Arm high, low, good
Limp pumping action
Jerky, late or slow
Weak
In-...effective
Anticipates (too much)
Leads man

IN GENERAL:
Confidence (G F P)
Style... (G F P)
Interested
Indifferent
Careful, careless
Inconsistent
Shows improvement

Student Check List*

These two sample rating lists are examples, drawn from social dance, of quick, easy classroom methods for daily, periodical, or final summaries of student's skill achievements. In the example to the left:

G = Good

F = Fair

P = Poor

Symbols are merely circled by the rater who may be either the teacher or a guest expert. Key words are underlined by rater. These will give a definite picture of student's performance.

Name:_____

Partner:_____

Dance:_____ Rating: check (✓)
                            Appropriate space.

Rhythm:	Lead: Good____
On____ Off____	Excellent____
Indefinite____	Weak____ Late____
Jerky____	Jerky____
Smooth____	Following: Good____
Variations:	Excellent____
None____ Few____	Slow response____
Many____	Leads____
Transitions smooth____	Style: Smooth____
Transitions awkward ____	Poised____
Footwork: Good____	Beautiful____
Step too long____	Careless ____
Step too short____	Jerky____
Body Positions:	Mechanical____
Limp____	Lacks confidence____
Tense____	
Comfortable____	

The example to the right is a variation of the above sample, in which a fellow student may be the rater. Check marks are used to indicate picture of achievement in the various skills indicated. The creative and imaginative teacher can easily adapt either of these samples to any area of dance skill.

_____

* Sample check list devised by Jane A. Harris. Washington State University, Pullman, Washington.

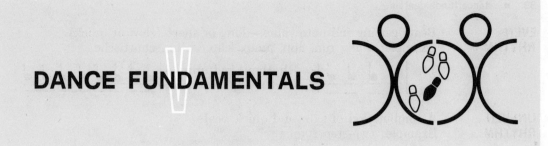

DANCE FUNDAMENTALS

RHYTHM AND METER

METER
Refers to time in music or grouping of beats to form the underlying rhythm within a measure.

It may be recognized by listening for the accent on the first beat, as in

2/4 (𝅗𝅥 𝅗𝅥) 2 beats to the measure – accent on 1st beat – quarter (1 2) note gets the beat.

3/4 (𝅗𝅥 𝅗𝅥 𝅗𝅥) 3 beats to the measure – accent on 1st beat – quarter (1 2 3) note gets the beat.

4/4 (𝅗𝅥 𝅗𝅥 𝅗𝅥 𝅗𝅥) 4 beats to the measure – accent on 1st beat – (1 2 3 4) quarter note gets the beat.

¢ Cut time plays the accented beats of the measure. Speed is often faster. Two beats to each measure. Same as fast 4/4 or 2/2 time.

6/8 (♪ ♪ ♪ ♪ ♪ ♪) 6 beats to the measure – accent on 1st beat (1 2 3 4 5 6) – eighth note gets the beat.

NOTE VALUES

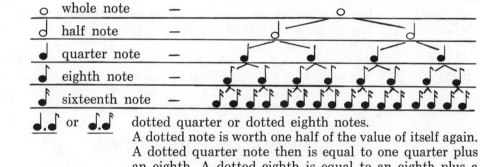

𝅝	whole note	—
𝅗𝅥	half note	—
♩	quarter note	—
♪	eighth note	—
♬	sixteenth note	—

𝅘𝅥𝅮·𝅘𝅥𝅮 or 𝅘𝅥𝅯·𝅘𝅥𝅯   dotted quarter or dotted eighth notes.
A dotted note is worth one half of the value of itself again. A dotted quarter note then is equal to one quarter plus an eighth. A dotted eighth is equal to an eighth plus a sixteenth.

♪♪♪ triplet   A group of three notes played in the usual time of two similar notes. It would be counted <u>one-and-a-half</u> for one quarter note.
3

RHYTHMIC PATTERN
The melody pattern or grouping of beats, as the melody of a song, corresponds to the underlying rhythm.

Example:

Meter or underlying beat 4/4

4/4 (♩ ♪ ♪ ♪ ♩   ♩) Melody or rhythm pattern
(___ ___   ___ ___) Meter or underlying beat

EVEN RHYTHM

Beats getting full note value — long or short (slow or quick)
Example: walk, run, hop, jump, leap, waltz, schottische

4/4 | ♩ ♩ ♩ ♩ | ← Rhythmic patterns → | ♪ ♪ ♪ ♪ ♪ ♪ ♪ ♪ |
　　　 — — — —　 ← Underlying beats →　 — — — — — — — —

UNEVEN RHYTHM

A combination of slow and quick beats
Example: two-step, rumba

4/4 | ♩ ♩ ♩ | rhythm pattern (quick, quick, slow)
　　 ♩ ♩ ♩ ♩ | underlying beat

A dotted beat borrows half the value of itself again.
There are long and short beats (slow and quick).
Examples: skip, slide, gallop, polka

2/4 | ♩. ♪ ♩. ♪ | rhythmic pattern — uneven beat due to dotted note
　　 ♩ 　 ♩ | underlying beat

BROKEN RHYTHM

A combination of slow and quick beats when the rhythm pattern takes more than one measure. A repetition will begin in the middle of measure.
Example: Magic step in the foxtrot.

4/4 | ♩ 　 ♩ | ♩ ♩ | rhythm pattern
　　 ♩ ♩ ♩ ♩ | ♩ ♩ ♩ ♩ | (slow, slow, quick, quick)
　　　　　　　　　　　 underlying beat

TEMPO

Rate of speed at which music is played.

MEASURE

One group of beats made by the regular occurrence of the heavy accent. It represents the underlying beat enclosed between two adjacent bars on a musical staff.

PHRASE

A musical sentence, can be felt by listening for the complete thought. Phrases may vary in length. A group of phrases may express a thought as a group of sentences may express a paragraph.

FORMS OF LOCOMOTION

Dancers forget their cares and find joy in the rhythmic swing of movement. Locomotor movement which forms the floor patterns in circles, rounds, squares, and longways is traditionally characteristic of our folk, square, and social dances. The many combinations of steps may vary in energy release, tempo, style, and direction. Movement through space is called locomotion and the following eight fundamental steps are simple ways that the individual may transfer the weight in moving from one place to another.

Eight Fundamental Steps

WALK:

1. Even rhythm.
2. Steps are from one foot to the other, the weight being transferred from heel to toe.

4/4 | ♩ ♩ ♩ ♩ |
　　 R　L　R　L
　　 step step step step

RUN:
1. A fast even rhythm.
2. A run may be compared to a fast walk except that the weight is carried forward on the ball of the foot.

4/4
R L R L R L R L

HOP:
1. Even rhythm.
2. A transfer of weight by a springing action of the foot from one foot (push off and land on ball of foot) to the same foot.

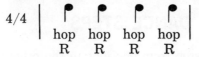

4/4
hop hop hop hop
R   R   R   R

JUMP:
1. Even rhythm.
2. Spring from one or both feet and land on both feet.
3. Feet push off floor with strong foot and knee extension, the heel coming off first, then the toe.
4. On landing, the ball of the foot touches the floor first, then the heel comes down, and knees bend to absorb shock of landing.

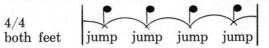

4/4
both feet   jump   jump   jump   jump

LEAP:
1. Even rhythm.
2. A transfer of weight from one foot to the other foot, pushing off with a spring and landing on the ball of the foot, letting the heel come down and bending the knee to absorb the shock.

4/4
springing   L   R   L   R

SKIP:
1. Uneven rhythm.
2. A step and a hop on the same foot.

2/4
step hop step hop   step hop step hop
R   R   L   L   R   R   L   L

SLIDE:
1. Uneven rhythm.
2. Movement sideward.
3. A step on one foot, and a draw of the other foot up to the first with a shift of weight done quickly on uneven beat.

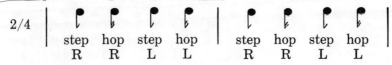

2/4
step close step close   step close step close
R   L   R   L   R   L   R   L

GALLOP:
1. Uneven rhythm.
2. Movement forward. Knee action, heel leading.
3. A step followed by a quick close of the other foot on the uneven beat.

2/4

step close step close | step close step close
R   L   R   L   R   L   R   L

These eight fundamental steps may be used alone or in combination to form the rhythmic foot patterns of the basic dance forms of folk, square, round, and social dancing.

BASIC DANCE STEPS

SHUFFLE:
1. An easy light one-step from one foot to the other moving forward.
2. Different from a walk in that the weight is transferred from the ball of the foot to the heel or kept on the balls of the feet.
3. The feet remain lightly in contact with the floor.

TWO-STEP:
1. 2/4 or 4/4 meter.
2. Uneven rhythm.
3. Step forward on left foot, close right to left, take weight on right, step left again. Repeat beginning with right.
4. The rhythm is quick, quick, slow.

Folk and square dance style:
2/4

step close step | step close step
L   R   L   R   L   R

Slow foxtrot style:
4/4

step close step | step side close
L   R   L   L   R   L

POLKA:
1. 2/4 meter.
2. A bright lively dance step in uneven rhythm.
3. Similar to a two-step with the addition of a hop so that it becomes hop-step-close-step. The hop comes on the up beat.

2/4

hop | step close step hop | step close step hop
L   R   L   R   R   L   R   L   L

SCHOTTISCHE:
1. 4/4 meter.
2. Smooth even rhythm.
3. Three running steps and a hop or a step, close, step, hop.

4/4

step step step hop | step step step hop
L   R   L   L   R   L   R   R

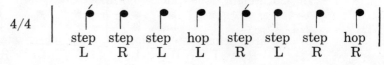

4. The schottische dance form is four measures (step step step hop, step step step hop, step hop, step hop, step hop, step hop).
5. Common and popular variations are to hold, turn, or swing the free leg on the fourth count instead of the hop.

WALTZ:
1. 3/4 meter — accent first beat.
2. A smooth graceful dance step in even rhythm.
3. Consists of three steps; step forward on the left, step to the side with the right, close left to right, take weight on left. The rhythm is an even three beats.

3/4 | fwd   side   close | fwd   side   close |
      L   R   L   R   L   R

4. The box waltz is the basic pattern for the box waltz turn. It is most successfully learned from a square pattern using the cue: forward side close, backward side close.

Start:

MAZURKA:
1. 3/4 meter.
2. Strong vigorous even three beat rhythm — accent second beat.
3. Step left, bring right up to left with a cut step displacing left, hop right while bending left knee so that left approaches the right ankle. Repeat on same side.

3/4 | step   cut   hop | step   cut   hop |
       L   R   R   L   R   R

BASIC DANCE TURNS

There are two kinds of partner turns based on the basic steps, pages 40 and above, the clockwise turn and the standard or counter-clockwise turn.

Schottische Turn

The clockwise turn is used almost exclusively for a schottische partner turn in folk or round dance. The schottische rhythm is even 4/4 time. The pattern is step, step, step hop; step, step, step hop; step hop, step hop, step hop, step hop. The last two measures of four are used for the partner turn. The starting position is generally a closed position or a shoulder waist position. By turning gradually, the couple may make only one turn clockwise on the four step hops, or by turning a half turn clockwise on each step hop, two full turns may be made.

Two-Step Turn

The clockwise turn is used almost exclusively for a two-step partner turn in folk and round dancing. The two-step rhythm is uneven 2/4 or 4/4 time with a *quick quick slow* pattern. The counter-clockwise turn is described in the Social Dance section. Refer to page 282.

THE CLOCKWISE TURN

A. *Half Turn*

2/4 time   Starting position: closed, man's back to center of circle. Directions are for man; lady's part reverse.

Measure:

1   Step left sideward, toe in slightly, and starting to turn clockwise (ct. 1). Close right, continuing turn (ct. and). Step left backward, toeing in, and pivot left foot completing ½ turn clockwise (ct. 2).

4/4 time   The same pattern takes only half a measure and is counted 1 and 2.

B. *Full Turn*

2/4 time   Starting position: closed, man's back to center of circle. Directions are for man; lady's part reverse.

Measure:

1   Take A. above to make ½ turn clockwise (cts. 1 and 2).

2   Step right forward, between partner's feet and turning clockwise (ct. 1). Close left to right, take weight left, coninuing turn (ct. and). Step right forward in line of direction, toe out and pivot right, completing ½ turn clockwise (ct. 2).

4/4 time   The same pattern takes only half a measure and is counted 1 and 2, 3 and 4.

Teaching cues: Side, close, turn — Side, close, turn.

Polka Turn

THE CLOCKWISE TURN is used almost exclusively for a polka partner turn in folk or round dance. The polka rhythm is uneven 2/4 time. The pattern is hop, step, close, step. With the addition of a quick hop (pick-up beat) before each two-step, all the directions described for the two-step turn may be applied for the polka turn. The starting position is generally a closed position or a shoulder waist position.

Waltz Turn

THE STANDARD TURN is the ballroom turn and may go either to the left in a counter-clockwise turn, or to the right in a clockwise turn depending on which foot leads the turn. These turns are described under the Waltz box turn, page 292.

THE CLOCKWISE TURN is the turn most often used for folk and round dances. It is sometimes confusing because it involves a clockwise turn starting with a left foot lead. This is contrary to the standard style turn described above.

A. *Half Turn* Backward (clockwise)

3/4 time   Starting position: closed, man's back to center of circle. Directions are for man; lady's part reverse.

Measure:

1   Step left, toe in, backward and turning clockwise with back to line of direction (ct. 1). Pivoting on left foot, step right sideward completing ½ turn (ct. 2). Close left to right, take weight left (ct. 3).

B. *Full Turn* Backward (clockwise)

Measure:

1   Take A. above to make ½ turn clockwise (cts. 1 2 3).

2   Step right, toe out, forward between lady's feet, turning clockwise to face line of direction (ct. 1). Pivoting on right foot, step left sideward, completing ½ turn (ct. 2). Close right to left, take weight right (ct. 3).

Teaching cue: Turn, side, close — Turn, side, close.

SUGGESTIONS FOR TEACHING BASIC DANCE STEPS

General Outline for Procedure

The level of ability and the degree of difficulty of the basic step will influence the manner in which a step is presented. The factors involved are interdependent and may be used in various combinations when teaching the steps. The sequence of the factors and the starting point for teaching will vary. Sometimes it is necessary to go back in the teaching process to an easier form. Several approaches may be necessary for everyone to learn the step.

ANALYSIS OF RHYTHM OF BASIC STEP

Explain and discuss accent, time signature, even or uneven rhythm, and foot pattern in relation to rhythm.

A. Listen to music
B. Clap rhythm with students
C. Write out on blackboard
D. Demonstrate action

METHOD OF PRESENTATION

A. Walk through with analysis and demonstration
B. Practice
C. Apply basic step in simple sequence
D. Use basic step in simple dance

INTERDEPENDENT FACTORS INFLUENCING PROCEDURE

A. Formation of group for teaching
   1. Line
   2. Single circle
   3. Double circle
B. Position of people
   1. Alone
   2. With partner

   a. Varsouvianna, couple, promenade, open, or conversation position
   b. Closed or shoulder-waist position

C. Accompaniment — with or without music
D. Cue — with or without verbal cue
E. Direction of movement
   1. In place
   2. Forward and backward
   3. Sideward or diagonal
   4. Turning

SELECTED EXAMPLES OF PROCEDURE FOR TEACHING BASIC DANCE STEPS AND TURNS

Sample Procedure for Teaching the Schottische

TO LEARN BASIC SCHOTTISCHE AND CLOCKWISE TURN.

1. *Single circle*, facing line of direction. Directions are for man; lady's part reverse.
   a. Beginning left, take two schottische steps moving forward in line of direction, Rock

forward on first step hop, rock backward on the second step hop, rock forward on the third step hop, and backward on the fourth step hop. Repeat.

b. Beginning left, take two schottische steps moving forward in the line of direction. Turn clockwise by rocking forward and backward twice to make one complete turn. Repeat. Discourage any body sway that may accompany the rock as soon as the pattern of turning is learned.

2. *Double Circle*, take open position, facing line of direction. Directions are for man; lady's part reverse.

Beginning left, take two schottische steps moving forward in line of direction. Take closed or shoulder-waist position. Turn clockwise by rocking forward and backward twice to make one complete turn. Repeat. Emphasize the importance of turning to face partner on the last schottische step so that the turn starts on the first step hop. Encourage more advanced dancers to make two turns.

3. Use a simple dance to practice schottische step. For example: Old Time Schottische, page 133.

Sample Procedure for Teaching the
Progressive Two-Step and Clockwise Turn

TO LEARN THE BASIC TWO-STEP.

1. The forward two-step may be taught simply by moving forward on the cue step, close, step, starting alternately left then right.

2. Take couple position with partner. Take the two-step face to face and back to back, progressing in the line of direction.

TO LEARN THE BASIC CLOCKWISE TURN.

1. *Circle formation*, all face the center of the circle, hands joined.
   a. Moving to the right, take four slides right, then four slides left. Repeat. Emphasize that the last slide is not a full slide but a getting ready step to change direction.
   b. Moving to the right, take only two slides right, two left. Repeat.
   c. Drop hands. Moving to the right in the line of direction, take four slides pivoting clockwise on the right to make a half turn on the last slide. Now facing out, start with the left, take four slides still moving in the line of direction. Pivot clockwise on the left the last time to make a half turn to original position. Repeat. Emphasize that the last slide each time is a pivot half way around clockwise.
   d. Moving in the line of direction, take two slides pivoting clockwise to face out, then two more slides in the line of direction, pivoting clockwise to face in. Repeat.

2. *Double circle formation*, man with his back to the center of the circle. Take closed position. Begin on man's left, lady's right.
   a. Moving toward line of direction, take four slides, pivoting around clockwise on the last slide so that the man faces the center of the circle. Take four slides to the man's right still in line of direction, pivoting on the last slide clockwise so that the man is back in original position. Repeat. Emphasize that the last slide is the pivot clockwise and that the man must lead the lady with his right arm as he goes around so that they can turn together.
   b. Moving to the man's left (line of direction), take two slides and pivot clockwise half around on the last slide. Then reaching in the line of direction, take two slides to the man's right and pivot clockwise to original position. Repeat.

3. Use a simple dance which has a progressive two-step turn to provide practice on this step. For example: Tuxedo Two-Step, page 150.

Sample Procedure for Teaching the
Progressive Waltz and Clockwise Turn

TO LEARN THE BASIC FORWARD WALTZ
1. First, learn the box pattern individually.
2. Take closed dance position with a partner. The gentleman steps forward on the left and the lady backward on the right.
   Gentleman: forward side close, backward side close
   Lady: backward side close, forward side close
3. To progress forward: *Gentleman:* forward side close, forward side close
   Lady: backward side close, backward side close

TO LEARN THE BASIC CLOCKWISE TURN
1. *Circle formation*, all face the center of circle.
   Beginning right, take one waltz step turning clockwise to face the outside of the circle. Emphasize that the toe turns out on the first step. Moving again in the line of direction, take one waltz step turning clockwise to face the inside of the circle. Emphasize that the left toe turns in and steps backward in the line of direction. Repeat. It takes two waltz steps to complete a full turn clockwise.
2. *Double circle formation*, man with his back to the center of the circle, take closed position.
   Directions are for man; lady's part reverse.
   Moving in line of direction, beginning left, take one waltz step turning clockwise so that the man faces the center of the circle. Emphasize that the man turns the toe in and steps backward in the line of direction on the first beat and that the lady steps with her right in between the man's feet on the first beat. Moving again in the line of direction, take one waltz step turning clockwise to original position. Emphasize that the man turns the right toe out into the line of direction on the first beat and the lady turns her left toe in stepping back in the line of direction on the first beat. The man must lead the lady with his right arm as he goes around so that they can turn together. Repeat.
3. Use a simple dance which has a progressive waltz turn to provide practice on this step. For example: Penny Waltz, page 162.

Sample Procedure for Teaching the Mazurka

1. *Line formation*, all facing forward.
   a. Moving to the right, step right (ct. 1), close left to right in such a way that the left foot displaces the right. The right leg consequently flies out to the right (ct. 2-3, accenting ct. 2).
   b. Moving to the right, repeat action of (a) adding hop on the left (ct. 3). Repeat continuing to move right. Beginning left, repeat sequence.
   c. Moving right, repeat action of (b) and on ct. 3 add sweep of right foot across in front of left. Beginning left, repeat sequence.
   d. Moving to right, repeat action of (c) stamping on (ct. 1) and on (ct. 3) take hop slightly backwards. Beginning left, repeat sequence.
2. *Circle formation*, take open position, facing in line of direction. Beginning man's left, lady's right, take mazurka steps forward in line of direction.
3. Use a simple dance to provide practice on this step. For example, Swedish Varsovienne, page 255.

Sample Procedure for Teaching the Polka and Polka Turn

THREE APPROACHES TO LEARNING THE BASIC POLKA
1. *Step by step rhythm approach*
   a. *Single circle*, all facing line of direction.

1) Analyze the polka very slowly and have class walk through the steps together in even rhythm (hop, step close step).

2) Gradually adapt the rhythm until there is a quick hop and a slower step close step.

3) Gradually accelerate the tempo to normal polka time. Add the accompaniment.

b. *Double circle*, take promenade, varsouvianna, or couple position, facing line of direction. Polka forward with partner.

c. Use a simple dance that has a polka step to provide practice on the step. For example: Jessie Polka, page 152.

2. *Two-step approach*

a. *Single circle*, facing line of direction.

Beginning left, two-step with music, moving forward in line of direction. Gradually accelerate the tempo to a fast two-step and take smaller steps. Without stopping change the music to polka rhythm and precede each two-step with a hop. If pianist is available, this rhythm change can be made with music. If pianist is not available, cue without music until step is learned, then use polka record.

b. *Double circle*, take promenade, varsouvianna, or couple position, facing line of direction. Polka forward with partner.

c. Use a simple dance that has a polka step to provide practice on the step. For example: Jessie Polka, page 152.

3. *Slide approach*

a. *Single circle*, all facing center, hands joined.

1) Take eight slides to the left and eight slides to the right. Take four slides to the left and four slides to the right. Take two slides to the left and two slides to the right. Repeat the last group of two slides over and over. *Emphasize that in order to change direction each time, a hop is added.* This last series of slides with the hop is a polka step.

2) Repeat this last series of slides moving forward toward the center of the circle and then away from the center.

b. *Double circle*, take promenade, varsouvianna, or couple position, facing the line of direction. Polka forward with partner.

c. Use simple dance that has a polka step to provide practice on the step. For example: Jessie Polka, page 152.

THE PROGRESSIVE POLKA TURN

1. Learn the basic polka step forward.

2. Repeat the process describing how to learn the two-step clockwise turn, page 44.

a. When a change of direction is made on the fourth slide or on the second slide, *add a hop.*

b. When a change of direction is made on a pivot, *add a hop*, as the pivot is made.

3. First practice individually and then with a partner.

4. Use a simple dance which has a progressive turn to provide practice on this step. For example: Cotton Eyed Joe, page 151.

DANCE FORMATIONS

These dance formations are representative of the dances in this book. There are many other variations.

KEY: The arrow on the circle and square indicate the direction that each faces.

GIRL ◯→   BOY ☐→

A. *No Partners*

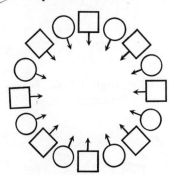

1. Single Circle.

2. Broken Circle.

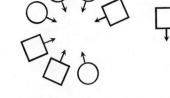

3. Line, side by side.

4. File, one behind each other.

B. *Couples in a Circle*

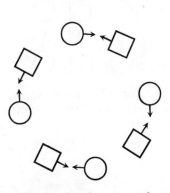

1. Single Circle, facing center.

2. Single Circle, man facing line of direction, lady facing reverse line of direction.

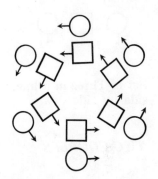

3. Double Circle, couples facing line of direction.

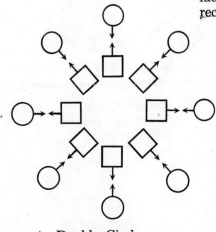

4. Double Circle, partners facing man's back to center.

C. *COUPLES IN A FILE – DOUBLE FILE*

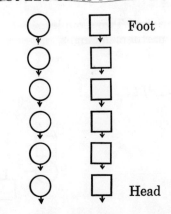

Foot

Head

Longway or Contra Set, couples facing head.

D. *COUPLES IN A LINE*

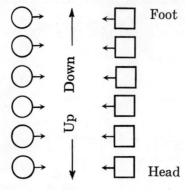

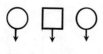

Longway or Contra Set, partners facing.

Couples 1, 3, 5 Cross Over

E. *THREE PEOPLE*

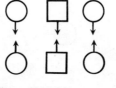

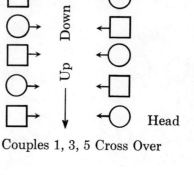

1. Set of Three in a line, side by side.

2. Set of Three, facing set of Three.

3. Single Circle, facing center.

F. *TWO COUPLES*

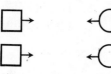

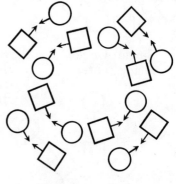

1. Sét of Two Couples, partners facing.

2. Sicilian Circle, Set of two couples, couples facing.

G. *FOUR COUPLES*

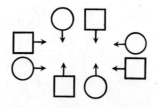

Set of Four Couples

DANCE POSITIONS[1]

1. BACK CROSS POSITION

2. BUTTERFLY POSITION

3. CLOSED POSITION

4. CONVERSATION POSITION

5. COUPLE POSITION

6. ESCORT POSITION

7. FACING POSITION

8. LEFT REVERSE OPEN POSITION

9. OPEN POSITION

[1] Detailed description for each position is given in the glossary.

DANCE POSITIONS

10. PROMENADE POSITION

11. REVERSE OPEN POSITION

12. REVERSE VARSOUVIANNA POSITION

13. RIGHT REVERSE OPEN POSITION

14. SHOULDER-WAIST POSITION

15. STAR POSITION

16. SWING OUT POSITION OR FLIRTATION POSITION

17. VARSOUVIANNA POSITION

18. WRAP POSITION

MUSIC IN RELATION TO DANCE

One problem which plagues the dance teacher more than any other is how to teach a student to hear and move to the beat of the music. Psychologically, it is a handicap for the person who cannot hear the beat and is constantly fumbling with all of the relationships in movement which depend upon "being on the beat." Perhaps there are some basic understandings which can be learned and explored.

What Should the Dancer Listen for in Music?

The underlying beat is usually carried by such instruments as the string bass, the piano, the drums. In the case of Latin rhythms, the beat is carried by the bongo drum, the clavs (sticks), or wood block. *THE BEGINNER:* The beginner should try to pick out a steady beat which is most dominant and synchronize his step with this down beat. Quite often people who think they have no sense of rhythm can clap a consistent pattern of beats but had not known what to listen for. If an individual can clap accurately to the basic beat, and understands that he can depend on this beat to be consistent throughout a piece of music, he will usually have his major problem solved. Regular practice moving with the beat will bring confidence for dancing.

When an individual cannot clap to a regular beat, cannot hear a beat, the only avenue of gaining help is to...

First: follow visually the clap of the teacher or someone in class.

Second: Try to relate this with listening for the basic beat of a very obvious piece of square dance or march music, until he can clap it himself. Mark time in place with feet and then try to walk to this beat.

Third: gradually progress to other music which has less obvious beat, melody or vocal.

Fourth: walk with a good partner and try to feel the relationship of the movement to the beat until he can move with the beat by himself.

The melody or the vocal can be very distracting to the individual who has difficulty with rhythm, as he tends to speed up or slow down. The more a dancer is concentrating on a dance step pattern, style, or lead, the easier it is to forget about listening to the music. A teacher may help in this case by calling his attention to listening for the music. Thorough understanding and practice of the difficult step without music will also permit greater freedom to listen to the music.

THE DANCER: When one has accomplished the hurdle of being able to dance to the beat of the music, the next step is to help the individual learn to listen to the rhythmic changes in the music.

1. He should be able to recognize the beginning and end of a phrase and anticipate this in his movement or call.
2. He should be able to recognize and adjust his movement to changes of tempo.
3. He should be able to identify the parts of a dance by the melodic changes in the music, and therefore be able to make smooth transitions in movement or position.
4. He should be able to note the quality of the various parts of the music and be better able to interpret the appropriate style.
5. He should learn from experience with different types of rhythm to correctly identify one basic rhythm from another.
6. And finally with experience he should be able to interpret the music and in combining dance steps feel the relationship of the step to the music.

How to Identify and Recognize Music for Dance

There are certain facts that must be learned in order to identify and recognize specific music for dance.

1. Each dance rhythm is in a definite meter. For example, the dancer will learn to recognize waltz music if he knows he

should listen for 3/4 time with an accent on the first beat.

2. Each dance has a pattern of movement, the quality or feeling of which should identify with the quality of the music. For example, the dancer needs to know the rumba is in a smooth rolling Latin quality, the samba is a faster bouncy rocking quality, the mambo is an off-beat heavy sultry quality. By trying to recognize this quality in the music, one can usually identify the appropriate music.

3. Some types of dances have particular instruments which carry the base or the melody. For example, the Latin American dances have the bongo drums, sticks, wood blocks, and maracas, one or two of which will carry the basic beat, and another the rhythm pattern.

4. In folk dance the music, the pattern of steps, and the style often relate to the meaning or the origin of the dance and this association helps the dancer to remember and identify the music.

How Can the Teacher Contribute to Rhythm Training and Appreciation Through Dance?

1. Be thoroughly familiar with the music used for any specific dance, in order to
   a. give verbal cues in the correct rhythm.
   b. give the starting cue at the appropriate time.
   c. cue the group with regard to the length of the musical introduction before the dance begins.
2. Direct the group to clap out difficult rhythms.
3. Point out rhythmic changes in the music and allow time for listening to the transitions from one part to another.
4. Point out and allow the class to listen to particular instruments or qualities in the music which will help them remember the dance.

5. Provide frequent opportunity for student identification of music rather than announcing the dance.
6. Plan the program to include interesting cultural contrasts in music and dance.
7. Use words and meanings to folk songs which accompany dance.
8. Add significant authentic sounds to the recorded music such as
   a. appropriate shouts or claps
   b. appropriate percussion instruments such as tambourine or drum beat
   c. appropriate words or yodeling.
9. Explain meanings of music or dance and add highlights of folklore or background information.
10. Allow sufficient practice and review of dances so that the group may know dances well.

POSTURE IN RELATION TO DANCE

THE BEAUTIFUL DANCER. A beautiful dancer is one of the most satisfying sights to watch. It is really not the intricate steps or figures which are noticed, but rather the rhythmical way the dancer seems to glide around the floor. There is an alertness, vitality, strength, and beauty which transmits the feeling of complete control of the entire body.

A PART OF ETIQUETTE. It is pleasant to think of good posture as part of a good dancer's etiquette, courtesy, and charm, and therefore, it is as important to him or her as the ability to execute the steps and

keep time to the music. To "see yourself as others see you" might be a terrible shock to many dancers, but it might demonstrate the glaring importance of good carriage and posture. Posture is a matter of getting all body parts in balance so that they are carried easily upright, instead of collapsing into the curves. A word picture often heard is "carry your living room upstairs and your dining room downstairs" which is a good reminder to keep the three body weights in line — the head, chest, and hips.

A SCIENTIFIC APPROACH. For a more scientific approach, stand side view before the mirror, toes straight ahead, weight going down through the ankles to the heels and over the outer borders of the feet. Hold the knees easy (not locked). Squeeze the abdomen and hips into place as if to move through a narrow passage; lift the chest and carry the head high. All points should be in vertical alignment from ear to ankle. In order to swing the leg effectively from the hip the trunk must be stabilized in a firm controlled hold so that the leg may move freely without causing a saggy resultant motion throughout the upper body.

KEY TO BALANCE AND CONTROL. The alert carriage of the body is equally as important as the foot and leg action or the beauty of the step pattern. Good posture is the key to body balance and control. It initiates a "readiness" throughout the whole body. It prepares the dancer to move easily from one step to another, to respond smoothly to the most subtle lead, and to adapt quickly to rhythm changes. Problems of leading and following are very closely tied up with proper carriage of the body.

A good dance posture means that the entire body is dancing, consequently any action initiated by the lead is transmitted to the follower and the response should be quickly synchronized.

EAR AND ANKLE LINE UP. The subtle thought of maintaining this alignment in an easy natural way gives the person the poise and confidence so rightfully desired by all. The dancer who practices this secret of body balance will not tire as easily. The dancer who adopts the "ear to ankle line up" as a slogan, whether dancing a favorite folk dance, in a square dance set, or on the ballroom floor, will have more assurance of what to do and how to do it, will wear a costume with greater charm and distinction, and will have a great deal more fun. It would be well if more teachers of dance would emphasize good posture among those they teach, as truly it is the body carriage which adds style to the dance pattern performed and gives the dancer that "finished, dressed up look."

Points to Remember

1. Keep yourself upright — do not lean forward or backward. Do not stick out in the "rear."
2. Keep your weight up — not dragging over your feet. This will cultivate that "light on your feet" feeling.
3. Keep yourself a moving weight — alert all the way through your body — not planted on every spot you take.
4. Transfer weight smoothly and evenly from foot to foot without unnecessary motion of the hips from side to side, or the body up and down.
5. Move on a narrow base with the feet and legs close together.
6. Practice walking backward — the lady must learn to keep her balance when taking long gliding steps backward.
7. Keep your eyes off the floor or feet.
8. Bend the ankles, knees, and hips when executing a dip — not the back and head — the trunk is held erect.
9. Be at ease but in complete control of all parts of the body.
10. Relax, listen to the music, and *enjoy* dancing!

WESTERN SQUARE DANCE

Square dance in America has developed primarily from two sources, the New England Quadrille and the Kentucky Running Set. The European influence may be noted in the figures while a Mexican-Spanish influence is apparent in the steps. The highly polished and sophisticated set dances of eighteenth and nineteenth century France are the antecedents of the New England Quadrille. The Kentucky Running Set, an old form of English dance called Running Set, has survived in the Kentucky mountains and throughout the Southern Appalachians. The Running Set is derived from a vigorous folk strain of round and chain dances from the lowlands of England and Scotland. The characteristic vigor of this dance form met with favor in the equally vigorous new world and spread quickly across the American frontier. Square Dance, the offspring of these dance forms, has embodied the characteristics of each, yet retained a personality all its own.

Definition . . . Western Square Dance is that part of the American Square Dance scene which reflects the color, custom, and casual life of the Western United States. Basically the fundamental movements, form, and techniques are like those found in other parts of the United States. It differs noticeably, however, in the enthusiastic use of elaborate patter and colorful colloquialisms as well as in the uninhibited imagination for creating figure patterns and movements that challenge the dancers' attentiveness and skill. Western Square Dance does not refute its heritage. On the contrary, over the years it has taken liberties with things from the past and molded from the original a not too distant relative which like the West is bigger, more boisterous, and benevolent.

The Patter Call . . . The patter type call is traditional in Western Square Dance. The patter call, in addition to giving directions or commands for movement, is embellished with colorful phrases and "folksy" references to western life. These bits of patter fill out the command or direction line and usually rhyme in couplet fashion with the preceding or the following line. Patter is not merely for ornamentation. It serves a real purpose in that it fills in the beats required for execution of a movement and therefore aids in proper timing of the call. Patter may precede a command or follow a command. When it precedes a command it cues that command. For example:

Rope a yearling, brand a calf,

Meet your honey with a *once and a half.*

When it follows a command it fills in the beats necessary for execution of that command. For example:

Allemande left as pretty as you can.

The "cue" call is a part of a patter call in which the rhyming word in the call gives a hint to the dancers as to what is coming next, before the actual direction is given. For example:

Allemande left and allemande *thar*

Right and left and form a star.

This advance clue makes it possible for greater continuity and flow from one figure into another. Most of the newer techniques in square dance have been created in this manner.

In addition to its usefulness and color, patter calls also reflect changes in our times. Before the horseless carriage became the mode of everyday travel the caller sang out:

Buckle up your belly bands

Loosen up your traces

All to your places

With a smile on your faces.

Today with the automobile a common item and a trip to the moon more of a fact than a fantasy, the modern caller sings out:

Throw in the clutch and put 'er in low
It's twice around on your heel and toe!

The Western Singing Call . . . The patter call has been traditionally associated with the Western Square Dance. However, in recent years the singing call has become increasingly popular among western square dancers. Singing calls have traditionally been identified with the eastern part of the United States. The chief characteristic of the singing call is that the commands or directions given follow the melody of the music. The call is phrased completely with the music. In other words, if there are sixty-four measures in the music then the call is phrased to fit one to sixty-four measures. A second characteristic, though not always true, is the fact that the call is associated with a particular tune. *"Hot Time in the Old Town Tonight"* is an example of a call title and a song title which are synonymous. *"Jessie Polka Square"* is an example of a call title and a song title which are not synonymous. The tune used for *"Jessie Polka Square"* is *"Jesuita en Chihuahua."*

The modern western singing call follows the general structure of its eastern counterpart. However, while the eastern singing call employs very simple figures, basic techniques and traditional tunes, western singing calls employ elaborate figures, breaks, trims, latest fundamental techniques and for musical background anything from modern cowboy tunes to popular ballroom dance music! The western and popular hit parade are a real source for present day western singing calls.

Regional Differences . . . The similarity in fundamental movement, form, and technique of square dance throughout the United States makes for a common bond and assures the dancer good fun and fellowship wherever he travels. Despite this basic similarity, however, the overall picture of square dancing is not one of uniformity. Like the English language, square dance has a different "accent" in each section of our country. The following items vary in different regions:

1. Tempo (speed) of dancing
2. Basic step
3. Promenade position
4. Type and duration of swing
5. Balance step
6. Variations on the do-si-do
7. Variations in style — involving:
   a. moving into and out of the promenade
   b. hand grasp on the allemande left, grand right and left, and do-si-do
   c. elbow and/or forearm grasp
   d. hand and/or wrist grasp for star figures
   e. use of a twirl
   f. use of a pause or dip on allemande left or when meeting partner on grand right and left

Dancers should be aware of these "accents" or regional differences if they are to enter into the spirit and good fellowship of the dance as enjoyed in other locales. The responsibility for pointing out these regional differences rests squarely upon those who teach.

Basic Step . . . The step which seems to be most basic to all regions is the *shuffle*. The shuffle step provides the beginner with an easy, smooth, even step which may be used for hours without fatigue. The dancer may easily add to the shuffle step any regional variations or unique stylings which please his rhythmic sense or better integrates his dance movement with that of a particular community. The basic step variations common to Western Square Dance range from the ultra smooth and sophisticated "gliding" steps to an exaggerated "limp" at the end of a two-step. Whatever the basic step, the emphasis should be on smoothness and response to the rhythm. Skipping, bouncing, and running are to be avoided since they are not only exhausting but often lead to rowdyism which is not in keeping with the spirit of the square dance.

The Caller . . . The patter caller directs the entire figure choosing materials without reference to any predetermined sequence. Therefore, it is absolutely necessary for the dancer to listen carefully to the caller. This adds a competitive element to the dance which has the effect of keeping the dancers attentive and alert and the caller versatile and profuse! To the dancer, competitive calling is an exciting challenge in which the dancer pits his skills against those of the caller. Although the caller may choose his materials and arrange the calls in any order he desires, the ultimate goal for both caller and dancer is to successfully complete the call. *The good caller, therefore, calls within the framework of the dancer's knowledge and abilities, choosing materials which are well known to the dancer.* The competition between the dancer and the caller *is not* directed at the caller's ability to call figures or breaks which are new to the dancer but rather to call from well known materials in such an exciting way that the arrangement alone will interest and challenge the dancer.

The Dancer . . . The dancer achieves his greatest satisfaction when his set can successfully complete the call. The *good* dancer needs to learn quickly the technique of *dancing to position.* This means that each dancer in the set will be aware of his relationship to *all others* in the square, and *to his home position* even when:

1. He is in a moving circle away from home position
2. He is facing out instead of in toward the center of the set
3. He is out of his original position or in relation to changes of direction
4. He has a partner other than his original partner
5. He is in lines, stars, or other figures which change the normal shape of the square.

When a mix-up occurs, all dancers should return quickly to home position and start with the call as soon as it is possible to get started again. Good square dancing and the ultimate enjoyment for all is possible when all dancers listen carefully to the call. Dancers should be approximately one call behind the caller. They need not hurry to catch up but keep moving and complete each call given before going into the next.

The Music . . . Music is the spark which sets off the lively and exciting action of the square dance. The old time "fiddle" band set the pace in the early days before records and record players were available. Even today the music of a "live" band is preferable though for certain situations economically impractical. Recorded music is available in ample quantity, and the high quality of present day recordings makes them very reasonable substitutes for live music. Western Square Dance music is predominantly 2/4 rhythm; however, many good tunes are written in 4/4 rhythm. Tunes written in 6/8 rhythm may also be used. The 6/8 rhythm is very easy to dance to but more difficult for patter calling. REMEMBER! The figure title and the tune title are not necessarily synonymous. For example: when calling the figure *"Sally Good'in"* the caller *may* use the "fiddle" tune "Sally Good'in." However, it is just as possible to use "Cripple Creek," "Soldier's Joy," or any other tune of similar rhythm. The tempo of the music will vary with the region in which one dances. In regions where the shuffle step is basic a faster tempo is more common. In regions where the two-step predominates a slower tempo is more common.

Figure Types . . . Western Square Dance figures may be grouped into relatively distinct figure types or patterns. A basic understanding of the several figure types and the structure of each will aid the teacher, caller, and dancer to more easily understand and master new and advanced figures. It is essential, from a teaching standpoint, that a variety in figure type be considered in planning a series of lessons. In like manner, it is essential that variety in figure type be considered when planning a festival, jamboree, or club program. The prospective teacher or caller should particularly keep in mind the necessity for variety in figure type while acquiring a repertoire of dance figures for future teaching and calling purposes.

Many square dance figures are "typical" rather than perfect examples of a particular type. The more elaborate figures are often a combination of several types. The descriptions of the figure types and the examples presented here are meant to serve as a guide for analysis and selection of figures which are relatively typical of the types found in Western Square Dance. The criteria used to determine the grouping of the various figure types follows.

A. The basic movement or lead action of an individual, couple, individuals, or couples which sets the figure in action and upon which the structure of the figures is based.

1. Visiting Figures

   a. Visiting couple: A figure in which each couple leads out in turn and dances a simple figure with each couple in succession around the set. The visiting couple figure may be varied in one of the following ways to make it more interesting and useful.

      1) Each couple, leading out in turn, dances a different figure. For example, couple one dances *Take a Little Peek* with each couple around the set. In like manner couple two may dance *Swing at The Wall* around the set. Couples three and four each execute a different figure.

      2) Each couple, leading out in turn, uses a different figure with each couple visited. Couple one would dance three different figures, one with each couple visited. Couple two, three, and four follow in like manner. Twelve different visiting couple figures are possible although several figures may be repeated.

      3) Each couple, leading out in turn, uses a different figure but visits only the couple on the right and then returns to home position. For example, couple one dances *Star by the Right* with couple two and then returns home. Four different figures are used in this sequence with couple visitation limited to a single visit to the couple immediately to the right.

   b. Single visiting: A figure in which one individual visits around the set dancing with each couple or with an individual or individuals of each couple visited, such as *Shoot the Owl* and *Adam and Eve*.

   c. Double visiting: A figure in which two couples are called out simultaneously and dance a figure pattern exclusive of the remaining couples, such as *Forward Up and Back*.

   d. Accumulative: A figure in which a single individual or a single couple begins the action of the figure and in turn increases the number of individuals or couples until all couples or the number of individuals indicated by the call are in action, such as *Sally Good'in*, *Sashay Partners Halfway Around*, and *Cowboy Loop*. This type is sometimes referred to as a "pick up" figure.

The Visiting Figure group, due to their simplicity and repetitious nature, offer the following *advantages*:

1) Dancers become thoroughly acquainted with their numbers, home positions, and the direction of progression around the square.

2) They offer ample opportunity for the caller to use trims which evolve from a circle of four.

3) Trims based on a circle of eight may also be injected before the "next couple" or "next individual" is called out.

4) Dancers become familiar with the term "lead" or "active" couple.

5) The competitive nature of the western patter call may be quickly and easily established.

6) The beginning caller quickly achieves the three basic fundamentals of good calling, for example, clarity, rhythm, and command, due to the repetitious nature and brevity of this group.

But the visiting figure group leaves the majority of dancers in the square standing too long. Present day dancers prefer more action.

2. Symmetrical Figures: A figure in which all four couples or all eight individuals simultaneously execute the same figure action. In addition, this figure type is characterized by a progression of the ladies, and sometimes the men, around the set so that each individual has a new partner for the repeat of the figure, such as *Arkansas Traveler*. Many figures fit in whole or in part into the symmetrical group.

B. The characteristic and distinctive design or pattern formation which readily identifies the figure.

1. Line Figures: A figure in which the action takes place between two opposing lines. The lines may be made up of three or four dancers, as in *The Route*. The single file or trailing type line formed in *Cowboy Loop* makes it possible to classify it in this group.

2. Star Figures: A figure in which one or more star formations are executed by three, four, or all eight dancers in the set. The star is the distinctive pattern formed and the word "star" usually appears in the title of the

dance figure: *Texas Star, Four Gents Star*, and *Double Star*.

3. Split the Ring Figures: A figure in which one couple moves across the set and goes between the opposite couple, separates and moves around the outside of the set. Then depending upon the call, the dancers may go around first *one* person, around *two* persons, or around the outside to home position. The foot or walking pattern of the dancers, in effect, cuts or divides the standing couple and then separates the moving couple. Few figures of this type are content with such simple movement and in general are more elaborate than the figure analysis here implies because of the action which follows the splitting motion, as in *Split the Ring, Split the Ring and Around Just One*, and *Split the Ring and Around Just Two. Split the Ring* is an example of this figure type.

4. Arching Figures: A figure in which a couple raises inside joined hands and moves over or ducks under a similar arch formed by an opposite couple, as in *Inside Arch and the Outside Under*. The arching of the joined hands is a distinctive feature of this group.

TEACHING NOTES

In square dance, as in many other forms of activity, the dancer must acquire a basic vocabulary of terms peculiar to the activity. The dancer must learn the meaning of and the appropriate reaction to the several fundamental techniques which form a necessary background from which he works and progresses. The following list of fundamental techniques[1] are the foundation stones upon which the intricate and colorful action of the square dance is based.

Basic Step	Pass Through	Square Through
Balance	Ladies Chain	Cross Trail Through
Swing	Ladies Grand Chain	Box the Gnat
Promenade	Sashay	Allemande Thar
Do Paso	Do-Si-Do	California Twirl
Do-Sa-Do	Back Track (Turn Back)	Bend the Line
Allemande Left	Once and a Half	Wheel Around
Grand Right and Left	Courtesy Turn	Dixie Chain
Right and Left Through	Star Through	

[1] Analysis of these and other key techniques may be found in the Glossary of terms.

Although the fundamental techniques are important, they are a means to an end rather than an end in themselves; therefore, they must be interwoven into the overall structure of the square dance. The Big Circle Method and the Set Method illustrate how these fundamental techniques may be incorporated into the whole structure of the square dance in a simple, clear, and effective manner.

Big Circle Method . . . In this method the dancers are arranged in a large circle around the room, each with a partner. The big circle formation may be employed exclusively for several consecutive class periods. Simple command calls based on the fundamentals taught may be arranged and called by the teacher. Thus the class may square dance for several beginning lessons without ever being in the set or square formation. After the techniques have been mastered, the class may be arranged into the traditional square formation, and the fundamental techniques are then correlated with the four basic parts of the square dance as the various dance figures are taught. Even after the class has become entrenched in the regular square formation, the circle formations may be used in the review and the warm up period before the class is arranged in sets.

The big circle formations may also be employed for only a part of each day's lesson. The circle formations may be used at the beginning of the class period for presenting and practicing selected new fundamental techniques to be used in the day's lesson. The class may then be arranged into sets and the techniques previously taught in the big circle integrated with the figure to be used in the lesson. The following outline illustrates how the fundamental techniques may be employed in several different types of circle formation for effective analysis and presentation.

1. SINGLE CIRCLE (and variations)
   Basic Step: Arrange couples in a single circle facing center. The basic step is the first fundamental to be dealt with irrespective of method used. Refer to page 40 and 41 for analyses and teaching suggestions.
   Balance: Arrange couples in a single cir-

cle facing center. Suggested teaching progression:
   a. Demonstrate balance with counts.
   b. Class practice.
   c. Class execute in response to call and music.
   d. Repeat (c) combining balance with a swing.

Swing: A single circle, couples facing center, may be used for a demonstration of the swing position and movement. Change the formation to a single circle, partners facing, for a detailed analysis of the swing position. After the swing position and movements have been mastered, it is important to have the dancers respond to a series of calls which require them to swing, starting from a stationary position, and to break into a swing from a circling movement. Here they may learn the difference in releasing a partner swing and corner swing.

Do Paso: Since the do paso is adaptable to circles of four, six, eight, or more, it is advisable to have the dancers practice it in the several circles in which it may be used. Teaching suggestions:
   a. Arrange couples in several single circles of more than eight couples but not more than sixteen couples.
   b. Designate one couple to be the lead or active couple.
   c. Direct the lead couple to lead to the right and circle four with the next couple. Call the do paso for the circle of four.
   d. Direct the lead couple to pick up the next couple and circle six. Call the do paso for the circle of six.
   e. Repeat, increasing the size of the circle.

Grand Right and Left—Allemande Left: The allemande left and the grand right and left are commonly called as one movement in the Western Square Dance. However, in reality they are two separate fundamentals. Therefore, to impress the dancers with the nature and action of these two fundamentals it is best to teach them separately. Teach the grand right and left first, then teach the allemande left. After dancers have responded to the calls in separate practice routines the two may be called as they are traditionally used. Although it is possible to teach these fundamentals in one large single circle, it is less fatiguing to both the dancer and caller to break the circles up into smaller groups or teach it in the regular square or set formation.

Sashay: Arrange couples in a single circle facing center. Teaching suggestions:

a. Demonstrate the sashay.
b. Ladies stand still, men move through action.
c. Repeat, men stand still, ladies move through action.
d. Both move through figure simultaneously in response to the call and music.

Do-Sa-Do: Arrange couples in a single circle, partners facing. Teaching suggestions:

a. Demonstrate the do-sa-do.
b. Class practice with partner, then with corner.
c. Execute movement in response to call and music.

Back Track — Turn Back — Once and a Half: These techniques are customarily used during a grand right and left and are executed as partners meet, therefore, a smaller single circle or the square formation may prove more effective for analyzing and presenting these fundamentals.

2. DOUBLE CIRCLE

Promenade: A double circle, partners facing, may be used for analyzing the hand positions to be used. Once the hand positions are taken the dancers simply face counter-clockwise and execute the promenade. Here is the opportunity to teach a twirl of the lady when going into or out of a promenade, if such a twirl is customarily used in that community. A series of calls which move the dancers from a circle or swing into a promenade helps the group as well as the individual couples achieve smooth transition from other movements into the promenade.

3. SICILIAN CIRCLE

Courtesy Turn: A commonly used turn in which partners, facing in the same direction, turn as a unit. The man takes the lady's left hand in his left, about left shoulder height, places his right hand in the small of her back, waist level, and in this position the couple turns as a unit, the man backing up, the lady moving forward and around to face as directed by the call. This movement ends or finishes off many dance movements, the do paso, ladies chain, etc.

Right and Left Through: In Western Square Dance, dancers take right hands in passing, although many dance groups have discontinued the custom of extending the right hand to the opposite person as this movement is executed. Whether customary or not, it is a helpful device in teaching this technique. After having learned the movement in this fashion, the dancer may bow to the dictates of regional custom as the occasion demands. It is especially helpful to teach the courtesy turn first. Suggested progression for teaching right and left through:

a. Men take one step to the left.
b. Couples advance toward each other grasping right hands with opposites, momentarily, as they pass right shoulders.
c. Man then courtesy turns lady.
d. The caller may call a, b, c, to original positions or a variety of other calls as he chooses.

Ladies Chain: The ladies chain may be executed directly across the set, to the right, or to the left as directed by the call or caller. The courtesy turn is used to end the figure. Teaching suggestions:

a. Ladies advance toward each other grasping hands, momentarily, as they pass.
b. Ladies give left hand to opposite man.
c. Man turns lady with courtesy turn.
d. The caller may call a, b, c, to original places or a variety of other calls as he chooses.

Pass Through: Dancers execute this movement independently. Each dancer passes the opposite's right shoulder and remains facing in the direction moved until caller gives the next call. Dancers do not touch right hands in passing.

Teaching suggestions:

  a. Two couples face, move toward each other passing right shoulders. Do not touch right hands. Each moves forward independently.

  b. Remain facing out until further directions are given by the caller.

  c. If directed to turn back by the caller, each dancer turns independently and moves back past opposite's right shoulder, remains facing out until caller directs next movement.

The Set Method . . . In this method the dancers are arranged in the regular "set" or "square" formation. The fundamental techniques and the four basic parts of the square dance, introduction, main figure, trimmings, and endings are integrated. Essentially, this means that the fundamental techniques are taught as they occur in the various parts of the whole dance. The following outline points out how the integration of the fundamental techniques and the four basic parts of the square dance may be achieved.

Basic Step: The basic step is the first fundamental technique to be dealt with irrespective of method used. In this method each square forms a single circle and practices the simple one step or shuffle step circling to the left and to the right. In regions where the two-step or combination of the one-step and the two-step is used it may be more effective to arrange the dancers into one large single circle or one long line for a more detailed analysis and demonstration of the two-step. Refer to page 40 and page 41 for analysis and teaching suggestions.

Balance, Swing, Promenade, Grand Right and Left, Allemande Left, Do-Sa-Do, Back Track, Turn Back, Allemande Thar, Once and a Half: These techniques may be taught as they occur in the many introductions, trimmings, and endings which go to make up the complete square dance sequence. Balance and Swing often appear consecutively in introductory calls, for example, "All eight balance — all eight swing." Both techniques may be analyzed and practiced at one time in direct reference to the call used. Back track, turn

back, and the once and a half embellish the grand right and left. It is advisable to wait until the dancers are thoroughly accustomed to the grand right and left before adding these techniques.

Right and Left Through, Ladies Chain, Ladies Grand Chain: These techniques are a featured part of the following dance figures: *Forward Up and Back, The Route,* and *Promenade the Outside Ring. Forward Up and Back* also makes use of the ladies grand chain. The latter fundamental can only be taught from the set formation.

Sashay: This technique may be introduced by way of the figure *Sashay Partners Halfway Around.* The sashay is the basic movement in the trimming "All around your left hand lady — see saw your pretty little baby."

Pass Through: This technique is employed in many dance figures. For example: *Ends Turn In, Corners of the World, Split the Ring and Around Just One,* and *Milagro Square.*

Do Paso or Do-Si-Do: The visiting couple type figure offers ample opportunity for employing the do paso and/or do-si-do. Any figure which finished with a circle of four may serve for either do paso or do-si-do. Any circle of six or eight offers opportunity for the use of do paso. Accumulative type figures such as *Cowboy Loop* and *Sashay Partners Halfway Around* permit the use of the do paso or the do-si-do in circles of four, six, and eight. The Shaw style do-si-do is adaptable only when a circle of four is formed.

In teaching the basic trims and figures it is wise to discuss the specific action in relation to maintaining the normal shape and size of the square. For example, in the promenade the men should pull in toward the center as they move around the ring, thus preventing the square from spreading out. Further, when one or more dancers promenades the outside of the ring, waiting couples should move in a few steps to close the square, thus minimizing the distance to be traveled. A third example, when teaching dancers the technique for swinging an opposite across the hall, the men should allow the man dancer to his immediate left to precede him as they move to the left half way around the square. Finally, it is important to help dancers learn the concept of space and movement in relation to the entire figure to be formed. Movements such as splitting the ring and moving around one or two dancers to form a line must be understood in terms of the entire figure being formed by these movements.

Teaching method coupled with thoughtful and detailed planning of the unit and daily lesson plan are the chief components of successful teaching. A check list of specific materials and techniques to be taught (devised from the general and specific objectives) assists in indicating progression and accomplishment.

THE SQUARE

Four couples form a square or set. Each couple forms one side of the square. All four couples face the center of the square, each man with his partner on his right. This is *home position* for each couple. Couples are numbered counter-clockwise or to the right around the square beginning with couple one. Couple one always has its back to the caller and the music. Couple two is to the right of couple one, couple three is opposite couple one, and couple four is to the left of couple one. Couples one and three are "head couples." Couples two and four are "side couples." The lady to the left of each man is the corner lady. The lady in the couple to the right of each man is the right hand lady. The lady directly across the square is the opposite lady.

Parts of the Square Dance

There are four parts to the square dance. The patter caller may select the various parts at random and arrange them into an interesting and exciting pattern. Introductory figures, trimmings, and endings are often used interchangeably. Those listed in this book are typical of Western Square Dance. The four parts of the square dance are:

1. Introduction. Refer to page 63.

2. The Main Figure, from which the dance often takes its name. Refer to pages 73-115.

3. Trimmings, often called Fill-ins, Breaks, etc., and are used as a chorus between sections of the main figure. Refer to pages 65-71.

4. Ending. Refer to pages 64-65.

A SAMPLE CALL ILLUSTRATING THE USE OF THE FOUR PARTS

Introduction:
Honor your partner, lady by your side
All join hands and circle wide
All the way around that great big ring
Home you go and everybody swing

Main Figure:
First and third go forward and back
Forward again in the same old track
Turn your opposite with the right hand
   around
Partners left and a left hand around
Corners all right and a right hand around
Partners left and left hand around
And promenade your corners
All around that ring
Home you go and everybody swing
   Repeat main figure for two and four

Trimming:
Walk all around your left hand lady
See saw your pretty little baby
Allemande left with your left hand
Dance right into a right and left grand
Meet your honey and give her a swing
Promenade home go around that ring
Home you go and everybody swing
   Repeat main figure for one and three
   Repeat main figure for two and four

Ending:
Allemande left with your left hand
Bow to your partner
And there you stand

INTRODUCTORY CALLS

Honor your partner, lady by your side
All join hands and circle wide
Break and trail along that line
The lady in the lead, the gent behind
Now you're home and now you swing
Round and round with the dear little thing.

Honor your partner and corners all
Swing your opposite across the hall
Treat your corner just the same
Home you go and everybody swing.

Honor your partner and give her a swing
Honor your corner, swing your partner!
Promenade two by two
Around that ring like you use to do.

Swing your partner by your side
All join hands and circle out wide
And Do Paso on all four sides
Grab your gal, don't let her fall
Promenade and home you go.

All jump up and never come down
Swing your partner 'round and 'round
And promenade, boys, promenade.

All join hands and circle to the left
Whoa-there! You're going wrong
Turn right back in single file — Indian style
Now swing that gal behind you.
Put her in the lead Indian style
Turn right back and swing awhile
Swing that gal behind you.
Trail along another half mile
Turn right back and swing awhile
Swing that gal behind you.
Trail along for an osage mile
Turn right back and swing awhile
This is the one you call your own
Take this gal and promenade home.
Little bit of heel, a little bit of toe
Join your hands and away we go
Now into the center and give a little yell!
Do it again, that's not too well,
Back up, boys, and swing your own
And promenade, go right on home.
Honor your partner and the lady by your
  side
All join hands and circle out wide
Break and swing and promenade home.

All to your places and straighten up your
  faces
Tighten up the bellybands, loosen up the
  traces
All join hands, we're off to the races
Circle left, go all the way around
Home you go and settle down
Swing that pretty girl 'round and 'round.

All join hands and circle to the left
Now up to the center and build a little nest
Rear right back and bust your vest
And swing the gal that you love best.

Honor your partner, give her a swing
Honor your corner, give her a swing
Now run back home and swing your own
And thank the Lord the bird ain't flown.

Swing your honey 'round and 'round
Any old way but upside down
Promenade her 'round and 'round
Promenade, you're going to town.

Clap your hands
Now slap your knees (twice)
Bump-si-daisy if you please
  (Partners bump hips together)
Swing on the corner high and low
Swing your own, I told you so
Now promenade.

Honor your partner, lady by your side
All join hands and circle wide
Spread right out like an old cow hide
Break and trail along that line
Lady in front and the gent behind
Home you go, you're doing fine
You swing yours and I'll swing mine.

All eight balance, all eight swing
Now promenade around the ring.

Swing your partner, don't be late
Swing on the corner like swingin' on the
  gate!
Now your own and promenade eight.

All join hands and circle to the south
Let a little moonshine in your mouth
Break and trail along that line
When you get home what'll you do
You swing her and she'll swing you.

GRAND RIGHT AND LEFT PATTER

Allemande left with your left hand
Right to your partner
And a right and left grand
Promenade eight when you come straight.

Swing on the corner like swingin' on the
  gate
Now swing your own if you're not too late
Allemande left with your left hand
Right to your partner, right and left grand.

Allemande left as pretty as you can
Right to your honey
And a right and left grand.

Allemande left as pretty as you can
Dance right into a right and left grand
Hand over hand around the ring
Meet your partner and everybody swing.

Lift your feet, set 'em down
Make those big feet jar the ground!
Allemande left without a sound
Grand right and left, go 'round and 'round.

On the corner with your left hand
Walk right into a right and left grand.

PROMENADE PATTER

Promenade around the ring
While the roosters crow and the birdies sing.

Here we go in a little red wagon
Rear wheel's broke and the axle's draggin'
Promenade, boys, promenade.

With your big foot up
And your little foot down
Promenade, go 'round and 'round.

Meet your honey and pat her on the head
If she don't like whiskey
Feed her corn bread, promenade.

With your right foot up
And your left foot down
Promenade your partner around.

Meet your honey and pat her on the head.
Promenade — that's what I said!

Meet ole Sal and meet ole Sue
Meet the gal with the run down shoe
Now promenade them two by two.

Promenade, go 'round and 'round
Like a Jay bird hoppin' on the frozen
  ground.

Ace of diamonds, jack of spades
Meet your honey and all promenade.

Meet that gal who's dressed in blue
She's the one that's stuck on you!
Promenade.

Two, four, six, and eight
All promenade when you get straight.

ENDINGS

Honor your partner, corners all
Honor your opposite across the hall
And that is all.

Promenade — you know where
And I don't care
Take her out and give her air.

All you folks listen to the call
Thank you, ladies — that will be all.

Grab your honey and promenade there
You know where and I don't care.

Now take your honey right off the floor
That's all there is, there ain't no more.

Honor your partner and your corner too
Now wave at the gal across from you
Thank you, folks, I'm all through.

Promenade her, you know where and I don't
 care
Take your honey to a nice soft chair.

Honor your partner, corner all
Wave at the gal across the hall
Thank you, folks, I guess that's all.

Allemande left with your left hand
Bow to your partner and there you stand.

Some will yell, some will holler
Thank the fiddler and kiss the caller.

Swing your honey and there you stand
Oh, by golly, ain't that grand.

TRIMS, BREAKS, FILLERS

The terms trim, break, or filler are synonymous. They are preferably short chorus figures used between sections of the main figure. Unlike the chorus of a song, they are not necessarily the same each time. They enliven and add spice to the call. Use more or longer trims to lengthen a short figure. When the main figure is long, use fewer and shorter trims.

Trims should be chosen to enhance the symmetry of the figure and to complement the formation being used at the time of insertion. Every trim is designed to flow logically from certain formations and positions. Choose trims to make smooth transitions from one movement to another. There should not be a break in position or rhythm to move into or out of a trim. With this criterion in mind, the following trims have been grouped in relation to the several formations and movement patterns which they complement.

Trims for Fours

Do-Si-Do
Do-si-do and a little more dough
Chicken in the bread pan peck'n out dough
Grab your partner and on you go
Promenade.

Circle left and around you go
Break it up with a do-si-do
Partner left and left hand around
Corner right and a right hand around
Promenade your honey as you come down.
 Note: Used for Shaw type do-si-do
  or do paso as desired.

Swap 'n' Trade
Now we swap and now we trade
Your pretty girl for my old maid
Yours is pretty and mine's so fine
You swing yours and I'll swing mine.

Ring, Ring
Ring, ring, pretty little ring
Break that ring with a corner swing
Ring, ring, pretty little ring
Break that ring with a corner swing.

Half Square Through
One and three go forward and back
Now half square through around the track
Right and left through with the outside two
Dive through, pass through to an allemande
 left.

Box the Gnat
Head two couples go forward and back
Right to opposite box the gnat
Pull her through and U turn back
 After box the gnat, opposites hang on
  with right, pull partner by to home
  position and turn in place.
First and third go forward and back
Cross trail through go around one
Come into the middle box the gnat
Right and left through, pass through
Split the ring, go around one
Meet partner, cross trail through
Allemande left.

Square Through
Heads go forward and back you do
Forward again and full square through
Now count four hands is what you do.

Heads two couples go square through
Right, left, right, and pass a few
Partner left and now you're through.

Star Through
Heads go forward, back with you
Go forward again and pass through
Around just one is what you do
Into the center and star through
Cross-trail through, look out, man
There's your corner, left allemande.

Dixie Chain

Heads (Sides) to the middle
Don't you roam
Cross trail through across from home
Round just one, go into the middle
Dixie chain in time to the fiddle
Ladies go left, gents go right
Round just one
Go back to the middle
Box the gnat, it's no riddle
Turn to the side
Do a left allemande.
     Continue as called.

Do Paso

Eight hands up and away we go
Circle left and don't be slow
Break right out with a do paso
Partner left, corner right
Back to your partner,
Turn that gal if it takes all night.

Ring, Ring

Ring, ring, pretty little ring
Break that ring with a corner swing
Ring, ring, pretty little ring
Break that ring with a corner swing
Now all four gents listen to the call
Swing your opposite across the hall
She ain't been swung since 'way last fall
And promenade home.

> *Note:* Call as described above or repeat
> "ring, ring, pretty little ring," etc.,
> four times until ladies are returned
> to original partners.

See Saw

Walk all around your left hand lady
    Gents move left behind corner lady and
    around her back to place.
See saw your pretty little taw
    Gents move right behind partner and
    around her back to place.

Box the Gnat

Box that gnat, box that flea
Box that pretty gal back to me.
    Box the gnat: Partners face, join right
    hands. Exchange places, lady turns coun-
    ter-clockwise under joined hands.
    Box the flea: Partners face, join left
    hands. Exchange places, lady turns coun-
    terclockwise under joined hands.

Sashay

Sashay partners halfway 'round
Resashay, go all the way 'round.

Sashay partners one and all
Resashay and don't you fall.

Trims for Eights

Throw in the Clutch

Throw in the clutch and put 'er in low
Gals walk around on your heel and toe
Twice around that ring you go.

> From star position in allemande thar,
> gents release ladies' left hand, ladies con-
> tinue counterclockwise, gents change di-
> rection move clockwise. Dancers may
> meet partner or corner and finish as
> directed by caller.

Swing Opposite

All four gents listen to my call
Swing your opposite across the hall.

The old cow kicked and the yearling bawled
Swing your opposite across the hall.

Star by the right across the ring
Give your opposite a great big swing.

Star by the left across the square
Swing your opposite standing there.

Down the center we'll roll the ball
Swing your opposite across the hall.
She ain't been swung since 'way last fall.

> *Note:* If dancers are with original part-
> ners when a "swing your opposite"
> call is made, use a second "swing
> your opposite" call or call "ring,
> ring" twice to return them to origi-
> nal partners.

Rip 'n' Snort

First couple go down the center with a
Rip 'n' Snort.

Down the center and cut 'em short
  All hands remain joined as couple 1 goes
  across and under arch formed by couple
  2.

Lady go gee and the gent go haw
  Couple 1, only, releases joined inside
  hands. Lady leads right, gent left as they
  pull their lines through the arch. Couple
  3 turns under own arch to face center of
  set once more.

Circle eight as you come straight.
  Repeat call for couples 2, 3, and 4. Couples always lead through arch formed by
  opposite couple. Example: 2 through 4,
  3 through 1, and 4 through 2.

Alamo Style

Allemande left in alamo style

Right to your honey and balance awhile
  Gents hold corners by the left, partners
  by the right. Gents face in, ladies face out.
  All hands are joined.

Balance in and balance out
  Gents step to center and back, as ladies
  step away from center and back.

Turn with the right hand half about
  Gents turn half around clockwise with
  partner. Gents now face out, ladies in.
  All hands are rejoined.

Balance out and balance in
  Gents step away from center and back.
  Ladies step to center and back.

Turn with the left hand half about
  Gents turn half around counterclockwise
  with right hand lady. Gents face in, ladies
  face out. All hands are rejoined.

Balance in and balance out
  Repeat as before.

Turn with the right hand half about
  Gents turn half around clockwise with
  opposite lady.

Balance out and balance in

Turn with the left hand half again
  Gents turn half around counterclockwise
  with corners. Meet and swing partners.

Swing your partner and promenade.

Sashay Right Around the Square

Allemande left with your corner there

Now Sashay right around the square
  Sashay or do-sa-do partner.

A right hand to that lady fair
  Partner by right, balance back and pass
  to next lady.

Sashay left around the square
  Sashay or do-sa-do around right hand
  lady.

A left hand to that lady there
  Left to right hand lady, balance back
  and pass to next lady.

Sashay right around the square

Right hand to that lady fair
  Repeat with opposite lady.

Sashay left around the square

Left hand to that lady fair
  Repeat with corner lady.

Sashay right around your own

Swing your gal and promenade home.

Gents Step Out (Back Track)

Eight hands up and away we go

Circle left and don't be slow

The other way back in single file

Lady in the lead, gents run wild

Gents step out and take a back track
  Gents reverse direction, moving clockwise
  around outside of set. Ladies continue
  counterclockwise.

Meet your honey with a right arm around
  Turn partners once and a half.

Allemande left as you come down

Right to your own go right on around

With a grand right and left.

Hi Diddle Diddle

Hi diddle, diddle

All eight to the middle

Stamp your feet in tune with the fiddle

Bust right out and swing your own

And leave my pretty little gal alone.

  Note: This call may be used as an intro-
    ductory call.

Thread the Needle

First old couple go down the center
And thread that needle and thread it wide
Sew it up on all four sides
Loop right under and pull it tight
Sew it up both left and right
Make that line if it takes all night.

> All hands joined. Couple 1 leads under the arch of couple 3. Couple 1, only, release inside hands. Lady goes right, gent left, pull lines through arch. Couple 3 turns half around to face opposite direction. Gent 1, again, leads line under second arch formed by lady 3 and the last person in line. Lady 1 does the same on gent 3's side. Continue to loop the lines under remaining arches until all are in a straight line facing forward, hands crossed in front.

> *Note:* Dance may end with the dancers in one straight line or caller may back the end dancers around and form a circle with dancers facing out. Call "eight hands up and away we go," dancers turn under own top arm without releasing joined hands to make original circle.

Bend the Line

One and three lead to the right
Circle four and make a line
Forward and back you're doing fine
Pass through and bend the line
Pass through and bend the line
> Pass through and bend line called two or four times puts sets in proper order.

Bend the Line

One and three lead to the right
Circle four and form a line
Forward and back you're doing fine
Pass through and bend the line
> Face couple in your line.
Pass through and bend the line.
> Call pass through and bend the line two or four times to put set in proper order.

All Eight Chain

(Chain All Eight)

Walk all around your corner lady
Walk right around your pretty baby
All eight chain your corner lady
> Corners join right hands, pass, give left to next, and courtesy turn, face center.
Four ladies chain across the land
Gents will turn with his left hand
Chain 'em back for a do-sa-do
Now chain all eight and here we go
Take your partner by the hand
Promenade around don't just stand.

Eight Chain Through

Heads to the center and back you do
Forward again do a full square through
Count four hands don't get mixed
Right and left through now you're fixed
> With side couples
Eight Chain through you an't through yet
All the way over and back you bet
> Continue across set and back to starting position.
Meet that couple right and left through
> (Side couple with whom chain began)
To a left allemande in front of you.

Bend the Line

One and three do a pass through
Split the ring and go around two
Hang on tight form two lines
Go forward and back keep in time
Pass through and bend the line
Pass through now and bend it tight
Circle up eight and keep it right.

Bend the Line

One and three lead out to the right
Circle up four with all your might
Break right out to a line of four
Forward and back and then no more
Pass through bend the line
Pass through bend the line
Pass through bend the line
Pass through bend the line.
> Continue as Caller directs.

Trims for Grand Right and Left

Once and a Half
Rope a yearling, brand a calf
Meet your honey with a once 'n a half
With an elbow hook and an elbow crook
The more you swing, the prettier they look
First old Sal, then old Sue
Now the gal with the run down shoe
Meet your own and promenade home.

Meet your honey coming down the pike
Swing her once 'n a half
And treat 'em all alike
Swing 'em high, swing 'em low
Swing those pretty little calico's
Meet your honey and on you go
Promenade home.

Catch All Eight
Hurry up boys don't be late
Meet your honey and catch all eight
With a right go half way 'round
Back with the left go all the way 'round
    Continue as called.

Double Back Track
Corn in the crib, wheat in the stack
Meet your honey and turn right back
Up the river and around the bend
Meet your honey turn back again
Meet your partner and promenade.

Listen folks to what I say
Meet your gal and go the other way
Whirl the rope and jerk the slack
Meet your partner and turn right back
Promenade boys, promenade.

Meet your honey and sing a little song
Turn right back you done gone wrong
Meet your honey and sing once more
Turn right back as you did before
Meet your partner and promenade.

Box the Gnat
Keep on goin' like this and that
Meet your honey and Box the Gnat
And go the other way.

Trims for Allemande Left

Allemande O

Allemande left and Allemande O
    O is the key word that identified this
    figure.
Go right and left and Do Paso
    Right to partner, pass by, left to next to
    begin Do Paso. This lady becomes new
    partner.
Her by the left, left arm around
Corner by right, right arm around
Back to partner left, full turn around
    Take a full turn with forearm grasp in
    order to continue around circle the nor-
    mal way.
On to the next, pass her by
Next with a left for a Do Paso
    Repeat action as above.
Her by left, left arm round
Corner by right, right arm round
Back to partner, full around
Meet next and Promenade.
    One time through figure returns dancer
    to original partner.

Allemande Thar

Allemande left and allemande thar
    "Thar" is the key word which identifies
    this figure movement.
Go right and left and form a star
Gents back up in a right hand star
    Right to partner, left to next lady – right
    hand lady – use forearm grasp, turn three
    quarters counterclockwise to form right
    hand star in center. Retain hold of la-
    dies' left arm, gents move backward, la-
    dies forward. Star turns counterclockwise.
Let that star to the Heavens whirl
    Gents break star, swing half around coun-
    terclockwise to face opposite lady.
Go right and left to a brand new girl
And form a star, back up boys not too far
    Right to opposite, left to next-original
    corner. Use forearm grasp, swing into
    center to form another right hand star.
Shoot that star and find your own
And promenade your pretty girl home.
    Gents swing half around counterclockwise
    to face partner. Promenade home.

Triple Allemande

Allemande left and the ladies star
  Ladies form right hand star in center.
  Star moves clockwise.
Gents walk around but not too far
  Gents walk counterclockwise around,
  ladies star.
Allemande left and the gentlemen star
  Left hand around original corner. Gents
  form right hand star. Star moves clock-
  wise.
The ladies walk around but not too far
  Ladies walk counterclockwise around,
  gents star.
Allemande left with your left hand
  Left around original corner.
Right to your partner
For a right and left grand.

Allemande Left — Allemande Right

Allemande left your corner
  Left arm around corner.
Allemande right your own
  Right arm around partner.
Hug and swing that corner girl
As tho' she were your own.
  Swing corner. Call may be repeated three
  times to return gents to original partners.

Allemande A

Allemande left and allemande A
  "A" is the key word which identifies this
  movement.
Go right and left and half sashay.
  Half sashay right hand lady.
Resashay go all the way around
  Resashay with right hand lady.
Gent star right to opposite lady
Left arm around
Right to the corner pull her by
And swing the next gal on the fly.

Wagon Wheel Break

Allemande left and a right to your girl
It's a wagon wheel so let it whirl
  Right to partner, use forearm grasp, turn
  once clockwise. Gents star left in center
  as they spin turn partners once clockwise.
  Ladies hook left hand in gent's right
  elbow. Couples move counterclockwise in
  star formation.
The hub flies out, the rim flies in
  Gents break star. Couples back out turn-
  ing counterclockwise once and a quarter
  to face partners in a single circle forma-
  tion.
It's a right and left, you're gone again
To another girl for another wheel
The faster you spin, the better you feel
  Right to partners, left to next — right
  hand lady — right to opposite. Use fore-
  arm grasp, turn into another wheel as
  described above.
Now the hub flies out the rim flies in
  Repeat as described above.
It's a right and left, you're gone again
  Right to opposite, left to corner.
Find your pretty girl, find your maid
Find your own and all promenade.

Turn Back to Allemande Left

Allemande left, grand right and left
Meet your honey, pat her on the head
Turn right back, that's what I said
To an allemande left with your left hand
Back to your partner for a
Right and left grand.
  Complete grand right and left until partners meet on opposite side of set. Take
  right hands and turn back, gents immediately turn the next lady — original corner — with an allemande left, then back
  to partner for another grand right and
  left.

Trims for Promenade

Red Hot

Promenade ready or not
Let's all promenade red hot!
  Gents turn ladies into center of set with
  left hands. Gents step slightly back and
  then to right to give ladies proper amount
  of space in center of set.
Swing your right hand lady. Right arm
  around
  Gents move forward, turn right hand
  lady with right forearm grasp.
Back to your partner, go all the way 'round
  Turn partners with left, once and a half
To your corner lady with a right arm
  around
  Turn corner once around.
Back to your partner. Go all the way
  around.
Promenade your corner as she comes down.
  Call may be repeated until ladies return
  to original partners.

Slip 'em Through

Promenade around — etc.
Now slip 'em through with your left hand
  Gents turn ladies to center with left hand.
  Ladies face clockwise.
Right to the next for a right and left grand
  Gents begin grand right and left with the
  next lady.
Meet your gal, the new one pal!
  Gents meet and promenade, a new part-
  ner, the lady with whom he began the
  grand right and left.
Promenade home.
  Call may be repeated until gents are
  returned to original partner.

Wheel Around

Promenade all and don't you frown
Head (Side) couples wheel around
Right and left through the couple you've
    found.
  Ladies chain, pass through, do-si-do, etc.,
  may be called instead of right and left
  through.

Promenade and keep up the pace
Heads (Sides) wheel around
Right and left through with the couple you
    face.
  Ladies chain, pass through, do-si-do, etc.,
  may be called instead of right and left
  through.

Promenade, but don't slow down
First and third, wheel around
Right and left through
Cross trail back to an Allemande left
  Man and lady pass through the couple
  they face and cross over man going behind lady. All eight are facing out. Man
  turns right, lady left to find corner for an
  allemande left.

CLASSIFIED INDEX OF SQUARE DANCE

ADAM AND EVE

FIRST GENT OUT TO THE RIGHT

AND SWING OLD ADAM WITH ALL YOUR MIGHT

Gent 1 swings gent 2 right hand around once. Use forearm grasp.

THEN SWING MISS EVE BEFORE YOU LEAVE

Gent 1 swings lady 2 with left hand around. Use forearm grasp.

HOME YOU GO AND EVERYBODY SWING

All couples swing with waist swing.

LEAD TO THE NEXT

Gent 1 visits couple 3, repeat call. Gent 1 visits couple 4, repeat call. Repeat call for gents 2, 3, and 4.

CORNERS OF THE WORLD

ONE AND THREE BALANCE AND SWING

STAR BY THE RIGHT IN THE CENTER OF THE RING

Couples 1 and 3 form right hand star in center of set. Turn star once around clockwise.

SIDE COUPLES WHIRL TO THE CORNERS OF THE WORLD

Side couples separate, gents whirl left, ladies right, to the corners of the square.

HEADS CROSS TRAIL THROUGH DON'T HESITATE

LEFT ON THE CORNER DON'T BE LATE

Couples 1 and 3 pass through in the center of the set. Partners exchange places, then turn corners once around with left hand.

SWING YOUR OWN FOR HEAVEN SAKE

Couples 1 and 3 swing own partner in opposite positions in set. Couples 2 and 4 return to home positions and swing own partner.

STAR BY THE RIGHT IN THE CENTER ONCE MORE

Couples 1 and 3 form right hand star in center of set, turn star once around clockwise.

SIDE COUPLES WHIRL AS YOU DID BEFORE

Side couples separate, gents whirl left, ladies right, to the corners of the square.

HEADS CROSS TRAIL THROUGH ACROSS THE LAND

LEFT ALLEMANDE AND A RIGHT AND LEFT GRAND

Couples 1 and 3 pass through in the center of set. Partners exchange places, then turn original corners once around with left hand. Meet partner for grand right and left.

Repeat call for couples 2 and 4.

References in Bibliography for Adam and Eve: 18 (p. 15), 36 (p. 81), 41 (p. 65), 94 (p. 228, and 100 (p. 38).
Corners of the World figure originated by Mr. Pat Pattison, Santa Fe, New Mexico.

BIRD IN THE CAGE
(Three Hands 'Round)

FIRST COUPLE, BALANCE AND SWING
LEAD TO THE RIGHT AND FORM A RING
WITH FOUR HANDS AROUND
CAGE THE BIRD WITH THREE HANDS 'ROUND
 Lady 1 steps in center. Couple 2 and gent 1 join hands and circle around
 lady 1.
BIRD HOPS OUT, CROW HOPS IN
 Gent 1 steps in center as lady 1 joins circle with couple 2.
RING UP THREE AND YOU'RE GONE AGAIN
CROW HOPS OUT WITH A RIGHT HAND CROSS
 Gent 1 steps out between the two ladies, all four form a right hand star
THEN BACK WITH THE LEFT AND DON'T GET LOST
 Reverse direction, form left hand star.
FORM A RING AND MAKE IT GO
 (Use appropriate trim.)*
LEAD TO THE NEXT
 Call may be repeated for couples 2, 3, and 4.

SASHAY PARTNERS HALF WAY AROUND

FIRST COUPLE OUT TO THE COUPLE ON THE RIGHT
CIRCLE FOUR WITH ALL YOUR MIGHT
SASHAY PARTNERS HALF WAY 'ROUND
RESASHAY, GO ALL THE WAY 'ROUND
CIRCLE FOUR AND MAKE IT GO
BREAK THAT RING WITH A
 (Use appropriate trim.)*
CIRCLE FOUR AND DON'T GET MIXED
 Couples 1 and 2.
PICK UP TWO AND MAKE IT SIX
 Gent 1 breaks circle, picks up couple 3 on left side. Circle six.
SASHAY PARTNERS HALF WAY 'ROUND
RESASHAY, GO ALL THE WAY 'ROUND
CIRCLE SIX AND MAKE IT GO
BREAK THAT RING WITH A
 (Use appropriate trim.)*
CIRCLE SIX AND DON'T BE LATE
PICK UP TWO AND MAKE IT EIGHT
 Gent 1 pick up couple 4 on left side.
SASHAY PARTNERS HALF WAY 'ROUND
RESASHAY GO ALL THE WAY 'ROUND
CIRCLE EIGHT AS YOU COME DOWN
 (Use appropriate trim.)*
 Repeat call for couples 2, 3, and 4.

---

* Refer to pages 65 and 66 for appropriate trims.

References in Bibliography for Bird in the Cage: 18 (p. 16), 27 (p. 84), 41 (p. 36).
 97 (p. 18).
References in Bibliography for Sashay Partners Half Way Around: 41 (p. 64), and
 97 (p. 15).

STAR BY THE RIGHT

FIRST COUPLE OUT TO THE COUPLE ON THE RIGHT

FORM A STAR WITH THE RIGHT HAND CROSS
    Join right hands, form a star, move clockwise.

BACK WITH THE LEFT AND DON'T GET LOST
    Join left hands, form a star, move counterclockwise.

FORM A RING AND AROUND YOU GO
    (Use appropriate trim.)*

LEAD TO THE NEXT
    Call may be repeated for couples 2, 3, and 4.

TEXAS STAR

LADIES TO THE CENTER AND BACK TO THE BAR
    Ladies walk to center and back to place.

GENTS TO THE CENTER AND FORM A STAR

RIGHT HANDS CROSSED
    Gents form right hand star in center of set. Use a wrist grasp, grasping
    the wrist of the gent in front.

BACK WITH THE LEFT AND DON'T GET LOST
    Gents reverse direction. Form left hand star.

MEET YOUR PRETTY GIRL, PASS HER BY
    Gents pass by own partner.

HOOK THE NEXT GAL ON THE FLY
    Gents take the next lady to be his partner. Ladies hook onto gent's right
    elbow with left or gents may place right arm around ladies' waist. Star
    continues counterclockwise.

THE GENTS SWING OUT, LADIES SWING IN

FORM THAT TEXAS STAR AGAIN
    Gents break the star. Couples turn, moving counterclockwise, once and
    a half. Ladies now form a right hand star in center. Couples move the
    star clockwise.

BREAK THAT STAR WITH A DO PASO

AND A LITTLE MORE DOUGH

TAKE YOUR PARTNER AND PROMENADE HOME
    Repeat call three times until ladies are returned to original partner.

---

* Refer to pages 65-66 for appropriate trim.
References in Bibliography for Star by the Right: 36 (p. 83), and 92 (p. 167).
Texas Star arranged from Texas Star Figure used by Herb Greggerson in *Herb's Blue
    Bonnet Calls,* Reference: 41 (p. 59).
References in Bibliography for Texas Star: 18 (p. 34), 27 (p. 89), 97 (p. 30), 82 (p. 92).

TAKE A LITTLE PEEK

FIRST COUPLE OUT TO THE RIGHT OF THE RING

'ROUND THAT COUPLE AND TAKE A LITTLE PEEK
Couple 1 separates, lady peeks right, gent peeks left around behind couple 2.

BACK TO THE CENTER AND SWING YOUR SWEET
Couple 1 swings.

AROUND THAT COUPLE AND PEEK ONCE MORE
Couple repeats "peeking action."

BACK TO THE CENTER AND CIRCLE FOUR
Couple 1 and 2 circle four. See page 57, for trims suitable to circle of four.

LEAD TO THE NEXT
Call may be repeated for couples 2, 3, and 4.

INSIDE OUT AND THE OUTSIDE IN

FIRST AND THIRD GO FORWARD AND BACK

FORWARD AGAIN IN THE SAME OLD TRACK

ONE DIVE IN FOR AN INSIDE OUT AND AN OUTSIDE IN
Couple 1 ducks under arch formed by couple 3 as they exchange places. Couple 3 then backs under arch formed by couple 1 as they move backwards to face again. Couples *do not* turn.

BOW YOUR BACK AND DO IT AGAIN
Couple 1 and 3 repeat above.

FORWARD UP TAKE YOUR OPPOSITE GIRL

TURN TO THE SIDE WITH A DISH RAG WHIRL
Gents take opposites, either one or both hands, turn to gent's left with dish rag turn. Gent 1 and lady 3 face couple 4, gent 3 and lady 1 face couple 2.

INSIDE OUT AND OUTSIDE IN
Gent 1 and lady 3 duck under arch of couple 4. Gent 3 and lady 1 duck under arch of couple 2. Repeat with couple 2 and 4 going under arch and back to place. Couples *do not* turn.

BOW YOUR BACK AND DO IT AGAIN
Repeat above with couples 2 and 4.

ALLEMANDE LEFT WITH YOUR LEFT HAND
Gents allemande left with lady directly in front (their original corners).

RIGHT TO YOUR PARTNER AND A RIGHT AND LEFT GRAND

MEET YOUR HONEY AND PROMENADE
Repeat for couples 2 and 4. Call "Two Dive In."
Repeat for couples 1 and 3. Call "Three Dive In."
Repeat for couples 2 and 4. Call "Four Dive In."

References in Bibliography for Take a Little Peek: 24 (p. 82) and 91 (Kit T, p. 25).

SWING AT THE WALL

FIRST COUPLE OUT TO THE COUPLE ON THE RIGHT

AROUND THAT COUPLE AND SWING AT THE WALL
   Couple 1 separates, gent left, lady right, meet and swing behind couple 2.

THROUGH THAT COUPLE AND SWING IN THE HALL
   Couple 1 walks between couple 2 and swings in center of set.

FORM A RING AND MAKE IT GO
   (Use appropriate trim.)*

LEAD TO THE NEXT
   Call may be repeated for couples 2, 3, and 4.

OH JOHNNY

Singing Call

Record: Blue Star 1690; Folkraft 1037; Imperial 1099; MacGregor 6525; Old
         Timer 8041; Lloyd Shaw 3301; Western Jubilee 703.

OH, YOU ALL JOIN HANDS AND CIRCLE THE RING
   Circle moves clockwise.

STOP WHERE YOU ARE AND YOU GIVE HER A SWING
   Gents swing partners.

NOW SWING THAT GIRL BEHIND YOU
   Swing corner girl.

GO BACK HOME AND

SWING YOUR OWN IF YOU HAVE TIME
   Swing with partners.

ALLEMANDE LEFT WITH YOUR CORNER GIRL
   Allemande left with corner.

DO-SA 'ROUND YOUR OWN
   Do-sa-do (sashay) around partner.

NOW YOU ALL RUN AWAY WITH YOUR SWEET CORNER MAID
   Promenade counterclockwise with corner lady for a new partner.

SINGING, OH, JOHNNY, OH, JOHNNY, OH!
   Repeat call to end of recorded music.

   NOTE: The dance may be done in the square formation or it may be
           danced in one large single circle, couples facing center. The
           latter formation makes it a good mixer.

* Refer to pages 65-66 for appropriate trims.

PROMENADE THE RING

FIRST COUPLE SEPARATE
AND PROMENADE THE OUTSIDE RING
LADY GOES RIGHT AND GENTS GO LEFT
    Couple 1 turn back to back, lady goes counterclockwise around outside
    of set, gent goes clockwise.
ALL THE WAY AROUND AND BACK AGAIN
    Walk around set to home position.
PASS YOUR PARTNER
    Couple 1 pass right shoulders.
AND SWING YOUR CORNERS
    Swing with waist swing.
NOW SWING YOUR PARTNER AND PROMENADE
    All couples swing and promenade.
    Repeat call for couples 2, 3, and 4.

FORWARD UP AND BACK

FIRST AND THIRD GO FORWARD AND BACK
FORWARD AGAIN AND RIGHT AND LEFT THROUGH
RIGHT AND LEFT BACK ON THE SAME OLD TRACK
TWO LADIES CHAIN AND CHAIN RIGHT BACK
    Lady 1 and 3 chain across and back.
RING UP FOUR AND AROUND YOU GO
    Couples 1 and 3 circle four.
    (Use trim suitable to circle of four.)*
    Couples 1 and 3 complete trim and move directly to home positions.
    Repeat call for couples 2 and 4.
    Note: After repeating call for second and fourth couples add this faster
           moving variation.
ONE AND THREE RIGHT AND LEFT THROUGH
TWO AND FOUR RIGHT AND LEFT THROUGH
ONE AND THREE RIGHT AND LEFT BACK
TWO AND FOUR RIGHT AND LEFT BACK
    Call rapidly. Couples 1 and 3 turn as couples 2 and 4 cross, etc.
HEAD LADIES CHAIN
SIDE LADIES CHAIN
HEAD LADIES CHAIN RIGHT BACK
SIDE LADIES CHAIN RIGHT BACK
    Call rapidly. Head ladies (ladies 1 and 3) turn as Side Ladies (ladies
    2 and 4) cross, etc.
ALL FOUR LADIES CHAIN, GRAND CHAIN LADIES.
CHAIN 'EM BACK DON'T BE SLOW
MEET YOUR HONEY FOR A
    (Use any appropriate trim.)*
PROMENADE AROUND THE RING
HOME YOU GO AND EVERYBODY SWING

---

* Refer to page 65-66 for appropriate trim.
Promenade the Ring was danced in Albuquerque, New Mexico, in 1947, origin unknown.
References in Bibliography for Forward Up and Back: 18 (p. 24), 41 (p. 45), 100 (p. 85).

BIRDIE IN THE CAGE AND SEVEN HANDS AROUND

FIRST COUPLE BALANCE AND FIRST COUPLE SWING

FIRST GENT OUT TO THE RIGHT OF THE RING
> Gent 1 leads to lady 2.

TURN THE RIGHT HAND LADY RIGHT HAND AROUND

PARTNER LEFT AND A LEFT HAND AROUND

OPPOSITE LADY RIGHT HAND AROUND

PARTNER LEFT AND A LEFT HAND AROUND

CORNER LADY RIGHT HAND AROUND
> Use forearm grasp on above turns.

SWING YOUR PARTNER WITH A TWO HAND SWING
> Gent 1 and lady 1 join both hands, turn twice around clockwise.

PUT HER IN THE MIDDLE OF THE PRETTY LITTLE RING

CAGE THE BIRD WITH SEVEN HANDS AROUND
> Gent 1 whirls lady 1 into center of set and circles seven hands around with couples 2, 3, and 4.

THE BIRD HOPS OUT THE CROW HOPS IN
> Lady 1 steps out, gent 1 steps into center of set.

SEVEN HANDS UP AND YOU'RE GONE AGAIN
> Lady 1 circles seven hands around with couples 2, 3, and 4.

CROW HOPS OUT WITH AN ALLEMANDE LEFT
> Gent 1 goes to original corner as all simultaneously do allemande left.

RIGHT TO YOUR PARTNER GRAND RIGHT AND LEFT

MEET YOUR HONEY AND PROMENADE HOME
> Repeat call for gents 2, 3, and 4.
>
> *Note:* Crow may "hop out" with a do paso, partner swing or corner swing, or any appropriate trim.

References in Bibliography: 97 (p. 25).

SHOOT THE OWL

FIRST COUPLE BALANCE, FIRST COUPLE SWING

FIRST GENT OUT TO THE RIGHT OF THE RING

THREE HANDS ROUND IF YOU KNOW HOW
    Gent 1 circles three with couple 2.

WHEN YOU GET RIGHT – SHOOT THE OWL

TWO HANDS UP, THE GENT SHOOTS UNDER
    Circle three once and a half. Couple 2 "Shoots" gent 1 under arch to center of set.

GRAB YOUR PARTNER AND SWING LIKE THUNDER
    Couple 1 swings in center of set.

GENT GOES ON, THE LADY FOLLOWS UP

FORM TWO RINGS WITH THREE HANDS AROUND
    Gent 1 circles three with couple 3.
    Lady 1 circles three with couple 2.

NOW TWO HANDS UP AND YOU BOTH SHOOT UNDER
    Circle three once and a half. Couple 2 and 3 "shoot" gent 1 and lady 1 under arch into center of set.

GRAB YOUR PARTNER AND SWING LIKE THUNDER
    Couple 1 swings in center of set.

THE GENT GOES ON AND THE LADY FOLLOWS UP
    Gent 1 circles three with couple 4. Lady 1 circles three with couple 3.

FORM TWO RINGS AND BOTH SHOOT UNDER
    Circle three once and a half. Couples 3 and 4 "shoot" gent 1 and lady 1 under arch into center of set.

GRAB YOUR PARTNER AND SWING LIKE THUNDER
    Couple 1 swings in center of set.

GENT GOES HOME AND LADY FOLLOWS ON
    Gent 1 goes to home position. Lady 1 circles three with couple 4.

FORM A RING AND CIRCLE THREE

SHOOT THAT PRETTY GIRL HOME TO ME
    Circle three once and a half. Couple 4 "shoots" lady 1 home to partner.

    Couple 1 swings in home position.

    Repeat call for gents 2, 3, and 4.

    (Use any appropriate trim.)

Dance arranged from figure given by Herb Greggerson in his book *Herb's Blue Bonnet Calls,* Reference 41 (p. 50).

Reference in Bibliography: 100 (p. 93).

MILAGRO SQUARE

FIRST FOUR LEAD TO THE RIGHT
Couples 1 and 3.

GO AROUND THAT COUPLE AND TAKE A LITTLE SWING
Couple 1 separates, lady goes right, gent goes left, and swings *three times* around behind couple 2. Couple 3 does the same around couple 4.

CENTER COUPLES FORM A RING AND CIRCLE ONCE AROUND
While couples 1 and 3 swing. Couples 2 and 4 circle *once* around in center of set.

PASS RIGHT THROUGH, JUST YOU TWO
Couples 2 and 4. Do not turn back.

AND AROUND THAT COUPLE AND TAKE A LITTLE SWING
Couple 2 moves forward, separates and swings behind couple 3. Couple 4 moves forward, separates, and swings behind couple 1.

CENTER COUPLES FORM A RING AND CIRCLE ONCE AROUND
While couples 2 and 4 swing. Couples 1 and 3 circle once around in center of set.

PASS RIGHT THROUGH, JUST YOU TWO
Couples 1 and 3. Do not turn back.

AND AROUND THAT COUPLE AND TAKE A LITTLE SWING
Couple 1 moves forward, separates, and swings behind couple 2. Couple 3 moves forward, separates, and swings behind couple 4.

CENTER COUPLES FORM A RING AND CIRCLE ONCE AROUND
While couples 1 and 3 swing. Couples 2 and 4 circle once around in center of set.

PASS RIGHT THROUGH JUST YOU TWO
Couples 2 and 4. Do not turn back.

AND AROUND THAT COUPLE AND TAKE A SWING
Couple 2 moves forward, separates, and swings behind couple 3. Couple 4 moves forward, separates, and swings behind couple 1.

CENTER COUPLES FORM A RING AND CIRCLE ONCE AROUND
While couples 2 and 4 swing. Couples 1 and 3 circle once around in center of set.

PASS RIGHT THROUGH, JUST YOU TWO
Couples 1 and 3. Do not turn back.

CIRCLE WITH THE NEXT AND AROUND YOU GO
BREAK RIGHT INTO A DO PASO
TAKE HER HOME AND EVERYBODY SWING
Repeat calls for couples 2 and 4 or side four.

Dance as revised with new trim taught by Herb Greggerson at the Square Dance Institute, University of Texas, March 1948.

SQUARE THROUGH AND BOX THE GNAT HASH

HEAD COUPLES GO FORWARD AND BACK
RIGHT AND LEFT THROUGH ACROSS THE TRACK
RIGHT AND LEFT BACK IN THE USUAL WAY
ROLL AWAY TO A HALF SASHAY
    Lady turns left face across in front of partners to exchange places.
RIGHT TO YOUR OPPOSITE, BOX THE GNAT
    End facing opposite.
HANG ON TIGHT FOR A HALF SQUARE THROUGH
    Opposite right, partner left, and face side couples.
RIGHT AND LEFT THROUGH WITH THE OUTSIDE TWO
    Outside two refers to side couples.
RIGHT AND LEFT BACK
SAME TWO DO HALF SQUARE THROUGH
YOU'RE FACING OUT IN LINES OF FOUR
FORWARD FOUR AND BACK LIKE THAT
BEND THE LINE AND BOX THE GNAT
CHANGE HANDS, BOX THE FLEA
CHANGE GIRLS, ALLEMANDE LEFT
    Turn to left hand lady who will be the original corner lady and allemande
    left.
GRAND RIGHT AND LEFT
    (Add any appropriate trim.)
    Repeat for side couples.

SALLY GOOD'IN

FIRST GENT OUT AND SWING SALLY GOOD'IN
Gent 1 swings right hand lady (Sally Good'in) with right hand around.

NOW YOUR TAW
Gent 1 swings own partner with left hand around.

SWING THE GIRL FROM ARKANSAS
Gent 1 swings the opposite lady (Arkansas) with right hand around.

THEN SWING SALLY GOOD'IN
Gent 1 swings Sally Good'in with left hand around.

AND THEN YOUR TAW
Gent 1 swings own partner with right hand around.

NOW DON'T FORGET YOUR OLD GRANDMA
Gent 1 swings corner lady (Grandma) with left hand around.

HOME YOU GO AND EVERYBODY SWING
All swing with a waist swing.

Repeat call with gents 1 and 2 leading out simultaneously.

Repeat again with gents 1, 2, and 3 leading out simultaneously.

Repeat, last time, with "ALL FOUR GENTS" leading out simultaneously.

Notes: Ladies' identity is the same for all gents, for example, Sally Good'in is the right hand lady and Grandma is the corner lady. When more than one gent is called out, they reach Arkansas (opposite lady) by following the gent on the left.

Dance may be done with lady leading out to swing Johnny Good'in. There are many regional variations of this figure. The primary differences are found in the location of Sally, Arkansas, and Grandma in the set. Other differences are in types of swings used (using waist swing throughout) and sequence of calling the leads.

References in Bibliography: 18 (p. 15), 41 (p. 28), 97 (p. 22).

COWBOY LOOP

FIRST COUPLE OUT TO THE COUPLE ON THE RIGHT
CIRCLE FOUR WITH ALL YOUR MIGHT
BREAK AND TRAIL THAT LINE TO THE NEXT
> Gent 1 breaks circle by unclasping left hand, trails (leads) line of four to couple 3.

TWO HANDS UP AND FOUR TRAIL THROUGH
> Couple 3 raises joined inside hands, line of four passes under arch. Couple 3 walks forward over line to position 1 in set.

TURN RIGHT AROUND AND COME BACK THOUGH
> Gent 1 pulls line around toward center of set and prepares to go under arch the second time. Couple 3 does California Twirl, walks back to position as line of four passes under arch to center of set.

AND TIE THAT KNOT LIKE THE COWBOYS DO
> Gent 1 turns right and pulls the line through arch formed by last couple in line.

CIRCLE UP FOUR AND AWAY WE GO
PICK UP TWO AND MAKE IT SIX
CIRCLE LEFT TILL ALL GET FIXED
> Gent 1 breaks circle with left hand and picks up couple 3 on left side.

BREAK AND TRAIL THAT LINE TO THE NEXT
> Gent 1 breaks circle with left hand, leads line of six through arch formed by couple 4.

TWO HANDS UP AND SIX GO THROUGH
> Couple 4 raises joined inside hands, line of six passes under arch. Couple 4 walks forward over line to position 2 in set.

TURN RIGHT AROUND AND COME BACK THROUGH
> Gent 1 pulls line of six around toward center of set and prepares to go under arch the second time. Couple 4 turns around, walks back to position as line of six passes under arch to center of set.

TIE THAT KNOT LIKE THE COWBOYS DO
> Gent 1 turns right and pulls the line through arch formed by last couple in line.

NOW CIRCLE UP SIX AND KEEP IT STRAIGHT
PICK UP TWO AND MAKE IT EIGHT
> Gent 1 breaks circle with left hand and picks up couple 4 on left side.

CIRCLE EIGHT AND HERE WE GO
> (Use any appropriate trim.)
> Repeat calls for couples 2, 3, and 4.

Dance arranged from calls given by Herb Greggerson in his book *Herb's Blue Bonnet Calls,* Reference 41 (p. 56).
References in Bibliography: 100 (p. 57), 97 (p. 21).

ARKANSAS TRAVELER

FIRST FOUR GO FORWARD AND BACK
Couple 1 and 3.
FORWARD AGAIN IN THE SAME OLD TRACK
TURN YOUR OPPOSITE RIGHT HAND AROUND
Gent 1 turns lady 3, gent 3 turns lady 1. Use a forearm grasp.
PARTNERS LEFT AND LEFT HAND AROUND
All turn partner, left forearm around.
CORNERS RIGHT AND RIGHT HAND AROUND
All turn corner, right forearm around.
PARTNERS LEFT AND LEFT HAND AROUND
All turn partner, left forearm around.
AND PROMENADE YOUR CORNERS
Promenade new partner to gent's home position.
Repeat call for couples 2 and 4.
Repeat from beginning until ladies are returned to original positions.

VARIATION:

ARKANSAS TRAVELER WITH A CROSS TRAIL THROUGH

ONE AND THREE GO FORWARD AND BACK
SIDES CROSS TRAIL THROUGH
GO AROUND THE OUTSIDE TRACK
Sides cross trail then separate and go all around the square, pass partner, and assume original position.
HEADS GO FORWARD
TURN YOUR OPPOSITE RIGHT, RIGHT HAND AROUND
PARTNER LEFT, LEFT HAND AROUND
Heads execute while sides are moving around the square to home positions.
CORNER RIGHT, RIGHT HAND AROUND
Heads pick up corners who are now back in position.
PARTNERS LEFT, LEFT HAND AROUND
PROMENADE CORNER AS SHE COMES AROUND
(Add any appropriate trim.)
Repeat call for side couples while heads execute cross trail through.

References in Bibliography: 41 (p. 36).

CATCH ALL EIGHT

FIRST COUPLE BALANCE AND SWING
DOWN THE CENTER AND SPLIT THE RING
  Couple 1 goes across set and walks between (splits) couple 3.
LADY GO GEE, GENT GO HAW
  Lady goes right, gent goes left.
MEET YOUR HONEY IN THE HALL
  Couple 1 meets in home position.
CATCH ALL EIGHT WITH THE RIGHT, GO HALF WAY AROUND
  All swing partner half turn around clockwise with right forearm grasp.
BACK WITH THE LEFT GO ALL THE WAY AROUND
  All swing partner one full turn counterclockwise with left forearm grasp.
SWING YOUR CORNER WITH A TWO HAND SWING
  Join both hands with corner, turn once around clockwise.
MEET YOUR PARTNER PASS HER BY
  Pass partner's right shoulder.
PICK UP THE NEXT GIRL ON THE FLY AND PROMENADE
  Promenade new partner (right hand lady) to gents' home position.
  Repeat for couples 2, 3, and 4.

YORKSHIRE PUDDING

FIRST AND THIRD BOW AND SWING
LEAD RIGHT OUT TO THE RIGHT OF THE RING
STAR BY THE RIGHT AND HERE WE GO
HEAD GENTS CENTER WITH A LEFT ELBOW
  Two gents turn each other in center.
BREAK THOSE STARS, AND FORM TWO LINES
  Stars of three break, line up three on the side.
HEAD GENTS HOME, YOU'RE DOIN' FINE
  Two gents break in center, go to home position.
FORWARD SIX AND BACK TO THE BAR
SIX TO THE CENTER WITH A RIGHT HAND STAR
WALK ALONG NOW NOT TOO FAR
  Six turn star around to home position.
HEAD LADIES OUT AND SWING YOUR MAN
  Head ladies drop out of star and swing partner.
FOUR HAND STAR IN THE MIDDLE OF THE LAND
  Side couples continue turning star.
MEET YOUR CORNER, LEFT ALLEMANDE
RIGHT TO YOUR PARTNER, RIGHT AND LEFT GRAND
  (Use any appropriate trim.)
  Repeat for side couples.

Catch All Eight arranged from figure used by Raymond Smith in his *Square Dance Handbook*. Reference 97 (p. 32). References in Bibliography for Catch All Eight: 41 (p. 40), 100 (p. 105).

Yorkshire Pudding, *Sets in Order, Yearbook of Square Dancing #1*, page 62. Reprinted by permission.

SIDES DIVIDE

FIRST FOUR FORWARD AND BACK
Couples 1 and 3.

FORWARD AGAIN ON THE SAME OLD TRACK

SWING IN THE CENTER AND SWING ON THE SIDE
Gent 1 swings lady 3, gent 3 swings lady 1. Simultaneously couples 2 and 4 swing. Use a waist swing throughout call.

NOW SWING YOUR OWN AND SIDES DIVIDE
Couples 1 and 3, in the center, swing own partners. Side couples separate, ladies to the left, gents to the right. Move one quarter of the way around set, meet opposites and swing.

CIRCLE FOUR IN THE MIDDLE OF THE FLOOR
Couples 1 and 3 circle four.

SIDES DIVIDE AND SWING SOME MORE
Sides separate. Move one quarter of the way around set, meet partners and swing.

DO PASO AND DON'T GET SORE
Couples 1 and 3 complete do paso in center of set.

SIDES DIVIDE AND SWING SOME MORE
Sides separate. Move one quarter of the way around set, meet opposite, and swing.

UP THE RIVER AND AROUND THE BEND

SIDES DIVIDE AND SWING AGAIN
Sides separate, meet partners in original home positions, and swing.

AND PROMENADE YOUR CORNERS ALL
All promenade corners. Gents now have new partners.

HOLD THAT GAL DON'T LET HER FALL

PROMENADE AROUND THE HALL
Promenade new partners to gents' home positions.
Repeat call for couples 2 and 4.
Repeat from beginning until ladies are returned to original positions.
Backward (clockwise)

Greggerson, H. F., *Herb's Blue Bonnet Calls,* Reference 41 (p. 55).
References in Bibliography: 18 (p. 32).

FORWARD UP SIX RIGHT HAND UP
AND LEFT HAND UNDER

FIRST AND THIRD BALANCE AND SWING

NOW WHIRL YOUR GIRL TO THE RIGHT OF THE RING

> Gent 1 twirls lady 1 to gent 2. Lady 1 stands to the left of gent 2 to form a line of three, facing center. Gent 3 whirls lady 3 to gent 4. Lady 3 stands to the left of gent 4 to form a line of three, facing center. Gents 1 and 3 remain in home positions. Join hands in each line.

FORWARD UP SIX AND BACK YOU GO

> Lines of three go forward and back.

TWO GENTS LOOP WITH A DO-SA-DO

> Gents 1 and 3 execute a do-sa-do.

NOW RIGHT HAND UP AND LEFT HAND UNDER

> Gent 2 twirls the left hand lady under the arch formed with right hand lady to gent 3. Right hand lady is twirled outside and over left hand lady to gent 1. Gent 4 twirls the ladies in the same manner with his left hand lady going to gent 1 and his right hand lady going to gent 3.

TWIRL THOSE GIRLS AND GO LIKE THUNDER

FORM NEW THREE AND DON'T YOU BLUNDER

> Gent 3 now has lady 4 on the right and lady 1 on the left. Gent 1 has lady 2 on the right and lady 3 on the left. Two new lines of three are formed.
>
> Repeat call three times beginning with "Forward up six and back you go," to return ladies to the right side of original partner. Then use any appropriate trim.
>
> Repeat call for couples 2 and 4.
>
> *Note:* Vary the call "Two gents loop with a do-sa-do" by calling "Two gents loop with a right elbow" or "Two gents loop with a left elbow."

THE "H"

FIRST COUPLE BALANCE, FIRST COUPLE SWING

DOWN THE CENTER AND SPLIT THE RING
> Couple 1 walks between couple 3.

LADY GO RIGHT, GENT GO LEFT, FOUR IN LINE YOU STAND
> Lady 1 stands beside gent 3, gent 1 stands beside lady 3. All join hands in a line of four.

FORWARD UP FOUR AND FALL BACK FOUR
> Line walks forward and back to place.

SASHAY FOUR TO THE RIGHT
> Gent 1 leads line to right behind couple 4.

FORWARD UP SIX, FALL BACK EIGHT
> Lady 1 joins left hand with gent 4's left hand. Gent 1 joins right hand with lady 4's right hand. All six move toward couple 2. All, including couple 2, fall back to couple 4's position.

FORWARD UP EIGHT, FALL BACK SIX
> All eight move toward couple 2's position. Couple 4 and line of four fall back to couple 4's position.

SASHAY FOUR TO THE RIGHT
> Gent 1 leads line of four to couple 1's position.

FORWARD UP FOUR AND FOUR STAND PAT
> Line moves forward, stands in center of set.

RIGHT AND LEFT THROUGH ALONG THAT LINE
> Couples 2 and 4. Gents pass on one side of line, partners on the other. Pass opposites' right shoulder.

RIGHT AND LEFT BACK, YOU'RE DOING FINE
> Turn partner and repeat back to home position.

OPEN THE GATE AND LADIES CHAIN THROUGH THE CENTER OF SET

CHAIN RIGHT BACK, YOU'RE NOT THROUGH YET
> Line opens, couple on right (lady 3 and gent 1) steps forward, couple on left (lady 1 and gent 3) steps back. Ladies 2 and 4 chain across and back through opening.

FALL BACK FOUR AND SASHAY TO THE RIGHT
> Line moves back and to right behind couple 2

FORWARD SIX, FALL BACK EIGHT

FORWARD EIGHT, FALL BACK SIX
> Repeat movements from couple 2's position.

SASHAY FOUR TO THE RIGHT
> Gent 1 leads line of four to couple 3's position.

FORWARD FOUR AND CIRCLE FOUR IN MIDDLE OF FLOOR
> Line circles four in center of set.

BREAK THAT RING WITH A (Use appropriate trim for four).

HOME YOU GO AND EVERYBODY SWING
> Repeat call for couples 2, 3, and 4.

References in Bibliography: 91 (Kit T, p. 12), 94 (p. 261), 100 (p. 81).

THE ROUTE

FIRST AND THIRD BALANCE AND SWING

LEAD RIGHT OUT TO THE RIGHT OF THE RING

CIRCLE FOUR AND FORM A LINE
> Circle three quarters around to form a line. Couples 1 and 3 are on the left end of line nearest home positions.

FORWARD EIGHT AND BACK YOU GO
> Lines advance forward and back to place.

FORWARD AGAIN AND DO-SA-DO
> Do-sa-do around opposites and back to place in lines of four.

CHAIN THOSE LADIES ACROSS THE HALL
> Ladies 1 and 4 chain as ladies 2 and 3 chain.

NOW CHAIN THOSE LADIES DOWN THAT LINE
> Ladies 1 and 2 chain as ladies 3 and 4 chain.

CHAIN THOSE LADIES ACROSS THE HALL
> Ladies 1 and 4 chain as ladies 2 and 3 chain.

CHAIN THOSE LADIES DOWN THAT LINE
> Ladies 1 and 2 chain as 3 and 4 chain.

NOW YOU'RE HOME AND DOING FINE
> (Use any appropriate trim.)
> Repeat call for couples 2 and 4.
> *Note:* The chain directions for the ladies are as follows:

CHAIN THOSE LADIES ACROSS THE HALL
> Ladies 4 and 3 chain as 1 and 2 chain.

NOW CHAIN THOSE LADIES DOWN THAT LINE
> Ladies 4 and 1 chain as 2 and 3 chain.

CHAIN THOSE LADIES ACROSS THE HALL
> Ladies 1 and 2 chain as 3 and 4 chain.

CHAIN THOSE LADIES DOWN THE LINE
> Ladies 1 and 4 chain as 2 and 3 chain.

NOW YOU'RE HOME AND DOING FINE

PROMENADE AROUND THE RING
> *Note:* Dance may be repeated substituting the right and left through for the ladies chain.

This is an abbreviated version of the figure which appeared in the first edition of *Dance A While*, pages 49 and 50.
Reference in Bibliography: 97 (p. 35).

PROMENADE THE OUTSIDE RING

FIRST AND THIRD COUPLES PROMENADE THE OUTSIDE RING
WHILE THE ROOSTERS CROW AND THE BIRDIES SING
> Couple 1 goes to the right, outside of set, around set, and back to home position.

WHEN YOU GET HOME LEAD TO THE RIGHT
AND RIGHT AND LEFT THROUGH WITH THE COUPLE YOU MEET
> Couple 1 with 2, 3 with 4.

RIGHT AND LEFT BACK ON THE SAME OLD TRACK
> Lines are parallel and run diagonally across the set.

TWO LADIES CHAIN AND CHAIN RIGHT BACK
> Simultaneously, lady 1 with 2 and 3 with 4.

FORWARD EIGHT AND BACK IN TIME
PASS RIGHT THROUGH AND BEND THE LINE
> Couple 4 faces 1, 3 faces 2.

NOW RIGHT AND LEFT THROUGH, YOU'RE DOING FINE
FORWARD EIGHT AND BACK ONCE MORE
PASS RIGHT THROUGH AND BEND THE LINE
> Couple 2 faces 1, and 3 faces 4.

GO RIGHT AND LEFT THROUGH TO YOUR OWN DOOR
ALLEMANDE LEFT, LOOK OUT NOW
RIGHT TO YOUR PARTNER, RIGHT AND LEFT GRAND

Promenade The Outside Ring, Greggerson, H. F., *Herb's Blue Bonnet Calls*. Revised with new trim. Reference: 41 (p. 30).

References in Bibliography for Promenade The Outside Ring: 18 (p. 26), 94 (p. 206), 100 (p. 80).

THREE LADIES CHAIN

FIRST COUPLE BALANCE, FIRST COUPLE SWING

LEAD RIGHT OUT TO THE RIGHT OF THE RING

CIRCLE FOUR HANDS ONCE AROUND
> Couples 1 and 2.

NOW TWO LADIES CHAIN, DON'T BE SLOW
> Ladies 1 and 2 chain.

NOW THREE LADIES CHAIN ACROSS THE FLOOR
> Gent 1 and lady 2 turn half left, chain ladies 2 and 4.
> Gent 1 and lady 4 turn half left, chain ladies 4 and 1.
> Gent 1 and lady 1 turn half left, chain ladies 1 and 2.
> Gent 1 and lady 2 turn half left, chain ladies 2 and 4.
> Gent 1 and lady 4 turn half left, chain ladies 4 and 1.
> Gent 2 and 4 turn the ladies chaining to them.

CHAIN THEM OVER, CHAIN THEM BACK

WHILE THE THREE GENTS STAND LIKE A ROCK IN THE SEA

CHAIN THOSE GALS 'TIL YOU'VE CHAINED ALL THREE

NOW FIRST OLD COUPLE LEAD TO THE NEXT

CIRCLE FOUR GO ONCE AROUND
> Couples 1 and 3.

CHAIN TWO LADIES ACROSS THE TRACK

CHAIN THOSE GALS — CHAIN 'EM BACK
> Ladies 1 and 3 chain.

FIRST OLD COUPLE ON TO THE NEXT

CIRCLE FOUR HANDS ONCE AROUND
> Couples 1 and 4.

NOW TWO LADIES CHAIN, DON'T BE SLOW

NOW THREE LADIES CHAIN ACROSS THE FLOOR
> Repeat action as described above for this part of the call.

HOME YOU GO AND EVERYBODY SWING
> Repeat call for couples 2, 3, and 4.

References in Bibliography for Three Ladies Chain: 94 (p. 347).

ENDS TURN IN

FIRST AND THIRD GO FORWARD AND BACK
SPLIT YOUR CORNERS ON THE OUTSIDE TRACK
> Gents 1 and 3 take opposites, turn to face side couples, go between the side couples.

AND FOUR IN LINE YOU STAND
> Gent 1 and lady 3 separate, gent left, lady right, and stand four in line with couple 4. Gent 3 and lady 1 do same with couple 2. Join hands in each line.

FORWARD EIGHT AND BACK WITH YOU
> Lines of four move forward and back.

FORWARD AGAIN AND PASS RIGHT THROUGH
> Pass right shoulders with person directly in front.

JOIN HANDS AND THE ENDS TURN IN
> Lines remain facing out, join hands and pass the lady and gent on the end of the lines through arch formed by center couple in each line of four to the center of set. Couples 2 and 4 have now exchanged sides of set. After arching, couples 2 and 4 turn to face center of set, lady on right side of partner.

CIRCLE FOUR IN THE MIDDLE OF THE FLOOR
> Gent 1 and lady 3 with gent 3 and lady 1.

GO ONCE AROUND WITH THE PRETTY LITTLE THING
PASS RIGHT THROUGH AND SPLIT THE RING
> Center couples go right and left through. Gent 1 and lady 3 go between couple 2. Gent 3 and lady 1 go between couple 4.

AND FOUR IN LINE YOU STAND
> Gent 1 and lady 3 separate, gent left, lady right, and stand in line with couple 2. Gent 3 and lady 1 do same and stand in line with couple 4. Join hands in each line.

FORWARD EIGHT AND BACK WITH YOU
FORWARD AGAIN AND PASS RIGHT THROUGH
JOIN HANDS AND THE ENDS TURN IN
> Ends turn in as before. Couples 2 and 4 are now back on home side of set.

CIRCLE FOUR IN THE MIDDLE OF THE FLOOR
> Gent 1-and lady 3 with gent 3 and lady 1.

GO ONCE AROUND AND FEEL THEIR HEFT
PASS RIGHT THROUGH FOR AN ALLEMANDE LEFT
> Center couples right and left through to face side couples. Gents allemande left with lady in front (original corners).

RIGHT TO PARTNER AND GRAND RIGHT AND LEFT
> Repeat call for couples 2 and 4.

Figure originated by Mr. Ed. Gilmore, Yucaipa, California.

RIGHT AND LEFT HOOK

HEAD TWO COUPLES BALANCE AND SWING
LEAD RIGHT OUT TO THE RIGHT OF THE RING
FORWARD UP WITH A RIGHT AND LEFT HOOK
> Couples move toward each other as if to do a right and left through, instead, they all hook elbows, the gents hook right with ladies right, and two ladies hook left to form a line of four. Couple 1 with 2 and couple 3 with 4.

GO HALFWAY AROUND AND SEE WHAT COOKS
> Lines turn clockwise a half turn until couples 1 and 3 face center of set.

BREAK APART AND PASS RIGHT THROUGH
AND HOOK IN THE CENTER LIKE YOU USED TO DO
> Couples 1 and 3 "hook" in center of set. Couples 2 and 4 courtesy turn to face center of set.

TURN ONCE AROUND AND SEE HOW IT LOOKS
> Couples 1 and 3 turn line once around clockwise.

NOW PASS THROUGH TO THE OUTSIDE CROOKS
> Couple 1 to couple 4 and couple 3 to couple 2.

GO HALF AROUND WITH THE SAME OLD HOOK
> Turn line half around clockwise until couples 1 and 3 are facing center of set.

YOU BREAK IT UP AND PASS ON THROUGH
YOU MEET IN THE CENTER AND HOOK THERE TOO
> Couples 1 and 3 "hook" in center of set. Couples 2 and 4 courtesy turn to face center of set.

GO AROUND ONCE AND DON'T GET SORE
PASS THROUGH TO THE OUTSIDE CIRCLE FOUR
> Couple 1 with 2 and couple 3 with 4.

HOME YOU GO AND CIRCLE TO THE SOUTH
> Join hands and circle 8 to the left.

LET A LITTLE MOONSHINE IN YOUR MOUTH
> Repeat call for couples 2 and 4. (Use any appropriate trim.)

Figure originated by Mr. Leon McGuffin of Austin, Texas.

SPLIT YOUR CORNERS

FIRST AND THIRD GO FORWARD AND BACK
FORWARD AGAIN ON THE SAME OLD TRACK
> Couples 1 and 3 meet in center of set.

SPLIT YOUR CORNER AND LEAVE YOUR TAW
> Gent 1 and lady 3 face couple 4, walk between (split) couple 4. Gent 3 and lady 1 do same going between couple 2.

THE LADY GOES GEE, THE GENT GOES HAW
> Ladies 1 and 3 turn right, gents 1 and 3 turn left to meet own partners in home positions.

SASHAY 'ROUND YOUR PRETTY BABY
> All couples begin action by sashaying around partners in home positions.

RIGHT ELBOW SWING THAT CORNER LADY
> All gents turn corners with right forearm turn.

A LEFT HAND TO YOUR PRETTY MAID
> Although the call indicates a hand swing, it is better to use a forearm swing.
> Turn partner once around.

A RIGHT TO YOUR CORNER AND ALL PROMENADE
> Promenade corner to gents' home position.
> Repeat call three times until ladies are returned to original partners.

References in Bibliography for Split Your Corners: 97 (p. 28).

SPLIT THE RING

FIRST COUPLE OUT BALANCE AND SWING
DOWN CENTER AND SPLIT THE RING
> Couple 1 walks across set and between (splits) couple 3.

LADY GO GEE AND THE GENT GO HAW
> Lady 1 goes right, gent 1 goes left, around outside of set back home.

SWING WHEN YOU MEET
SWING AT THE HEAD AND SWING AT THE FEET
> Couples 1 and 3 swing.

SIDE FOUR THE SAME
> Couples 2 and 4 swing.

DOWN THE CENTER AS YOU DID BEFORE
DOWN THE CENTER AND CAST OFF FOUR
> Couple 1 walks across set. Gent 1 goes left between lady 3 and gent 4. Lady 1 goes right between gent 3 and lady 2. Walk outside of set back home.

SWING WHEN YOU MEET
SWING AT THE HEAD AND SWING AT THE FEET
> Couples 1 and 3 swing.

SIDE FOUR THE SAME
> Couples 2 and 4 swing.

DOWN THE CENTER AS YOU USED TO DO
DOWN THE CENTER AND CAST OFF TWO
> Couple 1 moves forward to center of set. Gent goes left and between (splits) couple 4. Lady goes right between (splits) couple 2. Walk outside of set back home.

SWING WHEN YOU MEET
SWING AT THE HEAD AND SWING AT THE FEET
> Couples 1 and 3 swing.

SIDE FOUR THE SAME
> Couples 2 and 4 swing.
> (Use any appropriate trim.)
> Repeat call for couples 2, 3, and 4.

Split the Ring arranged with a slight variation from figure used by Herb Greggerson in *Herb's Blue Bonnet Calls,* Reference 41 (p. 36).
References in Bibliography for Split the Ring: 18 (p. 20), 36 (p. 77), 94 (p. 288), 97 (p. 26).

SPLIT THE RING AND AROUND JUST ONE

ONE AND THREE BALANCE AND SWING
UP TO THE CENTER AND BACK TO THE RING
FORWARD AGAIN AND PASS RIGHT THROUGH
SPLIT THE RING AND AROUND JUST ONE
>Couples 1 and 3 separate. Gents go left, ladies go right. Gent 1 and lady 3 meet behind couple 4. Gent 3 and lady 1 meet behind couple 2.

DOWN THE CENTER WE'LL HAVE SOME FUN
>Gent 1 and lady 3 go between couple 4 as gent 3 and lady 1 move between couple 2. Couples meet in center of set. Pass through.

SPLIT THE RING AND AROUND JUST ONE
>Gent 1 and lady 3 go between couple 2. Gent 3 and lady 1 go between couple 4. Gents 1 and 3 turn left, ladies 1 and 3 turn right to meet own partner.

DOWN THE CENTER, PASS RIGHT THROUGH
HOME YOU GO AND EVERYBODY SWING
>Couples 1 and 3 go to home positions.

ALLEMANDE LEFT WITH THE LEFT HAND HIGH
RIGHT TO YOUR PARTNER AND PASS HER BY
>Ladies stay in home positions do not move forward as in regular grand right and left.

LEFT TO THE NEXT AND HOLD ON TIGHT
TURN HER AROUND IF IT TAKES ALL NIGHT
>Gents turn right hand ladies once and a half around with left forearm grasp.

STAND RIGHT THERE UPON THE FLOOR
STAND RIGHT THERE WE'LL DANCE SOME MORE
>Gents have progressed one position to the right around set.
>Repeat call for gents 1 and 3 and their new partners.
>>"SAME TWO GENTS WITH A BRAND NEW DAME"
>Repeat call for gents 2 and 4 and their new partners.
>>"TWO AND FOUR BALANCE AND SWING"
>Repeat call for gents 2 and 4 and their new partners
>>"SAME TWO GENTS WITH A BRAND NEW DAME"

Figure originated by Mr. Herb Greggerson of Ruidoso, New Mexico. Revised with Pass Thru.

THERE'S YOUR CORNER

ONE AND THREE DO A HALF SASHAY
Gents 1 and 3 exchange place with partners.
UP TO THE MIDDLE AND BACK THAT WAY
FORWARD AGAIN AND PASS THROUGH
Pass opposites right shoulder.
SPLIT THE RING GO AROUND ONE
Gents right, ladies left, move between side couples into center.
COME INTO THE MIDDLE, BOX THE GNAT
Partners join right hands, exchange places, lady turns under gents right arm, end facing partner.
RIGHT AND LEFT THROUGH THE OTHER WAY BACK
Gent 1 with lady 3, gent 3 with lady 1, pass partners right shoulders.
TURN ON AROUND AND PASS THROUGH
Gent 1 with lady 3, gent 3 with lady 1, execute a courtesy turn, face center and pass through, face side couples, gent 1 with lady 3 face couple 4, gent 3 with lady 1 face couple 2.
SPLIT THE RING AND AROUND JUST ONE
COME DOWN THE MIDDLE WITH A RIGHT-LEFT THROUGH
Couples 1 and 3 pass right shoulders.
TURN YOUR GIRL AND CROSS TRAIL BACK
Couples 1 and 3 courtesy turn partner, pass opposites right shoulder change places man passing back of partner.
COME AROUND ONE, INTO THE MIDDLE
Gent 3 faces lady 3, gent 1 faces lady 1 in the center of set.
BOX THE GNAT, PULL HER BY
Partners join right hands, exchange places and facing partner, gents then pull partners by, all move to face original corners.
THERE'S YOUR CORNER, ALLEMANDE LEFT
(Add any appropriate trim.)
Repeat for side couples.

MOFFITT'S MANEUVERS

FIRST AND THIRD DO A HALF SASHAY
UP TO THE MIDDLE AND BACK THAT WAY
FORWARD AGAIN, BOX THE GNAT
> End facing opposite.

PASS THROUGH THE OTHER WAY BACK
SPLIT THE RING, GO AROUND JUST ONE
PUT THE LADY IN THE LEAD, DIXIE CHAIN
> Ladies lead as heads move between side couples.

LADY GOES LEFT, GENT GOES RIGHT
> Lady 1 around lady 2, lady 3 around lady 4, gent 1 around gent 4, gent 3 around gent 2.

AROUND ONE, PUT THE LADY IN THE LEAD
DIXIE CHAIN, LADY GO RIGHT, GENT LEFT
> Lady 1 around lady 4, lady 3 around lady 2, gent 1 around gent 2, gent 3 around gent 4.

AROUND ONE, LINE UP FOUR
> Gent 1, lady 3 between couple 2 to form one line. Lady 1, gent 3 between couple 4 to form opposite line.

FORWARD FOUR AND BACK WITH YOU
CENTER FOUR, SQUARE THROUGH
IT'S RIGHT, LEFT, RIGHT, LEFT YOU DO
SPLIT THE RING AND COME AROUND TWO
> Gent 3 left around couple 4, lady 3 right around couple 2, gent 1 left around couple 2, lady 1 right around couple 4.

COME DOWN THE MIDDLE AND CROSS TRAIL THROUGH
THERE'S YOUR CORNER, LEFT ALLEMANDE
GRAND RIGHT AND LEFT

Break

CATCH ALL EIGHT WITH A RIGHT HAND HALF AROUND
> Partners turn half around.

BACK WITH THE LEFT, GO ALL THE WAY AROUND
GENTS STAR RIGHT ACROSS THE TRACK
> Gents star right across set.

TURN OPPOSITE LEFT HAND ROUND
STAR RIGHT BACK TO AN ALLEMANDE THAR
> Gents star right again across to partner, turn partner with left forearm around far enough for gent to form an Allemande Thar Star.

SLIP THE CLUTCH TO AN ALLEMANDE LEFT
> All release star, move forward one person to find original corner.

GRAND RIGHT AND LEFT, PROMENADE
> Repeat for side couples.

Reference: *Sets In Order Yearbook, No. 3,* page 35.

FOUR GENTS STAR

FOUR GENTS STAR ACROSS THE SQUARE
>Four gents form right hand star and move clockwise. (All turns in this figure are done with forearm grasp.)

OPPOSITE LEFT AND LEAVE HER THERE
>Turn opposites with left once around.

STAR RIGHT BACK ACROSS THE SET
PARTNER LEFT YOU AIN'T THROUGH YET
>Turn partners left around once.

STAR RIGHT BACK THREE QUARTERS ROUND
YOUR RIGHT HAND LADY LEFT HAND AROUND
>Turn right hand ladies left once around.

STAR RIGHT BACK AS YOU COME DOWN
TURN YOUR CORNER LADY WITH A LEFT HAND AROUND
>Turn corners left once around.

STAR RIGHT BACK AS YOU DID BEFORE
MEET YOUR PARTNER WITH A DO PASO
PARTNER BY THE LEFT AND A LEFT ARM 'ROUND
CORNER BY THE RIGHT AND A RIGHT ARM 'ROUND
PARTNER BY THE LEFT, GO ALL THE WAY AROUND
PROMENADE YOUR CORNER AS SHE COMES DOWN
>Promenade new partners to gents' home position.
>Repeat call three times until ladies are returned to original partners.

DOUBLE STAR

FIRST AND THIRD DO A HALF SASHAY
>Gents pass ladies to left side, join inside hands.

FORWARD TO THE CENTER AND BACK THAT WAY
NOW RIGHT HAND STAR IN THE CENTER OF THE FLOOR
>Couples 1 and 3.

THEN STAR BY THE LEFT WITH THE OLD SIDE FOUR
>Couple 1 with 2 and couple 3 with 4.

BACK TO THE CENTER WITH A RIGHT HAND STAR
GO ONCE AND A HALF RIGHT WHERE YOU ARE
STAR BY THE LEFT WITH THE SIDES ONCE MORE
>Couple 1 with 4 and couple 3 with 2.

GO ONCE AROUND AS YOU DID BEFORE
BREAK TO THE CENTER AND THE TWO LADIES CHAIN
>Lady 1 and 3 chain in center of set.

CHAIN 'EM OVER AND DON'T CHAIN BACK
>Courtesy turn ladies, to face partner.

SQUARE THROUGH THREE QUARTERS AROUND
THERE'S YOUR CORNER, LEFT ALLEMANDE
>(Use appropriate trim.)
>Repeat for couples 2 and 4.

References in Bibliography for Four Gents Star: 100 (p. 97).

INSIDE ARCH AND THE OUTSIDE UNDER

COUPLE NUMBER ONE BALANCE AND SWING
LEAD RIGHT OUT TO THE RIGHT OF THE RING
  Couple 1 leads to couple 2.
CIRCLE FOUR GO HALFWAY AROUND
INSIDE ARCH AND THE OUTSIDE UNDER
  Couple 2 arches, couple 1 goes under. Couple 2 does a courtesy turn.*
INSIDE ARCH AND THE OUTSIDE UNDER
  Couple 1 arches, couple 4 goes under. Couple 1 does a courtesy turn.
INSIDE ARCH AND THE OUTSIDE UNDER
  Couple 4 arches, couple 2 goes under. Couple 4 does a courtesy turn.
INSIDE ARCH AND THE OUTSIDE UNDER
  Couple 2 arches, couple 1 goes under. Couple 2 does a courtesy turn.
LEAD TO THE NEXT, CIRCLE FOUR GO HALFWAY AROUND
  Couple 1 goes to couple 3, circles halfway around.
INSIDE ARCH AND THE OUTSIDE UNDER
  Couple 3 arches, couple 1 goes under.
LEAD TO THE NEXT AND GO LIKE THUNDER
CIRCLE HALF — GO HALFWAY AROUND
  Couple 1 leads to couple 2, now in couple 4's position, circles halfway around.
INSIDE ARCH AND THE OUTSIDE UNDER
  Couple 2 arches, couple 1 goes under. Couple 2 does a courtesy turn.
INSIDE ARCH AND OUTSIDE UNDER
  Couple 1 arches, couple 4 goes under. Couple 1 does a courtesy turn.
INSIDE ARCH AND THE OUTSIDE UNDER
  Couple 4 arches, couple 2 goes under. Couple 4 turns in home position.
INSIDE ARCH, OUTSIDE UNDER
  Couple 2 arches and couple 1 goes under. Couple 2 turns in home position.
HOME YOU GO AND EVERYBODY SWING
  Couple 1 returns to home position. All couples swing.
  Repeat call for couples 2, 3, and 4.

---

* Courtesy turns throughout figure may be changed to California Twirls.

THREE COUPLES ARCH AND ONE GO UNDER

FIRST COUPLE BALANCE AND SWING LIKE THUNDER

THREE COUPLES ARCH AND ONE GO UNDER

> Ladies of couples 2, 3, and 4 form a right hand star and at the same time form an arch by raising joined inside hands with partner. Couples 2, 3, and 4 face clockwise around set. Couple 1 goes to the right and under the arches as couples 2, 3, and 4 move the arches clockwise around the set over couple 1.

GENTS DROP OFF AT YOUR HOME BAR

> Gents drop out of figure at home positions.

LONE LITTLE LADY JOIN THAT STAR

> Lady 1 joins star, stepping in between lady 2 and 4.

LADIES STAR TO THE OPPOSITE MAN

TURN HIM ONCE WITH YOUR LEFT HAND

> Ladies turn opposites once around, forearm grasp.

FOUR GENTS STAR YOUR WESTWARD BOUND

> Gents form a right hand star.

TURN YOUR CORNER LADY LEFT ARM AROUND

> Gents pass opposites (original partners) and turn original corner (next lady) with left arm around.

PARTNER RIGHT GO ALL THE WAY AROUND

> Turn original partner, once and a half.

TURN YOUR RIGHT HAND LADY LEFT ARM AROUND

> Lady to right of original partner.

PARTNER RIGHT GO ALL THE WAY AROUND

> Turn original partner once and a half.

ALLEMANDE LEFT WITH YOUR LEFT HAND

> Original corner.

RIGHT TO YOUR PARTNER AND A RIGHT AND LEFT GRAND

MEET YOUR PARTNER AND MEET HER WITH A SMILE

GRAND RIGHT AND LEFT FOR ANOTHER HALF MILE

> Meet partner "smile," pass partner, and continue the grand right and left.

MEET OLE SAL, MEET OLE SUE

PROMENADE YOUR GAL WHEN YOU GET THROUGH

> Meet partner (second time), promenade home.
>
> Repeat call for couples 2, 3, and 4.

PITT'S PRACTICE PATTER NO. 1

ONE AND THREE DO A RIGHT HAND STAR
  Turn right hand star one full turn to corner.
ALLEMANDE LEFT LIKE AN ALLEMANDE THAR
BACK UP BOYS BUT NOT TOO FAR
  Gents turn corner left, retain grasp, form right hand star in center, gents
  back up, ladies move forward.
THROW IN THE CLUTCH PUT 'ER IN LOW
TWICE AROUND AND HERE WE GO
  Gents release lady's left hand. Ladies continue counterclockwise, gents
  move forward clockwise in a star.
ALLEMANDE LEFT LADIES STAR
GENTS WALK AROUND BUT NOT TOO FAR
  Gents turn corner left, ladies form right hand star move clockwise, gents
  move around set counterclockwise.
ALLEMANDE LEFT GENTS STAR
LADIES WALK AROUND BUT NOT TOO FAR
  Gents turn corner left and form right hand star, move clockwise, ladies
  move around set, counterclockwise.
ALLEMANDE WITH YOUR LEFT HAND
  Gents allemande left with original corner for the third time.
  (Add appropriate trim.)

PITT'S PRACTICE PATTER NO. 2

HEAD COUPLES SWING
NOW PROMENADE THE OUTSIDE RING
SIDES YOU DO A PASS RIGHT THROUGH
STEP IN BEHIND THE OLE HEAD TWO
  Couple 2 behind 3, couple 4 behind couple 1.
GENTS TURN BACK IN A RIGHT HAND STAR
  Gents left face turn to center, form a right hand star.
GALS PROGRESS JUST AS YOU ARE
  Ladies continue to move counterclockwise.
MEET YOUR HONEY ON THE FLY
CATCH HER NEXT AS SHE GOES BY
  Pass partner once, do as caller directs upon second meeting.

PITT'S PRACTICE PATTER NO. 3

HEAD TWO DO A CROSS TRAIL THROUGH
GO AROUND JUST ONE THAT'S WHAT YOU DO
MEET IN THE MIDDLE AND PASS RIGHT THROUGH
SPLIT THE COUPLE IN FRONT OF YOU
GO ROUND JUST ONE LIKE YOU DID BEFORE
AND CROSS TRAIL THROUGH IN THE CENTER ONCE MORE
ROUND JUST ONE AND ON TO THE MIDDLE
FULL SQUARE THROUGH TO THE TUNE OF THE FIDDLE
BOX THE GNAT AND SWING YOUR OWN
LEAVE MY PRETTY LITTLE GAL ALONE

Practice patter arranged by Anne Pittman, Arizona State University, Tempe, Arizona.

PITT'S PRACTICE PATTER NO. 4

ONE AND THREE LEAD TO THE RIGHT
CIRCLE FOUR AND FORM A LINE
FORWARD EIGHT AND BACK YOU GO
FORWARD EIGHT AND PASS RIGHT THROUGH
BEND THE LINE AND DIVE THROUGH
    Couple 1 face 2 and couple 3 face 4 and dive through.
BEND THE LINE AND PASS THROUGH
    Couple 1 face 4 and couple 2 face 3 and pass through.
BEND THE LINE AND RIGHT AND LEFT THROUGH
    Couple 4 face 3 and couple 1 face 2, execute a right and left through.
PASS THROUGH AND BEND YOU DO
    Couple 3 face 2 and couple 4 face 1.
NOW PASS THROUGH TO A BRAND NEW TWO
    Couple 1 face 2 and couple 3 face 4.
STAR THROUGH YOU AIN'T THROUGH YET
BOX THE GNAT AND DON'T BE SLOW
    All gents are facing partners.
SWING YOUR PARTNER AND HERE WE GO
CIRCLE EIGHT I TOLD YOU SO
    (Use any appropriate trim.)

PITT'S PRACTICE PATTER NO. 5

ALL EIGHT SWING NOW PROMENADE AROUND THE RING
HEADS WHEEL AROUND
DIVE RIGHT THROUGH THE COUPLE YOU'VE FOUND
    Couple 1 with 4, couple 3 with 2.
PASS THROUGH A BRAND NEW TWO
    Couple 1 with 2 and couple 3 with 4.
DIVE THROUGH AND BEND THE LINE
    Couple 1 with 4 and couple 3 with 2.
PASS THROUGH AND BEND THE LINE
    Couple 1 with 2 and 3 with 4.
FULL SQUARE THROUGH YOU'RE DOING FINE
CIRCLE EIGHT AND MAKE A RING
    (Add appropriate trim.)

Practice patter arranged by Anne Pittman, Arizona State University, Tempe, Arizona.

ALABAMA JUBILEE
Singing Call

Record: J Bar L 4117 (with calls); Folkraft 1136; MacGregor 638 (with calls) 640; Old Timer 8041 and 8043; Western Jubilee 900; Windsor 4144 and 4444.

FOUR LITTLE LADIES PROMENADE INSIDE OF THE RING
Ladies move in single file, counterclockwise, around inside of set.
BACK TO YOUR PARTNER AND GIVE HIM A SWING
SASHAY 'ROUND YOUR CORNER GIRL
Either sashay or do-sa-do.
BOW TO YOUR PARTNER BOYS, GIVE HER A WHIRL
NOW FOUR LITTLE GENTS PROMENADE INSIDE OF THE RING
Gents move single file, counterclockwise, inside of set.
SASHAY 'ROUND YOUR PARTNER, GIVE YOUR CORNER A SWING
Either sashay or do-sa-do.
YOU PROMENADE JUST YOU AND ME
Gents promenade corner lady.
TO THE ALABAMA JUBILEE, YEAH MAN
TO THE ALABAMA JUBILEE

Break
TURN THE LEFT HAND LADY WITH A LEFT HAND 'ROUND
Turn corner once around. All turns with forearm grasp.
A RIGHT TO YOUR PARTNER GO ALL THE WAY 'ROUND
Turn partner once and a half.
THE RIGHT HAND LADY WITH A LEFT HAND 'ROUND
Turn right hand lady twice around.
NOW SWING YOUR LITTLE HONEY
Waist swing.
'TILL HER FEET LEAVE THE GROUND
IT'S AN ALLEMANDE LEFT, A RIGHT AND LEFT GRAND
MEET YOUR LITTLE HONEY, TAKE HER BY THE HAND
YOU PROMENADE, JUST YOU AND ME
TO THE ALABAMA JUBILEE, YEAH MAN
TO THE ALABAMA JUBILEE
Repeat figure and break three times until ladies are returned to original partners.

ALOHA TO YOU
Singing Call

Record: Western Jubilee 909.

Introduction
ALLEMANDE YOUR CORNER, TURN YOUR PARTNER BY THE
      RIGHT
THE MEN STAR LEFT, THE LADIES SWAY
TURN YOUR PARTNER BY THE RIGHT, YOUR CORNER BY THE
      LEFT
    All turns with forearm grasp.
AND WEAVE DOWN THE LINE ALL THE WAY
    Dancers execute a "no hands" grand right and left *around* the set.
DO-SA-DO YOUR LADY IN THE MOONLIGHT
ALLEMANDE YOUR CORNER, TAKE YOUR OWN TONIGHT
PROMENADE YOUR LADY GO TWO BY TWO
    Take original partner to home place.
AND SHE'LL SAY "ALOHA TO YOU"

Figure
ONE AND THREE LEAD TO THE RIGHT AND CIRCLE TO A LINE
WITHOUT A STOP DO A DO-SA-DO
    First and third couples lead to the right circle and break to form a line
    facing across the set. Do-sa-do the opposite in the line across.
ALL THE WAY 'ROUND, MAKE AN OCEAN WAVE, ROCK IT UP
      AND BACK
    Following Do-sa-do continue around the person just far enough to form a
    line: gent 3, lady 2, lady 3, gent 2, are hooked together with hands up
    position. Gent 1, lady 4, lady 1, gent 4 are hooked together in the same
    way. They move forward and back in a balancing motion.
SWING THROUGH, ROLL IT ONCE AGAIN
    Dancers on end of line hook right elbows, turn half around. Center
    dancers then hook left elbows and turn half around.
SWING THROUGH, ROCK IT, AND WHEN YOU DO
    Repeat "swing through," such as ends turn half, then centers turn half,
    then "ocean wave" by moving up and back in the line.
CROSS TRAIL, SWING THE CORNER WAITING FOR YOU
    Couples move out of line toward home position, do a cross trail to face
    and swing corner.
PROMENADE YOUR LADY GO TWO BY TWO
    Take new partner to home place.
AND SHE'LL SAY "ALOHA TO YOU"
AND SHE'LL SAY "ALOHA TO YOU"
    Repeat figure for couples 1 and 3.
    Break — repeat Introduction.
    Figure — repeat twice for couples 2 and 4.
    Ending — repeat Introduction.

Original dance choreographed by Mr. Michael Michele of Western Jubilee Records,
    1210 E. Indian School Rd., Phoenix, Arizona.

ARE YOU FROM DIXIE?
Singing Call

Record: Lore 1076.

Introduction
YOU CIRCLE LEFT NOW, AND DON'T BE LATE NOW
AND DO A LEFT ALLEMANDE THEN, A RIGHT AND LEFT GRAND
AND WHEN YOU MEET HER, HERE'S HOW YOU GREET HER
YOU'LL DO A DO-SA-DO, THEN SWING YOUR MAID
GENTS STAR LEFT, ACROSS THE SET, AND THERE YOU BOX THE
      GNAT
      Gents box gnat with opposite.
THE GIRLS STAR LEFT, GO STRAIGHT ACROSS, LET'S BOX IT
      BACK
      Ladies star across, box the gnat with original partner.
PROMENADE HER, YOU SERENADE HER
YOU'LL KNOW THAT SHE'S FROM DIXIE TOO

Figure
HEAD COUPLES SWING NOW, PROMENADE THE RING NOW
GO HALF WAY 'ROUND, THEN A RIGHT AND LEFT THROUGH
YOU'LL TURN YOUR LADY, FOUR LADIES GRAND CHAIN
      Heads promenade outside to opposite's position. Then right and left
      through and courtesy turn in home place. All four ladies chain to oppo-
      site gent.
AND THEN THE SIDES SQUARE THROUGH, GO FULL AROUND
      Sides do a full four hand square through to end facing corners.
GO ALL THE WAY AROUND THE RING, SWING THAT CORNER
      MAID
      Swing corners, now, the *new* partner.
ALLEMANDE LEFT, THEN COME ON BACK, LET'S PROMENADE
      Allemande left the *next* corner and promenade the *new* partner to home
      position.
ARE YOU FROM DIXIE, I SAID FROM DIXIE
'CAUSE SHE'S FROM DIXIE TOO
      Repeat figure for couples 1 and 3.
      Break — repeat Introduction.
      Figure — repeat twice for couples 2 and 4.
      Ending — repeat Introduction.

Original dance choreographed by Mr. George Elliott, North Hollywood, California.
    Arranged from *Sets In Order* direction sheet.

COTTON PICKIN' POLKA
Singing Call

Record: Old Timer 8192.

Introduction
ALL JOIN HANDS, CIRCLE TO THE LEFT
TO THE COTTON PICKIN' POLKA
ALLEMANDE LEFT YOUR CORNER
GRAND RIGHT AND LEFT NO JOKIN'
HAND OVER HAND AROUND THE RING
WHEN YOU MEET YOU DO-SA-DO
GENTS STAR LEFT GO ONCE AROUND
BACK TO THE SAME LITTLE GAL YOU KNOW
AND WHEN YOU MEET YOU PROMENADE
TO THE COTTON PATCH AND FIND SOME SHADE
SWING THAT GAL AND TELL HER SO
AT THE END OF EVERY COTTON ROW

Figure
ONE AND THREE YOU STAR THROUGH
    End gent 1 facing lady 1, gent 3 facing lady 3.
PASS THROUGH, AND SPLIT THOSE TWO
    Gent 1 and lady 3 split couple 2. Gent 3 and lady 1 split couple 4.
GO AROUND ONE, LINE UP FOUR
    Gent 1 and lady 3 with couple 2. Gent 3 and lady 1 with couple 4.
FORWARD EIGHT AND BACK ONCE MORE
PASS THROUGH, TURN TO THE RIGHT
SINGLE FILE AROUND THE RING
    Dancer turn individually to own right, all move in single file clockwise
    around set.
GENTS STEP OUT AND BACK TRACK
    Gents turn to own left and move around set in opposite direction. Ladies
    continue clockwise.
MEET YOUR OWN WITH A LEFT ARM SWING
PROMENADE YOUR CORNER HONEY
WEIGHT HER UP AND SPEND YOUR MONEY
PROMENADE THAT LADY FAIR
TO THE COTTON PICKIN' POLKA SQUARE
    Repeat for couples 1 and 3.
    Break — repeat Introduction.
    Figure — repeat twice for couples 2 and 4.
    Ending — repeat Introduction.

Original dance choreographed by Mr. Johnny Schultz of Old Timer Records Co., Inc.,
    708 E. Weldon Avenue, Phoenix, Arizona.

EVERYWHERE YOU GO

Singing Call

Record: Western Jubilee No. 557; MacGregor 8475, 8485; Blue Star 1772.

Introduction
WHY DON'T YOU WALK AROUND YOUR CORNER GIRL
SEE SAW 'ROUND YOUR OWN
THE GENTS STAR RIGHT ONE TIME
TURN YOUR PARTNER BY THE LEFT
YOUR CORNER BOX THE GNAT
SAME GIRL DO-SA-DO
GENTS STAR LEFT
ONCE AROUND YOU GO
PASS YOUR LADY RIGHT ON BY
TAKE THE NEXT AND PROMENO
     Pass corner, take original partner.
SHE WILL FOLLOW YOU
EVERYWHERE YOU GO

Figure
WHY DON'T THE HEAD TWO COUPLES RIGHT AND LEFT
       THROUGH
THE SIDE TWO COUPLES SWING
HEADS PROMENADE GO HALF WAY 'ROUND
     Couples 1 and 3 promenade outside ring to home places
FOUR LADIES CHAIN ACROSS
TURN 'EM TWICE AROUND
     Ladies remain with opposite gents.
FACE YOUR CORNER AND ALL EIGHT CHAIN
     Give right hands to corner, pull her by, give left to the next lady for a
     courtesy turn, put her on the right, and face center of set.
WALK AROUND YOUR CORNER GIRL
     Walk around original corner
PASS ON BY YOUR OWN
     Pass by new partner
SWING AND WHIRL THE RIGHT HAND GIRL
     Lady in couple to gent's right. Original right hand lady.
PROMENADE BACK HOME
SHE WILL FOLLOW YOU
EVERYWHERE YOU GO.
EVERY ... WHERE ... YOU GO ...
     Repeat figure for couples 1 and 3.
     Break — repeat Introduction.
     Figure — repeat twice for couples 2 and 4.

Original dance choreographed by Mr. Gene McMullen, Houston, Texas. Arranged from
    Western Jubilee direction sheet as called by Mr. Michael Michele, of Western
    Jubilee Records, 1210 E. Indian School Rd., Phoenix, Arizona.

HOT TIME
Singing Call

Record: *Hot Time in the Old Town Tonight* — Folkraft 1037; Imperial 1096; MacGregor 652, 004-4, 445-4 (with calls); Old Timer 8025, 8030; Windsor 4115 and 4115.

FIRST COUPLE OUT, AND CIRCLE FOUR AROUND
Couples 1 and 2 circle four.

PICK UP TWO, AND CIRCLE SIX AROUND
Gent 1 breaks circle by unclasping left hand. Picks up couple 3 for a circle of six.

PICK UP TWO, AND CIRCLE EIGHT AROUND
Repeat above, pick up couple 4, circle eight.

THERE'LL BE A HOT TIME IN THE OLD TOWN TONIGHT

ALLEMANDE LEFT WITH THE LADY ON THE LEFT
Gents turn corner with left forearm.

ALLEMANDE RIGHT WITH THE LADY ON THE RIGHT
Gents pass partner on inside of set. Turn right hand ladies with right forearm.

ALLEMANDE LEFT WITH THE LADY ON THE LEFT
Gents pass partner on inside of set. Turn corners with left forearm.

AND GRAND RIGHT AND LEFT ALL AROUND

WHEN YOU MEET YOUR PARTNER, SASHAY ONCE AROUND
Either sashay or do-sa-do once around.

TAKE HER IN YOUR ARMS AND SWING HER 'ROUND AND 'ROUND

PROMENADE AROUND WITH THE PRETTIEST GIRL IN TOWN

THERE'LL BE A HOT TIME IN THE OLD TOWN TONIGHT
Repeat call for couples 2, 3, and 4.

Notes: Recorded music will allow for four complete calls of the figure as arranged above. When called with "live music" the following introduction and ending may be used by having the musicians add three eight measure phrases — one for the introduction and two for the ending.

Introduction
ALL JOIN HANDS AND CIRCLE EIGHT AROUND
BREAK AND TRAIL ALONG THAT LINE
WHEN YOU GET HOME EVERYBODY SWING
THERE'LL BE A HOT TIME IN THE OLD TOWN TONIGHT

Ending
ALLEMANDE LEFT WITH THE LADY ON THE LEFT
ALLEMANDE RIGHT WITH THE LADY ON THE RIGHT
ALLEMANDE LEFT WITH THE LADY ON THE LEFT
GRAND RIGHT AND LEFT ALL AROUND
WHEN YOU MEET YOUR PARTNER, SASHAY ONCE AROUND
BREAK UP YOUR SETS AND DANCE HER 'ROUND AND 'ROUND
SHE'S THE ONE — THE PRETTIEST GIRL IN TOWN
THERE'LL BE A HOT TIME IN THE OLD TOWN TONIGHT

Dance arranged from *Square Dance Handbook by Raymond Smith,* Reference 97 (p. 37).

JESSIE POLKA SQUARE
Singing Call

Record: Blue Star 1667; Folkraft 1263, 1071; MacGregor 657 (with calls),
657; Old Timer 8052 and 8073.

THE SIDE COUPLES ARCH AND THE HEAD COUPLE DIVE UNDER
Couples 2 and 4 form arch with partners, turn left. Couple 2 faces couple
1 and couple 4 faces couple 3. Couples move forward as couple 1 and 3
"dive" under arches.

DIP AND DIVE ROUND THE SQUARE

GO HOME AND DON'T YOU BLUNDER
Couples 1 and 3 arch as couples 2 and 4 "dive" under. Alternate "arching" and "diving" action until couples are in home positions.

IT'S AN ALLEMANDE LEFT, PUT YOUR ARM AROUND YOUR
PARTNER

IN A STAR PROMENADE, DO THE JESSIE POLKA DANCE
All allemande left. Gents form left hand star as they place right arms
around partners' waist. Star moves counterclockwise.

WITH A HEEL AND A TOE, YOU CAN START THE ROOM A
JUMPING
Couples execute following "Jessie Polka Step," (2/4 time). Touch left
heel forward (ct. 1), step left in place (ct. 2), touch right toe back (ct.
1), touch right beside left (ct. 2), touch right heel forward (ct. 1), step
right in place (ct. 2), touch left heel forward (ct. 1), swing left foot
across instep of right (ct. 2).

THE LADIES TURN RIGHT BACK, YOU CAN SEE THEIR BUSTLES
BUMPING
Couples dance forward four two-steps, ladies turn to right and back to
next gent on the last two of the four two-steps.

YOU DANCE THROUGH THE NIGHT AS IF IT WERE A MINUTE
Couples repeat the "Jessie Polka Step."

YOUR HEART IS REALLY IN IT, DO THE JESSIE POLKA DANCE
Couples repeat the four two-steps, ladies turn back as before on the last
two of the four two-steps.

NOW WATCH THAT CORNER GIRL AND AS SHE COMES AROUND
Couples repeat "Jessie Polka Step."

TAKE HER IN YOUR ARMS AND SWING HER 'ROUND AND
'ROUND
Couples repeat the four two-steps, ladies turn back on the last two to
take original corner for new partner.

NOW YOU PROMENADE HER HOME AND KEEP HER FOR YOUR
PARTNER

BALANCE AND YOU SWING 'TIL THE MUSIC STARTS AGAIN
Repeat call three times until ladies are returned to original partners.

Note: For variation the head couples may be called to begin the arching. Call side couples twice and head couples twice.

Figure originated by Mr. Red Warrick of Kilgore, Texas.

LITTLE RED WAGON
Singing Call

Record: Set In Order 2083, 153; Old Timer 8199.

Introduction
TO YOUR PARTNER BOW LOW, CORNER GAL DO-SA-DO
GO BACK SWING YOUR HONEY ROUND AND ROUND
GENTLEMEN CENTER LEFT HAND STAR
TRAVEL ONCE AROUND FROM WHERE YOU ARE
HOME YOU GO AND DO-SA-DO, TURN TO THE CORNER AND
    HERE WE GO
ALLEMANDE LEFT WITH YOUR LEFT HAND, AROUND THE RING
    WE GO
IT'S A GRAND OLD RIGHT AND LEFT, WALK WITH THE GIRL
    YOU KNOW
PROMENADE YOUR PRETTY GIRL, GO BACK HOME AND SWING
    AND TWIRL
FOR SHE'LL RIDE IN YOUR WAGON AGAIN

Figure
ONE AND THREE BOW AND SWING, FORWARD UP AND BACK
    AGAIN
PASS THROUGH, TURN RIGHT, GO 'ROUND ONE
CROSS THE CENTER SINGLE FILE, TURN LEFT GO 'BOUT A MILE
    After pass through, each person turns right and with lady in the lead,
    each couple walks around one person. Still in single file, cross the square,
    split the other couple, and then turn left and around one.
LEFT HAND STAR IN THE MIDDLE ONCE AROUND
    Form left hand star in center of set.
TURN YOUR CORNER BY THE RIGHT, YOUR PARTNER LEFT
    HAND SWING
    These are forearm turns.
PROMENADE YOUR CORNER GAL, PROMENADE HER GO ROUND
    THE RING
FOR SHE'LL RIDE IN YOUR LITTLE RED WAGON
TAKE HER HOME, SWING YOUR HONEY ONCE AROUND
    Repeat figure for couples 1 and 3.
    Break — repeat Introduction.
    Figure — repeat twice for couples 2 and 4.
    Ending — repeat Introduction.

Original dance choreographed by Mr. Lee Heisel, Sacramento, California. Arranged
    from *Sets in Order* direction sheet.

MAÑANA
Singing Call

Record: MacGregor 008-2, 1017; Old Timer 8163.

Introduction
NOW YOU HONOR YOUR CHIQUITA, GIVE YOUR CORNER GIRL
      A WEENK
ALLEMANDE LEFT YOUR CORNER, GRAND OLD RIGHT AND
      LEFT I THEENK
NOW WHEN YOU MEET YOUR ENCHILADA, DO-SA-DO HER NEAT
    Do-sa-do with partner.
SWING YOUR CHILI PEPPER AND PROMENADE THE STREET
    Swing partners, promenade home.

Figure
VAQUEROS STAR ACROSS THE SET, A LEFT HAND SWING THAT
      GIRL
    Gents star right, turn opposite once around, forearm turn.
STAR BACK HOME AGAIN, REAL QUICK ANOTHER LEFT HAND
      WHIRL
    Gents star right, turn partner once around, forearm turn
A RIGHT ARM AROUND YOUR CORNER
GIVE YOUR OWN A LEFT ARM SWING
NOW PROMENADE THAT CORNER GIRL AND EVERYBODY SING
    Promenade corners as new partners to gents' home position.
MAÑANA, MAÑANA, MAÑANA IS GOOD ENOUGH FOR ME
CHIQUITAS STAR ACROSS THE SET, A LEFT HAND SWING THAT
      MAN
    Ladies star right, turn opposite once around, forearm turn.
STAR BACK HOME AND TURN YOUR HOMBRE WITH THE OLD
      LEFT HAND
    Ladies star right, turn partner once around, forearm turn.
A RIGHT ARM AROUND YOUR CORNER
GIVE YOUR OWN A LEFT ARM SWING
NOW PROMENADE YOUR CORNER GIRL AND EVERYBODY SING
    Promenade corners as new partners to gents' home position.
MAÑANA, MAÑANA, MAÑANA IS GOOD ENOUGH FOR ME

Break
ALLEMANDE LEFT YOUR CORNER
AND PASS RIGHT BY YOUR OWN
    Pass partner's right shoulder.
ALLEMANDE RIGHT YOUR RIGHT HAND GIRL
    Allemande right original right hand lady.
AND LEAVE YOUR OWN ALONE
    Pass partner's right shoulder again.
NOW ALLEMANDE LEFT YOUR CORNER AND GIVE YOUR OWN A
      SWING
AND PROMENADE TO MEXICO AND EVERYBODY SING
    Promenade partners, original opposite, to gent's home.
MAÑANA, MAÑANA, MAÑANA IS GOOD ENOUGH FOR ME
    Repeat figure and break 3 times until ladies are returned to original
    partners.

POLKA ON A BANJO

Singing Call

Record: Western Jubilee 901; Bogan 1182.

Introduction

ALLEMANDE LEFT THE CORNER, ALLEMANDE RIGHT YOUR
      PARTNER
    Turn corner with left hand around, turn partner with right hand around.
    (Forearm grasp more stable.)
GENT'S STAR LEFT, TURN IT ONE TIME AROUND
PARTNER RIGHT AND BOX THE GNAT, PULL HER BY AND THEN
LEFT ALLEMANDE THE CORNER, GRAND RIGHT AND LEFT MY
      FRIEND
GRAND RIGHT AND LEFT YOU GO NOW
DO-SA-DO WHEN YOU MEET YOUR LADY OVER THERE
      PROMENADE
PROMENADE THE RING, TAKE HER RIGHT ON HOME, AND
      SWING
TO THE POLKA ON THE OLD BANJO

Figure

ONE AND THREE A HALF SASHAY DANCE FORWARD UP AND
      BACK
    Gents exchange places with partners.
BOX THE GNAT, DO A RIGHT AND LEFT THROUGH ON DOWN
    Gents box the gnat with opposite. Right and left through to home places
    and courtesy turn in place.
PASS THROUGH AND SEPARATE GO ROUND ONE YOU KNOW
COME INTO THE CENTER, STAR THROUGH, CROSS TRAIL JOE
    Couples 1 and 3 star through in center to face each other, ladies on
    gent's right. Then cross trail through to face original corner.
LEFT ALLEMANDE THE CORNER, WALK RIGHT BY YOUR
      PARTNER
SWING THE NEXT LITTLE LADY ROUND AND ROUND
    Promenade the right hand lady.
PROMENADE THE RING, TAKE YOUR HONEY HOME AND SWING
TO THE POLKA ON THE OLD BANJO
    Repeat figure for couples 1 and 3.
    Break — repeat Introduction.
    Figure — repeat for couples 2 and 4.
    Ending — repeat Introduction.

Original dance choreographed by Mr. Charles Dewey Drake. Arranged from Western
    Jubilee direction sheet as called by Mr. Drake.

YES SIR!
Singing Call

Record: Old Timer 8177.

Introduction
WALK ALL AROUND YOUR LEFT HAND LADY
SEE SAW YOUR OWN PRETTY BABY — GO BACK
AND SWING YOUR CORNER LADY 'ROUND — PROMENADE
    Promenade corner.
YOU PROMENADE DON'T SLOW DOWN
ALL FOUR COUPLES WHEEL AROUND
PROMENADE THE WRONG WAY 'ROUND THE TOWN
ONE AND THREE (TWO AND FOUR) WHEEL AROUND
    Either may be called.
SQUARE ON THROUGH THREE QUARTERS ROUND
RIGHT, LEFT, RIGHT, CORNERS ALL LEFT ALLEMANDE
    Allemande left with *original* corners.
GO BACK AND PROMENADE WITH YOUR PRETTY BABY
TAKE HER HOME AND SWING, WELL MAYBE
    Promenade original partner.
YES SIR! SHE'S YOUR BABY NOW

Figure
HEADS TO THE MIDDLE AND BACK YOU RUN
CROSS TRAIL THROUGH, AROUND JUST ONE
MAKE A LINE, GO FORWARD UP AND BACK
BOX THE GNAT ACROSS FROM YOU
SAME GIRL YOU CURLIQUE
    Both use right hands, gents do normal star through, lady walks under
    man's right arm, makes a 3/4 left-face turn. Couples end right shoulders
    to right shoulders, each facing in opposite direction in a single file line.
LINES TURN LEFT, SINGLE FILE
GIRLS IN THE LEAD, WATCH 'EM SMILE
GENTS TURN BACK, SWING THE GIRL THAT'S FACING YOU
THEN PROMENADE WITH THIS NEW GIRL
TAKE HER HOME AND SWING AND WHIRL
YES SIR! SHE'S YOUR BABY NOW
    Repeat figure for couples 1 and 3.
    Break — repeat Introduction.
    Figure — repeat twice for couples 2 and 4.
    Ending — repeat Introduction.

Original dance choreographed by Mr. Johnny Schultz of Old Timer Records Co., Inc.,
    708 E. Weldon Avenue, Phoenix, Arizona.

CONTRA DANCE

HISTORY
By Ralph Page*

Contra dances and northern New England are fast becoming synonymous terms in American dance terminology. Far from being quaint "reliques" rescued for the tourist trade from a limbo of forgotten Americana, they are today as vigorously alive and as much loved among us as were their ancestors — the English "longways for as many as will"; the Irish "cross-road" dances; and the vibrant Scottish reels — at the time of the settling of Maine, New Hampshire, and Vermont.

Special Appeal . . . Literally *a contra dance is a dance of opposition: a dance performed by many couples face to face, line facing line.* They came to this country from the British Isles; every one of the thirteen colonies knew them; they were danced by people from all walks of life and especially by the country people.

Contras are said to appeal to a special type of dancer, and that could be true. At least one has to be able to count to eight and to dance in time with the music. To live more or less unchanged for three hundred years or so, they must have something. Why have we retained our love of contras when elsewhere in the United States they have fallen from favor? I doubt if anyone could point to any one definite answer. Perhaps it is a combination of English resentment to change, Irish bull-headedness, and Scottish stubbornness, for in the beginning at least 90 per cent of our early settlers came from these three named portions of the British Isles.

The terms "Duple minor" and "Triple minor" are applied to contra dance forms. Think of the expressions in this manner: "Duple minor" is a contra dance in which every alternate couple is an active couple. All of the dances at the end of this chapter are "Duple minors." Many people think that they are the easiest kind of contras to do.

Over two thousand American contras have been recorded in dance books published in this country since 1790. Once you have mastered all of the contras given here you will be ready to progress to the intermediate contras which make up by far the greatest number of the above mentioned two thousand. The next step involved is the figure "cast off" which is a method of progression up and down the set. There is a "cast off" in each of the dances described — there had to be else you would dance with the same couple from beginning to end, and how boring can a dance become? But the "cast off" is hidden and you are not aware of it. You merely note that you are moving up and down the set and having a grand time doing so.

In Olde England . . . Contras, or longways, were the rage of England in the 17th century. The peasantry and bourgeois society of the country developed the contredanse to its highest points in complexity. For example, the number of corresponding country dances of England in 1728 numbered some 900 dances in all, and explored every form of cross-over and interweaving, with numbers of participants varying from four to an indefinite number. Sometimes each couple in succession led through the figures, sometimes alternate couples, and sometimes the whole group "for as many as will" performed them simultaneously.

Is it any wonder then, that during the 16th and 17th centuries the English were known as the "dancing English"? Country dances were the ordinary, every day dance

---

* Chapter VII — Contra Dance, has been written by Ralph Page, foremost authority on contra dancing in the United States. 117 Washington St., Keene, New Hampshire.

of the country folk, performed not merely on festal days, but whenever opportunity offered. The steps and figures, while many in number, were simple and easily learned so that anyone of ordinary intelligence could qualify as a competent dancer. Truly they were dances of the people.

Royal Flavor ... The Tudor royal family was passionately fond of dancing and introduced many Court Masques embodying many of the country dances of the day and period. In the reign of James I, it was said that it was easier to don fine clothes than to learn the French dances, and that therefore "none but Country Dances must be used at court."

There is a legend that Queen Elizabeth bestowed the office of Lord Chancellor on Sir Christopher Hatton, not for any surpassing knowledge of the law, but because he wore green bows on his shoes and danced the pavane to perfection. No wonder her Court produced so many fine dancers.

Playford Collection ... No doubt it was some royal personage who commissioned John Playford to collect and set down all the country dances of the country. This he did, and since he was a bookseller and a musician of considerable ability, he found no difficulty in publishing a series of books: The English Dancing Master — Plaine and Easy Rules for the Dancing of Country Dances, with the Tunes to Each Dance.

The first of these volumes was brought out in 1650 and the last in 1728. Obviously the books had great popularity and were continued by Playford's successors. While the majority of the dances in the Playford collection were not pure folk dances, they certainly had a folk basis. The Country dance ordinarily consisted of a series of figures arbitrarily chosen to fit a given tune; only in certain instances did a particular combination of figures prove so enjoyable as to achieve universal acceptance. The country people never lost their love of these old dances and they still survive from Cornwall to the Border Counties.

This, then, was the status of country dancing at the time of the first settlements in New England. No one will ever make me believe that the English colonials did not bring with them their love of dancing. Not all of the Puritans were "pickle-faced joy-killers."

So much for England. Let us turn northward and see what was happening in Scotland during this same period.

Our Debt to Scotland ... From time immemorial the Scots have followed all facets of Country and Highland dancing with delight and enthusiasm. Their fondness for it amounts almost to a passion. All efforts of the Kirk to put down "promiscuous dancing" have been failures. The Scot dances naturally and with intuition, which seems logical enough when we remember their great love of music. However, descriptions of the early dances of Scotland are very meager, though we know the names of many from the old ballad "Cokelkie Sow," wherein twenty dances are mentioned.

The reason for this poverty of description is that the Scots, while practicing the musical arts, had not reached the point of penning treatises on any of them; and then came the times of John Knox, when dancing was looked on as a sin and only spoken of to be inveighed against. We must remember that dancing or sports of all kinds had very much obscured the original significance of religious ceremonies and the Puritans were but endeavoring to return to the simplicity of ancient times when they sought to curtail somewhat the amusements of the people.

By 1723, however, a weekly dancing assembly was established in Edinburgh and was largely patronized and, in 1728, the Town Council of Glasgow appointed a dancing master with a salary of 20 pounds "to familiarize the inhabitants with the art." And by 1768 we read that the "Rev. John Mills includes dancing — and Church music, among the many things necessary for a Gentleman's education."

Dancing at weddings was a common custom among the Scottish people. In the 18th century dancing took place on the green when weather permitted, and the first reel was danced by the newly-married couple; next in line were the bridesmaids and their escorts. The first reel was called "shemit," from the supposed bashfulness of the young couple.

From the wedding to the death-bed is a sad journey, but extremes meet. On the night after a death in Scotland, dancing was kept up until the next morning, just as it was at a wedding. If the dead person was a man, his widow — if he left one — led the first dance; if the deceased was a woman, the widower began the measure.

Scottish Reels . . . When one thinks of country dancing in Scotland, one thinks of the "reel." The Scots dance their reels for the reel's sake. The dance is not with them an excuse for a social gathering, or means of carrying on a flirtation. The Scot arrives on the dance floor as he would on the drill square and he dances until he is tired out. When performed by two couples it is called a "foursome reel"; when danced by three couples it is called a "sixsome reel," etc., the difference being in the music with a corresponding difference in steps. It might also be noticed that the Scot did not depend always on the playing of some instrument to accompany his dances, but often "reeled" to his own music.

How the ballet step known as "Pas de Basque" found its way into the Scottish reels is a most intriguing and controversial question. The logical answer seems to be: from the French dancing masters. But perhaps this is too logical an answer. What was the reel step before the introduction of the Pas de Basque?

The longways dance was equally as popular in Scotland as in nearby England, and was danced and enjoyed in the Lowlands and Highlands alike. In fact, they have never ceased to be danced in the smaller communities.

The Irish Influence . . . The Irish possess a natural flair for both music and dancing, and the Irish Jig has a most wonderful influence over an Irish heart. You can get into all kinds of trouble and arguments over the origin of the word "jig." Whatever may be its origin, in Ireland it has long stood for a dance, popular with young and old in all classes.

Few meetings for any purpose took place in Ireland without a dance being called for. It was not unusual for young men, inspired by their sweethearts to dance away the night to the music of the pipes (the bagpipe is not a monopoly of Scotland). Every village had its piper who, on fine evenings after working hours would gather all the people of the town about him and play for their dancing. Before the gathering broke up, the piper would dig a small hole in the ground before him and at the end of the next dance all present were expected to toss coins into this hole to "pay the piper his due." One very old tune of this character was called "Gather Up The Money." Another tune often used was the one now known as "Blackberry Blossom."

Harp Tunes . . . The harp is really the national instrument of Ireland, and Irish harpers were unsurpassed in skill. Many of the tunes to which we now dance contras were once songs written for the harp.

An Irish wake meant dancing; not in delight because of the passing, but rather in his or her honor, and as a mark of esteem in which the deceased was held. If no musician was present at the time, then they danced anyway to their own music that was called "lilting" a tune. Some of these lilts have found their way into the dance music of Ireland.

It is difficult today to realize the extent to which Irish dance and music permeated English life in the 16th and 17th centuries. In the previously mentioned "Playford's Dancing Master," there are many Irish dance tunes given with a key to the dance which was performed to each tune (some fourteen in all, in the earlier editions).

It is in the realm of music that the Irish have contributed most to New England contras. Who does not know and love such tunes as "The White Cockade," "Irish Washerwoman," "The Girl I Left Behind Me," "Turkey in the Straw" and numberless more of similar nature? Some of these very tunes were brought over to New England by immigrants in the first wave of colonization.

Our Early Settlers . . . The English, Irish, and Scottish nationalities constituted the largest numbers of early settlers in northern New England. All three had an inborn love of dancing and were well versed in longways type dances: the English and their highly developed techniques and exactness of steps in reels and longways; the Irish with their well developed skill in music; the Scots with their highly developed techniques and exactness of steps in reels and longways; and the Irish and Scottish with their well-known fondness of holding to the old traditions and ways of their ancestors. Is it any wonder that contra dances flourished from the first in Maine, New Hampshire, and Vermont? Is it to be wondered that we still love them? With our preponderance of natives still of the same racial stock, how could it be otherwise?

I know of no New England contra that is completely Irish in character and figures. The side step-seven and threes — which is the basic step in Irish dancing — is entirely absent from our contras. Yet the music played for dozens is a direct importation from the "Ould Sod."

The Scottish Influence . . . The Scot, on the other hand, has had a big influence on the steps and figures of many of our line dances. Three favorites come quickly to mind: Money Musk, Petronella, Hull's Victory. The music that we play for Money Musk was written by a butler in the household of Sir Archibald Grant of Money Musk, in the Lowlands of Scotland. History tells us that the butler's name was Donald or Daniel Dow and apparently he was a musician of no mean ability for an early collection of Scottish and Irish airs published by Buntings of London contains many tunes attributed to him. The dance was originally known as "Sir Archibald Grant of Moniemusk Reel." As you would suspect, it was too unwieldy a title to have a long life and it was soon shortened to "Money Musk."

"Hull's Victory" is almost step for step the same dance as one known in Scotland as the "Scottish Reform." The same may be said of "Petronella." New England dancers for generations have called it "Pat'nella." Further proof of these statements may be found by reading the "Scottish Country Dance Books." The English also have an interesting "Money Musk." The Scottish dance "Strip the Willow" is an interesting version of "Virginia Reel," in turn a descendant of "Sir Roger de Coverly." A still closer relative to "Sir Roger" is the Scottish dance, "The Haymakers."

"Pousette" and "Allemande" were both methods of progression in Scottish country dances, neither of which is practiced now in our New England contras, though once they were common terms with us. Many old manuscripts of the last century contain both terms over and over again. I have copies of several of these dance manuscripts dated from 1795 to 1816 and they are full of combinations of dance terms, half or two-thirds of which are English terms and the rest Scottish; an interesting bit of data it seems to me. That was just after the Revolutionary War and no doubt in many districts of New England, the English were far from being loved, and other terms began to creep into our contra dances. Still others began to be omitted entirely and American substitutions replaced them. "Set" is one term in particular quite common in both English and Scottish dances, corresponding to the New England "balance."

French-Canadian Influence . . . Within the past hundred years New England has experienced another flood of immigration — the French-Canadians. Especially is this true of New Hampshire: thousands of French-Canadians from Quebec have poured across our borders, first to work in our lumber camps, later to become textile workers. So many are now here that within another two or three generations New Hampshireites of French-Canadian descent will outnumber all others. They are a delightful and fun-loving people and dearly love to sing and dance.

They have had little or no influence as far as bringing with them from Canada contra dances of their own. However, so adaptable are they in all things, that they have taken to our contras like "young ducks to water" and their contagious laughter and mimicry are now mingled with Irish tunes and English and Scottish figures and everybody loves it immensely.

French-Canadian fiddle tunes are used more and more for our New England dances, both square and contras. Some of our finest folk musicians are of French-Canadian derivation and they are without peer in this field.

Without a doubt the French-Canadians have had the strongest influence on *our long New England swings*. To them should go the credit — or "blame" — for the frequent 8 to 16 count swings.

Yankee Musicians . . . We have never lacked for fiddlers capable of playing the proper tunes for our contras. This could be because of our racial strains — for you can find a touch of the Gael in most of our fiddlers. Itinerant fiddlers traveled over the countryside, sure to find a warm feeling of welcome wherever night found them. Word soon spread of their presence in town, and neighbors came from far and near to listen and, often-times, to dance a contra or two with the fiddler standing in an out-of-the-way corner of the room. After playing a few figures, the musician would "pass the hat," collecting from each man whatever could be afforded. The total amount collected decided how long the fiddler would continue to play.

For larger parties in the local town hall, for the many balls, assemblies or any other name you cared to give them, other instruments were added and the traditional orchestra of mother's day consisted of first and second violins, cornet, "clarionet" — that's the way they spelled it then — double bass and, if the occasion warranted it, a violincello and flute. Later an organ was added, and by the turn of the century it was in turn replaced by the piano. My earliest recollection of dancing recalls an orchestra of two violins, clarinet, cornet, and piano.

And Yet They Live . . . For more than a half century dance manuals did their best to kill contra dances. Such dancing masters as Elias Howe, Edward Ferraro, Wm. B. DeGarmo, C. H. Cleveland, Jr., and Thomas Hillgrove proclaimed bitterly against them and considered them unfashionable. Characteristically, northern New Englanders paid no heed to such "high falutin' fiats," and continued dancing contras with as much verve and zest as ever.

There are those who hold that Puritanism took the merriness out of "Merry England," but it didn't take the merriness out of the stock that came from Old England to make New England. Neither did John Knox drive it completely out of the minds and customs of the Scottish immigrants. Nor could Cromwell drive it out of the lives of Irish folk coming to America by the thousands. Perhaps all this persecution only made our pioneer forefathers more determined than ever to carry on the customs of their native lands here in New England.

FUNDAMENTALS *

Formation of Set . . . Refer to diagram on page 47. The dancers stand five to six feet apart. Although as many couples may dance in a single contra set as space allows, it is better to learn in sets of six or eight couples. Contra sets are arranged so that the head of the set is nearest the caller.

In most of the dances included, couples 1, 3, 5, etc., cross over. Partners of the 1, 3, 5 couples change sides. Refer to diagram on page 48. The couples that cross over are referred to as *active couples*. They are active until they reach the foot of the set. They wait one turn without dancing, then become inactive and work their way up to the head of the set. The other couples are referred to as *inactive couples*. They work

their way to the head of set, wait one turn without dancing, and then become active couples, *cross over*, and start dancing, moving toward the foot of the set. Cross over means that the man and lady, who have waited without dancing, must change places before the figure begins again.

If there is an even number of couples dancing, every other time all people are working and every other time the end couples wait out. When there is an odd number of couples dancing, one couple will always be waiting out, first at the foot, then at the head.

Dancers will be working with the partner across the set or with the person below (toward the foot of the set) on the same

* Additional information may be found in references 55 and 91 of Bibliography.

side, or with the one above (toward the head of the set) on the same side.

Progression, or *casting off*, usually takes place by:

1) swinging a lady and finishing with her on the man's right
2) a right and left through
3) a ladies chain

To move in a *line of four*, the active couple separates and the inactive couple is in between them.

Basic Step . . . A rhythmic walking step in time with the music is used throughout the dance, except for special steps such as Swing and Balance.

Basic Techniques . . . Most of the basic techniques of contra dancing are the same as those in square dancing. The swing, promenade, ladies chain, right and left through, and sashay are some of the techniques that are commonly called. The techniques that are unique to contra dancing are described in the specific dances in which they are used.

Calls . . . The calls are basically cues that give direction to the dancer with a minimal amount of rhyming patter. Calls for each dance have been suggested; but the caller is free to use his own ingenuity in calling the cues. The caller must note the couple at the head of the set before the dance begins in order to get that couple back to place before the dance ends. The caller must learn to space the calls so the dance will move along continuously, and so the dancers will not have to wait at the end of each figure nor have to run to keep up.

Music . . . Contra dance music is written in 2/4, 6/8, and 4/4 rhythm. The 6/8 rhythm is counted like two beats, each beat being worth a triplet, first beat 1, 2, 3; second beat 4, 5, 6.

A contra dance fits a definite number of measures. In many cases a contra is done to a specific tune — *Hull's Victory, Money Musk, Chorus Jig, Fisher's Hornpipe, Old Zip Coon*, etc. In other cases an interchange of dance to other tunes is permissible if the phrasing is exactly the same. Therefore, it is necessary for the dancer to give each maneuver the *exact* designated number of beats in order to maintain the consistent relationship of dance to music.

DUD'S REEL

This is arranged by Ralph Page from the dance DUD'S REEL, by Dudley Briggs, Arlington, Massachusetts.

Music	Record: *Indian Reel* Folk Dancer MH 508.
	Piano: *Once Upon My Cheek*, One Thousand Fiddle Tunes.
Formation	Contra dance formation with couples 1, 3, 5, etc., cross over.
Steps	Balance, walk, buzz step swing.

DIRECTIONS FOR THE DANCE

Music 2/4   NOTE: Directions are same for both lady and man.

Metronome 128

MEASURES

1–2   Balance left hand lady. Beginning right, take one short step forward toward left hand lady (ct. 1), bring left foot up beside right (ct. 2). Beginning left, take one short step backward away from left hand lady (ct. 1), bring right foot beside left (ct. 2).

3–8   Swing left hand lady. Buzz step square dance swing. Leave lady on right (12 cts., two buzz steps to each measure).

1–4   All forward and back. All join hands up and down line. Beginning right, take three short steps forward (cts. 1, 2, 1) right, left, right, bring left beside right (ct. 2). Beginning left, take three short steps backward (cts. 1, 2, 1) left, right, left, bring right beside left (ct. 2).

5–8   Opposite ladies chain (8 cts.).

9–12   Same ladies chain back (8 cts.).

13–16 All forward and back (as in measures 1–4) (8 cts.).

9–16   Circle four with opposite couple. Beginning left, take eight walking steps to left in a circle of four (8 cts.). Then beginning right take eight walking to right (8 cts.).

THIS IS ONCE THROUGH THE DANCE.
REPEAT AS LONG AS DESIRED.

THE CALLS: Balance and swing the one below
            All forward and back
            Opposite ladies chain, and chain right back
            All forward and back once more
            With the opposite couple circle four hands around
            The other way back to place

Dance annotation form © 1948 by the Folk Dance Federation of California.

HAYMAKERS' JIG

This is a traditional contra, most popular in the state of Maine, where there are five different versions. It is popular too in New Hampshire. The version given here is the one most commonly found in both states.

Music	Record: *Come Up the Backstairs*, Folk Dancer MH 1071.
	Piano: *Miller's Reel*, One Thousand Fiddle Tunes.
Formation	Contra dance formation with couples 1, 3, 5, etc., cross over.
Steps	Balance, buzz step swing, walk.

DIRECTIONS FOR THE DANCE

Music 6/8*   NOTE: Directions are the same for both lady and man.

Metronome 124

MEASURES

1–2   Balance left hand lady. Beginning right, take one short step forward toward left hand lady (ct. 1), bring left foot up beside right (ct. 2). Beginning left, take one short step backward away from left hand lady (ct. 1), bring right foot beside left (ct. 2).

3–4   Repeat foot action of measures 1–2.

5–8   Swing left hand lady. Buzz step square dance swing (8 cts. two buzz steps to each measure). Lady ends on man's right.

1–2   Beginning right, active couple takes one short step forward toward partner in the middle of set (ct. 1), bring left foot up beside right (ct. 2). Beginning with left, take one short step backward away from partner (ct. 1), bring right foot beside left (ct. 2).

3–4   Repeat action of measures 1–2.

5–8   Swing partner. Active couple, buzz step swing in center with partner (8 cts.).

9–12   Down the center in line. Active couples face down the set, lady on man's right. Take the person you swung and all four walk down the center in a line (8 cts.). On cts. 7 and 8, drop hands and turn alone to face opposite direction.

13–16 Join hands. Walk back to place eight steps (8 cts.).

9–16   Opposite ladies chain (16 cts.).

THIS IS ONCE THROUGH THE DANCE.
REPEAT AS LONG AS DESIRED.

THE CALLS: Balance and swing the one below
            Balance and swing your own in the center
            Go down the center four in line
            Turn alone and come back home
            Within your line two ladies chain
            Turn them around and chain them back

---

* 6/8 time is counted like 2 beats, each beat being worth a triplet, first beat 1, 2, 3; second beat 4, 5, 6.

Dance annotation form © 1948 by the Folk Dance Federation of California.

ALL THE WAY TO GALWAY

This is an original dance by Richer Castner, Portland, Maine.

Music   Record: *Paddy on the Turnpike*, Folkraft 1151.
              Piano: *All the Way to Galway*, One Thousand Fiddle Tunes.
Formation   Contra dance formation with couples 1, 3, 5, etc., cross over.
              Walk, balance, buzz step swing.

DIRECTIONS FOR THE DANCE

Music 4/4   NOTE: Directions are same for both lady and man, except

Metronome 124   when specially noted.

MEASURES

1–4	Active couples (1, 3, 5, etc.) down the center with partner. Man beginning left, lady right, take eight walking steps down center of the set toward foot of set, inside hands joined.
5–8	Up the outside to place. Man beginning left, lady right, active couples separate, cut through the line and up the outside with eight walking steps to original place.
1–4	Do-si-do partner. Active couples step to center of set and di-si-do.
5–8	Do si-do the one below. Active couples now do-si-do with one next below.
9–10	Balance with the same (one below). Beginning right, take one step to own right (cts. 1, 2), swing left foot across in front of right (cts. 3, 4) DON'T HOP AND DON'T STAMP! Step on left foot (cts. 1, 2), swing right foot across in front of left (cts. 3, 4).
11–16	Swing the same. Buzz step square dance swing (12 cts. two buzz steps to each measure).
9–12	Half promenade. With the one you swung, face middle of the set. Walk across set, passing to right of opposite couple eight steps. Turn as couple to face the middle again (actually you take four steps across and four to turn).
13–16	Half right and left to place. Opposite couples right and left through (four steps to pass through, four steps to courtesy turn).

THIS IS ONCE THROUGH THE DANCE.
REPEAT AS LONG AS DESIRED.

THE CALLS: Down the center with your own, then up the outside right
              back home
              Now you go into the center with a do-si-do
              Do-si-do the one below, then balance, and you swing the same
              Take this lady, half promenade across the set
              Turn as couples and right and left home.

Dance annotation form © 1948 by the Folk Dance Federation of California.

THE TOURIST

Original dance by Ted Samella, Lexington, Massachusetts. The Tourist is arranged by Ralph Page.

Music	Record: *Lamplighter's Hornpipe*, Folk Dancer MH 1582.
	Piano: *Lamplighter's Hornpipe*, One Thousand Fiddle Tunes.
Formation	Contra dance formation with couples, 1, 3, 5, etc., cross over.
Steps	Walk, buzz step swing, balance.

DIRECTIONS FOR THE DANCE

Music 2/4   NOTE: Directions are the same for both lady and man.

Metronome 128

MEASURES

1–4   <u>Active couples (1, 3, 5, etc.) turn out and walk down outside of set</u>, behind their own respective lines eight steps. On steps seven and eight, each turns toward center of set.

5–8   Continue to turn to face head of set and come right back. Active couples take eight walking steps back to original place.

1–4   <u>Do-si-do your partner</u>. Active couples step to middle of set and do-si-do with own partner (eight steps).

5–8   <u>Circle four hands once around</u>. Opposite couples join hands in a circle. Beginning left, take eight walking steps to left.

9–10   <u>Balance left hand lady</u>. Beginning man's right, lady's right, each takes one short step toward other (ct. 1), bring left foot beside right (ct. 2). Beginning left, each takes one short step backward (ct. 1), bring right foot beside left (ct. 2).

11–16   <u>Swing that same left hand lady</u>. Buzz step square dance swing (12 cts., two buzz steps to each measure).

9–16   <u>Opposite ladies chain over and back.</u>

THIS IS ONCE THROUGH THE DANCE.
REPEAT AS LONG AS DESIRED.

THE CALLS: Down the outside of the set
Turn around and come right back
Into the center with a do-si-do
Circle four with the couple below
Balance and swing the left hand lady
Opposite ladies chain.

Dance annotation form © 1948 by the Folk Dance Federation of California.

THE MALDEN REEL

This is an original contra by Herbie Gaudreau, Holbrook, Massachusetts.

Music Record: *Maple Leaf Jig*, Folk Dancer MH 508.

Piano: *Smash the Windows Jig*, One Thousand Fiddle Tunes.

Formation Contra dance formation with couples 1, 3, 5, etc., cross over.

Steps Walk, buzz step swing.

DIRECTIONS FOR THE DANCE

Music 6/8*   NOTE: Directions are the same for both lady and man.

Metronome 124

MEASURES

1–4 Do-si-do one below. Men do-si-do lady on their left, passing right shoulder to right shoulder, take on step to own right and walk backward to original place (8 cts.).

5–6 Balance and swing with same. With the one you do-si-do, beginning right, take one short step forward (ct. 1), bring left foot up beside right (ct. 2), take one short step backward on left (ct. 1), bring right foot along side left foot (ct. 2).

7–8 Buzz step square dance swing with same person (4 cts.).

1–4 Circle four with opposite couple. Face middle after swing, and join hands with opposite couple. Beginning left, take eight walking steps in a circle once around (8 cts.).

5–8 Left hand star back to place. Same four people drop hands, turn in place to face opposite direction and join left hands across in a star. Beginning left, take eight walking steps back to place (8 cts.).

9–12 All promenade up and down. At end of left hand star, two couples separate and promenade in opposite directions by couples up and down the hall, eight walking steps (8 cts.). Active man and lady he swung, promenade UP the hall, active lady and man she swung promenade DOWN the hall.

13–16 Turn as a couple the other way back. All turn as couples and take eight walking steps, promenading back to original place (8 cts.).

9–16 Same two ladies chain over and back (16 cts.).

THIS IS ONCE THROUGH THE DANCE.
REPEAT AS LONG AS DESIRED.

THE CALLS: Do-si-do the one below
Then balance and you swing the same
Circle four with opposite two
The other way back with left hand star
All promenade up and down
Turn as couples the other way back
Same two ladies chain

* 6/8 time is counted like 2 beats, each beat being worth a triplet, first beat 1, 2, 3; second beat 4, 5, 6.
Dance annotation form © 1948 by the Folk Dance Federation of California.

ST. LAWRENCE JIG

This is an original contra by Ralph Page, Keene, New Hampshire.

Music   Record: *St. Lawrence Jig*, Folk Dancer MH 507.

                 Piano: *Maggie Brown's Favorite*, One Thousand Fiddle Tunes.

Formation   Contra dance formation with couples 1, 3, 5, etc., cross over.

Steps   Walk, buzz step swing.

DIRECTIONS FOR THE DANCE

Music 6/8*   NOTE: Directions are the same for both lady and man.

Metronome 124

MEASURES

1–4   Allemande left the one below. Active couples allemande left with one on their left (8 cts.).

5–8   Swing partner in the center. Active couples buzz step square dance swing in middle of set. Finish swing with lady on man's right. Both facing down set (8 cts., two buzz steps to each measure).

1–4   Down the center four in line. Four join hands. All take eight walking steps down toward foot of set. On cts. 7 and 8 all turn alone, face up set.

5–8   Come back home four in line. Line of four again join hands and take eight walking steps up center to place. On cts. 7 and 8, the two people on outside of line stop and swing the one in line nearest to them outward once around to face middle of set. (This is one way to cast off.)

9–16   Opposite couples right and left four. Couples right and left through and right and left back (16 cts.).

9–12   All forward and back. The long lines join hands. Beginning left, all take four short steps forward. Beginning right, all take four short steps backward to place (8 cts.).

13–16   Make a right hand star once around with opposite couple (8 cts.).

THIS IS ONCE THROUGH THE DANCE.
REPEAT AS LONG AS DESIRED.

THE CALLS: Allemande left the one below
             Then in the middle you swing your own
             Go down the center four in line
             Turn alone, the same way home
             Cast off and right and left four
             All join hands go forward and back
             Opposite couples star by the right

---

* 6/8 time is counted like 2 beats, each beat being worth a triplet, first beat 1, 3, 3; second beat 4, 5, 6.
Dance annotation form © 1948 by the Folk Dance Federation of California.

CRISS CROSS REEL

This is an original contra by Herbie Gaudreau, Holbrook, Massachusetts. Originally Criss Cross Reel was called "Becket Reel." It is known in Ontario as "Slaunch to Donegal" and in some parts of New Hampshire as "Bucksaw Contra."

Music	Record: *Reilly's Own,* Folk Dancer MH 10072.
	Piano: *Reilly's Own,* One Thousand Fiddle Tunes.
Formation	Contra dance formation BUT couples stand side by side with partner. Each couple MUST have an opposite couple. (Couples 2, 4, 6 cross over to get this position but 1, 3, 5 start as active couples.)
Steps	Walk, buzz step swing.

DIRECTIONS FOR THE DANCE

Music 2/4   NOTE: Directions are same for lady and man.

Metronome 124

MEASURES

1–4	<u>Allemande left</u> lady on left (8 cts.). Note: Individuals at extreme ends of each line cannot do this. They stand in place.
5–8	<u>All swing partners in line.</u> Buzz step square dance swing (8 cts. two buzz steps to each measure.)
1–8	<u>Opposite ladies chain over and back</u> (16 cts.).
9–12	Right and left through with left hand two. From lines each couple does a half right and left with couple in opposite line to your left of opposite couple. Courtesy turn partners to face middle of set (8 cts.).
13–16	<u>Right and left through</u> with opposite two. From lines each couple does a half right and left with couple then directly opposite. Courtesy turn partners to face middle of the set (8 cts.).
9–12	Same two couples <u>left hand star</u> once around (8 cts.). Two men join left hands, two ladies join left hands. This makes a star. Beginning left, take eight walking steps, star revolves counterclockwise once (8 cts.).
13–16	Same two couples <u>right hand star</u> back to place. Two couples break left hand star, join right hands to form right hand star. Beginning right, take eight walking steps back to place, star revolves clockwise (8 cts.).

THIS IS ONCE THROUGH THE DANCE.
REPEAT AS LONG AS DESIRED.

THE CALLS: Allemande left the lady on the left
Come back and swing the one you left
Opposite ladies chain over and back
Right and left through with the left hand two
Do the same across from you.
Same two couples star by the left — back by the right

THE NOVA SCOTIAN

This is an original contra by Maurice Henneger, Halifax, Nova Scotia, arranged by Ralph Page.

Music   Record: *Glise a Sherbrooke*, Folk Dancer MH 173.

Piano: *Speed the Plough*, One Thousand Fiddle Tunes.

Formation   Contra dance formation with couples 1, 3, 5, etc., cross over.

Steps   Walk, buzz step swing.

DIRECTIONS FOR THE DANCE

Music 2/4   NOTE: Directions are same for lady and man.

Metronome 124

MEASURES

1–4   Allemande left one below. Active couples allemande left with one below (8 cts.).

5–8   Swing partner in center. Active couples buzz step square dance swing with partner in center of set (8 cts., two buzz steps to each measure).

1–8   Down center three in line. Active couple and No. 2 lady (active man has a lady on either side of him, partner on his right, corner lady on his left) take four walking steps toward foot of set. Then in 4 cts. left hand lady under, right hand lady over. Man makes an arch with his right hand and his partner's left, left hand lady walks under this arch as man's partner walks to other side, taking left hand lady's place in line. Man now turns under his own right arm (4 cts.). All are now facing up set.
Change them over and bring them home. This has been done in action above, so line of three return to place with four walking steps.

9–12   Same ladies half chain. Two ladies do ladies chain to opposite side (8 cts.). DON'T return.

13–16   Circle four hands once around. Same four people, join hands and beginning left, walk eight steps once around.

9–16   Same two couples right and left four. Over and back (16 cts.).

THIS IS ONCE THROUGH THE DANCE.
REPEAT AS LONG AS DESIRED.

THE CALLS: Allemande left with the one below
Come back to the middle and swing your own
Go down the center three in line
Left hand under, right hand over, change them over and bring them home
The ladies chain and don't return
But circle four hands once around
Same two couples right and left four.

Dance annotation form © 1948 by the Folk Dance Federation of California.

NEEDHAM REEL

This is an original contra by Herbie Gaudreau, Holbrook, Massachusetts.

Music   Record: *Bob's Double Clog*, Folk Dancer MH 507.
      Piano: *Good for the Tongue*, One Thousand Fiddle Tunes.
Formation Contra dance formation with couples 1, 3, 5, etc., cross over.
Steps   Walk, buzz step swing.

DIRECTIONS FOR THE DANCE

Music 2/4 NOTE: Directions are same for lady and man.

Metronome 128

MEASURES

1–4	<u>All forward and back.</u> All join hands up and down line. Beginning right, take four short walking steps forward. Beginning left, all take four short walking steps backward (8 cts.).
5–8	<u>Swing left hand lady.</u> Each man swings his left hand lady with buzz step square dance swing (8 cts., two buzz steps to each measure). End swing with that lady on man's right. All should now be facing down the hall.
1–4	<u>Down center four in line.</u> All walk down the hall, hand in hand, four in a line (8 cts.).
5–8	<u>Turn as couples return to place.</u> Each man holding the pivot, brings lady on his right around in the pivot to face up the hall. Line now returns to place, hand in hand, four in line (8 cts.).
9–16	<u>Same two ladies chain.</u> Over and back (16 cts.).
9–12	<u>Pass through, turn alone.</u> Pass through the opposite couple (4 cts.). Turn alone (4 cts.).
13–16	<u>With right hand lady promenade home.</u> After turning alone each man takes NEW right hand lady and does a half promenade to original side (8 cts.).

THIS IS ONCE THROUGH THE DANCE.
REPEAT AS LONG AS DESIRED.

Note: This is a DOUBLE PROGRESSION contra. So cross over *immediately* when you reach either end of the line.

THE CALLS: All join hands, go forward and back
      Then all your left hand lady swing
      Put her on your right, join hands,
      Down the center four in a line
      Turn as couples the other way back
      And the same two ladies chain
      Everybody pass through — turn alone
      With the right hand lady promenade home.

Dance annotation form © 1948 by the Folk Dance Federation of California.

ROUND DANCE

DEFINITION

Round dance is the term used for a large number of American dances performed by couples. They move around the room in one direction in order to accommodate all the dancers, thus the name round dance.

HISTORY

As early as the eighteenth century in Europe, there were dances in which couples progressed in a counterclockwise circle around the room. Originally these were old time partner dances such as the schottische, the waltz, the varsouvianna, and the polka. The two step was added to these early dances in America. There were numerous step combinations for each dance, which could be put together to suit the dancer. The round dance movement has grown up along with square dancing and traditionally these dances have been a part of every evening of folk or square dancing.

TREND

The composed dances, which have set routines and a uniformity of movement, are very popular in round dance circles today. In ever increasing numbers they have been created to all types of music from old familiar folk tunes, through the popular classics, to western and modern swing. These dances may be called a "hybrid type" of dance evolving from combinations of steps, positions, and styles borrowed from both folk and ballroom dance forms. They represent the inventiveness of the dancing American and his desire for creative expression.

Problem . . . The degree of interest in American round dancing varies greatly throughout the country. Those who enjoy the modern round dances most are the intermediate-advanced club dancers who dance regularly and practice often so as to be able to keep up when they attend the state square dance festivals. Couples who do not have this much time often find it difficult to keep abreast of the ever increasing number of dances. Like the popular song, they come and go so fast that only a few survive the "fad" stage or continue to be danced beyond a few months. Wise teachers and leaders have partially solved the problem by teaching only those dances which survive the intense screening of the publication offices and come out as the "dance of the month." The schottische, varsouvianna, and polka have all but disappeared from the round dance scene and in their place such steps as the grapevine, the cut step, the dip, and the twinkle appear over and over in a variety of positions. One advantage of the set patterned dance is that there is less premium on the ability to lead or follow, since both man and lady know a set routine.

REFERENCES

Literature is filled with delightful anecdotes on American folk and round dance. Perhaps with a few helpful references, the alert teacher will delve further and find information that will keep some of these lovely old dances alive.

1. *Country Dance Book*, Reference in Bibliography: 101.
   Polka Mania and the Round Dance Era, page 127.
2. *Cowboy Dance*, Reference in Bibliography: 94.

Round Dances, page 70. (waltz, schottische, varsouvianna, polka)
Origins of Dances, page 25.
3. *Dance Encyclopedia*, Reference in Bibliography: 14.
Round Dance, page 409.
Polka, page 376.
Waltz, page 497.

4. *Round Dance*, Reference in Bibliography: 78.
Polka, page 67.
Waltz, page 101.
Varsouvianna, page 245.
Schottische, page 270.

RECONSIDER

A new look at some of the older round dances might be worth while. The schottische and the polka, for example, are free form dances meaning that the traditional step may be danced to any schottische record and the variations used in any order. Anyone knowing this step can enjoy the dance. It is often a relief not to have to dance a set routine of steps always to the same music, and follow in a line of other couples. Our young people can really let go an old time schottische or polka and those who sit on the sides are green with envy. They also provide a more vigorous type dance which the young people can enjoy with tremendous freedom. This section includes a representative sample of all time favorite round dances. Many of these beautiful figures are seldom seen any more but belong to the historical past. Since so few of the new round dances have lasted long enough to get into print, the authors have chosen to adhere to the old time favorites. There have been only a few new dances added to this section. They were selected for their "fun appeal" in the teen-age dance program.

CLASSIFIED INDEX OF ROUND DANCES – BASIC STEP

OLD TIME SCHOTTISCHE

Music   Record: Educational Dance Recordings FD-3; MacGregor
                      4005; or any schottische.

Position   Open, couple, or conversation.

Steps   Schottische.

DIRECTIONS FOR THE DANCE

Music 4/4   NOTE: Directions are for man; lady's part reverse.

MEASURES   *Basic Schottische*

1–2   Open dance position. Beginning left, move forward in line
               of direction with two schottische steps.

3–4   Closed position or waist position. Turn clockwise with four
               step-hops. Progress in line of direction.

Variations on Basic Schottische

I. Lady's Turn

1–2   Repeat action of measures 1-2 in Basic Schottische.

3–4   Four step-hops, man moves forward, while the lady turns
               clockwise under upraised left arm of partner. Lady may
               make one or two complete turns. Progress in the line of
               direction.

II. Man's Turn

1–4   Directions are the same as for the Lady's Turn except man
               turns clockwise under upraised right arm of lady.

III. Both Turn

1–2   Repeat action of measures 1-2 in Basic Schottische.

3–4   Four step-hops, partners turn away from each other, man
               to his left, lady to her right. Partners may make one or
               two complete turns.

IV. Diamond

1–2   Man and lady take one schottische step diagonally for-
               ward away from each other. Man and lady take one
               schottische step diagonally forward toward each other.
               Progress in the line of direction.

3–4   Repeat action of measures 3-4 in Basic Schottische.

V. Wring the Dish Rag

1–2   Repeat action of measures 1-2 in Basic Schottische.

3–4   Partners face, join two hands and with four step-hops
               turn back to back (turning to man's left, lady's right)
               and continue roll until face to face. Join hands swing
               through between couple, below waist, and quickly over-
               head. The couple may make one or two turns.

References in Bibliography: 96 (p. 272) (p. 100), 117 (Vol. II, No. 8, June '47, p. 6).
Dance annotation form © 1948 by the Folk Dance Federation of California.

MEASURES

VI. Rock

1–2   Repeat action of measures 1-2 in Basic Schottische.

3   Step forward on left, take weight (ct. 1-2). Step backward on right, take weight (ct. 3-4).
Repeat action of measure 3.
Note: Rocking effect is produced by swaying body forward and backward.

VII. Ballroom Schottische

1–2   Repeat action of measures 1-2 in Basic Schottische. On ct. 4, the hop is omitted and the free leg swings forward, toe pointed close to floor.

3–4   Closed position. Beginning left, pivot turn clockwise four steps, progressing in line of direction.

SCHOTTISCHE FOR FOUR

Two couples stand one behind the other, both facing the line of direction. Join inside hands with partner. The outside hands joined link the two couples together. The front couple is number one, the back couple is number two.

1–2   Repeat action of measures 1-2 in Basic Schottische.

3–4   Four step-hops. No. 1 couple releases partner's hand and turning away from each other, man left, lady right, they move around couple No. 2 on the outside and come in behind them. Joining hands with partner, they therefore become the back couple and No. 2 couple, the front couple. Or No. 1 couple may take step-hops backward through the upraised arms of No. 2 couple. This action will cause No. 2 couple to turn the dish rag in order to become straightened out. After turning No. 2 couple becomes the front couple. These variations, if repeated, will return couples to starting position.

     Repeat the entire action of measure 1–4 with No. 2 couple turning out or moving backward with step hops, to return couples to original positions.

MIXER:
The lady moves forward to a new partner on the second schottische step.

STYLE:
Three styles are used in this schottische: *Traditional* — the schottische step is danced as a step, close, step, hop. *Barn Dance* — the schottische step is danced as a step, step, step, hop or run, run, run, hop. *Ballroom Dance* — step close, lift. The hop is replaced by a slight lift of the body. Point toe of the free foot. The step-hops are replaced by a step-lift, with a rocking action forward and back.

The American style is to swing the free leg forward on the hop and the pattern is very smooth. The European style keeps the leg under the body and the hop has a bouncy action.

TEXAS SCHOTTISCHE VARIATIONS

This dance was first seen by the authors as part of an exhibition of old time Texas Schottisches danced and taught by Herb and Pauline Greggerson. There are many Texas Schottische variations such as McGinty, Douglas, Drunk, Blue Bonnet. As originally danced these steps were not done in any special sequence.

Music   Record: *Bummel Schottische*, RCA Victor EPA 4235; Victor 45-6177; *Oklahoma Mixer*, Folkraft 1035; *Starlight Schottische*, Western Jubilee 700.

Position   Varsouvianna.

Steps   Variations of grapevine, schottische step, and two-step.

DIRECTIONS FOR THE DANCE

Music 4/4   NOTE: Directions are same for man and lady.

MEASURES

I. Military Schottische

1   Point left toe in front of right foot (cts. 1–2). Point left toe sideways to left (cts. 3-4).

2   Step left foot behind right (ct. 1). Step right foot to right (ct. 2). Close left to right (ct. 3). Hold (ct. 4).

3–4   Beginning right, repeat action of measures 1–2.

5–6   Beginning left, two walking steps forward followed by one two-step.

7–8   Beginning right, repeat action of measures 5–6.

II. Peter Pan

1   Step forward left (cts. 1–2). Step forward right (cts. 3–4).

2   Step forward left, right, (cts. 1–2), step left and pivot to own right (ct. 3) swing or lift right leg (ct. 4). Couple now faces in reverse line of direction.

3   Moving backward, step right, lift left (cts. 1–2). Step left, lift right (cts. 3–4).

4   Step right, left, right, pivoting to own left (cts. 1-2-3-4). Couple now faces line of direction.

CALIFORNIA SCHOTTISCHE

VARIATION:

Measures 1–4, take action of measures 1–4, Part I.

Measures 5–8, take action of measures 1–4, Part II.

References in Bibliography: 96 (p. 279, 284), 117 (Vol. I, No. 6, April '47, p. 5-6), 84 (p. 6), 124 (Vol. VI, No. 7, July '54, p. 30).

CANADIAN BARN DANCE

The original Canadian Barn Dance was an English Dance. This version is a variation popular in the western United States.

Music	Record: Folkraft 1471X45; MacGregor 631; any lively two-step.
Position	Couple.
Steps	Two-step, three-step-turn, grapevine.

DIRECTIONS FOR THE DANCE

Music 4/4   NOTE: Directions are for the man, lady's part reverse.

MEASURES

I. Walk and Point

1   Beginning left, walk three steps in line of direction and point right toe forward.

2   Beginning right, back up three steps in reverse line of direction and point left toe forward.

II. Grapevine Step

3   Beginning left, still facing line of direction, move apart from partner. Step sideward left, step right behind left, step sideward left and swing right across in front of left.

4   Beginning right, repeat action of measure 3, moving toward partner.

III. Walk and Pivot

5   Open position, facing line of direction. Beginning left, take three steps in line of direction, turning on the third step to reverse open position, and point right toe in reverse line of direction.

6   Repeat action of measure 5, moving in reverse line of direction.

IV. Two-Step

7–8   Closed position. Beginning left, four two-steps turning clockwise, progressing in line of direction.

VARIATIONS ON PART II:

1. Beginning left, take a three step turn moving apart from partner. Point right toe toward partner and clap hands. Beginning right, take three step turn toward partner and assume open position.

2. Face partner. Beginning left, three walking steps backward, away from partner and bow or curtsey. Three steps forward toward partner and assume open position.

MIXER:
The change of partners is made on Part II by moving diagonally to right toward a new partner.

Reference in Bibliography: 23 (p. 18).
Dance annotation form © 1948 by the Folk Dance Federation of California.

CHOP SUEY POLKA

This dance was composed by Dottie and Van Vander Walker.

Music   Record: Blue Star 1592.
Position   Varsouvianna.
Steps   Two step, slide.

DIRECTIONS FOR THE DANCE

Music 2/4   NOTE: Directions are same for man and lady except where noted.

MEASURES   **Introduction**
1–4   Face partner, man's right holds lady's left, wait two measures. Balance apart on left, touch right, to left, balance forward right turning to varsouvianna position, facing line of direction, touch left to right.

I. **Two-Step and Slide Across**
1–4   Beginning left, take two two-steps forward, then releasing right hands, take two two-steps crossing the lady to the inside of circle to face reverse line of direction while the man does two two-steps in place.

5–6   Release hands. Beginning left, take four slides across, changing sides, sliding face to face. End with lady on outside facing reverse line of direction, man on inside facing line of direction. Hands are up at shoulder height, snap fingers on the slide.

7–8   Join right hands. Beginning right, take two two-steps circling around each other clockwise so as to move the man to the outside facing in reverse line of direction and lady inside facing line of direction.

9–10   Release hands. Beginning right, take four slides across, changing sides, sliding face to face (with fingers snapping). End with the lady on the outside facing line of direction and man inside facing reverse line of direction.

11–14   Join left hands and beginning left, take four two-steps circling around each other counterclockwise one complete circle. On the last two-step, the man makes a tight left spot-turn so as to assume the original varsouvianna position with partner facing in line of direction.

15–16   Beginning left, walk four steps forward left, right, left, right in line of direction.

MEASURES
17–32   Repeat action of measures 1–16, Part I, but finish in side by side position, inside hands joined, and face in line of direction.

II. **Step Kick and Chase**
1–2   Beginning left, step forward, kick right across in front of left, step right forward, kick left across in front of right.

MEASURES

3–4	Beginning left, take two two-steps forward.
5–8	Beginning left, take four two-steps, the first two with the lady chasing the man toward the center of the circle, then both turning one-half counterclockwise, take two two-steps with the man chasing the lady away from the center of the circle. On the last two-step both man and lady maneuver so that they are again facing in line of direction and join inside hands.
9–16	Repeat action of measures 1–8, Part II.

III. Slide and Step Touch

1–2	Beginning left, take three slides diagonally left toward center of circle, step left.
3–4	Beginning right, repeat action of measures 1–2, Part III, sliding diagonally right toward outside of circle.
5–6	Beginning left, step left, touch right to left, step right, touch left to right.
7–8	Release hands. Beginning left, the man takes two two-steps across in front of lady toward the outside of the circle turning right while the lady takes two two-steps across in back of him toward the center of the circle turning left and both end facing reverse line of direction, side by side, inside hands joined.
9–16	Repeat action of measures 1–8, Part III, traveling in reverse line of direction and moving alternately diagonally to outside of circle (left) then inside of circle (right). End facing in line of direction and assume varsouvianna position on last two-step. Entire dance repeats once from Part I.

ENDING:
Beginning left, take two steps forward and three walking steps left, right, left. Close feet together and jump back facing partner on last beat.

GLOW WORM

This dance was taught at the Lloyd Shaw Cheyenne Mountain School, August 1943, '46, and '47.

Music	Record: MacGregor 310; Old Timer 8004; RCA Victor EPA 4139; Shaw 106; Windsor 4613; Folkraft 1158; Flip 114.
	Piano: Lincke, Paul, *The Glow Worm*, Edward B. Mark Music Corp., RCA Bldg., Radio City, New York.
Position	Couple.
Steps	Walk, slide, two-step, grapevine, dip.

DIRECTIONS FOR THE DANCE

Music 4/4   NOTE: Directions are for man; lady's part reverse.

MEASURES   **Part I.**

1–2   Walk forward three steps, left, right, left. Touch right toe forward (ct. 4). Beginning right, repeat.

3–4   Partners face, join two hands. Take grapevine step left, right, left, and swing right across in front of left (ct. 4). Beginning right, repeat moving in reverse line of direction.

5–6   Beginning left, man and lady exchange places taking three steps, turn and point, lady turning counterclockwise under man's upraised right arm. Man walks across passing right shoulders with lady. Beginning right, repeat exchange to end in original position.

7–8   Closed position. Four two-steps turning clockwise and progressing in line of direction.

Part II.

9   Couple position. Walk forward three steps left, right, left, and touch right toe forward (ct. 4).

10   Partners face, join two hands. Beginning right, take two slides in reverse line of direction. Step right and dip backward left by shifting weight to left and point right toe forward (ct. 4), facing reverse line of direction. Body leans toward pointed foot.

11   Beginning right, repeat action of measure 9, continue in reverse line of direction.

12   Beginning left, repeat action of measure 10, taking dip with weight on right and point left toe forward, now facing line of direction.

References in Bibliography: 96 (p. 330), 23 (p. 28).
Dance annotation form © 1948 by the Folk Dance Federation of California.

MEASURES

13–14   Closed position. Beginning left, take six steps (cts. 1, 2, 3, 4, 1, 2) or two two-steps. Man steps in place, lady turns three times clockwise under man's upraised left arm (2 counts to each turn). Dip back on left (ct. 3). This is like a tango corte. Step forward right (ct. 4).

15–16   Beginning left, four two-steps turning clockwise, progressing in line of direction.

STYLE:

This is a very stately dance. Careful footwork and an upright body will give the dance a minuet-like quality.

HAPPY POLKA

This dance was composed by Julie and Bert Passerello, Long Beach, California, 1956.

Music   Record: *Sunny Hills*, Accent AC 1118*; Blue Star 1578.

Position   Varsouvianna position with man's right arm around lady's waist, holding her right hand.

Steps   Two-step.

DIRECTIONS FOR THE DANCE

Music 2/4   NOTE: Directions are the same for man and lady except as noted.

MEASURES

I. Heel and Toe, Two Step

1–4   Beginning left, touch heel forward, touch toe in place, take one two-step forward left, right, left. Repeat all starting right.

5–8   Beginning left, take four two-steps. Releasing right hands, the man takes two two-steps in place sending the lady across in front of him taking two two-steps to the center to face reverse line of direction. Lady continues on around with two two-steps to face line of direction as man follows her with two two-steps making a full left face turn to resume original position.

9–16   Repeat action of measures 1–8, Part I.

II. To the Center, Kick and Roll

17–18   Beginning left, walk three steps diagonally in toward center of circle left, right, left, and kick right across left.

19–20   Release hands and beginning right, both take a solo turn, three steps right, left, right, rolling clockwise a full turn diagonally back into original varsouvianna position facing line of direction.

21–24   Beginning left, take four two-steps forward in line of direction. This action should bring the couple out to the original line of the circle so that they do not become crowded.

25–32   Repeat measures 17–24, Part II, but on the last two-step, release the left hands and turn the lady clockwise one-half turn to face reverse line of direction in front of but slightly off to right side of man. Right hands are joined.

III. Walk, Kick and Roll Across

33–34   Beginning left, man takes three steps forward left, right, left (lady backward). Kick right forward.

Dance printed in *Sets in Order*, Reference 125 (October 1956, p. 46). Reprinted by permission.

Dance annotation form © 1948 by the Folk Dance Federation of California.

* Out of print.

MEASURES

35–36	Release hands and beginning right, both take a solo turn, three steps right, left, right, rolling clockwise a full turn changing sides with partner. The lady crosses in front of the man and they join left hands. The lady is now on the inside facing reverse line of direction, the man on the outside facing line of direction.
37–38	Beginning left, take two two-steps forward (lady backward).
39–40	Take two more two-steps changing hands and moving the lady across to the outside of the circle.
41–48	Repeat measures 33–40, Part III, but on the last two two-steps, roll the lady backward turning her clockwise into original varsouvianna position. Entire dance repeats twice.

ENDING:
On last two-step partners face, join man's right, lady's left hands. They step back away from each other two steps, right, left, and point right forward as in a bow.

TEACHING NOTE:
Part II and III are the same steps but done in a different position.

JOSEPHINE

This dance was composed by Mel and Helen Day.

Music Record: Coral 65511; Windsor 4-502 (Ballroom Series).
Piano: *Josephine.*

Position Promenade.

Steps Grapevine, two-step, three step turn.

DIRECTIONS FOR THE DANCE

Music 4/4 NOTE: Directions are the same for both man and lady.

MEASURES

I. Grapevine Step and Slow Walk

1 Beginning right, grapevine step (right, left, right) and swing left across in front of right.

2 Repeat to left.

3–4 Beginning right, four walking steps forward. On fourth step man releases right hand and turns half clockwise to face reverse line of direction.

II. Roll Across and Walk Around

5 Beginning right, repeat action of measure 1, each moving to own right away from partner. Left arm is extended.

6 Beginning left, release left hands and take a three step turn (left, right, left) spinning counterclockwise across to partner's place. Now swing right across in front of left. Join right hands.

7–8 Beginning right, four walking steps around clockwise to original position. While moving around, the man takes the lady's left hand under their joined right hands and turns her into promenade position.

VARIATIONS:

1. Measures 1–2, both man and lady take a three step turn and swing right. Then repeat to the left.

2. Measures 3–4, man spins lady twice clockwise under his right arm.

Reference in Bibliography: 23 (p. 37).
Dance annotation form © 1948 by the Folk Dance Federation of California.

LACES AND GRACES

This dance was taught at the Lloyd Shaw Cheyenne Mountain School, August 1943, '46 and '47.

Music   Record: Folkraft 1047; Folk Dancer MH 3002; Imperial 1006*; Lloyd Shaw 105.

     Piano: Salzer, Gustave, and Bratton, John, *Laces and Graces*, copyright MCMLLL by M. Witmark and Sons, New York. (6/8 time)

Position Couple.

Steps   Pivot, slide, two-step.

DIRECTIONS FOR THE DANCE

Music 4/4   NOTE: Directions are for man; lady's part reverse.

MEASURES

I. Pivot and Slide

1 Beginning left, touch toe in front, to the side, then in back of right (cts. 1–2–3). Drop hands and pivot on both toes, turning about face counterclockwise and end with weight on left (ct. 3), facing partner.

2 Join two hands, step sideways with right (ct. 1), touch left toe behind right heel (ct. 2). Repeat sideways left (cts. 3–4).

3–4 Beginning right, four slides in reverse line of direction. The fourth slide is not completed, weight remains on right. Turn to line of direction and beginning left, walk forward four steps in couple position.

5–8 Repeat action of measures 1–4.

II. Face to Face, Back to Back

9–12 Beginning left, eight two-steps, turning face to face and back to back four times, progressing in line of direction.

13–16 Closed position. Eight two-steps turning clockwise, progressing in line of direction.

STYLE:
The movement should be smooth and dignified, almost like a minuet.

MIXER:
Partners may be changed on Part II, measures 9–12 as follows:
Four two-steps moving face to face, back to back. Partners separate and back away from each other four steps and then move toward the next lady (or man) or the left. Move to new partner in four steps.

References in Bibliography: 96 (p. 337), 14 (Vol. III, p. 17).
Dance annotation form © 1948 by the Folk Dance Federation of California.
* Out of print.

LUCKY

This dance was composed by Pete and Ann Peterman, Fort Worth, Texas.

Music	Record: Blue Star 1624; Belco 204; *Little Black Book*, Columbia 4-42529.
Position	Open position, facing line of direction.
Steps	Two-step, grapevine.

DIRECTIONS FOR THE DANCE

Music 4/4

NOTE: Directions are for the man, lady's part reverse.

MEASURES

Introduction: Side by side position, inside hands joined. Wait two measures.

1–4
Beginning left, step sideward (counts 1–2), point right toward partner bowing (counts 3–4), step right back in place beside partner (counts 1–2), and touch left to right (counts 3–4). End in skater's position.

I. **Two-Step, Cross Step, Dip, Grapevine**

1–2
A. Beginning left, take two slow two-steps forward in line of direction.

3
Beginning left, cross left in front of right, step back on right, cross left in front of right, step back on right.

4
Dip or corte back on left foot (counts 1–2) and recover forward on right (count 3) and touch left to right (count 4), turning to face partner in butterfly position, man's back to center of circle.

5
B. Keeping both hands joined in butterfly position, step left sideward, close right to left taking weight on right, cross left over right, and hold.

6
Repeat, beginning right and crossing right over left.

7
Still in butterfly position, step sideward left, cross right behind left, step sideward left, cross right behind left.

8
Step sideward left (counts 1–2) releasing right hand and turning forward into line of direction. Step forward right, moving into skater's position, facing line of direction.

9–16
Repeat action of measures 1–8 remaining in butterfly position to start Part II.

II. **Grapevine and Wrap**

17
Beginning left, step left behind right, step right sideward, touch left to right.

Dance printed in *Sets in Order*, Reference 125 (February 1963, p. 32). Reprinted by permission.

Dance annotation form © 1948 by the Folk Dance Federation of California.

MEASURES

18   Keeping both hands joined, man repeats this grapevine step to the right in the reverse line of direction. He will make a quarter turn left at the same time, rolling the lady counterclockwise by lifting their joined hands (man left, lady right) up over her head and ending in the wrap position, facing line of direction.

19   Releasing man's left hand (lady's right), man steps in place left, right, left, touch right to left as lady unwraps rolling clockwise toward the outside of the circle, right, left, right, touch left to right ending in an apart position side by side and facing line of direction, inside hands joined.

20   Turning to face each other, the lady takes three steps left, right, left and touch right to left, going under their joined hands to the inside of the circle as he walks around her to the outside of the circle taking right, left, right, and touch. They end in butterfly position man facing center of hall.

21–24   Repeat action of measures 17–20 in reverse line of direction, ending in butterfly position, man with his back to center, two hands joined.

III.   **Grapevine Face to Face, Back to Back, Apart and Together**

25–28   In butterfly position, step sideward left, step right behind left, sideward left face to face. Drop left hand (lady's right) and pivot on left so as to be back to back and step sideward right, step left behind right, step sideward right, touch left to right pivoting back to face line of direction. Drop inside hands and take the grapevine step moving apart, step sideward left, right behind left, step sideward left, touch right to left, and repeat beginning right, coming together into closed dance position, man's back to center of circle.

29-30   In closed position, beginning left, take two two-steps turning clockwise.

31–32   Take slow two measure twirl, man taking left, right, left, right (counts 1, 3, 1, 3) in place as the lady twirls clockwise right, left, right, left (counts 1, 3, 1, 3) ending in skater's position facing line of direction to start to dance again.
The entire dance repeats twice from Part I.

ENDING:

Repeat once more action of measures 1–23. Then on measure 24, place feet together, turning to face partner, and jump back in place.

SHORTCAKE

This dance was composed by Dot 'N Date Foster. It has become popular in French Canada, in Wales, and in Germany, as well as having been a best seller in the United States.

Music	Record: Grenn 14012.
Position	Open position, facing line of direction.
Steps	Two-step.

DIRECTIONS FOR THE DANCE

Music 4/4   NOTE: Directions are for the man, lady's part reversed.

I. Shortcake Step, Walk, Side Close, Twirl

1   Beginning left, place left heel forward, then step back in place. Place right heel forward, then step back in place (cts. 1, and, 2, and).

2   With heels together, toes slightly out, with weight on ball of foot, move heels out (pigeon toe) then heels back together, then out, and back together.

3–4   Beginning left, take four slow steps forward. They are taken with a heel toe strutting style.

5–8   Repeat action of measures 1–4. End in butterfly position, man with back to center of circle.

9   Beginning left, step left sideward in line of direction, close right to left, step left sideward, touch right to left.

10   Repeat, beginning right and traveling in reverse line of direction.

11–12   Beginning left, man walks four slow steps forward in line of direction twirling lady two complete twirls under their joined hands (man's left, lady's right). The lady takes two steps to each twirl. End in butterfly position.

13–14   Beginning left, repeat action of measures 9 and 10.

15   Beginning left, repeat action of measure 11, twirling lady once.

16   Man and lady take last two steps in place assuming open position facing in line of direction.

1–16   Repeat action of measures 1–16, Part I.

II. Two-Step, Side Close Touch, Box, Draw

1–2   Beginning left, take two two-steps forward, end facing partner.

MEASURES

3–4	Release inside hands, join man's left, lady's right. Beginning left, step sideward left in line of direction, turning to face reverse line of direction. Swing joined hands forward. Touch right foot well behind left (counts 3, and). Turning to face partner, change hands (man's right, lady's left). Step sideward right in reverse line of direction. Swing joined hands forward, turn to face line of direction and touch left foot well behind right (counts 4, and). These are slow steps.
5–8	Repeat action of measures 1–4, Part II, except take last touch in place maneuvering to closed position, man's back to center of circle.
9–10	Beginning left, step sideward left, close right to left, step forward left, hold one count, step sideward right, close left to right, step backward right, hold one count.
11–12	Beginning left, step sideward left in line of direction, draw right to left (no weight change). Step sideward right in reverse line of direction, draw left to right (no weight change).
13–16	Repeat action of measures 9–12, Part II, except in place of last step draw, take a step touch maneuvering to open position.
1–16	Repeat action of measures 1–16, Part II.
1–32	Take action of measures 1–16, Part I twice. The sequence of the dance is: Part I twice, Part II twice, Part I twice.

ENDING:
Repeat action of measures 1–2, Part I (shortcake step) and then beginning left, walk forward two slow steps, turn to face partner and bow.

SUSAN'S GAVOTTE

This dance was composed by Susan Gentry of Oklahoma.

Music   Record: *Lili Marlene*, Folkraft 1096, 1414; MacGregor 310; Old Timer 8070; Western Jubilee 701; World of Fun M113.

Position   Couple.

Steps   Slide, two-step.

DIRECTIONS FOR THE DANCE

Music 4/4   NOTE: Directions are for man; lady's part reverse.

MEASURES

I. Walk Step

1	Beginning left, walk four steps forward.
2	Face partner and join two hands. Four slides in line of direction.
3–4	Repeat the action of measures 1–2 in reverse line of direction.

II. Step Swing, Walk, Turn, and Point

5–6	Beginning left, step in place, swing right over left; step right in place, swing left over right. Repeat.
7	Couple position or open position. Beginning left, walk three steps forward in line of direction. Turn toward partner and point right in reverse line of direction.
8	Beginning right, repeat action of measure 7 moving in reverse line of direction.

III. Face to Face and Back to Back

9–10	Beginning left, one two-step facing partner and one two-step turning so that the man and lady are back to back, progressing in line of direction.
11–12	Repeat action of measures 9–10.
13–16	Beginning left, four two-steps turning away from partner in a small circle and meet on the last step.

VARIATION:
The last four two-steps may be done in a closed position, turning clockwise, progressing in line of direction.

MIXER:
On the last four two-steps the man turns to his left and two-steps in a half circle moving back to lady behind; the lady turns to her right and two-steps in a circle, coming back to place to receive a new partner.

Reference in Bibliography: 23 (p. 66).

TUXEDO TWO-STEP

Music	Record: Decca DLA1423*; Windsor 4112.
	Piano: *Marching Through Georgia, Dixie.*
Position	Partners facing, two hands joined, or closed position.
Steps	Slide, two-step.

DIRECTIONS FOR THE DANCE

Music 2/4   NOTE: Directions are for the man; lady's part reverse.

MEASURE

I. Slide

1   Beginning left, two slow slides in line of direction.

2   Beginning left, four quick slides continuing in line of direction. The fourth slide is not completed, the weight remains on left, right foot free to change direction.

3–4   Repeat action of measures 1–4, beginning right in reverse line of direction.

II. Two-Step

5–8   Closed position. Beginning left, eight two-steps turning clockwise. Progress in line of direction.

NOTE: This is a good dance to use for learning the two-step. Beginners often find it hard to take eight two-steps turning. The two-steps may be danced in open position as a learning device.

VARIATION:
Face partner, two hands joined. Measure 5, step left, swing right across in front of left. Step right, swing left across in front of right.
Measure 6, repeat action of measure 5.
Measure 7–8, four two-steps turning clockwise, progressing in line of direction.

Reference in Bibliography: 96 (p. 323).
Dance annotation form © 1948 by the Folk Dance Federation of California.
* Out of print.

COTTON EYED JOE

According to Dorothy Scarborough's *On the Trail of Negro Folksongs*, Cotton Eyed Joe is an authentic slavery tune song. The fiddle tune is of semi-established origin. Music may be found in several references, one being Ira W. Ford's *Traditional Music of America*. According to Uncle Dave Dillingham of Austin, Texas, who learned the dance in Williamson County in the early 80's, Cotton Eyed Joe is nothing but a heel and toe "poker," with fringes added. For the most part, the fringes or variations over and above the heel and toe polka were originally clog steps which required skill, as well as an extroversion on the part of the dancer. The dance and variations listed here are the simpler ones, not including clog steps found and performed to a large extent in Texas.

Music	Record: Educational Dance Recordings F. D. 3; Folkcraft 1035, 1124, 1225, 1470; Imperial 1045*; MacGregor 8495, 604; RCA Victor EPA 4134; World of Fun M 118; Kalox 1062.
	Piano: Dave, Red River, *Cotton Eyed Joe*, Southern Music Co., San Antonio, Texas.
Position	Closed.
Steps	Polka, two-step, push step.

DIRECTIONS FOR THE DANCE

Music 4/4
MEASURES

NOTE: Directions are for man; lady's part reverse.

I. Heel and Toe Polka

1 Hop right, touch left heel out to the left (ct. and 1). Hop right, touch left toe behind right foot (ct. and 2). Polka to left (ct. and 3, and 4), in line of direction.

2 Repeat beginning with hop on left foot and travel in reverse line of direction.

II. Individual Turn

3–4 Three two-steps turning in a small circle. The man turns counterclockwise, the lady turns clockwise. Finish with three quick stamps in place, facing partner.

III. Push Step

5 Chug left foot sideward in line of direction (ct. 1), place the weight momentarily on the right (ct. and), push back onto left foot, chugging left sideward again and flip right heel out to the side (ct. 2). Push with the right (ct. and), chug left (ct. 3), push with right (ct. and), chug left (ct. 4). Weight remains on left.

6 Repeat action of measure 5, starting with the right foot, and moving to the right.

IV. Two-Step or Polka

7–8 Four two-steps in closed dance position turning clockwise, progressing in the line of direction. These may be polka steps.

Dance annotation form © 1948 by the Folk Dance Federation of California.
* Out of print.

JESSIE POLKA

Music Record: Blue Star 1588 and 1667; Education Recordings FD 2; Imperial 1168*; MacGregor 6325; *Teddy Bear Picnic*, Capitol 3085; Western Jubilee 701. Old Timer 8210; Folkraft 1093.

Piano: Any good polka.

Position Form groups of two or more in a line, with arms around each other's waist. Groups progress counterclockwise around the room.

Steps Two-step or polka.

DIRECTIONS FOR THE DANCE

Music 2/4 NOTE: Directions are the same for all.

MEASURES

I. Heel Step

1 Beginning left, touch heel in front, then step left in place.

2 Touch right toe behind, then touch right toe in place, or swing it forward, keeping weight on left.

3 Touch right heel in front, then step right in place.

4 Touch left heel to the left side, sweep left across in front of right. Keep weight on right.

II. Two-Step or Polka

5–8 Four two-steps forward in line of direction. Four polka steps may be used if preferred.

VARIATION:
This dance may be done in a conga line, one behind the other, with the leader moving in a serpentine on the four two-steps.

MIXER:
Couples in line alternating lady and man. The lady may turn out to the right on the last two two-steps and come back into the line behind her partner. The lady at the end of the line rushes up to the head of the line.

Reference in Bibliography: 23 (p. 36).
Dance annotation form © 1948 by the Folk Dance Federation of California.
* Out of print.

BLACK HAWK WALTZ

This dance was taught at the Lloyd Shaw Cheyenne Mountain School, August 1943, '46, and '47.

Music Record: Folkraft 1046X45; Folk Dancer MH 3002; Imperial 1006; MacGregor 3095; Old Timer 8186; Lloyd Shaw 104.

      Piano: *The Folk Dancer*, Vol. 6, No. 11, November, 1946, p. 10–12.

Position Closed.

Steps Waltz, balance.

DIRECTIONS FOR THE DANCE

Music 3/4   NOTE: Directions are for man; the lady's part reverse.

MEASURES

  I. **Balance Waltz**

1–4 Balance or rock forward on left, balance backward on right. Repeat balance forward and backward.

5–8 Beginning left, four waltz steps, turning clockwise, progressing in line of direction.

9–12 Repeat action of measures 1–4.

13–16 Beginning left, two waltz steps, followed by six walking steps forward.

    NOTE: The first 16 measures of Balance and Waltz steps may be done as follows: Balance forward and back, two waltz steps. Repeat three times.

  II. **Cross Step**

17 Man places left (lady right) across in front of right letting it take weight.

18 Place right across left in the same manner.

19–20 Cross again with left followed by step sideward to right with right, step with left behind right and finally, point right sideways to right (weight remains on left).

21–24 Beginning right, repeat action of measures 17–20 moving to left on the completion.

25–32 Repeat action of measures 17-24.

STYLE: During the crossing step, the foot is extended and the toe is pointed to the side. This is accompanied by a turn of the body in the new direction.

References in Bibliography: 14 (Vol. II, p. 3), 96 (p. 211), 116 (Vol. VI, No. 11, p. 10), 23 (p. 14).

Dance annotation form © 1948 by the Folk Dance Federation of California.

BLUE PACIFIC WALTZ

This dance was composed by Henry "Buzz" Glass of Oakland, California.

Music   Record: Old Timer 8070, 8208; Shaw 117; Western Jubilee 702; Windsor 4638.

                Piano: *Over the Waves.*

Position   Couple.

Steps   Waltz, three-step-turn.

DIRECTIONS FOR THE DANCE

Music 3/4   NOTE: Directions are for man; lady's part reverse.

MEASURES

I. Three Step Turn and Swing

1   Beginning left, step left and swing right across left, turning slightly away from partner.

2–3   Beginning right, take a three step turn clockwise (lady counterclockwise) exchanging places with partner (holding ct. 2, move on cts. 1-3-1). Swing left across right, turning slightly away from partner (cts. 2–3). The rhythm of this figure is known as the canter waltz. Lead: Man draws lady across in front of him into the turn with his joined hand, releasing just in time to make the turn and then catches the opposite hand after the turn.

4–5   Beginning left, repeat action of measures 2-3, swinging right across.

6   Step right, turning to face partner. Touch left to right, keep weight on right. Take closed position.

7–8   Two waltz steps turning clockwise, progressing in line of direction.

9–16   Repeat action of measures 1–8.

II. Twinkle Step

17   Semi-open position, facing line of direction. Step left forward, swing right forward.

18   Step right forward, step left in place facing partner, step right in place facing reverse line of direction (cts. 1-2-3). This movement is called the twinkle step (waltz time).

19   Step left across right in reverse line of direction, step right in place, facing partner. Step left in place to face line of direction in open position.

References in Bibliography: 23 (p. 15), 125 (Vol. III, No. 6, June '51, p. 4).

MEASURES

20	Step forward right, touch left to right, keep weight on right.
21–28	Repeat action of measures 17–20 twice.
29	Step left forward, swing right forward.
30	Man: Step right across left, close to left toe (ct. 1). Pirouette on toes turning one-half counterclockwise (cts. 2–3). Lady: Three little steps (right, left, right) and follow man's turn counterclockwise, walking around him.
31–32	Closed positions. Two waltz steps turning counterclockwise. Open into couple position to repeat dance from beginning.

NOTE: For simplification of measures 30–32, step right forward, touch left to right, keep weight on right and take closed position. Two waltz steps turning clockwise.

BOLERO

This dance was taught at the Lloyd Shaw Cheyenne Mountain School, August 1943, '46 and '47.

Music	Record: *Estudiantina Waltz*, Decca 1986*; Shaw 401; Folkraft 1448X45.
	Piano: Waldteufel, Emil, *Estudiantina*, Oliver Ditson Co., Theodore Presser Co., distributors, Philadelphia, Pa.
Position	Couple, partners facing.
Steps	Balance, waltz.

DIRECTIONS FOR THE DANCE

Music 3/4   NOTE: Directions are for man; lady's part reverse.

MEASURES

I. Step Swing, Balance, Draw

A. 1 Step sideways left in line of direction, swing right across left and pivot counterclockwise on left, to back to back position.

2 Step sideways right in line of direction, close left to right, keeping weight on right, and hold.

3 Step sideways left in reverse line of direction, draw right to left, taking weight right.

4 Step sideways left again, draw right to left, keeping weight on left, and hold.

5 Step sideways right in line of direction, swing left across right and pivot clockwise on right, to face to face position.

6 Step sideways left, close right to left, keeping weight on left, and hold.

7 Step sideways right in reverse line of direction, draw left to right, taking weight on left.

8 Step sideways right again, draw left to right, keeping weight on right, and hold.

II. Step Swing

9–12 Step left, swing right across in front of left. Repeat three times, alternating right, left, right.

III. Turn Partner

13–14 Take two waltz steps, man waltzing in place as lady turns clockwise twice under his upraised right arm.
NOTE: Partners may turn away from each other, lady right, man left, taking two waltz steps progressing in line of direction.

IV. Stamps

15–16 Stamp four times (left, right, left, right), facing partner.

Reference in Bibliography: 96 (p. 190).
Dance annotation form © 1948 by the Folk Dance Federation of California.
* Out of print.

V. Waltz

MEASURES

B. 17–32   Closed position. Beginning left, take sixteen waltz steps, turning clockwise, progressing in line of direction.

NOTE: Since A and/or B part of music vary on different records and sheet music, repetition of the action should vary accordingly.

STYLE: This dance is done with the Spanish styling as the music suggests.

GOLDEN GATE WALTZ

This dance was composed by Bob and Helen Smithwick, San Diego, California.

Music	Record: Grenn 14040.
Position	Side by side position, inside hands joined.
Steps	Waltz, balance.

DIRECTIONS FOR THE DANCE

Music 3/4 — NOTE: Directions are for the man; lady's part reversed.

MEASURES

Introduction

1–4 — Wait two measures then beginning left, step sideward, touch right to left, step right sideward, touch left to right.

I. Waltz Out and In and Turn

1–2 — Beginning left, take one waltz out diagonally to the left in the line of direction (almost back to back), and one waltz diagonally to the right in line of direction, turning face to face and changing hands (man's left, lady's right).

3–4 — Beginning left, step backward in line of direction turning to face reverse line of direction. Drop hands and finish out waltz measure turning clockwise (lady counterclockwise). Take one more waltz measure right, left, right, continuing the turn to face partner, and the man maneuvering to closed position with his back to the line of direction.

II. Waltz Turn and Twirl

5–8 — Beginning left, starting backward in line of direction, take three waltzes, turning clockwise once and a half, progressing in the line of direction, and then twirl the lady under the man's left arm clockwise on one more waltz as he maneuvers along side of her to the inside of the circle in open position, facing line of direction.

9–16 — Repeat action of measures 1–8, Parts I and II, but finish in butterfly position with man facing partner and line of direction at the end of the twirl.

III. Twinkle and Cross Touch

17–20 — Turn butterfly position slightly on a diagonal so man faces out. Beginning left take three twinkle waltzes* moving diagonally out, in, out crossing and traveling forward on the line of direction. On the fourth waltz measure, beginning right, cross to diagonal position and touch left to right, holding the third count. (The lady crosses in back for the twinkle step, moving backwards.)

Dance printed in *Sets in Order*, Reference 125 (September 1962, p. 104).
    Reprinted by permission.
* Reference to Scissors or Twinkle Waltz, page 294.
Dance annotation form © 1948 by the Folk Dance Federation of California.

MEASURES

21–24	Repeat action of measures 17–20, Part III, but travel backwards in the reverse line of direction moving diagonally out, in, out and back touch. End facing partner and line of direction. (The man crosses in back for the twinkle step, moving backwards.)

IV. **Waltz Corte, Turn Open, Corte and Twirl**

25–26   In closed position, man facing line of direction, beginning left, corte* back on left foot, count one, and hold two counts. Take one waltz forward in line of direction, right, left, right, turning the lady to open position.

27–28   Beginning left, take one waltz forward in open position. Beginning right, step through forward and maneuver on the remaining two counts to closed position, man with his back to the center of the circle.

29–30   Beginning left, corte back on left foot, and hold two counts. Beginning right, take one waltz, maneuvering so man will be in closed position with his back to line of direction.

31–32   Beginning left, take one waltz turning clockwise to face line of direction. Beginning right, man takes one waltz right, left, right while twirling the lady once around clockwise to end in side by side position with inside hands joined.

Entire dance repeats twice from Part I.

ENDING: The couple takes slow twirl and bow.

MERRY WIDOW WALTZ

This dance was taught at the Lloyd Shaw Cheyenne Mountain School, August 1943, '46 and '47.

Music   Record: Old Timer 8050; Lloyd Shaw 101 (slow).
Position   Closed.
Steps   Balance, waltz, dip, hop.

DIRECTIONS FOR THE DANCE

Music 3/4   NOTE: Directions are for man; lady's part reverse.
MEASURES

Part I.

1–4	Balance backward on left, balance forward on right. Repeat.
5–6	Open position. Beginning left, step forward in line of direction and swing right forward. Step forward right and swing left.
7–8	Closed position. Continuing in same direction, step left, close right to left, taking weight right. Step left, close right to left, keeping weight on left, and hold.
9–12	Reverse open position. Moving in reverse line of direction, step right, swing left, step left, swing right, step right and pivot to open position, swinging left leg slightly forward and out in a semicircle away from partner. Dip back on left, taking weight and extend right forward, touching toe to floor.
13–16	Closed position. Coming out of dip immediately and beginning *right*, take three waltz steps, turning clockwise, progressing in line of direction. Then step left, close right to left, taking weight on right.

Part II.

17–20	Repeat action of measures 1–4.
21–24	Open position. Moving in line of direction, step forward left, swing right, hop left, lifting slightly (cts. 1-2-3). Walk forward right, left, right (cts. 1-2-3), step left and pivot to reverse open position, swinging right leg forward and out in a semicircle away from partner (cts. 1-2-3). Dip back on right and extend left forward, touching toe to floor (cts. 1-2-3).
25–27	Moving in reverse line of direction, walk left, right, left (cts. 1-2-3). Step right and pivot to open position, swinging left leg forward and out in a semi-circle away from partner (cts. 1-2-3). Dip back on left (cts. 1-2-3).
28	Closed position. Beginning right, take one waltz step.
29–31	Pivot turn clockwise taking nine little steps (cts. 123, 123, 123).
32	Beginning right, man takes one waltz step in place turning, the lady clockwise under his upraised left arm.

References in Bibliography: 96 (p. 185), 14 (Vol. II, p. 2), 116 (Vol. VI, No. 6, June '46, p. 9), 23 (p. 44).

MEXICAN WALTZ
American

Although called the "Mexican Waltz" and done to the Mexican tune "Chiapanecas," this is a composed American dance.

Music	Record: Folk Dancer MH 1016; Folkraft 1093X45, 1483X45; MacGregor 608; Old Timer 8100; Lloyd Shaw 118.
	Piano: Herman Michael, *Folk Dances for All*, Chiapenecas, p. 16.
Position	Couple.
Steps	Waltz, balance step or rock.

DIRECTIONS FOR THE DANCE

Music 3/4   NOTE: Directions are for man; lady's part reverse.

MEASURES

I. Step Swing and Clap

1 Beginning left, step forward in line of direction, and swing right foot across left.

2 Beginning right, repeat.

3–4 Step on left with a slight stamp (ct. 1). Pause (ct. 2). Clap own hands twice (ct. 3 and 1). Pause (ct. 2 and 3).

5–8 Partners turning toward each other in place, face reverse line of direction and join inside hands. Beginning right, repeat action of measures 1–4.

9 Partners face, join two hands. Beginning left, balance or rock away from partner (ct. 1), pause (cts. 2 and 3).

10 Beginning right, balance or rock forward toward each other with arms stretched out to the side at shoulder level.

11–12 Beginning left, balance or rock away from each other (ct. 1), pause (ct. 2). Partners clap own hands twice (cts. 3 and 1). Pause (cts. 2 and 3).

13 Join hands again and balance or rock forward on right, arms outstretched at side.

14 Beginning left, balance or rock away.

15–16 Step forward right (ct. 1), pause (ct. 2). Lady extends arms around man's neck as man extends arms around lady's waist. Both clap twice (cts. 3 and 1). Pause (cts. 2 and 3).

II. Waltz

17–28 Closed position. Beginning left, take twelve waltz steps, turning clockwise, progressing in line of direction.

29–30 Man takes two waltz steps in place, turning lady under his upraised left arm.

31–32 Step left in place with a slight stamp (ct. 1), pause (ct. 2), clap own hands twice (cts. 3 and 1), pause (cts. 2-3).

MIXER:
On action of measures 29–30, lady turns under partner's arm and moves forward to a new partner.

References in Bibliography: 52 (p. 16), 96 (p. 387).
Dance annotation form © 1948 by the Folk Dance Federation of California.

PENNY WALTZ

This dance was composed by Penny and Ross Crispino, Nampa, Idaho.

Music   Record: Black Mountain Records RL 1010.
Position   Closed position.
Steps   Waltz, balance.

DIRECTIONS FOR THE DANCE

Music 3/4   NOTE: Directions are for man, lady's part reversed.

MEASURES

I. Balance and Waltz Turn

1   Beginning left, take one waltz balance forward. (Step forward left, step right beside left, step left in place.)

2   Beginning right, take one waltz balance backward. (Step backward right, step left beside right, step right in place.)

3   Beginning left, take one waltz balance in line of direction. (Step sideward left, step right beside left, step left in place.)

4   Beginning right, take one waltz balance in reverse line of direction.

5–8   Beginning left, take four waltzes, turning clockwise twice around and progressing in line of direction. Maneuver on the last waltz so as to end in open position, facing the line of direction.

II. Step Swing and Waltz Turn

9–10   Beginning left, step left and swing right foot forward (no weight change). Then step right and swing left forward.

11   Beginning left, take one waltz measure (left, right, left) forward in line of direction.

12   Step right forward, touch left to right, maneuvering to closed position, man's back to line of direction.

13–16   Beginning left, take four waltzes, turning clockwise twice around and progressing in the line of direction.
Entire dance repeats five times through.

ENDING:

Twirl lady on measure 16 the last time through and bow to partner.

Dance printed in *Sets in Order*, Reference 125 (August 1956, p. 30).
   Reprinted by permission.
Dance annotation form © 1948 by the Folk Dance Federation of California.

SPANISH CIRCLE WALTZ

Music   Record: *Spanish Circle Waltz*, Folkraft 1047X45; Shaw 119; RCA Victor EPA 4131.

Piano: *Over the Waves.*

Position   Couple.

Formation   Double circle, couples arranged in a set of four, one couple facing line of direction, the other, reverse line of direction.

Steps   Balance, waltz.

DIRECTIONS FOR THE DANCE

Music 3/4   NOTE: Directions are same for both lady and man except where specially noted.

MEASURES

I. Balance Forward

1–2   Beginning left, couples balance forward, swinging joined inside hands forward and up. Balance backward, swinging joined inside hands backward up and down.

II. Change Partners and Turn

3–4   Couples release partner's hand. Waltz forward one waltz step, join inside hands with opposite; as the man turns opposite lady under his raised right arm, they execute a second waltz step ending with new lady to his right. One couple now faces the center of the circle, the other has backs to center of circle. Each individual has moved one quarter of the way around the small circle formed by the two couples (the man clockwise, lady counterclockwise).

5–16 Repeat action of measures 1–4 three times.

III. Star by the Right

1–4   Place right hands in center of circle grasping wrist of person ahead. Beginning left, waltz four steps clockwise.

IV. Star by the Left

5–8   Place left hands in center of circle. Repeat action of measures 1–4, Part III, moving counterclockwise to original place.

V. Waltz Around Opposite Couple

9–16 Closed position. Beginning left, man dips backward left, lady dips forward right, and takes seven waltz steps, turning clockwise and progressing counterclockwise once around the set. From original position, waltz half way around again counterclockwise to meet a new couple.

NOTE:
This is a progressive couple dance. Couples progress in the direction originally faced, for example, line of direction or reverse line of direction.

References in Bibliography: 14 (Vol. III, p. 21), 96 (p. 372), 125 (Vol. V, No. 6, June '53, p. 34).
Dance annotation form © 1948 by the Folk Dance Federation of California.

VELETA WALTZ

The first part is an old English ballroom dance. This dance was taught at the Lloyd Shaw Cheyenne Mountain School, August 1943, '46, and '47.

Music   Record: Folk Dancer MH 3001; Folkraft 1065X45; Lloyd Shaw 145.

                Piano: Lloyd Shaw, *Round Dance Book*, p. 176.

Position   Couple.

Steps   Draw step, waltz, three step turn.

DIRECTIONS FOR THE DANCE

Music 3/4   NOTE: Directions are for man; lady's part reverse.

MEASURES

I. Draw Step

1–2	Beginning left, two waltz steps forward in line of direction, swinging joined hands forward and back.
3–4	Face partner, two hands joined. Step left (ct. 1), draw right to left (ct. 2), take weight on right (ct. 3). Step left (ct. 1), draw right to left, keeping weight on left (cts. 2 and 3). Body leans toward drawing foot.
5–8	Beginning right, repeat action of measures 1–4 in reverse line of direction.
9–10	Closed position. Beginning left, two waltz steps, turning clockwise.
11–12	Beginning left, two draw steps in line of direction. Whole body leans toward reverse line of direction.
13–16	Beginning left, four waltz steps, turning clockwise. Progress in line of direction. Turn lady under man's upraised left arm on last waltz step.

II. Limp Step

1–2	Closed position. Moving forward in line of direction, step left (cts. 1-2), close right to left, taking weight on right (ct. 3). Repeat.
3–4	Step left to side, step right across in front of left, step left again to side (cts. 1-2-3). Pivot to reverse open position, pointing right foot to right (cts. 1-2-3).
5–8	Beginning right, repeat action of measures 1–4, Part II. Action of measure 4 will be a pivot to open position and left toe pointing to left.

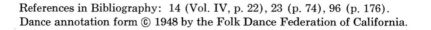

References in Bibliography: 14 (Vol. IV, p. 22), 23 (p. 74), 96 (p. 176).
Dance annotation form © 1948 by the Folk Dance Federation of California.

MEASURES

9–12   Closed position. Beginning left, two waltz steps, turning clockwise, followed by two draw steps, progressing in line of direction. Body leans in reverse line of direction.

13–14   Beginning left, two waltz steps, turning clockwise. Progress in line of direction.

15–16   Progressing in line of direction, step left foot to the left side (ct. 1), step right foot behind left (ct. 2). Beginning left, take a three step turn counterclockwise (lady clockwise) away from partner (cts. 3-1-2) and close right to left taking weight on right (ct. 3). End facing in couple position.

III. **Butterfly**

1–2   Beginning left, move forward with two waltz steps, turning counterclockwise (lady clockwise) away from partner.

3–4   Beginning left, repeat action of measures 3–4, Part I. Hands are free and arms extended to the side.

5–8   Beginning right, repeat action of measures 1–4, Part III, moving in reverse line of direction.

9–12   Closed position. Beginning left, two waltz steps, turning clockwise, and two draws in line of direction. The body leans in reverse line of direction.

13–14   Step left to side (ct. 1), step right behind left (ct. 2), step left in place (ct. 3). Step right to side (ct. 1), step left behind right (ct. 2), step right in place (ct. 3).

15–16   Beginning left, pivot turn clockwise left, right, left (cts. 1-2-3). Dip back on right (cts. 1-2-3).

WALTZ OF THE BELLS

This dance was composed by "Doc" Alumbaugh, Alhambra, California.

Music	Records: Folkraft 1061X45, 1420X45; Old Timer 8049; Lloyd Shaw 2-109; Windsor 4605; World of Fun M 113.
Position	Couple.
Steps	Waltz, three-step-turn, rock step.

DIRECTIONS FOR THE DANCE

Music 3/4   NOTE: Directions are for man; lady's part reverse.
MEASURES

I. Swing and Waltz

1–2 Beginning left, step forward and swing right forward. Step right backward and swing left slightly across in front of right. Joined hands swing forward and back.

3–4 Repeat action of measures 1–2.

5–6 Beginning left, two waltz steps. Partners turn away from each other making one full turn, lady right, man left, and progress in line of direction. End with two hands joined facing partner.

7–8 Step left, draw right to left. Step left, draw right to left, keeping weight on left. (Holding ct. 2, move on cts. 1, 3, 1, 3). This is known as canter rhythm.

9–16 Beginning right, repeat action of measures 1–8, progressing in reverse line of direction.

II. Step Close and Lady Turn

17–18 Partners facing, join two hands. Beginning left, step sideward left, in line of direction. Close right to left. Step sideward left, close right to left (holding ct. 2, move on cts. 1, 3, 1, 3).

19–20 Man takes step left, close right, step left, touch right in place keeping weight left. Lady takes a three step turn clockwise under man's upraised left arm (cts. 1-3, 1) to face partner. Close left to right, keeping weight on right (cts. 2-3).

21–24 Repeat action of measures 17–20, moving in reverse line of direction, lady turning under man's right arm. Note: In the original dance, man turned lady with the trailing arm, but it is generally not danced this way.

III. Rock Step and Waltz

25–26 Partners facing, man's right hand holds lady's left. Rock back on left away from partner, then rock forward on right toward partner.

27–28 Repeat action of measures 25–26. Take closed position on the last rock step together.

29–30 Two waltz steps, turning clockwise, progressing in line of direction.

31–32 Six little steps, man stepping in place and turning lady clockwise under his upraised left arm.

References in Bibliography: 23 (p. 77), 125 (Vol. I, No. 11, Nov. '49, p. 15).
Dance annotation form © 1948 by the Folk Dance Federation of California.

VARSOUVIANNA

This dance is also known, especially in Texas, as "Put Your Little Foot."

Music   Record: Folk Dancer MH 3012; Folkraft 1034, 1165; Mac-Gregor 389, 3985; Old Timer 8001; Russell 707; Lloyd Shaw 103; Western Jubilee 700; Windsor 4615; World of Fun M 107.

      Piano: Lloyd Shaw, *Cowboy Dances*, page 392.

Position   Varsouvianna.

Steps   Mazurka.

DIRECTIONS FOR THE DANCE

Music 3/4 NOTE: Directions are same for both lady and man.

MEASURES

	I.	**Long Phrase**
A.	1	Swing left heel across in front of right instep (ct. 3, pick up beat). Step left, close right to left, weight ends on right (cts. 1-2).
	2	Repeat action of measure 1.
	3–4	Swing left heel across in front of right instep (ct. 3, pick up beat). Step left, right, left (cts. 1-3-3) and point right foot to right (cts. 1-2).
	5–8	Beginning right, repeat action of measures 1–4.
	II.	**Short Phrase**
B.	9–10	Repeat action of measures 3–4.
	11–16	Beginning right, repeat action of measures 9–10 through three times.

VARIATIONS FOR MEASURES 3–8, Part I:

1. Crossover. Beginning left, the man moves the lady across in front of him to his left side with three steps. Beginning right, he moves her back to his right side.
2. Turnback. During the three steps, make half turn clockwise and point in opposite direction. Beginning right, turn counterclockwise. Note: Forward or backward movements with a pivot on first or third step may be used.

VARIATION FOR MEASURES 9–16, Part II:

Swing In and Out. Beginning left, repeat action of measures 3–4 as follows:

Man: Take steps in place.

Lady: Release man's right hand and take three steps toward center of circle to face reverse line of direction, out to the left and slightly in front of man. Beginning right, take three steps turning counterclockwise under man's upraised left arm and finish in original position. Repeat action toward center and back to original position.

MIXER:

On measures 15–16 in the Swing In and Out Variation, lady may move in reverse line of direction to a new partner and turn counterclockwise into place beside him in varsouvianna position.

NOTE:

Since the A and B parts of the music vary on different records, the repetition of the action should vary accordingly.

References in Bibliography: 27 (p. 62), 94 (p. 78), 96 (p. 245).

THREE STEP

Music   Record: Imperial 1046; MacGregor 6115; Lloyd Shaw, 141, 142, 3303, 3304.

Piano: Stevens, George, *Moon Winks*, published by Will Rossiter, Chicago, Illinois.

Position   Closed.

Steps   Slide, pivot, dip.

DIRECTIONS FOR THE DANCE

Music 3/4   NOTE: Directions are for the man; lady's part reverse.

MEASURES

I. Slide Turn

1   Beginning left, two slides in line of direction, step left and pivot half around clockwise. Keep weight on left. Man is now facing inside of circle.

2   Beginning right, take two slides still in line of direction. Step right in place.

II. Pivot and Dip

3   Beginning left, three steps pivoting clockwise half way around so as to put man's back to center of circle.

4   Dip backward on right and recover with two final steps, left and right.

VARIATION OF PART I:

Closed position, man facing line of direction. Beginning left, two slides diagonally forward toward center of circle. Step left and pivot a quarter turn counterclockwise. Beginning right, two slides diagonally forward away from center of circle. Step right pivoting clockwise so man has back to center of circle.

VARIATION OF PART II:

1. Man takes three steps in place instead of three steps pivoting. Lady takes a three step turn under own right arm. Take closed position. Dip, step, step.

2. Closed position, man facing line of direction. Beginning left, step, step, and dip forward left (the lady backward on right) in line of direction. Step, step, dip backward right (lady forward on left) in reverse line of direction.

STYLE:

This dance is done with very smooth dignified style.

Reference in Bibliography: 96 (p. 194).

Dance annotation form © 1948 by the Folk Dance Federation of California.

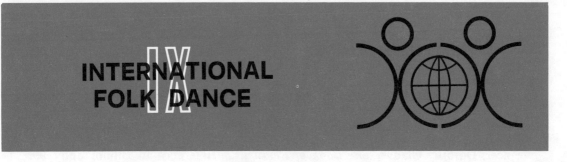

INTERNATIONAL FOLK DANCE

DEFINITION

The term International Folk Dance applies to those dances which come from countries other than the United States of America. The dances in this section are classified by basic step, number of people involved, and nationality on page 177.

HISTORY

Along with other traditional folk arts, folk dances were practically swept away in the urbanization trend at the end of the 19th century. Then movements arose to preserve the knowledge of the past.

An understanding and appreciation of people's origins, mores, political and religious history, and physical environment enhance the teaching as well as actual dancing of International Folk Dances. Dancing becomes a richer experience as the world becomes smaller and our contact with people from other lands becomes more frequent. Dance is a common bond and a language in itself in understanding others. Foreign students offer an excellent opportunity to learn about different cultures. Refer to Notes on The Dance, page 1, for general background information for folk dance.

Start a collection of background information relating to each country that includes history, climate, topography, occupations, customs, costumes, music, instruments, festivals and holidays, and dance characteristics. Add interesting items of folklore, pictures, and celebrations from newspapers and magazines. Suddenly it is apparent that customs continue long after the superstition which created them ceases to exist; that the influences of culture are reflected in the folk arts; that folk dance follows ethnological rather than political boundaries; that there are similar dances, such as Sword dances, all over Europe in varying forms. The following sources are suggested for gathering information:

Encyclopedias
History Books
Magazines:

    Country Dancer. Reference in Bibliography 116.
    Folk Dancer. Reference in Bibliography 117.
    Let's Dance. Reference in Bibliography 120.
    National Geographic, 16th and M Streets N.W., Washington 36, D. C.
    Viltis. Reference in Bibliography 127.
Duggan, Anne, Schlottman, Jeannette, and Rutledge, Abbie.
    _____ *Folk Dances of the British Isles.* Reference in Bibliography 24.
    _____ *Folk Dances of European Countries.* Reference in Bibliography 25.
    _____ *Folk Dances of Scandinavia.* Reference in Bibliography 26.
    _____ *Folk Dances of the United States and Mexico.* Reference in Bibliography 27.
Haire, Frances H., *The Costume Book.* Reference in Bibliography 43.
Holden, Rickey, and Vouras, Mary, *Greek Folk Dances.* Reference in Bibliography 57.
Joukowsky, Anatol M., *The Teaching of Ethnic Dance.* Reference in Bibliography 62.

Lawson, Joan, *European Folk Dance — Its National and Musical Characteristics.* Reference in Bibliography 70.

Leeming, Joseph, *The Costume Book for Parties and Plays.* Reference in Bibliography 71.

Lidster, Miriam, and Tamburini, Dorothy H., *Folk Dance Progressions.* Reference in Bibliography 72.

Sachs, Curt, *World History of the Dance.* New York: W. W. Norton and Company, Inc., 1937.

Spicer, Dorothy Gladys, *The Book of Festivals.* Reference in Bibliography 99.

Handbooks of European National Dances. New York: Chanticleer Press, 1948.
    This series includes: Dances of Austria, Bulgaria, Czechoslovakia, Denmark, England, Wales, Finland, France, Germany, Greece, Hungary, Italy, Netherlands, Norway, Portugal, Scotland, Spain, Sweden, Switzerland.

STYLE

It is as important to execute the styling and mannerisms inherent in the dance of another country as it is to be able to dance the steps and pattern sequences. One of the great dangers in this era of enthusiasm for folk dancing is to treat all dances alike regardless of their origin and background. Mary Ann Herman of Folk Dance House, New York City, compared this particular problem to the seasoning of food and pointed out that if all food were seasoned only with salt and pepper, all food would taste the same and be uninteresting. If twirls, hoops, and yells are added to every dance, the dances, like the food, lose their individuality and become uninteresting.

Basically style, if not inherent, must be developed by the dancer to achieve the fullest enjoyment from the dance. The following suggestions will help the dancer acquire proper style.

1. Realize that the application of style begins with posture and good body mechanics. Refer to page 52.
2. Study each nationality, its history and way of life.
3. Acquire an understanding of the background of folk dancing in general and the specific dance in particular.
4. Study the costumes and note their influence on dance movement peculiar to each nationality.
5. Develop an awareness of the characteristic styles, step patterns, formations, and quality of movement of each country or area. Although these characteristics are not limited to any one country, there are general characteristics which will serve as a guide for the development of style.
6. Apply this information in the development and continued practice of style.

The above knowledge will reflect itself in the style and manner in which the dance is executed; and the dancer will receive more pleasure from dancing and develop greater interest and appreciation for people of many lands and the way they live.

The average dancer has difficulty in developing style and may feel that it is a nebulous thing, or that the dance is for fun — an end in itself. The teacher will have greater success in developing style among dancers if only a few specific suggestions are made for each dance presented. For example, point out the exact position of the hands in relation to the waist and clothing; the action of the hands and arms as in the manipulation of the skirt; any unusual body position as in arching the upper torso in a drawstep; the position and interaction of the individual in relation to partner and group; the details of footwork in terms of length of step, foot mechanics, quality of step; the amount of energy expended in a movement; the facial expression including the focus of eyes and direction the head faces. After these suggestions have been assimilated by the dancer, additional suggestions may be made with more gratifying results.

A very brief description of the kinds of dance, steps, and formations is presented for selected countries. Some very general comments about style are indicated. It is hoped that this beginning will stimulate additional research by students.

DANCE CHARACTERISTICS

England . . . English folk dancing may be divided into three forms: *Sword, Morris,* and *Country dance.* The *Sword dance,* the oldest form, is thought to have been introduced into England in Roman times. The Sword dance is a combination drama and dance. It is for men only and involves a simple running step with complex figures. This dance is related to Mummer's Play, and thus the actors and dancers intermingle in parts. It was performed at Christmas time in accordance with the anteceding customs of pagan agricultural festivals, with their fertilization of crops, and their luck charms. The Sword dances also seem to be related to the calendar, the conquest of the old year by the new.

The *Morris* dances, also performed by men alone, are lively and gay and were originally a fertility rite, a part of a religious ceremony. They are thought to be an off-shoot of the Sword dances because of their many similarities. The team of dancers execute the precise routine carrying sticks that are knocked together rhythmically, or large handkerchiefs that are waved in various patterns. Bells and bright ribbons are tied to the calf of each leg.

The character of the *English Country Dance* is entirely different. Men and women alike participated in the Country dances. They were danced in circles, lines, squares, or as couple dances. The dances were simple and for the people to enjoy, but they became more complex as they moved into the cities. The style of Country Dancing is characterized by a light running step sometimes described as a dance walk. It is taken on the ball of the foot with an easy springing motion. The dancers may inject a two-step or polka occasionally as suggested by the music. The body is held erect and dignified. The arms hang at the side, moving freely with the action of the body. The English people move precisely with the beat and the phrasing of the music. It appears that flirtation or coquetry is related to all movements.

Germany . . . The folk arts of Germany have not been influenced by many different cultures because Germany did not suffer great invasions or settlements of people as did other countries. But the struggle for power between the Pope and the Emperor has left its mark on German folk dancing. There have been more bans on German dancing than any other European country.[1]

The *turning couple dance* is one of the characteristics. Social dancing still follows the feature of couples rotating around the room. The most popular dance steps used are the waltz, polka, and schottische. The German Landler changed from 3/4 to 4/4 time. Instead of a waltz step, a flat footed walking step is used. In some areas the Landler is referred to as Schupplattler or shoe clapping dance.

The dances follow the same form and pattern as Country dances, Longway Sets, Quadrille, or Cotillion. The dances tend to be lusty with a heavy peasant quality, punctuated by a stamp or heavier step. In the North, the dances tend to be serious and in the South gaiety accompanies the leaping and waltzing rhythms.

Where Germany borders Austria and Switzerland in the Bavarian region, the styles of all three blend and the dances appear gay and hearty, heavy in step, particularly on the first beat of a measure. The hand is clenched in a fist position and placed at the waist slightly forward from the hip with the elbows forward.

Greece . . . Modern folk dancing in Greece may be classified according to their rhythm. There are the *Syrtos* or *Kalamatianos,* 7/8 time; the *Tsamiko,* 3/4 time; and the *Chasapikos* (sometimes referred to as the Butcher's Dance), 2/4 time. Most of the dances follow the circle or broken circle formation; although men and women used to dance alone, they now dance together without partners. In the broken circle, the leader is on the right hand end, holding two handkerchiefs, one in his right hand, hand out

---

1 Lawson, Joan, *European Folk Dance — Its National and Musical Characteristics.* Reference in Bibliography 70, p. 121.

away from the body, to wave and signal variations in step, and the other joins the leader to the next person in the line. The leader improvises steps in time with the music displaying his ingenuity and skill. Occasionally the leader moves to the opposite end and the next person in line is now the leader. There is usually a basic step that is repeated over and over.

The Syrtos and Tsamikos types are the most popular and national in scope. The couple and solo dances are in the minority.

Style . . . In general, dances of the mountainous regions are comprised of jumpy movements in contrast to the slow even rhythm of the plain regions. The step is with a flat foot. In the hopping steps, the lady slides her feet along, the man's foot leaves the ground. The steps for the ladies are simple and dignified and for the man they tend to show feats of strength.

Music . . . There is a very interesting relationship between the Greek song and dance. The steps are slow and quick and correspond with the length of syllables of words rather than the beats. Many dances are performed with the accompaniment of people sitting on the side singing or with the folk instruments.

Ireland . . . There are three types of Irish folk dances: *Jigs*, *Reels*, and *Hornpipes*. The Jigs and Hornpipes are characterized by clog or tap steps, and the Reels by shuffle or gliding steps. The dances follow traditional formations of solos, couples, and group or set.

Style . . . Characteristics of the Irish people, such as their keen sense of humor, happiness, wit, imagination, and superstition, prevail in their dances and music. The dancer is erect, hands at the side. The range of movement is minimal. The distinguishing characteristic is the intricate and exact footwork. In the most difficult dances there are about seventy-five taps per quarter minute. The control of the variety of sounds produced by the taps of heels and soles on the floor and against each other is of utmost importance in competitive dancing. The group dances such as round, square, and longway formations are based on simple steps and are popular with the people.

Italy . . . The Italian dance reflects the influence of the invaders from Asia, Northern Europe, and Africa. The dances are simple in form and pattern. The dances may be classified in these groups: Processional and Religious dances, Sword dances, Chain dances in closed or open circles, and Couple dances. The Tarantella, originating in the Southern part of Italy, is one of the best known dances.

Style . . . The dancers are free and easy. The body is held loosely, often swaying from side to side with arms held high in the air and the head erect. In the mountainous areas and in the Sword dances, the steps are precise. Pantomime and flirtation are a part of the dance, especially in courting dances. The dances sometimes are accompanied by castanets or tambourines used by the dancers themselves.

Israel . . . The Jewish folk dances reflect the many different cultures that the Jews have experienced, first as agricultural people in their own land, then absorbing the ways of others as they wandered and settled all over the world, and once again as agricultural people as many have returned to the New State of Israel.

Many of the Israeli folk dances have been created, first following the hora style and later encompassing accents and rhythms of the Orient. Every event inspired the creation of a new dance. A group of dances came from Song of Songs. Many came from the Jews of Yemen who were transported by airplane from the Southwest corner of Arabia to Israel. Although the Yemenites had many things in common with the Arabs, their religion was different, and they could read and write. The Yemenites were a link with the biblical Hebrew. They had maintained old religious and cultural patterns, songs in the language of the bible, and dances of oriental rhythm. Their dances were slow, gentle, gradually accelerating as danced to a drum, hand clapping, and singing. Their basic dance forms inspired a new trend in Israeli dances and the Yemenite step in many variations became a basic step.

The melodies have a strong rhythmic pulse. Some original steps have been crystallized and used in line, circle, and couple dance formations. It is important to remember that many divergent cultures have definitely influenced these dances. The most popular Jewish folk dances are old dances of other countries as well as the newly created ones.

Lithuania . . . Folk dancing in Lithuania was quite related to their way of life and reflected the life, chores, and various aspects of farm life. Although the older dances were slow and restrained, in later years they became livelier. Eventually, the polka arrived on the scene from Poland and became an integral part of Lithuanian folk dance. According to Vyts Beliajus, the polka was "flat footed with more body bounce than foot hop"[2] because the farmers wore wooden shoes and if their feet came too far off the ground, the shoes would fall off. "The steps were small, rapid and close to the ground. It consisted of three such bouncy steps with a low hop on the fourth, which often terminated with a quick step on the ground."[2]

Mexico . . . A great variety exists in Mexican dance. Some of the dances are very primitive Indian dances; some, although originally of European and Spanish origin, are combined with the Indian dance, the latter of which is the dominating characteristic; and others are pure Spanish in style, temperament, and rhythm.

Dance among the Indians related to worship and war. When the Spaniards arrived, they tried to demolish the native Indian culture and substitute the Spanish customs and mores. Although Christianity was introduced and the Aztec priests driven away, the pagan dance connected with religious ceremonies persisted and is still performed.

The *zapateados* are the most popular dances today.[3] Although they are Mexican in spirit, theme, and structure, they are similar to Spanish dancing.

Style . . . The men clasp their hands behind and the women hold their skirts up. The body posture is forward. The footwork is quick with steps small and close to the ground. Frequently there is a flirtatious aspect about the dance.

Russia . . . A great variety of dance is found in Russia because there are no natural boundaries and intermarriage and movement of people have existed for a long time. Therefore, the folk dance reflects many cultures: the Slavs, the Turks, Ugrian tribes, the Mongolians, and Tartars. Many of our dances have come from the Ukraine, for it is here that the Cossacks lived. Cossack dancing is reflective of the spirit of the fearless soldier and superb horseman. It is exuberant, exciting, and characterized by fast running, leaping or pas-de-bas steps and by the difficult knee bend or Prysiadka steps used by the men. Also characteristic are the turns, spinning, stamping, and heel clicking. The Ukrainian dancers are unsurpassed for their vitality, competitive spirit, and endurance of the performers. The Western influence is relatively limited to the court dances and the contacts with Poland. The dance patterns include circles, processionals, couple, and some figure dances.

Style . . . The Russian dances are characterized by emotional expressiveness. The movements are fluid from the hot countries and very vigorous from the cold countries. Russian dances are not always set.

Music . . . There was a period when Tsar Paul I forbade national instruments in an effort to Germanize Russia. People joined together to sing as accompaniment for the dances. Russian music is similar to Eastern music.

SCANDINAVIA

Scandinavia is made up of three distinct racial groups: the Nordics, the Finns, and the Lapps. These racial groups give rise to five different nationalities: Finland, Denmark, Norway, Sweden, and Iceland. There are relatively few differences in the dances of these countries except those influenced by climate, geography, and work conditions.

---

[2] *Let's Dance*, Reference in Bibliography 120, April 1959. *The Lithuanian Song and Dance*, p. 6. This article is based on a longer one written by Vyts Beliajus, editor of *Viltis*.

[3] Duggan, Anne, Schottmann, Jeannette, and Rutledge, Abbie, *Folk Dances of the United States and Mexico*. Reference in Bibliography 27, p. 105.

Denmark . . . The dancing is similar to that of the Dutch. The action is very smooth with no bounce. Frequently there is a stamp at the beginning of a phrase. Since Denmark is on the continent, it tends to reflect the dancing of the continent with more squares and quadrilles. The same dances appear all over Denmark but with different variations. Walking, running, galloping, and skipping are fundamentals commonly used. The waltz and polka are also prevalent. Dances are more often classified by geographical origin than by type.

Finland . . . The dancing is definitely influenced by the Finn-Ugrian origin as well as by the Nordic, Teutonic, and Eastern neighbors. The Finns tend to display more verve in their dance. Many of the dances have a polka rhythm. The polka step is characterized by small steps with lots of bounce. The most common dances are Purpuri, a mixture of figure dances from other countries like waltz, Russian quadrille, polska, and the march. According to Gordon E. Tracie,[4] the minuet is still danced today in Finland.

Norway . . . The Norwegian love of the mountains and the sea is reflected in a somewhat freer and more spontaneous dance style. During a pivot, the knees bend more, the body leans to each side slightly, and a slight bounce is present with each step.

There are three types of dances: the Song Dance, the Bygdedans or Country Dance, and the Turdans or Figure Dance. The Song Dance is the oldest form. It is interesting to note that during the Reformation the Song dances which were once prevalent in Europe died out. The only place the Song Dance survived was in the Faroe Islands. This dance is similar to the Slavic Chain dance in that the dancers are in a closed circle and repeat a basic step over and over. The song sung by the dancers is the only accompaniment. The Country dances are the oldest living form with uninterrupted tradition. The Halling, Gangar, Springer, and Pols are examples. The Figure dances are composed of quadrilles, contra, and square formations.

The Hardingfele, Hardanger fiddle, is unique in Norway. This fiddle has four strings on top of four or five strings. The top strings are bowed, and the lower ones act in a resonating capacity. The fiddle is usually highly ornamented, with decorations such as carved scrolls, dragon heads, or simple painted decorations.

Sweden . . . Authorities classify Swedish folk dances in different ways. One of the simplest methods divides the dances into three groups: the Traditional dances, the Choreographed dances based on folk elements, and the Singing Games. The Singing Games are one of the oldest forms and young and old still dance them today particularly at Midsummer time around the Maypole[5] and at Christmas time when everyone joins hands at the end of an evening and serpentines upstairs and downstairs through the house or, as it may occur on the farm, they move outside and weave in and out around the out buildings. Traditional dances consist of revived dances such as Quadrilles and living ones like the Hambo. Daldans is a good example of a dance created for the period around 1840. The music came from Darlana, the steps were invented by a Ballet Master some time during the period of 1840 to 1850.

The influence of Polish dance in Sweden was felt about 1648 when Sweden and Poland were in close contact. The polska, which means Polish, is the hallmark of Swedish folk dancing. It has been the prevailing dance idiom for the past two centuries. Although the step stems from complicated Polish dances perfected by the military, the etiquette and elegant movements of court dances of France, Italy, and Germany have strongly influenced the evolution of the polska. It consisted of many figures, the first part slow with walking steps; the second part a fast movement for rapid turning. Many variations of the polska, each with a different name, are still danced.

Style . . . The dislike for excessive display of emotion in public probably has contrib-

---

[4] Gordon E. Tracie, authority on Swedish Folk Dancing, Seattle, Washington. Mr. Tracie made this observation while studying in Finland during the summer of 1963.

[5] The Swedish word for Maypole is "majstang" which is a green or decorated pole around which the people dance at Midsummer time. Technically this pole has nothing to do with the month of May.

uted to the simplicity of the step as danced today and has sobered the livelier dance forms that come from Norway. There is a definite dignity and reserve displayed in the execution of Swedish dances. Lightness, buoyancy, and the proud manner in which the upper body is held erect give Swedish dances a highly distinctive character.

Music ... The Fiol, fiddle, is by far the most predominant folk instrument in Sweden. The traditional fiddler is able to convey to the listener that elusive element of "folk character" which distinguishes one culture from another. Although other instruments are now used for accompaniment, originally the musical accompaniment was limited to the fiddle or singing by the dancers.

Scotland ... Scottish dancing may be divided into three categories: *Highland dances*, *Reels*, and *Country dances*. The Reels are the oldest surviving Scottish social dances and may be traced back to the 16th century. They are said to be of Celtic origin and are also shared by the Danes. The Country dances came to England about the 18th century. They also had Sword dances, ritual dances that were connected with old folk customs, and dance games (play party games) as well as others that do not fall into the above categories.

Style ... The Scots are very enthusiastic about their dance and have always entered into it with a great deal of zest. The steps are precise, light, and quick. The carriage of the body is very erect and the supporting leg straight. The toes are pointed at all times. The hand and arm positions are exact; fists are at the hips or arms curved over head, thumb and third finger touching. The life, spirit, and technique of the dancer are major factors in the success of Scotch dancing.

Music ... The dances should be done to the music of the bagpipes in order to express the Scottish quality and rhythm of their dance music. The violin is now played in many parts of Scotland for the reels.

Today ... It is interesting to note that many of their folk dances are a regular part of an evening of social dancing today. A waltz country dance, a Petronella, a Skip the Willow, or a Highland Schottische are some that are currently seen.

Spain ... The dancing in Spain may be grouped according to the regions. The lay person is most aware of the dances from the Southern province of the peninsula, Andalusia which are referred to as *Flamenco*, *Classical Espanol*, and *Folk dances*. The Central Uplands, Castile, Extremadura, and Leon, dance the *Charradas*. This area is the melting pot of Spanish dancing as dances from neighboring provinces are also danced. The dances of Cantabria, Asturias, and Galicia, the North Western regions, are much simpler than in the South. The most common types are *Fandangos*, *Jotas*, *Circle* dances, and *Square* dances. The *Jota* is actually known all over Spain, but is claimed by the Aragonese as theirs. Two well known types of Catalonia are the *Sardana* and *Contrapas*. In Valencia, the *Jota*, *Bolero*, *Fandango*, and *Folias* are also found.

Style ... The influence of the Moors, who dominated the peninsula for seven hundred years, is shown in dancing by the famous back bends, play of delicate hands and fingers, hand clapping, and heel rapping out broken rhythm. In the solo dances, the woman is dominate and the man accompanies her with an occasional opportunity to display his skill. A flirtatious quality exists. The carriage of the head, torso, and arms as well as the emotional expression are all important characteristics of Spanish dance. Although the origin of castanets is lost, it is important in many of the dances.

Switzerland ... It is important to recognize the four different races that inhabit Switzerland: French, German, Italian, and Romanish. Switzerland is the meeting place of these four peoples and cultures. The dances reflect these influences, some distinct, others melded together. Some of the common types of dance are landler, square, longways, chain or round and allemande, alewander or allemandler.

The Swiss dances are simple with precise movements. A string instrument called the zither is used for accompaniment as well as various types of horns. Sometimes singing is done with the dances too.

Yugoslavia . . . After the first World War, six republics were banded together to form a new monarchy, Yugoslavia, in the central and Northwestern part of the Balkan peninsula. These were Serbia, Croatia, Bosnia and Hercegovina, Slovenia, Macedonia, and Montenego. The people all spoke languages derived from a common source. Their folk dancing and art had much in common, too. The *Kolo* is everywhere but is at its best among the Serbians. Yugoslavia was influenced by Greece, Italy, Turkey, Hungary, and Austria at different times. The dance was also influenced by the church. In areas where the Greek Orthodox Church predominates, the men and women danced in separate lines, sometimes a man leading the ladies' line, and a lady leading the man's line. In Croatia, Slovenia, and Northern Serbia the Catholic Church and Western influence were strong. Here the men and women alternated frequently in the lines. Couple dances from Austria, Italy, and Hungary are also present. The Hungarian influence brings elements of Western dance, such as hand clapping, stamping, swinging, waltz, and polka. The Mohammedan religion also left its mark.

The Kolo is believed to have originated in Serbia. The closed circle in its primitive form moved around an object of worship to ensure the magic from within the ring; the open circle offered an escape for evil and an entrance for good.

There are two types of dances; those in which the dancers dictate their own rhythm and those in which the dancers follow the music. There are open and closed Kolos, parallel lines, processions, solos, and dances for two or three people.

Style . . . The Kolos combine Slavic dance traits of liveliness, gaiety, quickness, and gymnastic footwork with the Turko-Balkan style of a circle without partners. The dancers are relaxed from head to foot. The basic step is alternated occasionally with a hop, spring, jump, stamp, or clap. The leader frequently carries a handkerchief and improvises figures. The men and women dance the same step but the women execute it with modesty and keep their eyes lowered and the men display great vivaciousness and vigor. Three styles are prevalent in the execution of the Kolos: the *shaking* with tiny jumps referred to as the "Kolo bounce," the *hopping*, and the *stepping* in which the body trembles with each step. The hand hold varies, sometimes hand in hand, held low; sometimes around their neighbor's neck, crossed arms, or holding neighbors' belts.

Music . . . The dances are performed to one or more native instruments or to singing. Some of the native instruments are gajde — bagpipe, duduk or svirala — native flutes, goc — a bass drum, gusle and tambura — string instruments, and def — tambourines. In some areas there is only the sound of the feet or clapping of hands.

CLASSIFIED INDEX OF INTERNATIONAL DANCES

* NOTE: A medley of Israeli or Russian dances is very effective for exhibition.

ALEXANDROVSKA
Russian

This is a Russian ballroom dance, probably named in honor of Czar Alexander.

Music	Record: Folk Dancer MH 1057; Folkraft 1107; Kismet 129.
	Piano: Fox, Grace, *Folk Dancing in High School and Colleges*, p. 10.
	Beliajus, V. F., *Dance and Be Merry*, Vol. 1, p. 22.
Position	Partners face, two hands joined.
Steps	Waltz, draw step, cantor waltz.

DIRECTIONS FOR THE DANCE

Music 3/4   NOTE: Directions are for man; lady's part reverse.

MEASURES   **I. Face to face, Back to Back**

1   Beginning left, take one draw step to left.

2   Step left to side (ct. 1), release man's left hand, lady's right, pivot on left back to back, swinging joined hands and right foot forward (cts. 2–3). Join other hands shoulder high. Release right hand.

3   Beginning right, take one draw step in line of direction.

4   Step right to side, touch left to right, weight remaining on right.

5–8   Beginning left, repeat action of measures 1-4 in reverse line of direction. NOTE: In measure 6, joined hands are swung down and back as partners pivot, bringing them face to face.

9–16   Repeat action of measures 1-8.

II. Lady's Turn

1   Partners face, inside hands joined, outside hands on hip. Beginning left, take one draw step on line of direction (ct. 1–3).

2   Man repeats draw step to left as lady turns clockwise once with two steps (right, left) under man's right arm (ct. 1, hold, 1–3).

3–4   Repeat action of measures 1-2, Part II. On last draw, man touches right to left, lady takes three steps in the turn (right, left, right).

5–8   Man beginning right, lady left, repeat action of measures 1-4, Part II, in reverse line of direction.

9–16   Repeat action of measures 1-8, Part II.

References in Bibliography: 6 (p. 22), 14 (Vol. I, p. 11), 65 (p. 98).
Dance annotation form © 1948 by the Folk Dance Federation of California.

MEASURES

III. Skating

1   Promenade position. Beginning left, take one waltz step forward in line of direction.

2   Take one waltz step turning toward partner to face reverse line of direction. Movement continues in line of direction.

3–4   Take two waltz steps backward, moving in line of direction.

5–8   Repeat action of measures 1–4, Part III, in reverse line of direction.

9–16   Repeat action of measures 1–8, Part III.

IV. Waltz

1–2   Closed position. Beginning left, take one draw step to side, step left to side, touch right to left, weight remaining on left.

3–4   Beginning right, repeat action of measures 1–2, Part IV, to right side.

5–8   Take four waltz steps, turning clockwise, progressing in line of direction.

9–16   Repeat action of measures 1–8, Part IV.

ARI ARA
Israeli

This dance was taught at Oglebay Folk Dance Camp, Wheeling, West Virginia, 1948. It is based on the Jewish Folk Dance Album by Miss Katya Delakava and Mr. Fred Berk, Ultra Album U-6.

Music   Record: Folk Dancer MH 1052.
Position   Partners face, right hands joined.
Formation   Double circle, man's back to center.
Steps   Three step turn, turn, skip.

DIRECTIONS FOR THE DANCE

Music 2/4   NOTE: Directions are the same for both lady and man.

MEASURES

Part I

1	Beginning right, leap towards partner, step left, step right in place.
2	Leap back on left away from partner, step right, step left in place.
3–8	Repeat action of measures 1–2 three times. As this step is done couples turn clockwise, making a quarter or half turn for each two measures.
1–8	Repeat action of measures 1–8. Partners end in original positions.

Part II

9–10	Drop hands. Beginning right, take two steps sideways to right (partners move away from each other), jump lightly on both feet and brushing left foot across right while rising from jump.
11–12	Beginning left, take a three step turn, counterclockwise, back to place.
13	Jump in place crossing legs. Jump to stride position (legs apart).
14	Jump, bring feet together (ct. 1). Clap hands ct. 2.
15-18	Link right arms, outside arms raised. Beginning right, couples turn clockwise with four skips or step hops.

MIXER:
Each dancer moves to the left one position on the last two skips to meet a new partner.

Reference in Bibliography: 16 (p. 45).
Dance annotation form © 1948 by the Folk Dance Federation of California.

AT THE INN
German

This dance is done to a gay German folk song, "Catherine's Wedding." The words of the song relate the happy events which took place at the Inn named "To the Crown." The dance comes from Sonderburg on the Island Alsen. This dance was taught at Oglebay Folk Dance Camp, Wheeling, West Virginia, 1948.

Music	Record: Folk Dancer MH 1022; Kismet 135 B; World of Fun 115.
	Piano: Dunsing, Paul, *German Folk Dances*, Vol. I, p. 18.
Position	Partners face.
Steps	Step hop, balance, waltz.

DIRECTIONS FOR THE DANCE

Music 6/8   NOTE: Directions are for man; lady's part reverse, except when specially noted.

MEASURES

1–2	Clap own hands, clap partner's right hand, clap partner's left hand, clap both hands of partner.
3–4	Join hands outstretched shoulder height. Both beginning left, take four step hops turning clockwise.
1–4	Repeat action of measures 1–4.
5–6	Partners face, right hands joined. Beginning left, man takes four waltz steps in line of direction while lady, beginning right, turns clockwise twice under her right arm with four waltz steps.
7–8	Closed position. Take four waltz steps turning clockwise.
5–8	Repeat action of measures 5–8.
9	Couple position. Beginning left, balance away from partner and balance toward partner, progressing in line of direction.
10	Beginning left, take two waltz steps making one complete turn away from partner, progressing in line of direction.
11–12	Repeat action of measures 9–10 moving forward.
13–16	Partners face reverse line of direction, inside hands joined. Beginning right, repeat action of measures 9–12, moving in reverse line of direction.

References in Bibliography: 30 (Vol. I, p. 18), 33 (p. 35), 54 (p. 140), 65 (p. 95).
Dance annotation form © 1948 by the Folk Dance Federation of California.

BITTE MAND I KNIBE
(Little Man in a Fix)
Danish

A very popular little dance, both in Denmark and all over United States. Knibe means to be in a "spot" or "fix."

Music   Record: Aqua Viking V400; Folk Dancer MH 1054; Tanz 58401.

                Piano: Burchenal, E., *Folk Dances of Denmark*, p. 44, and *Folk Dances from Old Homelands*, p. 62. La Salle, D., *Rhythms and Dances for Elementary Schools*, p. 115.

Formation   Two couples, lady to right of partner. Men hook left elbows and place right arm around partner's waist, ladies place left hand on man's left shoulder.

Steps   Run, tyrolian waltz, waltz.

DIRECTIONS FOR THE DANCE

Music 3/4   NOTE: Directions are same for man and lady, except when specially noted.

MEASURES

I. Run Around

1–8   Beginning left, take small running steps forward, moving counterclockwise.

1–8   As *running steps are continued*, men grasp left hands and raise left arms, holding ladies' left hand with their right and two ladies move under arch and pass each other. Ladies turn counterclockwise to face center, men lower left arms and ladies grasp each other's right hand on top of men's left hand grasp. All four continue to take small running steps, moving counterclockwise.

II. Tyrolian Waltz

9–12   Men release left hand, ladies right. The two couples turn back to back. Each couple takes couple position, inside hands shoulder height, outside hand on hip, thumb pointing backward, fingers forward. Man beginning left, lady right, take four tyrolian waltz steps moving forward (away from the other couple). Arms reach forward and draw back with each step. They do not swing forward.

13–16   Closed position. Man beginning left, lady right, take four waltz steps, turning clockwise, progressing in line of direction.

9–16   Repeat action of measures 9–16.

Note: As the dance repeats, each couple dances with another couple. If a couple cannot find a couple for the first figure, they are *in a fix!* They go to the center and dance the running steps alone, with two hands joined. The next time the man will avoid being the *man in a fix* by hooking arms with another couple quickly for the first figure.

References in Bibliography: 6 (p. 32), 13 (p. 63), 14 (Vol. I, p. 7), 65 (p. 118), 69 (p. 115), 82 (p. 371).

BRANDISWALZER *
Swiss

Brandis is a small town in Switzerland. This lilting dance is a medley of four waltz figures common to many cantons in Switzerland. It is one of the rare Swiss dances that have no set melody. Louise Huggler of Brienz, Canton Bern, presented this dance at the 14th Annual Folk Camp, Canton Bern, Switzerland, in 1953. Then Jane Farwell introduced this dance across the United States at many folk dance camps, institutes and workshops.

Music	Record: Folk Dancer MH 1113
	Piano: Farwell, Jane, *Folk Dancing for Fun*, p. 32.
Position	Couple, inside hands joined, held at shoulder height, free hands (knuckles) on hips, facing line of direction.
Steps	Waltz, step swing, step hop.

DIRECTIONS FOR THE DANCE

Music 3/4 NOTE: Directions are for man; Lady's part reverse.

MEASURES

I. Open Waltz and Waltz Turn

1   Beginning left, take one waltz step forward, swinging joined hands forward. (A series of waltz steps in the line of direction is sometimes referred to as "open waltz.")

2   Take one waltz step forward, swinging hands back, turning toward partner.

3–4   Turning toward partner to face reverse line of direction, release joined hands and join man's left with lady's right, free hands on hips and take two waltz steps backwards in line of direction.

5–8   Shoulder waist position. Take four waltz steps turning clockwise, progressing in line of direction.

9–16   Repeat action of measures 1–8.

VI

II. Step-Swing and Waltz

1   Man's back to center, partners facing, join two hands. Beginning left, step and swing right foot across left, close to floor, swinging both arms forward.

2   Repeat action of measure 1 in opposite direction.

3–4   Place hands on hips. Take two waltz steps turning away from each other (man counterclockwise, lady clockwise) progressing in line of direction.

5–8   Closed position. Beginning left, take four waltz steps, turning clockwise, progressing in line of direction.

9–16   Repeat action of Figure II, measures 1–8.

* This dance was arranged from the dance as written by Jane Farwell, *Folk Dances For Fun*, Cooperative Recreation Service, Inc., Delaware, Ohio.
References in Bibliography: 34 (p. 33), 99 (Apr. 1955, p. 13).

MEASURES

III. Step Hop and Waltz

17–18　　Couple position, lady holding man's right forefinger with her left hand, free hands on hips. Joined hands held above head. Beginning left, take two step hops, swinging joined hands forward and backwards.

19–20　　Take one step hop, then one waltz step, man moves forward, lady turns clockwise under upraised right arm of partner.

21–24　　Shoulder-waist position. Beginning left, take four waltz steps turning clockwise, progressing in line of direction.

23–32　　Repeat action of measures 17–24.

IV. Waltz

17–22　　Closed position, man's left, lady's right arms slightly extended. Beginning left, take six waltz steps, turning clockwise, progressing in line of direction. On sixth waltz step, man places lady's right hand in middle of her back, releases it, and takes her right hand in his left.

23–24　　Take two waltz steps, lady turning away from her partner clockwise once, man dancing in place and guiding lady in her turn. Release hands as lady faces man and resume closed position.

25–32　　Repeat action of Figure IV measures 17–24.

STYLE:
Free hands are always placed on hips, knuckles toward the body. The steps are simple and quiet movement.

CABALLITO BLANCO
Mexican

Caballito Blanco is a Mexican variation on a Portuguese melody. It means "little white flower." This dance was introduced by Helen Erfer, Los Angeles, California.

Music	Record: *Fado Blanquito*, Folkraft 1173X45, Standard T 124*, Decca 2164*. Piano: *Caballito Blanco* by Retana, published by Edward B. Marks.
Formation	Couples in a line, lady in front of man, all face forward. Lady crosses arms, left arm right, shoulder height. Man grasps lady's right hand with his left, lady's left hand with his right.
Steps	Step hop, walk, buzz step, dos-a-dos, jump hop.

DIRECTIONS FOR THE DANCE

Music 4/4   NOTE: Directions are same for both man and lady, except when specially noted.

MEASURES

Introduction

1–3 Man gives lady slight pull with his right hand to start lady turning clockwise, and then releases both hands. Lady beginning right, takes six step hops turning clockwise, moving forward away from man. Man with hands clasped low behind him sways slightly with music in place. Dancers move about six to eight feet apart.

4 Partners face. Beginning right, stamp lightly in place, right, left, right (cts. 1–2–3) and hold (ct. 4).

5–8 Beginning left, partners pass right shoulders stepping left (cts. 1–2, slow), right (cts. 3–4, slow), left (ct. 1, quick), right (ct. 2, quick), left (cts. 3–4, slow). Beginning right, partners continue on past each other to opposite positions stepping right (cts. 1–2, slow), left (cts. 3–4, slow), right (ct. 1, quick), left (ct. 2, quick), right (cts. 3–4, slow), and face partner on last step.

Vamp

1 Beginning right, man slaps thigh four times alternating right, left, (cts. 1 and 2 and), slaps hands twice (cts. 3–4). Lady holding skirt lightly in front with two hands, steps right in place, points left toe in front of right, steps left, points right toe in front of left. *Note:* Although lady has weight on right foot at end of measure 8, she must shift weight quickly to left so that she may step *right* here in measure 1.

2 Repeat action of measure 1, Vamp.

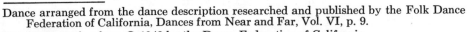

Dance arranged from the dance description researched and published by the Folk Dance Federation of California, Dances from Near and Far, Vol. VI, p. 9.
Dance annotation form © 1948 by the Dance Federation of California.
* Out of print.

MEASURES

Figure I. Long Fado Step, Buzz Step, Turn

A 1   Man clasps hands behind him. Lady holds skirt with two hands. Beginning right, take six step hops in the following pattern: Step diagonally right (ct. 1), hop right (ct. 2), step left in front right (ct. 3), hop left (ct. 4). Left shoulders are forward when left foot is in front, right foot is raised behind. Partners look back at each other over own shoulder.

2   Step right behind left (ct. 1), hop right (ct. 2), step left diagonally left (ct. 3), hop left (ct. 4).

3   Step right in front of left (ct. 1), hop right (ct. 2), step left behind (ct. 3), hop left (ct. 4). Right shoulders are forward when right foot is in front, left foot is raised behind. Partners look back at each other over own shoulder. *Note:* The above three measures, six step hops, represent *one* fado step.

4–9   Repeat action of measures 1–3 two times.

10   Repeat action of measure 1.

11–13   Beginning right, each take six slow buzz steps, turning clockwise, three complete turns. Finish facing partner.

14   Stamp in place, right, left, right (cts. 1–2–3) and hold (ct. 4).

Figure II. Jump Hop Step

B 1   Jump to stride position, knees bent, toes turned out, heels about two-three inches apart (ct. 1), hop onto left straightening left leg and point right toe in front of left toe, right knee turning outward (ct. 2). Repeat action of counts 1 and 2, hopping on right and pointing left toe down in front of right toe (cts. 3–4).

2   Jump to stride position (ct. 1), hop left three times, turning clockwise one, right knee bent (cts. 2–3–4).

3–4   Repeat action of measures 1–2, hopping onto right foot, then left, and hopping on right, turning counterclockwise.

5–8   Beginning left, partners repeat action of measures 5–8 in Introduction, passing right shoulders to exchange places.

9–12   Repeat action of measures B 1–4.

13–16   Partners do a do-sa-do, passing right shoulders first, with step pattern of measures 5–8. On last step, man turns one quarter turn left, lady one quarter turn right. Partners are now side by side facing same direction and right angles to original position. Lady on man's right.

Figure III. Short Fado Step

C 1–3   Skater position. Beginning right, take one fado step (six step hops) as described in Figure I, measures 1–3.

4   Stamp in place right, left, right, and hold.

5–8   Beginning left, repeat action of measures C 1–4.

MEASURES

Vamp

1–2   Partners face. Repeat action of Vamp, (measures 1–2), moving backwards till about six to eight feet apart.

A   1–14   Figure I. **Long Fado Step**
Beginning right, repeat action of measures A 1–14.

B   1–16   Figure II. **Jump+Hop Step** (without do-sa-do)
Repeat action of measures B 1–16, omitting do-sa-do in measures 13–16. Instead man and lady change places.

C   1–8   Figure III. **Short Fado Step** (opposite each other)
Partners face and are several feet apart. Beginning right, repeat action of Figure I, measures C 1–8.

B   1–16   Figure II.   **Jump Hop Step**
Repeat action of II, measures B 1–16. On do-sa-do in measures 13–16 partners *end* side by side, lady on man's right, facing same direction and at left angles to original position. Since dancers started from opposite positions, they will face opposite end of hall this time.

C   1–18   Figure III.   **Short Fado Step**
Skater position. Repeat action of Figure I, measures C 1–8. On last stamp sequence, lean away from partner to pose, still maintaining skater position.

NOTE:

1. One Fado step is equal to six step hops. When this is done once it is the Short Fado. When done three times, it is the Long Fado.

2. Whenever the man's and lady's hands are free, the man places hands behind his back, held together low. The lady holds her skirt in front with two hands.

3. When the man and lady change places on the do-sa-do, the style is that of a stroll with a flirtatious air with partner.

4. *Teaching suggestions:* The dance is essentially simple, consisting of an Introduction, Vamp, and three Figures. The dance has been adjusted slightly in order to fit the record, Standard T 124.

5. *Routine:* Introduction
     Vamp
     Figure I
     Figure II
     Figure III
     Vamp
     Figure I
     Figure II   (without do-sa-do)
     Figure III   (opposite each other)
     Figure II
     Figure III

CALL TO THE PIPER
Scottish

Frank Kaltman learned this dance from Mr. Armstrong at Pinewoods about 1954. In the absence of the specific tune. they selected the tune "Ab Schenken" as a desirable one. Through the Folkraft recording, Frank Kaltman has introduced this charming dance to the American public.

Music	Record: Folkraft 1065X45.
Position	Varsouvianna.
Steps	Walk, pas-de-basque.

DIRECTIONS FOR THE DANCE

Music 2/4   NOTE: Directions are same for man and lady except when specially noted.

MEASURES

I. Walk

1–2 Beginning right, take four walking steps in line of direction. This is a very proud walk, foot brushing floor slightly with each step.

3–4 Beginning right, brush foot forward lightly (ct. 1), back across left foot (ct. 2), forward (ct. 1), and step in place (ct. 2).

5–8 Beginning left, repeat action of measures 1–4. On last count release hands and face partner.

II. Pas-de-basque

9–12 Beginning right, take four pas-de-basque steps, which carry them around a square and at same time around each other.

1. First pas-de-basque, beginning right, making one quarter turn right and end facing out. This puts man and lady back to back.

2. Second pas-de-basque, beginning left, backward and turn one quarter turn right again to face partner. Now dancers are opposite from original starting position.

3. Repeat action of first pas-de-basque, ending back to back on third side of square.

4. Repeat action of second pas-de-basque, ending in starting position face to face.

(Continued next page)

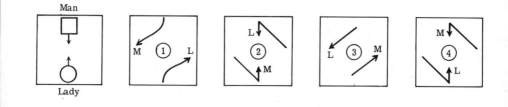

Dance arranged from the dance description by Folkraft Records, Frank Kaltman.
Dance annotation form © 1948 by the Dance Federation of California.

MEASURES

13–14	Partners facing, join right hands. Beginning right take one pas-de-basque right and one pas-de-basque left.
15–16	Man walks four steps in line of direction while turning lady under joined right arms. Lady takes four steps turning clockwise once. Assume original dance positions.

NOTE:

1. This dance has tremendous dignity.

2. *Teaching suggestion for pas-de-basque:* Practice pas-de-basque individually, forward beginning right and backward, left. Then practice step individually to turn going around a square. Finally try it with a partner.

CIRCLE FROM SARID
Israeli

This dance was taught at Oglebay Folk Dance Camp, Wheeling, West Virginia, 1948. It is based on the Jewish Folk Dance Album by Miss Katya Delakava and Mr. Fred Berk, Ultra Album U-6.

Music	Record: Folk Dancer MH 1053.
Formation	Single circle, arms resting on shoulders of person on either side.
Steps	Jump.

DIRECTIONS FOR THE DANCE

Music 4/4   NOTE: Directions are same for both lady and man.

MEASURES

1   Beginning right, step forward as the left foot comes off the floor, step left backward, step right in place, hold.

2   Jump (debka) to right, feet together, bending knees. Jump to left.

3   Beginning right, step forward as the left foot comes off the floor, step left backward, step right backward with the left foot coming off the floor, step left forward.

4   Step right forward as left foot comes off floor, step left backward, bring right to left, weight remains on left, hold last beat.

5–8   Repeat action of measures 1–4.

9   Beginning right, step forward, step back left, step back right, step back left.

10   Travel backward, right, left, right (cts. 1–2–3, hold ct. 4). Circle enlarges as arms slide away from shoulders until hands are grasped, arms extended shoulder height.

11–12   Beginning left, step to side, step right behind left. Repeat this step two times. Then step left and hop left. Circle moves clockwise.

13–14   Beginning right, step to side, step left behind right. Repeat this step three times. Circle moves counterclockwise.

15–16   Beginning right, step forward and draw the left to right. Repeat draw step three times, end with weight on left foot. The arms gradually slide back to original position as circle diminishes in size.

Dance annotation form © 1948 by the Dance Federation of California.

CORRIDO
Mexican

This dance was introduced to the California Folk Dance Federation by Avis Landis, a former member of the Research Committee of the California Folk Dance Federation. The Corrido is actually a folk ballad. Several steps are commonly done spontaneously to this type of music, namely, soldado, grapevine, and the side close step. The dance was learned in California by the authors.

Music	Record: Star 8412; Folkraft 1485X45.
	Piano: California Folk Dance Federation Reference II, Vol. IV (p. 1).
Position	Closed, man's back to center of circle.
Steps	Step-close, grapevine, shuffle.

DIRECTIONS FOR THE DANCE

Music 4/4   NOTE: Directions are for man; lady's part reverse.
MEASURES

Part I

I. **Step-close**

A 1–5 Beginning right, take ten step-close steps in reverse line of direction.

II. **Grapevine**

B 1–7 Beginning right, take seven grapevine steps (crossing in front first) in line of direction.

8 Step right across in front of left, stamp left, stamp right in place, and hold.

III. **Step-close and Soldado**

C 9–10 Beginning right, take four step-close steps in reverse line of direction.

11 Beginning right, take four shuffle steps (soldado), couples moving diagonally to center of circle. (Man moves backward, lady forward).

12 Take four shuffle steps (soldado) moving diagonally away from center of circle to man's left.

13–17 Repeat action of measures 11–12 five times, progressing forward in line of direction while moving diagonally in and out of circle.

18 Moving away from center of circle, step forward on right, stamp left, stamp right, and hold.

IV. **Grapevine**

B 1–18 Repeat action of measures 1–8, Part I.

Part II

I. **Step-close**

A 1–5 Repeat action of measures 1–5, A, Part I.

References in Bibliography: 14 (Vol. IV, p. 1), 65 (p. 112).
Dance annotation form © 1948 by the Folk Dance Federation of California.

MEASURES

II. Cross-step with One Turn

B 1 Partners face, man's hands clasped behind back, lady's skirt held out to side. Beginning right, moving in line of direction, step right across in front of left (accent), left coming off floor in back (ct. 1), step left in place (ct. 2), step right in place (ct. 3), cross left in front of right, right coming off floor in back (ct. 4).

2 Starting a full turn, step right behind left (ct. 1), step left in place, pivoting counterclockwise to face away from partner (ct. 2), step right to side, pivoting counterclockwise to face partner (ct. 3), step left, facing partner (ct. 4).

3–6 Repeat action of measures 1–2, B, Part II, twice.

7 Repeat action of measure 1, B, Part II.

8 Step right across in front of left, stamp left, stamp right in place, and hold.

III. Step-Close and Soldado

C 9–18 Repeat action of measures 9–18, C, Part I.

IV. Grapevine with Two Turns

B 1–7 Partner's face, right hands joined at shoulder height, man's left placed behind back, lady's right holds skirt. Beginning right, moving in line of direction, man takes seven grapevine steps. Lady takes one grapevine step (measure 1), and four steps turning clockwise twice under man's right arm (measure 2). Lady repeats this action twice, and takes one grapevine step on measure 7.

8 Step right across in front of left, stamp left, stamp right in place, and hold.

Part III

I. Step-close

A 1–5 Repeat action of measures 1–5, A, Part I.

II. Grapevine

B 1–8 Repeat action of measures 1–8, B, Part I.

III. Step-close and Soldado

C 9–18 Repeat action of measures 9–18, C, Part I.

IV. Grapevine

B 1–7 Inside hands joined, held at shoulder height and man's left hand placed behind back, lady's right holds skirt. Beginning right, take seven grapevine steps in line of direction. Dancers turn toward and away from each other as lady alternately holds skirt out to side and then folds it across the front of her body with the action of the grapevine steps.

8 Step right across in front of left, stamp left, stamp right in place and hold.

DEN TOPPEDE HØNE
(The Crested Hen)
Danish

Den Toppede Høne means "The Crested Hen" referring to the fact that in Denmark the men wore red stocking caps with a tassel representing his rooster comb. The ladies added to the fun of the dance by trying to pull the man's cap off as he went through the arch. If successful, then the lady became "crested" hen.

Music	Record:	Folkraft 1159, 1194; RCA Victor 45-6176; Tanz 58 402; Victor EPA 4143; World of Fun M 108.
	Piano:	Burchenal, Elizabeth, *Folk Dances of Denmark*, p. 49. LaSalle, Dorothy, *Rhythms and Dances for Elementary Schools*, p. 150. Neilson, N. P., and Van Hagen, W., *Physical Education for Elementary Schools*, p. 300.
Formation		Set of three, two ladies and a man, hands joined to form a circle.
Step		Step hop.

DIRECTIONS FOR THE DANCE

Music 2/4   NOTE: Directions are same for both lady and man.

MEASURES

A   1–8   I. Beginning left, step hop around circle clockwise, taking a vigorous stamp on first beat. Dancers lean away from center as they circle.

1–8   Jump, bringing feet down sharply on first beat, step hop around circle counterclockwise.

B   9–10   II. Continuing step hop, ladies release joined hands, place free hand on hip, and right hand lady dances through arch made by man and left hand lady.

11–12   Man turns under his left arm, following right hand lady through arch.

13–14   Left hand lady dances through arch made by man and right hand lady.

15–16   Man turns under his right arm, following left hand lady through arch.

9–16   Repeat action of measures 9–16.

MIXER:
The man may progress forward to the next group at the completion of Part II.

References in Bibliography: 12 (p. 49), 14 (Vol. I, p. 5), 26 (p. 49), 32 (p. 44), 33 (p. 21), 54 (p. 104), 69 (p. 150), 82 (p. 300).
Dance annotation form © 1948 by the Folk Dance Federation of California.

DJURDJEVKA KOLO
Yugoslavian

Music	Record: Folk Dancer MH 1011; RCA Victor EPA 4130 or LPM 1620.
Formation	Broken circle, joined hands held down.
Step	Walk.

DIRECTIONS FOR THE DANCE

Music 2/4   NOTE: Directions are same for both lady and man.

MEASURES

I. Walking

1–4 Beginning right, take eight walking steps in line of direction. Circle moves counterclockwise.

5–8 Beginning right, take eight walking steps in reverse line of direction.

II. Pointing

9–10 Beginning right, point right in front of left. Point right to side. Point right in front of left. Place (step) right beside left, take weight on right.

11–12 Beginning left, repeat action of measures 9–10.

13–14 Beginning right, repeat action of measures 9–10.

15–16 Beginning left, repeat action of measures 9–10.

NOTE:

1. The walking steps are very short, weight heavy on heel, bend knee to produce bouncing or jigging effect.

2. In Part II, when pointing, give a slight rhythmic lift on the supporting foot.

3. *Variation for Part II*. A backward skip may be substituted for or alternated with the Pointing. *Backward Skip:* Place right behind left, hop on right and at same time chug right slightly forward to displace left, lift left off floor. Repeat beginning left behind right. Actually a "step-hop" beginning each time by placing foot behind supporting foot. Dancer remains in same place. The dancer *does not* travel backward, during backward skip.

DOUDLEBSKA POLKA
Czechoslovakian

Doudlebska polka, pronounced *Doo-dleb-ska*, is a simple mixer learned in Czechoslovakia by Jeannette Novak and introduced to American folk dancers through Folk Dance House, New York.

Music	Record: Folk Dancer MH 3016, Educational Dance Recordings FD-2; Folkraft 1413, 1413X45, LP-13.
Formation	Couples in closed position form one large circle or several smaller circles. Directions are for one large circle.
Steps	Polka, walk.

DIRECTIONS FOR THE DANCE

Music 2/4   NOTE: The directions are for man, lady's part reverse.
MEASURES
  1–4

Introduction

    I. **Polka**

1–16   Beginning left, take sixteen polka steps turning clockwise, traveling in line of direction.

    II. **Walk and Circle**

17–32   Open position, lady's free hand on hip. Man stretches left arm out to place hand on left shoulder of man in front as couples take thirty-two walking steps moving in line of direction. This action moves dancers toward center to form a ring of couples. As ring revolves counterclockwise, everyone sings "tra-la-la, etc."

    III. **Men Clap, Ladies Circle**

33–48   Men face center of circle and clap hands throughout figure as follows: Clap own hands (ct. 1), clap own hands (ct. and), clap hands of man on both sides, shoulder high (ct. 2). Ladies with hands on hips, take one half turn clockwise to face reverse line of direction and take sixteen polka steps, progressing forward in reverse line of direction around men's circle.

On last measure, each lady steps behind a man, and men turn around and begin dance again with new partner.

VARIATION:

1. Measures 1–16, for beginners a heavy two-step and the Varsouvianna position or inside hands joined may be substituted.
2. Measures 33–48, the men may slap a thigh occasionally, duck down, or cross their own hands over when they clap neighbors' hands.
3. Measures 17–32, if group is large, form several small circles.
4. Measures 33–48, if more than one circle is formed, ladies may "cheat" by moving from one circle to another.

References in Bibliography: 15 (Vol. A-2, p. 10), 65 (p. 138), 72 (p. 170).

Dance arranged from the dance description by Michael Herman and reproduced by permission of Folk Dance House, 108 West 16th Street, New York City, New York.

Dance annotation form © 1948 by the Folk Dance Federation of California.

NOTE:

1. Those without partners go to the center (the "lost and found" department) and meet the other one without a partner.

2. If there are extra people, extra men without a partner may join dance during star figure, and extra ladies may join ring as ladies polka around outside.

3. Encourage group singing during the march, especially loud. It makes the dance fun!

DR GSATZLIG
Swiss

Dr Gsatzlig means "exactly" and is from Appenzell in Switzerland. Jane Farwell learned this dance there and introduced it across the United States in 1954. Later Jane corrected one of the figures slightly, which accounts for two different versions. Although the music is written in 2/4 meter, it has the quality of a schottische.

Music	Record: Folk Dancer MH 1114.
	Piano: L. Witzig and A. Stern Pub. Hug and Co., Zurich *12 Schweitzer Tanze.*
Position	Closed, man's back to center of circle, man's left, lady's right arms extended towards line of direction.
Steps	Side step, schottische.

DIRECTIONS FOR THE DANCE

Music 2/4   NOTE: Directions are for man; lady's part reverse.

MEASURES

	1–4		**Introduction**

		I.	**Dr Gsatzlig** (side step)
A	1–2		Beginning left, take four side steps forward, moving in line of direction.
	3		Take two side steps in reverse line of direction, swinging joined hands sharply down, elbow bending, upper arm shoulder high.
	4		Take two side steps in line of direction, arms extended toward line of direction. Joined hands always point in the direction travelling.
	5–8		Beginning right, repeat action of measures 1–4, travelling in reverse line of direction.
A	1–8		Repeat action of measures 1–8.

		II.	**Heel and Toe Schottische**
B	9		Closed position. Beginning left, take one heel and toe.
	10		Take one step-close-step-close in line of direction. Weight remains on left.
	11–12		Swinging joined hands sharply down, elbow bending, upper arm shoulder high, face reverse line of direction. Beginning right, repeat action of measures 9–10, moving in reverse line of direction.
	13–16		Closed or shoulder waist position (latter preferred). Beginning left, take four slow two steps (Swiss schottische steps) turning clockwise, progressing in line of direction.

References in Bibliography: 15 (p. 31), 72 (p. 149).
Dance arranged from the dance description by Jane Farwell.
Dance annotation form © 1948 by the Folk Dance Federation of California.

MEASURES

B 9–16   Repeat action of measures 9–16.

III. Dr Gsatzlig (side step)

A 1–8   Repeat action of Figure I, measures 1–8.

IV. Schottische

C 17–18   Man faces line of direction, crossed arms held on chest; lady faces man, back to line of direction, hands on hips, knuckles toward the body. Beginning left, take two schottische steps (step-close-step hop) (Swiss polka) in line of direction. Both move diagonally toward center, then away from center, always progressing forward.

    19–20   Take four slow step hops in line of direction, man stamping left on first step, lady turning clockwise twice.

    21–24   Repeat action of measures 17–20.

C 17–24   Repeat action of measures 17–24, with right hands joined, free hand on hip. The lady turns clockwise under man's raised arm.

V. Dr Gsatzlig

A 1–8   Repeat action of measures 1–8.

ROUTINE:
AABBACCAABBACCA. The record, Folk Dancer MH 1114, allows for this sequence.

STYLE:
The Swiss dance movements are small and precise. Keep the steps simple without much extension of the knee or foot. The side steps are little steps; do not scrape the foot, but lift each foot. Turn head and focus eyes on the direction of travel during the side steps. The abrupt change of direction and focus of a large group is very effective. Keep free hands on hips. Keep step hops low and subdued. Jane Farwell refers to it as a *leisurely dance*.

NOTE:

1. It is fun to sing "la-la-la" during the specific tune for Dr Gsatzlig.

2. Add a few shouts "ya'hoo'hoo'hooy" anytime.

3. In Switzerland they call a polka a schottische and a schottische a polka. Since this book is used primarily by Americans, the terms schottische and polka as defined by Americans are used.

EL BAILE DEL PALO
Guam

El Baile Del Palo translated literally means the "Dance Stick." El Baile Del Palo or the Guam Stick Dance, as it is commonly referred to since its introduction in this country, is done by two dancers. Each dancer holds two sticks, one in each hand, and in a rhythmic staccato of sharp striking sounds, they dance about each other alternately striking the ground, their own sticks, and those of their partner. As the dance progresses, the dancers assume more difficult and unique positions around which they rhythmically demonstrate their nimbleness and great sense of timing to produce an exciting and beautifully coordinated series of figures. The significance and meaning of the dance has been lost over the long period of time consumed by passing it from one generation to another.

The dance was brought to this country and introduced on the campus of Arizona State University, Tempe, Arizona, by Mr. Juan C. Guerrero, a student, from Barrigada Village, Guam. The dance was learned by Mr. Guerrero from members of his family. Mr. Guerrero, with the assistance of Miss Anne Pittman of the Women's Physical Education Department, arranged the dance notations which appear here in published form for the first time.

In Barrigada Village the dance is equally shared and enjoyed by women as well as men dancers, though the striking action and direction of the sticks make it more readily appropriate for men dancers. Couples may be comprised of two men, a man and lady, or two ladies. The modern Barrigada woman simply slips on a pair of slacks and joins in the fun. The wearing of slacks or shorts is advisable or the whole action of the dance will lose its effectiveness.

Music . . . The rhythmic sound of the striking of the sticks provides the music for El Baile Del Palo. The soft strumming of a guitar often accompanies the dance but is background music in reality. Mr. Guerrero says the tune sometimes used sounds very much like our Varsouvianna or Put Your Little Foot. The striking of sticks is very effective alone. The count is an even 4/4 meter rhythm. It is quite possible to perform the sequence of figures in 3/4 time by double striking sticks each time the directions call for the dancer to *cross strike own sticks.*

Sticks . . . The sticks should be thirty inches long. Longer sticks may be used depending on the height of the dancer. Sticks should be at least one-half inch thick and preferably round and smooth. Dowel rods, readily available at hardware and lumber supply stores, make excellent sticks for this dance. Dowel rods come in various widths and generally one piece four feet long cut in half makes a very suitable and inexpensive pair of sticks. From a safety point of view, the one-half inch thick dowel rod is much more sturdy and will break less frequently under constant use. In addition to the safety factor, it also produces a sharper and more audible sound, thus giving the dance its basic charm and effectiveness.

Position . . . Couples stand side by side facing forward. The dancer on the left is the *lead* dancer. The *lead* dancer is responsible for cuing and counting repeats in each figure as well as throughout the dance. The *lead dancer* is referred to as *A* and the partner as *B*.

SPECIAL NOTES ON PERFORMANCE

1. At all times the sticks must be struck together sharply! Each dancer must *swing*, not *hold*, the stick so that each count or beat makes a sound. Make free use of wrist action in operating the sticks.

2. Body weight should shift naturally and easily with the action of the sticks. There is no set foot pattern to follow when dancers move around each other with walking steps; they simply move naturally and smoothly with the rhythm and action of the dance. Jerky motions and undue emphasis on *getting in position on the turns* tends to distract attention from the very intricate and effective action made by the sticks.

3. Distance between dancers at all times should be sufficient to allow for easy striking. Undue reaching causes the dancers to look stiff and off balance. The distance between the dancers is the length of stick between outside of feet.

4. The *dance sequence is continuous from one figure to the other*, therefore it is best to practice and learn a figure for at least two counts beyond the end of that particular figure in order to get the transition from one figure to the next. Perfect this much before adding another figure. In this way the dance becomes progressively easier to do.

5. *A's* stick is swung parallel with tip slightly up. *B's* stick is held at an angle and is swung so that it makes an arc downward.

6. In general, right hand stick should cross over left hand stick except where the crossing seems awkward or unnatural.

7. Dancers strike the ground with ends of sticks. When striking ground, sticks are parallel to each other and at forty-five degree angle with striking surface.

.8. If one wishes to shorten the dance, omit K through N in Figure V.

Figure I. STRIKE GROUND, CROSS STRIKE STICKS

Dancers strike the ground with ends of sticks. When striking ground, sticks are parallel to each other and at forty-five degree angle with striking surface. Dancers then *cross* and *strike* their *own sticks*. The sticks are clearly off the ground for cross strike own sticks. The body is slightly bent forward during the routine. *Do not stand up to cross strike own sticks*. Sticks barely leave the floor to cross. The action is similar to "cross sticks" in hockey. Action as follows:

Count 1 Strike ground
Count 2 Cross strike own sticks

Count 3 Strike ground
Count 4 Cross strike own sticks
Count 5 Strike ground
Count 6 Cross strike own sticks
Count 7 Strike ground
Count 8 Cross strike own sticks

Figure II. LEG SWING, CROSS STRIKE

Dancers swing right leg forward and cross strike sticks under right leg. Stand erect and cross strike sticks in front of body below waist line. Swing left leg forward and cross strike sticks under left leg. Action as follows:

Count 1 Swing right leg forward, cross strike sticks under right leg.
Count 2 Stand erect, cross strike sticks in front of body below waist line.
Count 3 Swing left leg forward, cross strike sticks under left leg.
Count 4 Stand erect, cross strike sticks in front of body below waist line.
Count 5 Stand erect, swing sticks behind hips and cross strike.
Count 6 Stand erect, swing sticks in front of body and cross strike.
Count 7 Strike near stick of partner. As strike is made, *A* makes half turn clockwise to face opposite direction. Dancers are now standing side by side with left shoulders almost touching. NOTE: *A* holds stick parallel to surface as *B* holds stick *up* at slight angle.
Count 8 Cross strike own sticks.

Figure III. ALTERNATE LEFT AND RIGHT SHOULDER IN OPPOSITION

Dancers step sideways overlapping back of inside legs and strike partner's stick as it swings through between their own legs. Step back into position and cross strike own sticks. Strike partner's near stick, then cross strike own sticks. Dancers step sideways again into a back to back position, swinging their sticks down and out to their right and left sides respectively to contact partner's stick. Again they step back into position and cross strike own stick. Strike partner's near stick as both dancers turn to face in opposite direction, ending Figure III, Part A, with right shoulders in opposition ready to repeat action as described in Figure III, Part B. Illustrations below are for Figure III, Part A, showing the turn on count 8 to begin Part B.

A. Partners stand side by side, left shoulders in opposition

Count 1 Step to own left into stride position, strike sticks between knees. NOTE: Swing right hand stick between own knees; swing left hand stick through partner's knees from behind.

Count 2 Step to own right, cross strike own sticks.

Count 3 Strike near stick of partner. NOTE: A holds stick parallel to surface as B holds stick "up" at slight angle.

Count 4 Cross strike own sticks.

Count 5 Step to own left, stand erect in a back to back position. Swing sticks down and to the right and left sides of body to contact partner's sticks below waist level.

Count 6 Step to own right into position, cross strike own sticks.

Count 7 Strike near stick of partner. As this strike is made both dancers make half turn counter-clockwise, ending right shoulders in opposition.

Count 8 Cross strike own sticks.

B. Partners stand side by side, right shoulders in opposition

Count 1 Step to own right into stride position, strike sticks between knees. NOTE: Swing left hand stick between own knees; swing right hand stick through partner's knees from behind.

Count 2 Step to own left, cross strike own sticks.

Count 3 Strike near stick of partner. NOTE: A holds stick parallel to surface as B holds stick up at slight angle.

Count 4 Cross strike own sticks.

Count 5 Step to own right, stand erect in a back to back position. Swing sticks down and to right and left sides of body to contact partner's sticks below waist level.

Count 6 Step left into position, cross strike own sticks.

Count 7 Strike near stick of partner. As strike is made both dancers make half turn clockwise, ending left shoulders in opposition.

Count 8 Cross strike own sticks.

C. Partners stand side by side, left shoulders in opposition

Counts 1-8 Repeat action as described in Part A of this figure.

D. Partners stand side by side, right shoulders in opposition

Figure IV. WALK, STRIKE, CIRCLE COUNTERCLOCKWISE

Dancers circle counterclockwise around each other and back to original positions by walking in semi-crouched position as they take measured "cat-like" steps. They strike sticks to ground, cross strike own sticks, and hit partner's near stick as they circle each other. The walk should be smooth and even as the dancers follow the natural rhythm and action of the beats. Three repeats of action of counts 1 to 4 will place dancers back in original positions. Action as follows:

Count 1 Strike end of sticks to ground.

Count 2 Cross strike own sticks.

Count 3 Strike near stick of partner.

Count 4 Cross strike own sticks.

Repeat action of Counts 1 to 4 twice.

Beginning the third repeat, the action is as follows:

Count 1 Couples side by side, left shoulders in opposition. A kneels on right knee as sticks strike ground. B remains standing as sticks strike ground.

Count 2 Cross strike own sticks.

Count 3 Strike near stick of partner. NOTE: A holds sticks up at slight angle as B swings stick parallel to surface for strike.

Count 4 Cross strike own sticks.

Figure V. KNEEL, STRIKE, TURN, STRIKE

Couples maintain position, *A* kneeling on right knee, *B* standing erect with left side toward *A*. *A* should kneel facing toward *B's* left side for best results in executing action required. Action as follows:

A. *A kneels and faces B's left side*

Count 1 *A* swings left stick parallel and across in back of *B's* legs, as *B* steps slightly sideways left into stride position and swings right hand stick down between knees to contact *A's* stick.

Count 2 Cross strike own sticks.

Count 3 Strike near stick of partner.

Count 4 Cross strike own sticks.

Count 5 *A* swings left stick parallel across in back of and to outside of *B's* legs, as *B* steps slightly sideways left and swings right stick down to right of body to contact *A's* stick. NOTE: This contact is made outside and slightly back of *B's* right knee.

Count 6 Cross strike own sticks.

Count 7 Strike near stick of partner. As strike is made *B* makes half turn counterclockwise to face opposite direction. *A* remains in kneeling position but may shift slightly to left for greater comfort.

Count 8 Cross strike own sticks.

B. *A kneels and faces B's right side*

Count 1 *A* swings right stick parallel and across in back of *B's* legs, as *B* steps slightly sideways right into strike position and swings left hand stick down and between knees to contact *A's* stick.

Count 2 Cross strike own sticks.

Count 3 Strike near stick of partner.

Count 4 Cross strike own sticks.

Count 5 *A* swings right stick parallel across in back of and to outside of *B's* legs, as *B* steps slightly sideways right and swings left stick down to right of body to contact *A's* stick. NOTE: This contact is

Count 1

Count 2

Count 3

Count 4

Count 5

Count 6

Count 7

Count 8

made to outside and slightly back of *B*'s left knee.

Count 6   Cross strike own sticks.

Count 7   Strike near stick of partner. As this strike is made *B* makes half turn clockwise to face opposite direction. *A* remains in kneeling position but may shift slightly to right for greater comfort.

Count 8   Cross strike own sticks.

C. *A kneels and faces B's left side*
Repeat action as described in Part A of this figure.

D. *A kneels and faces B's right side*
Repeat action as described in Part B of this figure.

E. *Dancers stand and face each other*
Repeat action of Figure IV. On fourth repeat of Figure IV, *B* kneels and *A* remains standing for action.

F. *B kneels and faces A's left side*
Count 1   *B* swings left stick parallel and across in back of *A*'s legs, as *A* steps slightly sideways left into strike position and swings right stick down and between knees to contact *B*'s stick.

Count 2   Cross strike own sticks.

Count 3   Strike near stick of partner.

Count 4   Cross strike own sticks.

Count 5   *B* swings left stick parallel across in back of and to outside of *A*'s legs, as *A* steps slightly sideways left and swings right stick down to right of body to contact *B*'s stick. NOTE: This contact is made on outside and slightly back of *A*'s right knee.

Count 6   Cross strike own sticks.

Count 7   Strike near stick of partner. As strike is made *A* makes half turn counterclockwise to face opposite direction. *B* remains in kneeling position but may shift slightly to left for greater comfort.

Count 8   Cross strike own sticks.

G. *B kneels and faces A's right side*
Count 1   *B* swings right stick parallel and across in back of *A*'s legs, as *A* steps slightly sideways right into strike position and swings left stick down between knees to contact *B*'s stick.

Count 2   Cross strike own sticks.

Count 3   Strike near stick of partner.

Count 4   Cross strike own sticks.

Count 5   *B* swings right stick parallel across in back of and to outside of *A*'s legs, as *A* steps sideways right and swings left stick down to right of body to contact *B*'s stick. NOTE: This contact is made outside and slightly back of *A*'s left knee.

Count 6   Cross strike own sticks.

Count 7   Strike near stick of partner. As strike is made, *A* makes half turn clockwise to face opposite direction. *B* remains in kneeling position but may shift slightly to right for greater comfort.

Count 8   Cross strike own sticks.

H. *B kneels and faces A's left side*
Repeat action as described in Part F of this figure.

I. *B kneels and faces A's right side*
Repeat action as described in Part G of this figure.

J. *Dancers stand and face each other*
Repeat action of Figure IV.

K. *A kneels and faces B's left side*
Repeat action as described in Parts A, B, C, and D of this figure.

L. *Dancers stand and face each other*
Repeat action of Figure IV. On fourth repeat of Figure IV, *B* kneels and *A* remains standing for action.

M. *B kneels and faces A's left side*
Repeat action as described in Parts F, G, H, and I of this figure.

N. *Dancers stand and face each other*
Repeat action of Figure IV, *except* this time they face each other standing erect as dancers complete the fourth repeat.

Figure VI.   DANCERS FACE, TWIST AND STRIKE, LEFT AND RIGHT

Dancers stand facing each other a comfortable distance apart. Without stepping to face right or left, they twist at the waist and strike sticks to floor to right or left side, as directions indicate, cross strike own sticks, then strike partner's near stick as they twist to repeat action on other side.

Count 1   Twisting to own left, strike sticks to ground. Sticks are parallel to each other.

Count 2   Cross strike own sticks.

Count 3   Twisting to right, strike near stick of partner.

Count 4   Cross strike own stick to right side of body.

Count 1   Strike ground on right side.

Count 2   Cross strike own sticks.

Count 3   Twisting to left, strike near stick of partner.

Count 4   Cross strike own stick to left side of body.

Count 1   Strike sticks to ground on left side.

Count 2   Cross strike own sticks.

Count 3   Twisting to right, strike near stick of partner.

Count 4   Cross strike own stick to right side of body.

Count 1   Strike ground on right side.

Count 2   Cross strike own sticks.

Count 3   *A* twisting left to face audience, *B* taking a quarter turn clockwise to face audience, strike near stick of partner. NOTE: Dancer moves, as action goes on to face audience.

Count 4   Cross strike own sticks. *A* crosses own sticks to right side of body while *B* crosses own sticks in front of body below waist line.

Figure VII.   ENDING

Count 1   Strike sticks to ground. NOTE: Sticks are parallel to each other.

Count 2   Cross strike own sticks.

Count 3   Strike near stick of partner. NOTE: *A* holds stick parallel with surface as *B* holds stick up at slight angle.

Count 4   Cross strike own sticks.

Repeat action of Counts 1 through 4 *twice*.

Repeat action of Counts 1 through 3. On Count 4, cross sticks, without making sound, in front of chest.

Count 1

Count 2

Count 3

Count 4

Count 5

Count 6

Count 7

Count 8

FAMILJEVALSEN
Swedish

Familjevalsen means "the family waltz" and is pronounced *fah-MILL-yeh-vahls-en*. Although this dance may be found throughout the Scandinavian countries, the Swedish version is described here as taught by Gordon E. Tracie, Seattle, Washington.

Music	Record: Any lively Swedish Waltz. RCA LPM 9910, RCA FAS-663, Aqua Viking V-830. Piano: Farwell, Jane, *Folk Dances for Fun*, p. 26.
Formation	Couples in single circle, lady to right of partner, hands joined, held at shoulder height, elbows v-shaped.
Steps	Waltz balance, waltz.

DIRECTIONS FOR THE DANCE

Music 3/4   NOTE: Directions are for man; lady's part reverse.

MEASURES

I. Balance

1   Beginning left, take one waltz balance turning toward corner.

2   Beginning right, take one waltz balance turning toward partner.

3–4   Repeat action of measures 1–2.

II. Waltz

5–8   Take closed position with corner. Arms, mans' left, lady's right, are extended straight out, shoulder height. Man places left thumb against the palm of the lady's right hand and closes his hand around the back of her hand. Beginning left, take four waltz steps turning clockwise, progressing in line of direction. On last waltz step, form single circle, man placing partner on right side.
Repeat dance from beginning with new corner.

STYLE:
This should be a very smooth, yet lively, dance. Be sure to exchange smiles or greetings with corner and partner on the waltz balance. Remember that the body rises and lowers during a waltz balance. The waltz is light, graceful, and fast.

References in Bibliography: 34 (p. 27), 72 (p. 209).
Dance annotation form © 1948 by the Folk Dance Federation of California.

FAMILIE SEKSTUR
Danish

Familie Sekstur means "family sixsome" and is pronounced *fa-MILL-yeh-SEKS-toor*. This Danish mixer is similar to American Square dance figures and steps. Jane Farwell comments that this dance is done frequently at most Scandinavian festivals.

Music	Record: Aqua Viking V 400; RCA LPM 9910. Piano: Farwell, Jane, *Folk Dances for Fun*, p. 20.
Formation	Couples in single circle, lady to right of partner, hands joined, held at shoulder height, elbows v-shaped. Dancers stand close to each other.
Steps	Buzz step, walk.

DIRECTIONS FOR THE DANCE

Music 6/8   NOTE: Directions are same for both lady and man.

MEASURES   Introduction

1–8   Beginning right, take sixteen buzz steps to side (right crosses over left, right knee bending slightly). Circle moves clockwise. Take small light steps, keep circle small with elbows bent, and lean back slightly for better action.

I. In and Out

9–10   Beginning right, take four steps toward center, slowly extending joined hands above head. On fourth step everyone nods head to greet everyone.

11–12   Beginning right, take four steps backward, to return to original formation, arms gradually lowering to original position (elbows bent, joined hands shoulder height). On fourth step, nod head to partner.

13–16   Repeat action of measures 9–12.

II. Grand Chain

17–24   Face partner and join right hands shoulder high, elbows bent, and continue around circle with grand right and left. Count out loud one to seven for each person met, keeping the seventh person for new partner. This keeps mixers in order. It is especially fun if counted in a Scandinavian language. Danish counting:

one-*en*, pronounced *enn*   five-*fein*, pronounced *femm*
two-*to*, pronounced *toe*   six-*sexs*, pronounced *sex*
three-*tre*, pronounced *tray*   seven-*syv*, pronounced *syou*
four-*fire*, pronounced *feer*

III. Swing

1–8   Left reverse open position, with man's left arm, lady's right, extended straight out at shoulder level. Swing new partner in place, taking 16 buzz steps, ending with lady on man's right. All join hands to form single circle.

Repeat action of measures 9–24, In and Out and Grand Chain. The dance continues with the Swing, In and Out, and Grand Chain order till end of record.

References in Bibliography: 15 (p. 19), 34 (p. 21), 72 (p. 79).

FJÄSKERN
Swedish

Fjäskern is pronounced *FYESS-kehrn*. It is a simple mixer that appeals to beginners and old timers as the music progresses from a very slow pace to almost too fast; thus it may appropriately be called in English "Hurry-Scurry." This dance was learned from Gordon E. Tracie, Seattle, Washington.

Music	Record: Aqua Viking V 200.
	Piano: *Samkväms och gillesdanser*, Svenska Ungdomsringen, Stockholm.
Position	Couple, inside hands joined, held shoulder height, outside hands on hips with fingers forward, thumbs back.
Formation	Double circle, couples facing line of direction.
Steps	Walk, run.

DIRECTIONS FOR THE DANCE

Music 4/4   NOTE: Directions are same for both lady and man.

MEASURES

I. Forward and Back

1–4   Beginning left, take sixteen walking steps, moving forward in line of direction. As music accelerates, these walking steps will become running steps.

1–4   Turn toward partner to face reverse line of direction and join inside hands, free hands on hips. Take sixteen walking steps, moving forward in reverse line of direction.

II. Kick and Change Places

5   Face partner, man's back to center of circle, hands on own hips. Beginning left, step left in place and kick right foot out, step right in place and kick left foot out.

6   Clap own hands (ct. 1) and partners change places with four running steps, moving clockwise, always facing each other.

7–8   Repeat action of measures 5–6 to return to original position.

5–8   Repeat action of measures 5–8. Man then moves forward to next lady for a new partner.
Repeat dance from beginning with new partner.

GAY GORDONS
Scottish

The authors learned this dance from Marion Henderson, University of British Columbia, 1951.

Music Record: Folkraft 1162; RCA Victor EPA 4129; Windsor 4607.*
     Piano: *Folk Dancer*, Volume 7, No. 4, p. 11.

Position Varsouvianna.

Steps   Walk, two-step, pas-de-basque.

DIRECTIONS FOR THE DANCE

Music 2/4 NOTE: Directions are same for both man and lady, except when specially noted.

MEASURES

I. Walk

1–2 Beginning left, walk four steps forward in line of direction. On fourth step pivot clockwise to face reverse line of direction. Lady is now on man's left.

3–4 Continue walking backwards in line of direction four steps.

5–8 Repeat action of measures 1–4 in reverse line of direction.

II. Two-step

9–12 Man beginning left, takes four two-steps in line of direction, as lady, beginning right, turns clockwise under man's right arm four two-steps. Or man, beginning left, lady right, pas-de-basque out and in and man takes four walking steps in line of direction as lady turns twice clockwise under man's right arm.

13–16 Closed position. Man beginning left, lady right, take four two-steps turning clockwise, progressing in line of direction. Or take two two-steps turning clockwise, then man walks four steps forward progressing in line of direction as lady twirls under raised right arm. Assume Varsouvianna position.

Note: This dance may be done with Inside hands joined instead of Varsouvianna position.

References in Bibliography: 116 (Vol. 7, No. 4, p. 11).
Dance annotation form © 1948 by the Folk Dance Federation of California.
* Out of print.

GERAKÍNA
(Kalamatiano)
Greek

Gerakina is pronounced *Gair-ah-kee'-na* and is a girl's name. Syrto is a type of Greek dance in which the feet glide one after another. Anatole Joakowsky learned Gerakína Syrto in 1926 in the village Zarnitza (Peloponez) and introduced it at the Stockton Folk Dance Camp in 1956.

Music Record: Folkraft 1060, 1060X45, Hrepakina (Gerakína) RCA 26-8220.

Formation Broken circle, hands joined at shoulder height, elbows bent, lead dancer at right end.

Steps Walk, step hop.

DIRECTIONS FOR THE DANCE

Music 7/8   NOTE: Directions are same for lady and man.

MEASURES

I.

1 — Beginning right, step diagonally forward to right (cts. 1–2), hop right (ct. 3), step left across in front of right (cts. 4–5), step right to right side (cts. 6–7). Circle moves counterclockwise.

2 — Step left behind right (cts. 1–2–3). Point right toe in place (cts. 4–5) and draw right heel over left foot (cts. 6–7).

3–8 — Repeat action of measures 1–2 three times.

II.

9 — Hands joined, held down, turn slightly to face right. Beginning right, take three walking steps: one long step right (cts. 1–2–3), short step left (cts. 4–5), and short step (cts. 6–7). Circle continues to move counterclockwise.

10 — Beginning left, take one long walking step (cts. 1–2–3). Point right toe near left toe turning right heel out (cts. 4–5). Turn right heel in (cts. 6–7).

11 — Repeat action of measure 9.

12 — Beginning left, take one long walking step (cts. 1–2–3). Draw right foot to left (cts. 4–5). Turning to face center. step right in place but do not transfer weight (weight remains on left foot) (cts. 6-7).

13–14 — Facing center, repeat action of measures 9–10 moving forward and raising arms to shoulder height.

15–16 — Beginning right, take six walking steps (long, short, short, long, short, short) moving backwards. Accent each long step with a knee bend.

17–18 — Point right toe near left toe, turning right heel out (cts. 1-2-3), in (cts. 4-5), out (cts. 6-7), in (cts. 1-2-3), out (cts. 4-5), and draw right heel over left instep (cts. 6-7).

Reference in Bibliography: 57 (p. 29).

Dance annotation form © 1948 by the Folk Dance Federation of California.

MEASURES

19–20   Drop hands. Hold left arm extended in front with wrist bent, fingers point upward; bend right arm and place hand behind back. Beginning right, each dancer takes six walking steps (long, short, short, long, short, short), turning clockwise one complete turn.

NOTE:

1. The rhythm in 7/8 time is counted 1-2-3, 4-5, 6-7. The walking steps are uneven, long (cts. 1-2-3), short (cts. 4-5), short (cts. 6-7).

2. The introduction, on the RCA record, is six measures of seven counts.

GREENSLEEVES
English

Music   Record: Educational Dance Recordings FD-1; RCA Victor 45-6175; RCA Victor LPM 1624; World of Fun MH 106; Lloyd Shaw 79/80.

Formation   Double circle, sets of two couples, facing line of direction; inside hands joined, outside hands are free. Number couples one, two, alternately around circle to form sets.

Steps   Walk.

DIRECTIONS FOR THE DANCE

Music 4/4   NOTE: Directions are same for man and lady.

MEASURES

1–8   Beginning left, take sixteen walking steps forward in line of direction.

9–12   Each set of two couples form right hand star and take eight walking steps. Star revolves clockwise.

13–16   Form left hand star and take eight walking steps. Star revolves counterclockwise. End with couple one in front of couple two, both couples facing line of direction.

17–18   Inside hands joined, couple one bends low and takes four steps backward as couple two raises joined hands to form an arch and takes four steps forward. This action is known as "turning the sleeves inside out."

19–20   Couple two bends low and takes four steps backward as couple one raises joined hands to form an arch and takes four steps forward.

21–24   Repeat action of measure 17 and 20.

          Mixer: To convert to a mixer, couple 2 moves forward on last four steps of measures 23–24.

References in Bibliography: 54 (p. 91), 65 (p. 65).
Dance annotation form © 1948 by the Folk Dance Federation of California.

GYPSY WINE
(Sparkling Wine or Pustza)

The dance was arranged by the California Folk Dance Federation and is not authentic. It was introduced in Austin, Texas, as Pustza by Mrs. Bertha Holck. It appeared in the first edition of *Dance A While* under the title Pustza.

Music	Record: RCA Victor 25-0038*, Victor 25-0031A*, and MacGregor 610.
Position	Left reverse open.
Steps	One step (glide), slide, two-step, pivot turn, dip.

DIRECTIONS FOR THE DANCE

Music 4/4   NOTE: Directions are for man; lady's part reverse.

MEASURES

I. Walking

1–2   Beginning left, walk four smooth steps in line of direction. Pivot on fourth beat (right foot) a half turn to right, ending in right reverse open position. Beginning left, continue in line of direction four smooth walking steps backward. Pivot on fourth beat (right foot) a half turn to left, ending in left reverse open position.

3–4   Repeat action of measures 1–2.

II. Slide

5–6   Closed position. Beginning left, take four slides in line of direction. Repeat slides in reverse line of direction.

III. Two-step

7   Beginning left, take two quick two-steps, turning clockwise.

IV. Pivot Turn and Dip

8   Beginning left, take three steps pivoting clockwise, dip back on right, lady dips forward left, into left reverse open position. The dance begins again as the man recovers from the dip onto his left foot. The ending may be simplified by taking either a four step pivot (no dip) or a three step pivot and lady turns under man's left arm into a left reverse open position for repeat of dance.

VARIATION:
Measures 5–6, all the slides may be taken in line of direction. Beginning left, take three slides in line of direction, step left pivoting a half turn clockwise; beginning right, take three slides and hop in line of direction, step right pivoting a half turn clockwise.

HAMBO
Swedish

The Hambo (its full name is Hambopolska), often called the national dance of Sweden, is known far beyond the borders of its homeland. It is danced in neighboring Scandinavian countries, in Swedish national groups around the world, and here in the United States is a top favorite among folkdancers. The Hambo is the most common living example of the once all-popular Swedish "polska" — a distinctly Nordic musical and dance form dating back to the 16th century. Since the Hambo is a living folkdance, yesterday's version is not the same as that danced today, according to Gordon E. Tracie*. The form common in the U.S. is a relatively old style one called "nighambo," referring to the characteristic "dip" on the first beat and came over with Swedish immigrants a half century ago.

Music	Record: Aqua-Viking 800; Aqua-Viking 820 (mod. fast), Aqua-Viking 812 (mod. slow), Capitol T 10039 LP; Folk Dancer MH 2002, 2003, 2004; Folkraft 1048, 1164; RCA FAS 663; RCA Victor EPA 4147.
Position	Couple, inside hands joined at shoulder height, outside hands on hip, thumb pointing backwards, fingers forward.
Steps	Step swing or waltz balance.

DIRECTIONS FOR THE DANCE

Music 3/4   NOTE: Directions are for man; lady's part reverse, except when specially noted.

MEASURES

I. Introduction

1 Beginning left, take one step swing (dal step) or waltz balance, turning body slightly away from partner, letting inside hands reach forward.

2 Take one step swing or waltz balance slightly forward, turning body slightly toward partner, drawing inside hands backward.

3 Take three steps or waltz step in line of direction.

II. Hambo (Polska) Step

4 Shoulder waist position

Man's Part: Count 1, beginning right, step (with flat foot and bent knee) forward in line of direction with foot turned outward to start clockwise pivot. Place foot between lady's feet. *Count 2*, step left slightly forward in line of direction (almost in place) pivoting almost 360 degrees clockwise. Body rises, coming up on ball of left foot. *Count 3*, touch ball of right foot *firmly* close behind left heel.

Lady's Part: Count 1, beginning left, step almost in place pivoting 180 degrees clockwise, bending left knee slightly. *Count 2*, right foot describes an arc skimming floor and touches toe close behind left heel. Body starts to rise. *Count and*, as body continues to rise, push slightly with

* Gordon E. Tracie, Authority on Swedish Folk Dancing, Seattle, Washington.
  Dance annotation form © 1948 by the Folk Dance Federation of California.

MEASURES	left foot and leap into air. *Count 3*, complete 180 degrees turn while both feet are in air, landing on right foot placed forward in line of direction between man's feet.
5–7	Repeat action of measure 4 three times.
8	Beginning right, take three steps almost in place. Take couple position, facing line of direction.

STYLE:

1. The Hambo is a very graceful, smooth flowing dance. The music should be a moderate speed, not fast. At the proper tempo the dancers appear very relaxed and to be using little effort. The extra turns and twirls are to be discouraged.
2. The upper *torso* is always *upright*. The torso is lowered or settles with the bending of the knee to accompany the primary accent (ct. 1). It rises on count 2. This body movement is subtle.
3. Both dancers should always be in control of their own body weight. The body is well "grounded" by planting each foot firmly in the step pattern. The touch of the man's right foot (ct. 3) acts to stabilize the body while pivoting. His weight is actually on both feet momentarily.
4. The lady should not let her right lower leg "fly up" or flick in the air as it describes the arc (ct. 2).
5. The man guides the lady while in the air. He does not lift her as she receives her impetus for height from her push (ct. and).
6. Once the basic footwork is learned, the perfection and styling of the dance takes several years of regular practice and conscious effort to improve one's style.

SUGGESTIONS FOR TEACHING* THE HAMBO (POLSKA) STEP

1. Understand basic rhythm.

Man: 3/4

Step	pivot	touch
R	L	R
1	2	3

Lady: 3/4

Step	touch	leap	step
L	R		R
1	2	and	3

2. Men stand single file facing a wall; ladies stand single file, facing opposite wall.
   a. Analyze basic step (without partner) for each group. Practice basic step in place.
   b. Analyze basic step (with turn) for each group. Emphasize exact placement of each foot in relation to line of direction and a *specific wall*. Face original wall with each hambo step.
3. Double file, couples in shoulder waist position.
   a. Practice step with partner.
   b. Practice individually and then together alternately.
4. Double circle, couples in shoulder waist position.
   a. Practice step progressing around room.
   b. Then analyze INTRODUCTION to Hambo and practice complete dance.

---

* Refer to page 36 for Suggestions for Teaching Basic Dance Steps.
References in Bibliography: 14 (Vol. II, p. 18), 36 (p. 19), 72 (p. 246).

HARMONICA
Israeli

The movements in the dance are symbolical of the action of an accordian.

Music	Record: Folk Dancer MH 1091; Folkraft 1109, 1109X45.
	Piano: Lapson, Dvora, *Dances of the Jewish People*, p. 13.
Formation	Single circle, hands joined and held down.
Steps	Grapevine (Tscherkessia), run, hop.

DIRECTIONS FOR THE DANCE

Music 4/4   NOTE: Directions are same for both lady and man.

MEASURES

I. Grapevine (Tscherkessia)

1   Moving counterclockwise, cross left in front of right (ct. 1), step right to side (ct. 2), cross left behind right (ct. 3), leap right to side with slight accent (ct. 4).

2   Continue moving counterclockwise and step hop left (cts. 1–2), step hop right (cts. 3–4).

3–8   Repeat action of measures 1 and 2 three times.

II. Cross Step, Hop

9   Beginning left, cross left over right (ct. 1), step right in place (ct. 2), step left in place (ct. 3), and hop slightly on left (ct. 4), turning body to left side on hop.

10   Beginning right, cross right over left (ct. 1), step in place (ct. 2), step right in place (ct. 3), and hop slightly on right (ct. 4), turning body to right side on hop.

11   Beginning left, repeat action of measure 9.

12   Moving clockwise, step hop right (cts. 1–2), step hop left (cts. 3–4).

13–15   Beginning right, repeat action of measures 9–11.

16   Moving counterclockwise, step hop left (cts. 1–2), step hop right (cts. 3–4).

III. Friendship Circle, Swaying

17   Place hands on upper arms of adjacent dancers. Dancers sway to left (cts. 1–2), sway to right (cts. 3–4). Action of feet may be step left, touch right to left; then step right, touch left to right.

18   Beginning left, moving clockwise, take four running steps.

19–24   Repeat action of measures 17–18 three times.

Dance arranged from the dance description by Dvora Lapson, *Dances of the Jewish People,* Reference 68 (p. 13).

Dance annotation form © 1948 by the Folk Dance Federation of California.

HAVA NAGILA
Israeli

Hava Nagila means "come let us be joyful." This couple dance is done to an old Hora melody, Hava Nagila. After the dance is learned, groups will enjoy singing the words as they dance.

A. Hava Nagila	Let's be joyful
Hava Nagila	Let's be joyful
Hava Nagila Venismecha	Let's be joyful
Repeat A	
B. Hava Neranena	Let's sing
Hava Neranena	Let's sing
Hava Neranena Venismecha	Let's sing and be joyful
Repeat B	
C. Uru Uru Achim	Wake up, Wake up, brothers
D. Uru Achim Belev Sameach	Wake up, brothers, with a happy heart
Repeat D three times	
E. Uru Achim	Wake up, brothers
Uru Achim Belev Sameach	Wake up, brothers, with a happy heart

Music Record: Folkraft 1110, 1110X45, 1116; Israel LP 2/3

     Piano: Lapson, Dvora, *Dances of the Jewish People,* p. 18.

Formation Double circle, partners facing, man's back to center, two hands joined. Partners stand close together, elbows bent, and hands close in.

Steps Walk, leap, hop, jump, run.

DIRECTIONS FOR THE DANCE

Music 4/4 NOTE: Directions are for both lady and man except when specially noted.

MEASURES

    I. **Pull Away and Circle**

A 1   Beginning right, take four steps backward, knees bend slowly taking body into crouch position by fourth step. Back remains fairly straight.

  2   Beginning right, take four steps forward, moving immediately into left reverse open position (ct. 1). Stand straight with left elbow bent and close to body, right arm is straight across in front of partner. Turn clockwise in reverse open position (cts. 2, 3, 4).

  3–4 Repeat action of measures 1–2.

  1–4 Repeat action of measures 1–4. On 4th measure, however, partners face line of direction and take cross back hold position.

    II. **Leap and Turn, Balance and Run**

B 1–2 Beginning right, leap forward, body bending forward (ct. 1), step left in place (ct. 2), step right back in place (ct. 3), step left in place (ct. 4). Repeat.

Dance arranged from the dance description by Dvora Lapson, *Dances of the Jewish People,* Reference 68 (p. 19).

References in Bibliography: 13 (Vol. VII, p. 9), 15 (Vol. B-1, p. 57).

Dance annotation form © 1948 by the Folk Dance Federation of California.

MEASURES

3   Drop left hands. Beginning right, take four steps, lady making three-fourth turn to face man who turns one-quarter clockwise to face her. Partners join left hands under right.

4   Beginning right, take four steps, lady in place, man turning a full turn clockwise under their joined upraised hands. Now in original starting position, with joined hands crossed.

5–6   Man beginning left, lady right, take four balances. (Man — left, right, left, right; lady — right, left, right, left.)

7–8   Hook right elbows and extend left arm diagonally upward and outward. Take eight running steps around each other, turning clockwise once around to face original starting position. Drop hands and move apart about three feet.

        III. **Clap, Hop, and Turn**

C   1   Bend over to right and clap hands to one's own right side about knee level (cts. 1–2). Repeat bending to left (cts. 3–4).

2   Bend forward and clap in front (ct. 1), gradually raise hands to outstretched arm position, in three upward lefts (cts. 2, 3, 4). Head follows hand positions.

3   Hands on hips. Jump in place (ct. 1). Take three hops on right, extending left foot forward (cts. 2, 3, 4).

4   Repeat action of measure 3, hopping on left foot and extending right.

5–6   Repeat action of measures 3 and 4.

7   Repeat action of measures 3 letting left foot trail behind while turning clockwise around in place once on three hops.

8   Repeat action of measure 4, letting right foot trail behind while turning counterclockwise around in place once on three hops.

HORA
Israeli

The Jewish people, dispersed over the earth for many years, have kept their religion alive, but many of the folk traditions have become broken or lost. When the people returned to Israel, they brought dances from their former homelands.

The Sephardic Jews, who left Spain during the Inquisition, settled in the Balkan area. They danced the Balkan Hora, adopting it and incorporating it in their festivities.

The word *hora*, a Croatian-Serbian word, means "tempo" or "movement." Although the earlier Hora dances were probably a part of primitive agricultural rites (the leaps and high jumps in the dance suggest and were supposed to induce high growth of corn); the Hora became more subdued and restrained as the people danced it indoors in small spaces. As danced in Israel today, it has absorbed the flavor of the people living there, and is once again danced out of doors.

There are many Hora melodies and variations of step. The dance presented here was taught at U.C.L.A., Los Angeles, California, 1943, and by Dvora Lapson, dance director of the Jewish Education Committee, Jewish Education Institute, New York City, 1946.

Music	Record: Folk Dancers MH 1052; Folkraft 1110, 1116, 1110X-45, 1118, 1106, 1431X45; 1476X45, LP-12, LP-2; Victor EPA 4140.
	Piano: Chochem, Corinne, and Roth, Muriel, *Palestine Dances*, p. 15.
	Beliajus, V. F., *Dance and Be Merry*, Vol. I, p. 37.
Formation	Single circle, hands on shoulders of person on either side, arms straight.
Music 4/4	NOTE: Directions are same for both lady and man.

DIRECTIONS FOR THE DANCE

MEASURES

1–3   Moving counterclockwise, step right to side, place left behind right, and step right. Kick left in front of right while hopping on right. Step left to side, kick right across left while hopping on left. NOTE: This same pattern is repeated throughout the dance.

NOTE:

Begin the Hora slowly in order to establish the rhythm, keep the tempo slow and the music soft, then gradually accelerate the rhythm and increase the volume. If the group is large, it is interesting to have several concentric circles, some circles beginning with the right foot moving clockwise, and others beginning with the left foot moving counterclockwise.

STYLE:

If the movement of the dance begins mildly, with a tiny hop it can build gradually to a larger hop as the tempo increases.

If dancers extend arms and lean back, keeping head up, the momentum is easier. Dancers should hold up their own arms, not press down on shoulders of the person to each side.

References in Bibliography: 6 (p. 36), 16 (p. 15), 65 (p. 71), 68 (p. 18).

IL CODIGLIONE
Italian

Il Codiglione means "the cotillion" and is pronounced *ill Coh-dill-yo-neh.* Vyts Beliajus first saw this dance at Chicago's Hull House about 1928 by an Italian group of dancers and introduced it at Idyllwild in 1954.

Music	Record: Folkraft 1172, 1403, 1426; Tarantella Barese, Harmonia 2074.
Formation	Double circle of couples, Varsouvianna position, facing line of direction.
Steps	Walk pas-de-basque.

DIRECTIONS FOR THE DANCE

Music 6/8

NOTE: Directions are same for man and lady.

MEASURES

1–4	Introduction

I. Walk

1–16	Beginning left, take 32 walking steps forward in line of direction.
17–24	All join hands to form a single circle and take sixteen walking steps to right. Circle moves counterclockwise.
25–32	Take sixteen walking steps to left. Circle moves clockwise.

II. Two Circles

1–8	Ladies form circle and take sixteen walking steps to left, circle moving clockwise. Men form circle around ladies and take sixteen walking steps to right, circle moving counterclockwise.
9–16	Each circle moves in the opposite direction, ladies counterclockwise, men clockwise.

III. Basket

1–8	Men join hands and raise over and in front of ladies to form basket as ladies join hands. Lady remains to right of partner. Take sixteen walking steps to right. Circle moves counterclockwise.
9–16	Ladies' hands remain joined. Men raise joined hands over ladies' heads, release hands, and reach under ladies' arms to rejoin hands in front of ladies and form basket again. Take sixteen walking steps to left. Circle moves clockwise.

IV. Walk

1–16	Repeat action of measures 1–16, Part I.
17–24	Men turn and walk clockwise single file in reverse line of direction while ladies continue to walk counterclockwise in line of direction.
25–32	Reverse. All turn half around and men walk counterclockwise while ladies walk clockwise. Ladies turn on the last measure to Varsouvianna position, facing line of direction.

MEASURES

V. Walk, Pas-de-basque, Dos-a-dos

1–3   Varsouvianna position. Take six walking steps forward in line of direction.

4   Release hands. Partners turn to face and back away from each other two steps. End facing partner, man's back to center.

5–8   Snap fingers with arms outstretched above head and beginning right, take four pas-de-basque steps in place.

9–12   Lower arms to side and partners do-sa-do, passing right shoulders first, taking eight steps.

13–16   Partners do-sa-do, passing left shoulders first, taking eight steps and progress to new partner on left by moving diagonally left on last four steps.

1–16   Repeat action of measures 1–16.

VI. Ending

1–2   With feet slightly apart take weight on right foot and clap hands (counts 1, 2, 3); pause (counts 4, 5, 6), step left and clap hands (counts 1, 2, 3); pause (counts 4, 5, 6).

3–4   Repeat action of measures 1–2.

5–8   Hook right elbow with partner and turn clockwise seven steps, then stop. Turn back on partner and clap hands overhead on last beat.

NOTE:

Directions above are given for the Folkraft record. The Harmonia Record is arranged slightly differently and is as follows:

Parts I, II, III danced as above.

Omit Part IV.

Part V — danced as above.

Repeat Parts I, II, III, V.

Ending: In varsouvianna position, take 16 walking steps forward in the line of direction (measures 1–8). Then hook right elbow with partner and take 14 walking steps turning clockwise (measures 9–15). On the last measure stop and turn back on partner and clap hands overhead on the last beat (measure 16).

STYLE:

There needs to be smooth transitions when changing directions. The walking steps are on the ball of the foot, a flat walk is heavy and ugly. The hands are joined shoulder high, elbows down, and not an extended arm. The body is carried high. The success of this dance depends upon the style of execution. The body is *high* and *light*.

KEHRUU VALSSI
(Spinning Waltz)
Finnish

This little waltz is done in both Finland and Sweden, where it is often called by an original French name "Mingon." The music is a well known Swedish Folksong, "Spinn, spinn, dotter min" (Spin, spin, daughter mine), and more often than not, it is sung while dancing it. Two versions are presented.

Music   Record: Imperial 1036; MacGregor 607; Rytmi RLP 8044 (recorded in Finland); World of Fun M 110.

Formation   Double circle, partners face, man's back to center, both hands joined.

Steps   Walk, balance, three step turn.

DIRECTIONS FOR THE DANCE

Music 3/4   NOTE: Directions are for man; lady's part reverse.

MEASURES

I. Step Swing, Walk Three, Lady Turns

1–2   Step to left, swing right across left, step to right, swing left across right.

3–4   Man, beginning left, takes three steps sideways to left and swings right across left. Lady, beginning right, takes a three-step turn clockwise and finishes swinging left across right. Both advance in line of direction.

NOTE: May be counted as follows:

	1–2	3	1–2		3
Man:	Left	Right	Left	Swing	Right
Lady:	Right	Left	Right	Swing	Left

5–6   Beginning right, repeat action of measures 1–2.

7–8   Repeat action of measures 3–4 in reverse line of direction, except that lady takes three steps to left and man takes three-step turn clockwise.

II. Balance and Walking Turn

9–10   Partners face, join two hands. Balance forward together, arms swinging out to side, balance backward apart, arms swinging in together.

11–12   Arms swing out to side shoulder height and partners moving into left reverse open position, take six walking steps, turning clockwise. Finish in original position.

13–14   Partners balance apart and then together.

15–16   Lady takes two waltz steps, turning clockwise under man's left arm and progresses in line of direction to next man. Man takes one small balance step backward and one balance step forward to receive new partner.

References in Bibliography: 1 (Vol. IV, p. 11), 33 (p. 23), 65 (p. 94), 72 (p. 211).
Dance annotation form © 1948 by the Folk Dance Federation of California.

VARIATION:
MEASURES

3–4	Man's left hand, lady's right hand joined, free hand on hip. Man takes two draw steps to left, lady twirls under raised arm.
5–6	Repeat action of measures 1–2.
7–8	Man's right hand, lady's left hand joined, free hand on hip. Lady takes two draw steps to right, man turns under raised arm.
9–10	Closed position. Take two draw steps, moving in line of direction. Step left (ct. 1), hold (ct. 2), close right to left (ct. 3), step left (ct. 1), hold (ct. 2), close right to left without taking weight (ct. 3).
11–12	Take two draw steps, moving in reverse line of direction.
13–16	Take four waltz steps, turning clockwise, progressing in line of direction. Do not twirl at end.

NOTE:

As commonly danced in Scandinavia, it is even simpler, almost exactly as our Swedish Waltz. The Scandinavians never dance this as a mixer.

KLUMPAKOJIS
Lithuanian

Klumpakojis means "wooden footed" or "clumsy footed." It is frequently translated erroneously as "wooden shoes." It is a form of the finger polka type folk dance found the world over. Notice its similarity to the Swedish Klappdans, the Dutch Hopp Mor Annika, and the Danish Siskind.

Music	Record: Folkraft 1419; Columbia 16083*; Imperial 1007*; RCA Victor LPM 1624 and EPA 4142.
Formation	Double circle, couples side by side, inside joined, free hands on hips, facing line of direction.
Steps	Walk, stamp, polka.

DIRECTIONS FOR THE DANCE

Music 2/4   NOTE: Directions are for man, lady's part reverse.

MEASURES

I. Walk

1–4   Beginning left, take eight brisk walking steps in line of direction, turning towards partner to face reverse line of direction on last step.

5–8   Join inside hands, free hands on hips. Take eight walking steps in reverse line of direction.

1–8   Face partner, joining right hands, right elbow bent, left hand on hip. Partners take eight steps, walking around each other clockwise. Join left hands and take eight steps, walking counterclockwise.

II. Stamps, Claps

1–4   No action (cts. 1, 2, 1, 2). Then stamp three times. No action (cts. 1, 2, 1, 2). Clap own hands three times.

5–8   Shake right finger, right elbow bent, at partner (cts. 1, 2, 3) hold (ct. 4). Shake left finger, left elbow bent, at partner (cts. 1, 2, 3), hold (ct. 4). Clap right hand of partner and turn solo counterclockwise in place once with two steps. Facing partner, stamp feet three times quickly.

1–8   Repeat action of measures 1–8.

III. Polka

1–8   Varsouvianna position. Beginning left take sixteen polka steps forward in line of direction. On last two polka steps, man moves forward to new partner.

NOTE:

1. Zest is added to the dance if dancers shout "Hey Hey" or "Ya-Hoo" spontaneously during the polka sequence.

2. This dance may be used to introduce either the two-step or polka step.

Reference in Bibliography: 65 (p. 148).

Dance annotation form © 1948 by the Folk Dance Federation of California.

* Out of print.

KOHANOCHKA
Russian

Kohanochka means "beloved" and is a Russian ballroom dance. The authors learned the dance in New York City.

Music	Record: Folk Dancer MH 1058; Folkraft 1423; Imperial 1021; Kismet 101.
	Piano: Herman, Michael, *Folk Dances for All*, p. 62.
Position	Couple, outside arms swing freely with action of dance.
Steps	Russian polka, pas-de-basque, four-step turn.

DIRECTIONS FOR THE DANCE

Music 2/4   NOTE: Directions are for man; lady's part reverse except when specially noted.

MEASURES

I. Russian Polka or Pas-de-Basque, Forward and Turn

1   Beginning left, take one Russian polka or pas-de-basque forward. Inside hands swing forward shoulder height, outside hands swing back freely.

2   Beginning right, take one Russian polka or pas-de-basque forward. Inside hands swing back, outside hands swing across chest.

3–4   Beginning left, take two Russian polka steps or a four step turn, making one complete turn (man turning counterclockwise, lady clockwise). Swing joined inside hands forward on count one, release hands for solo turns, and rejoin hands.

5–8   Repeat action of measures 1–4.

II. Rock Forward and Back, Polka

9–10   Varsouvianna position. Man and lady beginning left, step forward, lifting right off floor, step back right, lifting left off floor, (rocking horse effect).

11–12   Take two Russian polka steps in line of direction.

13–16   Repeat action of measures 9–12.

III. Clap Step

17–20   Partners face, man's back to center of circle. Clap hands twice. Man crosses arms on chest, lady places hands on hips. Beginning left, take three Russian polka steps backward away from partner.

21–24   Repeat claps, take two Russian polka steps forward passing *left* shoulders, stamp three times.

17–20   Repeat claps, take three Russian polka steps backward passing *left* shoulders. End facing partner.

21   Repeat claps.

22   Pause (ct. 1), partners strike right hands (ct. 2).

23–24   Make one complete turn to own left, counterclockwise, stamp three times in place.

STYLE:

The movement should flow forward smoothly without hesitation. If the pas-de-basque is used, it should be danced smoothly as dancers move progressively forward.

References in Bibliography: 14 (Vol. I, p. 12), 52 (p. 61), 65 (p. 104).

KOROBUSHKA
Russian

Korobushka, also spelled Korobotchka, means "little basket" or "peddlar's pack." According to Michael Herman* this dance originated on American soil by a group of Russian immigrants following the close of World War I, to the Russian folk song, "Korobushka."

Music	Record: Folkraft 1170, 1170X45; Folk Dancer MH 1059; Imperial 1022; Kismet 106; World of Fun M 108; Stinson 8001.
	Piano: Beliajus, V. F., *Dance and Be Merry*, Vol. I, p. 20.
Formation	Double circle, partners facing, man's back to center. Two hands joined or man crosses arms on chest, lady places hands on hips.
Steps	Hungarian break step, schottische, balance, three-step turn.

DIRECTIONS FOR THE DANCE

Music 2/4   NOTE: Directions are for man; lady's part reverse.
MEASURES

I. Schottische Step

1–2	Beginning left, take one schottische away from center of circle. Extend right foot on hop.
3–4	Beginning right, take one schottische step toward center of circle.
5–6	Repeat action of measures 1–2.
7–8	Hungarian break step (cross-apart-together).

II. Three Step Turn

9–10	Drop hands. Man and lady beginning right, take one three-step turn or one schottische step moving away from each other.
11–12	Beginning left, repeat three-step turn or schottische back to place.
13–14	Join right hands. Man and lady beginning right, balance together, balance back.
15–16	Man and lady beginning right, change places with four walking steps, lady turning counterclockwise under man's arm.
17–24	Repeat action of measures 9–16, returning to original starting position.

MIXER:
One may progress to a new partner on the last three-step turn, measures 19–20, by taking turn in place, balancing with new partner, and changing sides. The man progresses to the lady in front of him at the completion of the three-step turn in place. Before dancers cross over, the man may identify his new partner as the next lady in the line of direction.

* Herman, Michael, *The Folk Dancer,* Vol. I, April 1941.
  References in Bibliography: 6 (p. 20), 14 (Vol. I, p. 14), 25 (p. 116), 23 (p. 21), 51 (p. 28).
Dance annotation form © 1948 by the Folk Dance Federation of California.

KREUZ KOENIG
German

Although Kreuz Koenig has been translated as "King's Cross," Michael Herman writes on the basis of further research that it is a German idiomatic expression which means "King of Clubs." The figures in the dance describe the shape of the King of Clubs. This dance was learned by the authors in New York City.

Music	Record: Folk Dancer MH 1022.
	Piano: Herman, Michael, *Folk Dances for All*, p. 89.
Formation	Set of two couples facing, lady to right of partner, hands joined in a circle of four.
Steps	Leap, run, step hop, mazurka.

DIRECTIONS FOR THE DANCE

Music 3/8   NOTE: Directions are the same for both lady and man.

MEASURES

Figure I.   Circle Four, Leap, Cross and Run (Slow waltz tempo)

1–2   Circle moves clockwise. Beginning left, leap on left (ct. 1), cross right behind left (bend left knee as right sweeps behind left) (ct. 2), turn body slightly toward left and take four running steps (cts. 3, 1, 2, 3).

3–8   Repeat action of measure 1–2 three times.

Figure II.   Run in Line of Four (Slow waltz tempo)

1–8   Ladies stand on right side of partner. Men hook left elbows, place right arm around partner's waist and grasp opposite lady's left hand behind her partner's back. Beginning left, take twenty-four running steps forward, turning the foursome counterclockwise.

Figure III.   Step Hop Across (Viennese tempo)

9–10   All drop hands and couples face. Men grasp left hands and beginning left, take two step hops exchanging places. Ladies take two small step hops in place.

11–12   Men grasp right hands with opposite lady and turn once clockwise with two step hops.

13–14   Men grasp left hands and return to original position with two step hops. Ladies take two step hops in place.

15–16   Men join right hands with partner, ladies turn once clockwise under raised right arms and curtsy as men bow.

Note: Men stand in place as ladies turn.

9–16   Repeat action of measure 9–16.

Dance arranged from the dance description by Michael Herman, *Folk Dances for All*, Reference 45 (p. 88).

References in Bibliography: 65 (p. 130), 72 (p. 238).

MEASURES

Figure IV. Circle Four, Mazurka (Mazurka tempo)

17	Form a circle of four, hands joined. Circle moves clockwise. Beginning left, step left (ct. 1), draw right to left (ct. 2), hop right, sweeping left across right (ct. 3). This is one mazurka step).
18–20	Repeat action of measure 17 three times.
21–22	Partners face and join two hands. Beginning left, take two mazurka steps, turning clockwise.
23–24	Take six running steps, continuing to move clockwise. Lean away from partner.
17–24	Repeat action of measures 17–24. During the six running steps the men place partner's right hand in his right and swing the ladies back to back in the center of the four.

Figure V. King of Clubs (Viennese tempo)

This figure begins with ladies standing back to back holding partner's right hand in their right and the opposite man's left hand in their left. NOTE: *Partners maintain right hand grasp throughout Figure V.*

25–28	Men turn slightly to left and beginning left, take twelve running steps forward, turning the foursome clockwise. Ladies run in place as they pivot in the center.
29–32	Men drop opposite lady's left hand and swing partners out as they move to center, back to back, and quickly grasp opposite lady's left hand. (The men and ladies have exchanged positions.) The foursome continues to move clockwise with twelve running steps. NOTE: Men accent the change by stamping left on the first running step to the center.
25–32	Repeat action of measures 25–32.

NOTE:

1. At the end of Figure V, all hands are dropped and the men turn in place to face center of foursome. All then join hands in a circle of four. Men now have a new partner on the right. The dance is repeated from the beginning with the new partner.

2. According to Paul and Gretel Dunsing, authorities on German Folk dancing Figure III is a grand right and left in the original version. The popular version is presented here.

LA RASPA
Mexican

Frequently La Raspa is called Mexican Hat Dance by the public. Mexican Hat Dance, Jarabe Tapatio, is an entirely different dance. This dance was taught by Martha Hill, New York University, 1944-45.

Music	Record: Folkraft 1119; 1119X45; Honor Your Partner 104; Old Timer 8100; RCA Victor EPA 4139; World of Fun M 106.
	Piano: Sedillo, Mela, *Mexican and New Mexican Folk Dances*.
Position	Partners face, man holds clasped hands behind back, lady holds skirt, or two hands joined.
Steps	Bleking step, running step.

DIRECTIONS FOR THE DANCE

Music 2/4   NOTE: Directions are same for both lady and man.

MEASURES

A 1–4   I. Beginning right, take one bleking step.

   5–8   Turn to face opposite direction (right shoulder to right shoulder) and repeat action of measures 1–4, Part A.

   9–12   Repeat action of measure 1–4, Part A, facing opposite direction (left shoulder to left shoulder).

   13–16   Repeat action of measures 1–4, Part A, facing partner.

B 1–4   II. Hook right elbows, left hands held high. Take eight running steps, clapping on eighth step.

   5–8   Reverse direction, hook left elbows. Take eight running steps, clapping on eighth step.

   9–16   Repeat action of measures 1–8, Part B.

VARIATION:
Measures 1–8.   Take sixteen running steps, right elbows hooked. Measure 9–16.   Reverse and take sixteen running steps.

ICEBREAKER:
No partners, all stand in single circle. Turn slightly left and right for action of measures 1–16, Part A; run in line of direction and reverse line of direction for action of measures 1–16, Part B. Halfway through record everyone may take a partner.

References in Bibliography: 14 (Vol. II, p. 7), 33 (p. 18), 54 (p. 90), 65 (p. 72), 93 (p. 29).

Dance annotation form © 1948 by the Folk Dance Federation of California.

MAN IN THE HAY
German

Music	Record: Folk Dancer MH 1051.
	Piano: Burchenal, E., *Folk Dances of Germany*, p. 28.
Formation	Set of four couples in square dance formation.
Steps	Skip, slide.

DIRECTIONS FOR THE DANCE

Music 6/8   NOTE: Directions are same for both lady and man, except when specially noted.

	MEASURES	
		Introduction
	1—4	All join hands and swing arms forward and back briskly, standing in place. The movement is small and staccato. Keep elbows straight and stand in close formation.

I. Circle

A	1—16	Beginning left, take sixteen skips clockwise. Repeat counter-clockwise.

CHORUS

B	9—10	Head couples take closed position. Man beginning left, lady right, take three slides to center and pause or stamp.
	11—12	Man beginning right, lady left, take three slides back to place and pause or stamp.
	13—16	Man beginning left, lady right, take six slides across set to opposite side, men passing back to back. Step left, bring right foot to left and hold. Do not turn.
	17—20	Repeat action of measure 13—16, returning to home position, ladies passing back to back. Man leads with right foot, lady left.
	9—20	Side couples repeat action of measures 9—20, B.

II. Ladies' Circle

A	1—8	Four ladies join hands in circle. Beginning left, take sixteen skips clockwise. Men clap.

CHORUS

B	9—20	Repeat action of measures 9—20, 9—20, B.
	9—20	

III. Men Circle

A	1—8	Four men join hands in circle. Beginning left, take sixteen skips clockwise. Ladies clap.

CHORUS

B	9—20	Repeat action of measures 9—20, 9—20, B.
	9—20	

References in Bibliography: 11 (p. 28), 14 (Vol. VI, p. 20), 65 (p. 190), 119 (Je. '51, p. 13).

MEASURES

IV. Basket

A 1–8 Head couples form circle, men's arms around ladies' waists, ladies' arms around men's shoulders. Beginning left, take sixteen skips or slides clockwise. A Buzz Step may be used here with the right foot in front of the left.

CHORUS

B 9–20 Repeat action of measures 9–20, 9–20, B.
  9–20

V. Basket

A 1–8 Side couples repeat action of measures A 1–8, Figure IV.

CHORUS

B 9–20 Repeat action of measures 9–20, 9–20, B.
  9–20

VI. Circle

A 1–8 Take sixteen skips clockwise and end with a bow to the center of the circle with hands still joined.

VARIATION:

Arrange all the squares so that they are directly behind and beside another square, so that the couples may slide through several squares and return to original position during the chorus.

Measures 13–16, B, man beginning left, lady right, take eight slides across set and on through as many sets as they can go, men passing back to back. Measures 17–20, B, repeat action of measures 13–16, returning home, ladies passing back to back.

MAYIM
Israeli

These words may be sung with the dance which appears on the following page.

I.   1–4   V-Shav-tem Mayim Bi-Sa-Son, Mi-ma-Yi-Wey Ha-Y'Shu-ah
     3–4   V-Shav-tem Mayim Bi-Sa-Son, Mi-ma-Yi-Wey Ha-Y'Shu-ah

II. 5–6   Ma-Yim Ma-Yim Ma-Yim, Ma-Yim, V-Ma-Yim Bi-Sa-Son
     7–8   Ma-Yim Ma-Yim Ma-Yim, Ma-Yim, V-Ma-Yim Bi-Sa-Son

III. 1   Hey! Hey! Hey! Hey!
     2   Mayim Mayim Mayim Mayim
     3   Mayim Mayim Bi-Sa-Son
     4   Mayim Mayim Mayim Mayim
     5   Mayim Mayim Bi-Sa-Son

MAYIM

Mayim is a Jewish folk tune. Translated Mayim means "Water." The dance movements express the joy of finding water in arid land and emulate the motion of waves as they break upon the shore. The dance originated in a "Kibbutz" on the shores of Galilee.

Music	Record: Folkraft 1108, 1475X45, LP-12; Israel 114; Israel LP 5/6; World of Fun MH 119.
	Piano: Lapson, Dvora, *Dances of the Jewish People*, p. 8.
Formation	Single circle, hands joined and held down.
Steps	Grapevine (tscherkessia), run.

DIRECTIONS FOR THE DANCE

Music 4/4   NOTE: Directions are same for both lady and man.

MEASURES

I. Grapevine (tscherkessia)

1–4   Moving clockwise, cross right in front of left (ct. 1), step left to side (ct. 2), cross right behind left (ct. 3), step left to side with a light springy step, accenting step (ct. 4). Repeat three times.

II. To Center and Back

5   Beginning right, move to center with four running steps. Leap slightly, bending the knee on first step. Lift joined hands gradually above heads as dancers move to center.

6   Beginning right, repeat action of measure 5, moving away from center. Lower joined hands gradually down to sides.

7–8   Repeat action of measures 5–6.

III. Run, Toe Touch, Clap

1   Beginning right, move clockwise with three running steps (cts. 1–3), turn to face center, weight remains on right (ct. 4).

2   Hop on right and touch left across front to right side (ct. 1), hop on right, touch left to side (ct. 3), hop on right, touch left in front to right side (ct. 3), hop on right, touch left to side (ct. 4).

3   Repeat action of measure 2, Part III.

4   Hop on left, touch right in front to left side and clap hands directly in front at arm's length (ct. 1), hop on left, touch right to side and swing arms out to sides shoulder high (ct. 2), hop on left, touch right in front to left side and clap hands directly in front at arm's length (ct. 3), hop on left, touch right to side and swing arms out to sides shoulder high (ct. 3).

5   Repeat action of measure 4, Part III.

NOTE: The words for Mayim appear on the preceding page. Singing enhances the dance.

Dance arranged from the dance description by Dvora Lapson, *Dances of the Jewish People*, Reference 68 (p. 8).

References in Bibliography: 14 (Vol. VII, p. 14), 15 (Vol. A-2, p. 21), 54 (p. 190), 119 (Jan. '47 (p. 190), 119 (Jan. '52, p. 14).

MISERLOU
Greek

The origin[1] of Miserlou is most interesting inasmuch as it originated at Duquesne University, Pittsburgh, Pennsylvania. In 1945, Professor Brunhilde Dorsch contacted a Greek-American student, Miss Mercine Nesotas, who taught several Greek dances to their dance group, hoping to find a Greek dance for a program. The group enjoyed the dance Syrtos Haniotikos the most; Miss Nesotas called it the "Kritikos." Since the appropriate music was not available, someone suggested that the steps be adapted to a slower piece of music, Miserlou. This dance was taught by Monty Mayo, Pittsburgh, Pennsylvania, at Oglebay Folk Dance Camp, Wheeling, West Virginia, in 1948. It is danced all over the world now, and by Greeks too!

Music	Record: Columbia 7217F,* Folkraft 1060X45, 1021; RCA Victor EPA 4129; Festival 3505; Kolo Festival 804.
	Piano: *Miserlou* by M. Roubanis, Colonial Music Publishing Company, 168 West 23rd, New York City, N. Y.
Formation	One large broken circle, hands joined, lead dancers at right end of line.
Steps	Two-step, grapevine.

DIRECTIONS FOR THE DANCE

Music 4/4   NOTE: Directions are same for both lady and man.

MEASURES

1   Beginning right, step in place (ct. 1). Hold (ct. 2). Pointing left toe in front of right, describe an arc to left toward right heel (cts. 3–4). Circle moves counterclockwise.

2   Step left behind right (ct. 1). Step right to side (ct. 2). Step left across in front of right (ct. 3), and pivot counterclockwise a half turn on left to face reverse line of direction (ct. 4).

3   Beginning right and moving clockwise, take one two-step.

4   Step back on left (ct. 1). Step right to side, body facing center (ct. 2). Step left across in front of right (ct. 3). Hold (ct. 4).

NOTE:
The dancer at the right end of the broken circle leads the line in serpentine fashion, coiling it counterclockwise, then reversing and uncoiling it clockwise, while executing the dance pattern.

VARIATION:
Measure 4   Beginning left, take one two-step backward, moving counterclockwise, and on last step pivot right on ball of left foot to face center.

[1] Holden, Rickey and Mary Vouras, *Greek Folk Dances,* Newark, New Jersey, Folkraft Press, 1965.
References in Bibliography: 65 (p. 88), 57 (p. 61, 85).
Dance annotation form © 1948 by the Folk Dance Federation of California.
* Out of print.

NORWEGIAN POLKA
(Scandinavian Polka)

The Norwegian Polka is also known as the Scandinavian Polka, Seattle Polka, and Ballroom Polka. Gordon E. Tracie* suggests that the Americanized version may come from a simplification of the Norwegian dance Parisarpolka, meaning "Parisian polka." The Norwegian immigrants probably brought the Parisarpolka to America where it changed somewhat in form, but retained the original Scandinavian polka music.

Music	Record: Aqua Viking V-812; Aqua Viking V-806; Capitol T-10039LP; Folk Dancer MH 2001 and 2004; Harmony 45-7; Folkraft 1411; or any good Scandinavian polka.
Position	Couple.
Steps	Walk, pivot turn.

DIRECTIONS FOR THE DANCE

Music 2/4   NOTE: Directions are for man; lady's part reverse.

MEASURES

1–2	I.	Beginning left, take three walking steps in line of direction.
3–4		Beginning right, repeat in reverse line of direction.
5–6		Beginning left, walk four steps in line of direction. Face partner on fourth step and take shoulder waist position. NOTE: To take a six step pivot turn, dancers may walk forward two steps and start pivot on measure 6.
7–8	II.	Shoulder waist position. Beginning left, take a four step pivot turn clockwise, progressing in line of direction. Partners should lean away from each other in turn. Man should end with back to center of room.

VARIATIONS:

1. Measures 1–2 Take two steps in line of direction and a two-step in place facing partner.

    Measures 3–4 Repeat in reverse line of direction.

2. Measures 1–2 Take three step turn in line of direction. Clap at end of turn.

    Measures 3–4 Repeat in reverse line of direction.

3. Measures 1–4 In Seattle Polka, a stamp is added at the end of the first three walking steps, and a clap, clap at the end of the second three walking steps.

TEACHING SUGGESTIONS:
To simplify for the beginner, it is helpful to teach two walking steps in measures 5–8 in couple position, followed by a two-step pivot in shoulder waist position and repeat. Gradually change the sequence to the regular four or six step pivot.

---

* Gordon E. Tracie, authority on Swedish Folk Dancing, Seattle, Washington.
  References in Bibliography: 14 (Vol. II, p. 11), 51 (p. 5), 45 (p. 27), 72 (p. 88).
  Dance annotation form © 1948 by the Folk Dance Federation of California.

OSLO WALTZ
Scottish-English

The Oslo Waltz is a Scottish-English Family Waltz done to a Norwegian folk song. This type of "family waltz" folk dance is found in almost every European country.

Music	Record: Folk Dancer MH 3016.
Formation	Single circle, couples facing center, lady to right of partner, hands joined.
Steps	Waltz, waltz balance, draw.

DIRECTIONS FOR THE DANCE

Music 3/4 NOTE: Directions are for man, lady's part reverse except when specially noted.

MEASURES

I. Waltz Balance

1   Man beginning left, lady right, take one waltz balance forward.

2   Take one waltz balance backward.

3–4   Man takes two waltz balances in place and guides lady on left to his right side. Lady takes two waltz steps (six steps), turning clockwise one complete turn in front of man, moving to right side of man. All rejoin hands immediately to form single circle.

5–16   Repeat the action of measures 1–4 three times.

II. Balance and Turn

1   Single circle. Man faces lady on right for new partner and join two hands. Beginning left, take one waltz balance to left side, toward center of circle.

2   Take one waltz balance to right side.

3–4   Drop hands and turn solo towards center of circle, man beginning left, turning counterclockwise, lady beginning right, turning clockwise with one waltz step and two steps. Hold last count. Or three steps in canter rhythm (step cts. 1, 2; step ct. 3; step cts. 1, 2, 3). Join two hands.

5–8   Repeat action of Part II, measures 1–4, balancing away from center first. Man turns clockwise, lady counterclockwise, moving away from center of circle.

Dance arranged from the dance description by Michael Herman and reproduced here by permission of Folk Dance House, 108 West 16th Street, New York City, N. Y.
References in Bibliography: 15 (Vol. A-2, p. 2), 65 (p. 146), 72 (p. 210).
Dance annotation form © 1948 by the Folk Dance Federation of California.

MEASURES

III. Waltz

9–10   Join two hands. Beginning left, take two slow draws toward center.

11–12   Take two slow draws away from center. The man needs to maneuver so that his back is to the center of the ring on measures 11–12 so he can make the following turn smoothly.

13–16   Closed position. Beginning left, take four waltz steps, turning clockwise, progressing in line of direction.
All face center in single circle, join hands, and repeat dance from beginning.

NOTE:

1. This is a perfect dance for both beginners and experts. For beginners, the balance in Part I may be done as a step forward and step backward. Using the waltz balance is an easy method of teaching the waltz.

2. The dance is more fun if partners and corners look at each other during the balance; and each lady greets each man as she passes. Make him feel important.

PATAIS MANI BALELINI
Latvian

Patais Mani Balelini means "brother, make me." It is the name of a song in which the words say, "Brother, make me a purse...; Brother, make me a glove...; Brother, make me a shoe...." This dance is executed with great gusto and was originated to express the desire of the people to be free. Susan Vitmus, a student at Arizona State University, presented this dance as learned from her father, a native of Latvia.

Music   Record: *Helena Polka*, Folkraft 1123.
Formation   Single circle of four, two couples, all face center, hands joined.
Step   Walk, polka, jump.

DIRECTIONS FOR THE DANCE

Music 2/4   NOTE: Directions are same for both man and lady.

MEASURES

I. Circle, Walk

1–8	Beginning right, take twelve walking steps to right, circle, moving counterclockwise. While turning to face opposite direction, clap hands three times.
1–8	Rejoin hands and form circle. Beginning right, take twelve walking steps to left, circle moving clockwise. While turning to face opposite direction, clap hands three times.

II. Mill, Polka

9–16	Dancers face counterclockwise. Man holds corner lady's (lady behind him) left hand in his left hand; outside hand on hip. Beginning right, take six polka steps around the circle, moving in line of direction. Clap hands three times while turning to face opposite direction.
9–16	Resume hand position, holding right hands. Repeat action of measures 9–16.

III. Couples Turn, Jump

17–24	Partners stand with right hips touching. Both extend right arms around waist of partner; extend left arm overhead. Each couple pivots clockwise in place, taking six jumps; claps hands three times, turning to face opposite direction.
25–32	Repeat action of measures 17–24 in opposite direction.

Dance annotation form © 1948 by the Folk Dance Federation of California.

PLJESKAVAC KOLO
Yugoslavian

Pljeskavac, a Serbian folk dance, is a quick, easy, and charming introduction to the Kolo.

Music   Record: Folk Dancer MH 1009; Folkraft 1548X45.

Formation   Broken circle, joined hands held down.

Steps   Walk, stamp.

DIRECTIONS FOR THE DANCE

Music 2/4   NOTE: Directions are same for both man and lady.

MEASURES

     I. **Walk, Step in Place**

1   Beginning right, take two walking steps (slow, slow) diagonally forward. Circle moves *counterclockwise*.

2   Face center. Beginning right, take three steps (quick, quick, quick) in place.

3   Beginning left, take two walking steps backward (slow, slow).

4   Beginning left, take three steps (quick, quick, quick) in place.

1–4   Repeat action of measures 1–4.

     II. **Stamps and Claps**

5–6   Face center. Beginning right, take two walking steps (slow, slow) toward center. Stamp three times right, left, right (quick, quick, quick).

7–8   Beginning left, take two walking steps (slow, slow) backward, away from center. Clap hands three times (quick, quick, quick).

5–8   Beginning right, repeat action of measures 5–8.

NOTE:

1. Each walking step is done with a bounce and tremble of the entire body.

2. The leader may use a skip step instead of a walking step. Dancers follow the leader and use skip step too.

3. Spontaneous Kolo shouts (Veselo ... hoopat svp – hup, hup, hup, tss, tss, tss, ... or ceceya) add to the interest of this dance.

Dance arranged from the dance description by Michael Herman, and reproduced here by permission of Folk Dance House, 108 West 16 Street, New York City.

References in Bibliography: 51 (p. 35), 72 (p. 76).

RANCHERA
Argentine

The Ranchera dance was brought to local folk dancers by Dr. Juan Rael, a Stanford professor, and his daughter, Maria.

Music Record: Imperial 1085.

Formation Double circle, couples facing line of direction, with left hands joined and extended slightly and forward to left, right hands joined at lady's waist (over right hip). For tunnel figure, divide group into eight to twelve couples, and designate first couple for each group.

Steps Waltz.

DIRECTIONS FOR THE DANCE

Music 3/4 NOTE: Directions are for man; lady's part reverse.

MEASURES

I. Introduction

1–12 Beginning left, take twelve waltz steps in line of direction.

II. Lady Turns

1–16 Beginning left, take sixteen waltz steps, man moving forward in line of direction, lady turning clockwise under man's raised left arm. Lady takes four waltz steps to make one complete turn. On last waltz step, take original position.

III. Couple Turns

1–8 Beginning left, take eight waltz steps, turning counterclockwise *once* in place, slowly. Man backs up and lady moves forward.

9–16 Reverse direction and turn clockwise with eight waltz steps. Man moves forward and lady backs up. On last waltz step, take open position, facing line of direction.

IV. Twist

1–12 Beginning left, man takes twelve waltz steps forward in line of direction. Beginning right, lady takes twelve waltz steps starting forward in line of direction on measure 1, and turning to left reverse open position on third beat of first measure. Then measure 2 in left reverse open position, turning back to open position on third beat. This pattern alternates back and forth for twelve measures. The music has an accented beat on third count which indicates the pivot to new position.

13–16 Take original position. Take four waltz steps in line of direction.

Dance arranged from the dance description researched and published by Folk Dance Federation of California, *Dances Near and Far, International Folk Dance Series,* Vol. A-1, p. 24.

Reference in Bibliography: 14 (Vol. V, p. 24).

MEASURES

V. Tunnel

1–16 Use waltz step throughout entire figure. First couple turns to face reverse line of direction and forms an arch with inside hands joined. First couple moves forward in reverse line of direction with arch (*over*), as remaining couples in their group bend and move in line of direction *under* the arches. As each couple reaches end of arches, they turn to face reverse line of direction, form an arch and move in the reverse line of direction. The arches form a tunnel. When first couple reaches end of line of couples in *their group* going under arches, they turn to face line of direction, take original dance position, and follow the other couples through the tunnel (arches). All couples follow the same procedure upon reaching end of line. When first couple reaches end of tunnel, they continue moving in line of direction with waltz steps.

17–28 Take twelve waltz steps in line of direction. All couples will finish moving through tunnel and all of the first couples will have led the group around into the original circle. Face center of circle on last waltz step.

VI. Lady to Center, Man Away

1–8 Hands on hips, take four waltz steps, man backing away from center, lady moving toward center of circle. Take four waltz steps, man moving forward, lady moving backwards. Single circle will be reformed. Take skater waltz position.

9–16 Repeat action of Part III, measure 1–8.

VII. Lady to Center, Man Away

1–8 Repeat action of Part VI, measures 1–8. When returning to position, man takes larger steps in order to move past lady to inside of circle. On last waltz step, both turn to face line of direction and take skater waltz position.

9–16 Repeat action of Part 4, measures 1–12. Twist step is for only eight waltz steps.

VIII. Lady Moving Around Man

1–12 Join left hands. Take twelve waltz steps, lady moving counterclockwise around man, making three complete revolutions (4 measures for each complete revolution); man moves very *slowly* forward. Man's left arm moves above head like the arm action for twirling a lariat. On last step, face partner, man's back to center of circle. Man bows and lady curtseys, sweeping skirt with free hand.

NOTE:

1. There is a slight break in the music between the 16th and 17th measures of the tunnel figure, making it necessary to change foot movement to fit, about two counts.

2. The Argentine waltz step differs from the traditional waltz step in that one steps left on a *flat foot* (ct. 1), steps right on ball of foot (ct. 2), steps left on ball of foot (ct. 3). This step is used throughout the dance.

RHEINLAENDER FOR THREE
German

Rheinlaender for Three in German is "Rheinlaender Zu Dreien." Zu Dreien means "for three" and Rheinlaender is another word for "schottische." Gretel and Paul Dunsing indicate that the dance was originated by an East Prussian Youth group.

Music	Record: Folk Dancer MH 1050.
	Piano: Dunsing, Gretel and Paul, *Dance Lightly*, p. 20.
Formation	Set of three, man between two ladies, facing line of direction, inside hands joined, outside hands on hip.
Steps	Schottische, run, step hop.

DIRECTIONS FOR THE DANCE

Music 4/4   NOTE: Directions are same for man and ladies, except when specially noted.

MEASURES

<u>Figure I.</u> **Arches**

A   1–2   Beginning left, take two schottische steps diagonally to the left, then right, in line of direction.

      3–4   Take two schottische steps, right hand lady moving through arch formed by man and left hand lady. Man turns under his left arm. Then left hand lady moves to other side. All face reverse line of direction.

      5–8   Repeat action of measures 1–4, moving in reverse line of direction.

      1–8   Repeat action of measures 1–8.

<u>Figure II.</u>   **Run, Women Turn**

B   9   Beginning left, take four running steps in line of direction.

      10   Ladies take four running steps turning once (toward the man) under raised arms.

      11   Take four running steps backward in reverse line of direction.

      12   Ladies take four running steps turning once (away from man) under raised arms.

      13–16   Repeat action of measures 9–12.

<u>Figure III.</u>   **Mill**

      9–12   Man and left hand lady join right hands held at shoulder height (called a mill). Beginning left, take two schottische steps, turning clockwise. Join left hands, take two schottische steps, turning counterclockwise. Right hand lady takes four schottische steps in place.

      13–16   Man and right hand lady join right hands. Repeat action of measures 9–12, Figure III. Left hand lady dances in place.

<u>Figure IV.</u>   **Arches**

Dance arranged from the dance description by Paul and Gretel Dunsing, *Dance Lightly*, Reference 29 (p. 21).

References in Bibliography: 51 (p. 30), 119 (July '53, p. 8).

Dance annotation form © 1948 by the Folk Dance Federation of California.

MEASURES

C 17–24   Repeat action of measures 1–8, A, Figure I, twice.

Figure V. **Man Dances with One Lady**

D 25   Man beginning left, right hand lady right, take one schottische step moving away from each other as left hand lady, beginning right, dances behind right hand lady with one schottische step to right.

26   All take one schottische step back to place. Man pretends to prepare to turn right hand lady, who extends arms for closed position; instead, man turns suddenly to face left hand lady.

27–28   Man and left hand lady take closed position. Man beginning left, lady right, take four step hops, turning clockwise, progressing in line of direction. Right hand lady takes four step hops, turning clockwise and crosses in front of couple to the inside. Ladies are now on opposite sides and all face line of direction.

29–32   Repeat action of measures 25–28, man dancing with other lady. Now all return to original positions and face line of direction.

25–32   Repeat action of measures 25–32.

ROAD TO THE ISLES
Scottish

Road to the Isles is a favorite marching song of the Pipe Bands. The tune called "Bens of Jura" was composed by Pipe Major MacLellan about 1890 with words by Dr. Kenneth McLeod. The original words are very similar to the song "Border Trail." The dance is relatively new in composition and is similar to the Scottish Polais Glide and the Douglass Schottische. The authors learned the dance in New York City and in California, 1944–46.

Music	Record: Folk Dancer MH 3003; Folkraft 1095, 1095X45, 1416; Imperial 1005; World of Fun M 110.
	Piano: Rorhbough, Lynn, Cooperative Recreation Service, *Sing it Again, Handy II*, p. 16.
Position	Varsouvianna.
Steps	Schottische.

DIRECTIONS FOR THE DANCE

Music 2/4   NOTE: Directions are same for both lady and man.

MEASURES

I. Point, Grapevine

1	Point left toe forward to left.
2–3	Step left behind right (ct. 1), right to right side (ct. 2), left in front of right (ct. 1), and hold (ct. 2).
4	Point right toe forward to right.
5–6	Step right behind left (ct. 1), left to left side (ct. 2), right in front of left (ct. 1), and hold (ct. 2).
7–8	Point left toe forward (body leans backward), point left toe back (body leans forward).

II. Schottische

9–12	Beginning left, take two schottische steps in line of direction. Without releasing hands, turn clockwise on hop (ct. 2 measure 12) to face reverse line of direction. Lady is now on man's left.
13–14	Beginning left, take one schottische step in reverse line of direction. Without releasing hands, turn counterclockwise on hop to face line of direction. Lady is now back in original position on man's right.
15–16	Stamp in place right, left, right.

STYLE:

The Scottish flavor may be added by precise and petite foot movement. Kicking the heel up on the hop of the schottische step so as to flick the kilt is characteristic.

References in Bibliography: 14 (Vol. III, p. 20), 35 (p. 24), 65 (p. 90).
Dance annotation form © 1948 by the Folk Dance Federation of California.

RUMUNSKO KOLO
Roumanian

Kolo means "wheel, turning, or circle," and is a folk dance of the Slavic people. There are many different Kolo tunes, patterns, and rhythms; yet they follow a definite form. According to Mary Hinman* the Kolo was an integral part of the pagan ritual in honor of Light. Eventually the dance was done on all occasions. The Bulgarians, Armenians, and Roumanians refer to these dances as Horo; the Jewish and Grecians use the word Horah or Horo; and the Serbs call them Oro. Most of the Kolos are performed in a broken circle.

Music	Record: Balkan 525, 45–576; Folk Dancer MH 1010, Folkraft 1402.
Formation	Broken circle, joined hands held down.
Steps	Schottische, rock, stamp, step hop.

DIRECTIONS FOR THE DANCE

Music 4/4
MEASURES

NOTE: Directions are same for both lady and man.

Introduction
Dancers stand in place and feel the basic rhythm for the first four measures and start with Part II or they may begin on the first beat with Part I.

I. Step Hop, Schottische

1–4   Face line of direction. Beginning right, take two step hops and one schottische step turning on hop to face reverse line of direction. Moving backward in line of direction and beginning left, take two step hops and one schottische step turning on hop to face center. On each hop, free foot swings forward. Circle moves counterclockwise.

II. Rock, Stamp

5   Face center. Beginning right, cross right over left (ct. 1), rock back onto left (ct. 2), rock forward onto right (ct. 3), hop right and swing left forward into position to repeat (ct. 4).

6   Beginning left, cross left over right (ct. 1), rock back onto right (ct. 2), rock forward onto left (ct. 3), hop left and swing right forward into position to repeat (ct. 4).

7–8   Beginning right, cross right over left (ct. 1), rock back onto left (ct. 2), rock forward onto right (ct. 3), place left beside right (weight remains on right) (ct. 4). Stamp left three times (cts. 1, 2, 3), hold (ct. 4).

9–12   Beginning left, repeat action of measures 5–8. Finish with stamp on right.

STYLE:
The dancers are close together, standing straight, hands joined below waist level. The basic body movement comes from below the hips, knees relaxed. The foot work is close to the floor. The body doesn't sway on the rock, but the rock comes from the knees.

---

* Hinman, Mary, *Group Dances, Gymnastics, and Folk Dances,* Vol. IV, A. S. Barnes, N. Y., p. 89.

References in Bibliography: 14 (Vol. VII, p. 22), 119 (Mr. '52, p. 14), 72 (p. 141).

Dance annotation form © 1948 by the Folk Dance Federation of California.

SELJANCICA KOLO
Yugoslavian

Seljancica is pronounced *Seh-lyahn'-chee-tsah*.

Music	Record: Folk Dancer MH 1006; Folkraft 1401X45, LP-13.
	Piano: Beliajus, V. F., *Dance and Be Merry*, Vol. 1, p. 50. Hinman, Mary, *Group Dances, Gymnastics and Folk Dances*, Vol. IV, p. 90.
Formation	Broken circle, joined hands held down, leader at right end of line.
Steps	Step hop, schottische.

DIRECTIONS FOR THE DANCE

Music 2/4   NOTE: Directions are same for both lady and man.

MEASURES

Part I

1–2   Beginning right, take one schottische step, swinging left leg forward on hop. Circle moves counterclockwise.

3–4   Beginning left, take one schottische step, swinging right leg forward on hop. Circle moves clockwise.

1–4   Repeat action of measures 1–4.

Part II

5   Beginning right, step right in place and swing left across in front of right, lifting right heel.

6   Step left in place and swing right across in front of left, lifting left heel.

7–8   Repeat action of measures 5–6.

Part III

9   Face line of direction. Hop left and touch right heel forward (ct. 1), bring right toe down to floor (ct. and), step forward left close to right (ct. 2), hold (ct. and). Circle moves counterclockwise.

10–12   Repeat action of measure 9 three times.

13   Face reverse line of direction. Hop right and touch left heel forward (ct. 1), bring left toe down to floor (ct. and), step forward right close to left (ct. 2), hold (ct. and). Circle moves clockwise.

14–16   Repeat action of measure 13 three times.

STYLE:

The dancers are close together, standing straight, hands joined below the waist level. The foot work is close to the floor.

References in Bibliography: 6 (p. 50), 14 (Vol. II, p. 29), 72 (p. 113), 62 (p. 31).

SENFTENBERGER
German

Music	Record: Imperial 1101; Folk Dancer MH 1049.
Position	Couple, inside hands joined at shoulder height, outside hands on hips.
Steps	Walk, step swing, polka, slide.

DIRECTIONS FOR THE DANCE

Music 4/4
MEASURES

NOTE: Directions are for man; lady's part reverse.

Part I. Walk, Step Swing

A 1–2
Moving forward, beginning left, walk four slow steps (cts. 1-2-3-4, 1-2-3-4).

3–4
Step left to side away from partner (ct. 1) close right to left (ct. 2), step left in place (ct. 3), hop on left swinging right forward (ct. 4 and), step right in place swinging left back (ct. 1), hop right turning counterclockwise to face reverse line of direction (ct. 2 and), step left in place (ct. 3), and hold (ct. 4 and).

5–8
Beginning right, repeat action of measures 1–4, moving in reverse line of direction.

Music 2/4

Part II. Hop Tap, Polka

B 1–2
Closed position. Beginning right, step hop in place (ct. and), tap left in place (ct. 1), hold (ct. 2). Repeat. Or beginning left, take two mazurka steps, moving forward.

3–8
Beginning left, take six lively polka steps, turning clockwise, progressing in line of direction.

1–8
Repeat action of measures 1–8, B.

Music 4/4

Part I. Walk, Step Swing

A 1–8
Couple position, outside hands on hip. Repeat action of Part I, A, measures 1–8.

Music 2/4

Part III. Slide, Polka

B 1–2
Open position. Take four slides in line of direction.

3–4
Jump on both feet or stamp left (ct. 1), hop left in place, swinging right leg forward (ct. 2), step right in place (ct. 1), hop right in place swinging left leg back (ct. 2).

5–8
Closed position. Beginning left, take four polka steps, turning clockwise, progressing in line of direction.

1–8
Repeat action of Part III, measures 1–8, B.

References in Bibliography: 14 (Vol. VI, p. 31), 120 (Mar. '51, p. 13), 72 (p. 177).

SIAMSA BEIRTE
Irish

Siamsa Beirte is pronounced *sheem-suh-Burr-tuh*. Beirte means "for two"; Siamsa is a "frolic" literally. So the translation is "a frolic for two." Siamsa Beirte is a 2/4 hornpipe time, *not* a reel. Una and Sian O'Farrell introduced Siamsa Beirte at the Stockton Folk Dance Camp in 1956.

Music	Record: *Bluebell Polka*, Folkraft 1422.
	Piano: *Bluebell Polka*, Reference in Bibliography 116, May 1951, p. 16.
Formation	Double circle, partners facing, man's back to center, right hands joined at shoulder height and left hand hanging relaxed by side.
Step	Polka.

DIRECTIONS FOR THE DANCE

Music 2/4

MEASURES

NOTE: Directions are for man; lady's part reverse.

Introduction

1–8   Always listen to eight measures of music before beginning to dance.

"Threes" and Rock

1   Beginning right, hop in place, step to left on left, step right almost behind left, step left (cts. and 1 and 2). Do not dip on second step.

2   Beginning left, repeat action in other direction (cts. and 1 and 2).

3–4   Beginning right, hop in place, bringing left behind right, step on left, hop left, bringing right behind left, step on right, hop right, bringing left behind right, step on left, rock to side on right, rock to side on left (cts. and 1 and 2 and 1 and 2). The rock is side to side with feet close together, the right foot crossed in front of the left. Raise weight onto ball of foot and rock. The lady begins on the left foot but steps one foot behind the other as does the man.

5–8   Beginning with *left hop*, repeat action of measures 1–4 in reverse line of direction.

"Threes" and Change Over

9   Repeat action of measure 1.

10   Beginning with *left hop*, take one schottische step to change places. Man moves around lady as she turns counterclockwise under joined right hands.

11–12   Repeat action of measures 9–10 and return to original position.

Dance arranged from the dance description researched and published by the Folk Dance Federation of California, *Let's Dance,* March 1955.
Dance annotation form © 1948 by the Folk Dance Federation of California.
Reference in Bibliography: 72 (p. 148).

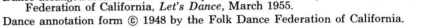

MEASURES

Irish Turn

13–16　　Take both hands, crossed so that man's right joins lady's right on top and man's left joins lady's left underneath. Hold at shoulder height, elbows bent. Man pulls right hand toward him and down and under the left, rolling up so that the girl's forearms are resting on him. Beginning with right hop, take four polka steps, turning clockwise, progressing in the line of direction. Irish folk dance teachers refer to this polka (hop 1, 2, 3) as "turning threes." Both pull away slightly, remaining in a true facing position for this turn.

STYLE:

The body is held erect but not stiff, the head high and the steps are small, lively and clean cut, and the toes pointing down.

NOTE:

The rhythm hop step step step is taken in even rhythm (and 1 and 2) even though it is referred to as a polka.

SNURRBOCKEN
Swedish

Snurrbocken, like the Hambo, is a form of Swedish polska. "Snurr" means a whirling motion, "bock" means a bow; thus the name can be translated "The Whirl and Bow." It is pronounced *SNOOR-book-en* (oo as in look). According to Gordon E. Tracie, the second (bowing) part of the dance is a bit of rustic satire in which the farm folk burlesqued the gentry and their affected mannerisms. Traditionally, it was at just this point that the fiddler could have *his* fun with the dancers by setting the timing and tempo of his bow sequence — often with long delays — and it was up to the dancers to follow him!

Music	Record: Aqua Viking V 200; Folk Dancer MH 1047; RCA LPM 9837.
	Piano: *Svenska folkdanser och sallskapsdancer,* Svenska Ungdomsringen, Stockholm.
Position	Shoulder waist.
Steps	Polska step, running step.

DIRECTIONS FOR THE DANCE

Music 3/4
MEASURES

NOTE: Directions are for man; lady's part reverse.

I. Polska Turn

1–8 Beginning left, take eight polska steps turning clockwise progressing in line of direction. Analysis of polska step: *Man's part:* Count 1, step forward left, pivoting clockwise. Count 2, continue pivoting on left and place ball of right foot near left foot (weight remains on left foot, right foot helps to maintain balance). Count 3, step forward right. *Lady's part:* Count 1, step on both feet, preparing to pivot clockwise. Count 2, step right, pivoting clockwise. Count 3, step left, pivoting clockwise.

II. Run

9–16 Conversation position, with free hand on hips, (fingers forward, thumb back). Beginning left, take twenty-four light small, running steps forward in line of direction.

III. Bows

17 Place hands on own hips and turn slowly toward partner, man with back to center, lady facing the center.

18 Slowly bow low to each other with dignity.

19 Each turn one half turn, clockwise away from each other.

20 Slowly bow while back to back.

21 Each turns one half more turn to face each other. Take shoulder waist position to repeat dance.

NOTE:

1. This polska step, sometimes called Delsbopolska after a district in the province of Halsingland, is related to the Hambo step but begins with the man's *left,* and has a pivot, whereas the hambo-polska begins with the man's *right* and has a "dip" (first beat) at the beginning of each step.

2. The recording by Folk Dancer begins with a bow instead of a polska.

References in Bibliography: 14 (Vol. VII, p. 23), 72 (p. 249).

SØNDERBORG DOBBELTVADRILLE
Danish

Sønderborg Dobbeltradrille means "Sønderburg Double Quadrille." Sønderburg is a little town on the Danish island of Alsen. It is danced in Denmark, Northern Germany, and Sweden. The first version presented is based on Sønderburg Double Quadrille*, dance description by Paul and Gretel Dunsing. The second version is Danish from Gordon Tracie, Seattle, Washington.

Music Record: Aqua Viking 406; Folkraft 1163; His Master's Voice A.L. 1291 (no longer pressed); World of Fun M 115, Tanz EP 58 607.

    Piano: Dunsing, Gretel and Paul, *Dance Lightly*, p. 16.

Formation Two lines facing each other, four couples in each line. Head couples are two couples on each side of line nearest head of set. Foot couples are two couples on each side of line forming remainder of set.

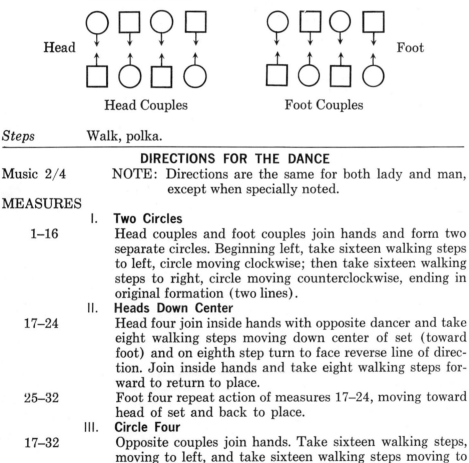

Head   Foot

    Head Couples   Foot Couples

Steps Walk, polka.

DIRECTIONS FOR THE DANCE

Music 2/4 NOTE: Directions are the same for both lady and man, except when specially noted.

MEASURES

I. Two Circles

1–16 Head couples and foot couples join hands and form two separate circles. Beginning left, take sixteen walking steps to left, circle moving clockwise; then take sixteen walking steps to right, circle moving counterclockwise, ending in original formation (two lines).

II. Heads Down Center

17–24 Head four join inside hands with opposite dancer and take eight walking steps moving down center of set (toward foot) and on eighth step turn to face reverse line of direction. Join inside hands and take eight walking steps forward to return to place.

25–32 Foot four repeat action of measures 17–24, moving toward head of set and back to place.

III. Circle Four

17–32 Opposite couples join hands. Take sixteen walking steps, moving to left, and take sixteen walking steps moving to right, ending in original position.

* Dance is based upon the dance description by Paul and Gretel Dunsing, *Dance Lightly*, Reference 29 (p. 14).

References in Bibliography: 29 (p. 14), 54 (p. 138), 72 (p. 178).

Dance annotation form © 1948 by the Folk Dance Federation of California.

MEASURES

IV. **Chain**

33–40   Opposite couples execute grand right and left in small circles, four dancers each. Opposite dancers join right hands, pass, left hand to partner, and so forth, ending in place and bowing to partner.

41–48   Repeat action of measures 33–40. See note below.

V. **Polka**

33–48   Couples take closed position or shoulder waist position. Man beginning left, lady right, take sixteen polka steps turning clockwise, progressing in line of direction around oval circle formed by two lines, back to place.

NOTE:

Measures 41–48. The record, His Master's Voice A.L. 1291, does *not* allow for this repeat. It goes directly into the polka. The World of Fun M 115 and the piano score fit the directions given.

VARIATION:

Measures 33–40, opposite couples may execute right and left through across set, then back to place, instead of grand right and left.

DANISH VERSION

Formation

Two lines facing each other, two couples in a line. Sets of four couples may be arranged in lines, the length of the hall or like spokes in a wheel. Arranged the length of the hall, dancers wait once through the dance at the end of the hall; whereas in the wheel formation, everyone dances continuosly.

I.

1–16   Each set of four joins hands to form a circle. Same action as Figure 1, measures 1–16.

II.

17–32   Same action as Figure 11, measures 17-32.

III.

17–32   Same action as Variation, measures 33–40.

25–32   Each seat of four, join hands to form a circle. Beginning left, take sixteen walking steps, circle moving clockwise, once and a half around. Couples end on opposite side.

IV.

33–48   Couples take closed position. Take sixteen polka steps turning clockwise and dance around opposite couple two times, ending back to back with opposite couple. Each couple now faces a new line, and a new set is formed as the dance is repeated from the beginning.

SQUARE TANGO
English

The Square Tango is an old English dance.

Music   Record: *Jealousy*, Windsor 4-536; El Choclo CEM 37023.
Position   Closed.
Steps   Draw step, twinkle step.

DIRECTIONS FOR THE DANCE

Music 2/4   NOTE: Directions are for man; lady's part reverse.

MEASURES

I. Box Step

1–2   Beginning left, step forward, step side on right, close left to right. (Slow, quick, quick). Step back on right, side left, and close right to left.

3–4   Step left sideward, draw right slowly to left. Step right sideward, draw left slowly to right.

5–8   Repeat action of measures 1–4.

II. Walk and Dip

9–11   Beginning left, take six walking steps forward in line of direction.

12   Dip forward on left and step back on right coming into an open position.

III. Twinkle

13–14   Open position. Step left (slow), step right (slow), step left in place (quick), step right in place (quick). Cross left over right (slow), turning inward toward partner to reverse open position.

15   Step right slightly forward in reverse line of direction (quick), step left in place (quick). Cross right over left (slow), turning inward toward partner to face line of direction.

16   Closed position. Step forward left (quick) in line of direction, step sideward right (quick), close left slowly to right (slow), keeping weight on right.

STYLE:
On the draw steps, Part I, the body leans to the side of the drawing foot. The left arm arches overhead as the body leans to the right. The left arm extends toward the floor as the body leans to the right.

References in Bibliography: 23 (p. 61), 119 (Vol. VII, Dec. '51, p. 13).
Dance annotation form © 1948 by the Folk Dance Federation of California.

SRPKINJA KOLO
Yugoslavian

Srpkinja means Serbian girl. This dance was created in the late 1800's using Serbian folk steps in a special arrangement that would appeal to more sophisticated people and could be used in the ballrooms of the city along with the other social dances of the day. In the ballrooms it was originally danced in a quadrille formation. Eventually the rural people were dancing it too, adapting it to their form, a big circle.

Music	Record: Folk Dancer MH 1008.
Formation	Single circle, couples facing center, lady to left of man, joined hands held down in peasant version, at shoulder height in formal version.
Steps	Walk, kolo step.

DIRECTIONS FOR THE DANCE

Music 2/4   NOTE: Directions are same for both lady and man.

MEASURES

I. **Walk, Center and Back**

1–2   Beginning right, take three walking steps in line of direction. Circle moves counterclockwise. Touch left toe to right.

3–4   Beginning left, take three walking steps in reverse line of direction. Touch right toe to left.

5–6   Face center. Beginning right, take three walking steps toward center. Touch left toe to right.

7–8   Beginning left, take three walking steps backward away from center. Touch right toe to left.

1–8   Repeat action of measures 1–8.

II. **Step Touch, Walk**

9–10   Face center. Beginning right, step to side and touch left toe to right. Repeat to the left.

11–12   Beginning right, take three walking steps in line of direction. Touch left toe to right.

13–14   Face center. Beginning left, step to side and touch right to left. Repeat to right.

15–16   Beginning left, take three walking steps in reverse line of direction. Touch right toe to left.

9–16   Repeat action of measures 9–16.

Dance is based upon the dance description by Michael Herman, reproduced here by permission of Folk Dance House, 108 West 16th Street, New York City, New York. Dance annotation form © 1948 by the Folk Dance Federation of California.

MEASURES

III. Bows, Basic Kolo

17–18	Beginning right, ladies take two steps turning counter-clockwise, into circle to face partner. Both bow.
19–20	Beginning right, ladies take two steps, turning counter-clockwise (thus backs into) to position in circle to left of partner. Lady is now on right side of partner. Pause.
21–22	Beginning right, men take two steps, turning counter-clockwise into circle to face partner. Both bow.
23–24	Beginning right, men take two steps turning counter-clockwise to position in circle to left of partner. Lady is now on left side of partner.
25–26	All join hands. Beginning right, take one kolo step to right.
27–28	Beginning left, take one kolo step to left.
29–30	Beginning right, take one kolo step to right.
31–32	Beginning left, take one kolo step to left.
1–16	Repeat action, measures 17–32.

NOTE:

1. *Kolo step:* Moving right, hop on left foot, leap onto right foot, step on left foot behind right, step on right in place, hop on right foot.

2. Part III, measures 25–32, a simple grapevine step may be substituted for the kolo step for the less experienced dancer.

STYLE:

In both the peasant and formal version, there is an elegant quality (posture) that is maintained throughout the dance.

SWEDISH WALTZ

This dance has been popular in the United States for at least 50 years. Gordon E. Tracie* in his study of dances in Scandinavia in 1948 discovered that such a "Swedish Waltz" was not danced in Sweden. However, an elderly couple from the country (Dalarna) recognized it as the nearly forgotten "Norsk Vals" (Norwegian Waltz) which they had danced in their youth. Scandinavian immigrants undoubtedly brought the dance to this country at the turn of the century.

Music   Record: Any good Swedish Waltz moderately slow in tempo. Aqua Viking 803 (slow), 807, 810.

Position   Couple, inside hands joined at shoulder height.

Step   Waltz, step swing or waltz balance.

DIRECTIONS FOR THE DANCE

Music 3/4   NOTE: Directions are for man; lady's part reverse.

MEASURES

1   Beginning left, take one step swing (dal step) or waltz balance (step touch) almost in place turning body slightly away from partner, inside hands reaching forward as arms are extended forward shoulder height.

2   Beginning right, move slightly forward, taking one step swing of waltz balance and turn body slightly toward partner, inside hands drawing backward as arms are extended backward shoulder height.

3–4   Beginning left, take two waltz steps or six steps in waltz rhythm in line of direction. More advanced dancers turn away from partner (man left, lady right) once while moving in line of direction. This turn is facilitated by man stepping back in line of direction right, lady left, on second waltz step before continuing turn.

5–8   Closed position or shoulder waist position. Beginning left, take four waltz steps, turning clockwise. Lady turns out under man's left arm on last waltz step to assume couple position.

---

* Gordon E. Tracie, authority on Swedish Folk Dancing, Seattle, Washington.
Dance annotation form © 1948 by the Folk Dance Federation of California.

SWEDISH VARSOUVIENNE
Swedish

All of the Scandinavian lands have virtually identical Varsouvienne, which is different but related in both music and step pattern to the well known American Varsouvianna or Put Your Little Foot.

Music	Record: Folk Dancer MH 1023, Folkraft 1130X45.
	Piano: Bergquist, Nils, *Swedish Folk Dances*, p. 12.
	Herman, Michael, *Folk Dances for All*, p. 32.
Position	Conversation, outside hands on hip, thumb pointing backward, fingers forward.
Steps	Walk, waltz, mazurka.

DIRECTIONS FOR THE DANCE

Music 3/4   NOTE: Directions are for man; Lady's part reverse.

MEASURE

I. Walk and Heel

1–2
Beginning left, take three steps, man dancing almost in place, the lady takes a full turn counterclockwise and moves across in front of man to his left side. Man places left arm around lady's waist and lady places right arm on man's left shoulder, outside hands on hip. Place right heel with toe raised (lady's left) slightly forward. Outside hand is always on hip.

3–4
Beginning right, repeat action of measures 1–2, lady turning clockwise, returns to original position. Place left heel with toe raised forward.

5–8
Repeat action of measures 1–4.

II. Mazurka

9–10
Beginning left, step forward with slight accent, draw right to left, hop right sweeping left across right. Repeat.

11–12
Repeat action of measures 1–2.

13–16
Beginning right, repeat action of measures 9–12.

III. Waltz

17–24
Closed position. Beginning left, take eight waltz steps, turning clockwise, progressing in line of direction.

VARIATION:

Measures 9–10, instead of sweeping foot across, kick left foot forward and back fast. In Sweden, this is referred to as "fryksdal-step."

References in Bibliography: 7 (p. 11), 36 (p. 65), 52 (p. 31).
Dance annotation form © 1948 by the Folk Dance Federation of California.

THREE MEET
English

Three Meet is a dance of greeting from Northern England.

Music	Record: Columbia DB 569*, Folkraft 1112, 1262. Piano: Gadd, May, *Country Dances of Today*, Book 2, p. 15.
Formation	English running step, buzz step. facing another set of three. All sets form large circle alternately one faces line of direction, the other reverse line of direction.
Steps	Sets of three, two ladies and a man or vice versa, arms linked,

DIRECTIONS FOR THE DANCE

Music 4/4   NOTE: Directions are same for lady and man.

MEASURES

I. Forward, Back and Change Sides

1–2   Take four steps, moving forward, four steps moving backwards. Take eight steps on a diagonal to right passing opposite set and turning counterclockwise a half turn to face same set on opposite sides.

5–8   In new place, repeat action of measures 1–4 to return to original place.

II. Elbow Swing

9–10   Taking eight steps, the middle dancer turns right hand partner with right elbow swing twice around in place.

11–12   Middle dancer takes eight walking steps, turning left hand partner with left elbow swing twice around. On last two steps, the three in set cuddle up (arms reach around each other, middle dancers arms underneath) to form a basket of three.

III. Basket in Line of Three

13–16   In cuddle position, sets progress diagonally to right passing each other, while turning counterclockwise with a buzz step (right foot crossed in front of left), and meet new set coming in opposite direction.

Repeat dance, each set dancing with new set.

NOTE:

The English Country dancers are particular about attacking each new phrase of music on time.

STYLE:

The English running step is a light, bouncy, dignified half walk-half run step. The body is in a dignified easy posture. The free hand of each outside dancer in the set hangs free to the side. The middle dancer holds the arms of the two partners in closely to his sides so that the threes can move easily as a unit. As a dance of greeting, the spirit is as gay as the music. The dancers enjoy visiting around the circle to each new set of three.

Dance arranged from the dance description by May Gadd, *Country Dances of Today, Book 2.* 55 Christopher Street, New York: Country Dance Society of America, May 1951.

References in Bibliography: 37 (p. 6), 51 (p. 3), 72 (p. 81).

Dance annotation form © 1948 by the Folk Dance Federation of California.

* Out of print.

TO TING
Danish

To Ting means "two things." This refers to the two different rhythms, 3/4 and 2/4. The dance was learned by the authors in New York City in 1944, '45, and '46.

Music	Record: Folk Dancer MH 1018; RCA FAS-664; Sonart 303.
	Piano: Herman, Michael, *Folk Dances for All*, p. 52.
Position	Couple position, outside hands on hips.
Steps	Waltz, walk, pivot turn.

DIRECTIONS FOR THE DANCE

Music 3/4 NOTE: Directions are for man; lady's part reverse.

MEASURES

Part I

1 Moving forward, beginning left, take one waltz step turning away from partner, swinging inside arms forward, hands at shoulder level.

2 Moving forward, take one waltz step turning toward partner, swinging inside arms back.

3–4 Repeat action of measures 1–2.

5–8 Closed position. Beginning left, take four waltz steps, turning clockwise, progressing in line of direction.

1–8 Repeat action of measures 1–8.

Part II

Music 2/4

9–12 Conversation position, outside hands on hips. Beginning left, take four walking steps forward.

13–16 Shoulder waist position. Beginning left, turn clockwise with four steps in a pivot turn.

9–16 Repeat action of measures 9–16.

VARIATION:

9–12 The Danes take four step hops.

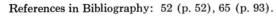

References in Bibliography: 52 (p. 52), 65 (p. 93).
Dance annotation form © 1948 by the Folk Dance Federation of California.

TOTUR
Danish

Totur or "Two Dance" is a mixer from the district of Vejle, Denmark. They refer to this dance as Totur Fra Vejle. Dancers usually get new partners at the completion of the grand right and left figure. It is customary to give each person you meet in the "chain" or grand right and left figure, a friendly greeting.

Music	Record: Folk Dancer MH 1021; Tono 16092; Imperial 6038; Kismet 135.
	Odeon GEOK 239 (recorded in Denmark).
	Piano: *The Folk Dancer*, Vol. V, December 1945, p. 10.
Formation	Single circle, couples facing center, lady to right of partner, hands joined, held at shoulder level.
Steps	Walk, two-step, polka.

DIRECTIONS FOR THE DANCE

Music 2/4   NOTE: Directions are for man; lady's part reverse except in the introduction.

MEASURES

Introduction

1–8   Beginning left, take sixteen walking steps or eight polka steps clockwise.

1–8   Repeat action of measures 1–8 counterclockwise.

Figure I

9   Single circle. Open position, men facing line of direction, joined hands toward center of circle. Beginning left, take one two-step toward center of circle.

10   Continue in same direction with two walking steps.

11–12   Beginning right, moving away from center, repeat action of measures 9–10 back to place in reverse open position.

13–16   Beginning left, take four polka steps, turning clockwise, progressing in line of direction.

9–16   Repeat action of measures 9–16.

Figure II

1–8   Partners face, grasp right hands and grand right and left around circle with walking or polka steps.

1–8   Continue grand right and left. NOTE: At the end of this figure, dancers may have a new partner for repeat of the dance.

Repeat Figure I and II alternately for remainder of record.

This dance was arranged from the dance as used in *The Folk Dancer,* Vol. 5, December 1945, p. 10-11.
References in Bibliography: 14 (Vol. IV, p. 19), 51 (p. 42), 65 (p. 137).

TROIKA
Russian

Troika means "three horses." The dance symbolizes three horses which traditionally drew sleighs for the Russian noble families.

Music   Record: Folk Dancer, MH 1059; Folkraft 1170, 1170X45; World of Fun M 105.

Piano: Herman, Michael, *Folk Dances for All*, p. 7.
Neilson, N. P., and Van Hagen, W., *Physical Education for Elementary Schools*, 1954, p. 373.

Formation   Set of three, man between two ladies, facing line of direction, inside hands joined, outside hands on hip.

Steps   Run.

DIRECTIONS FOR THE DANCE

Music 4/8   NOTE: Directions are same for man and ladies.

MEASURES

I. **Run Forward**
1–4   Beginning right, take sixteen running steps in line of direction. The first four runs may be done diagonally right, second four, diagonally left, and last eight straight forward.

II. **Arch**
5–6   Right hand lady moves under arch made by raised arms of man and left hand lady with eight running steps. Man runs in place and follows right hand lady turning under his left arm. Left hand lady runs in place.

7–8   Left hand lady moves under arch made by raised arms of man and right hand lady with eight running steps. Man runs in place and follows left hand lady turning under his right arm. Right hand lady runs in place.

III. **Circle**
9–11   Set of three join hands in circle and run twelve steps clockwise.

12   Stamp left, right, left, hold.

13–16   Repeat action of measures 9–12, moving counterclockwise.

STYLE:
The knees should be lifted high and the body and head held high.

MIXER:
The man may move forward to the next group of three as the stamps are taken in the last figure.

References in Bibliography: 14 (Vol. I, p. 20), 32 (p. 43), 33 (p. 14), 52 (p. 6), 65 (p. 151), 82 (p. 373).
Dance annotation form © 1948 by the Folk Dance Federation of California.

TSCHERKESSIA
Israeli

Tscherkessia or Cherkessia is a dance for men from Circassia. They were followers of the Mohammedan faith and seeking religious freedom in the Czarist days of Russia. They left southeastern Russia and migrated to Palestine and Syria. The Circassians were noted for their horsemanship. The rhythmic movement of the dance portrays either horses or riders. The dance was taught at U.C.L.A., Los Angeles, California, 1943, and by Dvora Lapson of the Jewish Education Institute, New York City, 1946.

Music	Record: Israel 116, Israel LP 7; RCA Victor EPA 4140; Sonart 303; Kismet 130.
	Piano: Beliajus, F. V., *Dance and Be Merry*, Vol. I, p. 12. Chochem, Corrine, and Roth, Muriel, *Palestine Dances*, p. 31. Lapson, Dvora, *Dances of the Jewish People*, p. 34.
Formation	Groups of four or five dancers in a line, arms linked about one another's waist or any number of dancers in a single circle.

DIRECTIONS FOR THE DANCE

Music 2/4   NOTE: Directions are same for both lady and man.

MEASURES

A 1–2   I. Step right across left, step left in place, step back right, step left in place. Line or circle moves left. As cross step is taken, body leans forward, left knee bends to give flexibility to movement. As backward steps are taken, body should lean back as far as possible.

    3–8   Repeat action of measures 1–2 three times.

B 9   II. Line or circle moves to the right. Beginning right, step to the side, cross left behind right.

  10–16   Repeat action of measure 9 seven times.

Variations for Part II

1. Sixteen scissor kicks (cut steps) in front.
2. Sixteen scissor kicks (cut steps) in back.
3. Combination of scissor kicks in front and back.
4. Eight slow skips to the right (one per measure).
5. Keep feet together, move both toes, then both heels to the right.
6. Semi-crouch position, execute a shuffle step, moving to the right.

NOTE:
The action described in Part II may be used each time or a different action selected from the variations may be used for each repeat of the B music. The dance should be started in a slow tempo. Each repetition becomes faster until a climax of great excitement is reached. If done in a line, each group moves independently, allowing the action of Part II to carry them anywhere on the floor.

References in Bibliography: 6 (p. 12), 16 (p. 30), 116 (Vol. 6, No. 12, Dec. 1946, p. 11). Dance annotation form © 1948 by the Folk Dance Federation of California.

WEGGIS DANCE
Swiss

This dance was originated in the United States by the Swiss Folk Dance Group of New York City in 1933. The tune is the familiar and favorite Swiss yodeling song, "Weggis." Weggis is the name of a village in the canton of Lucerne, Switzerland. The words of the song tell of a favorite trip between two villages, Weggis and Lucerne. The steps are characteristic of Swiss folk dance patterns. The dance was learned by the authors in New York City.

Music	Record: Folk Dancer MH 1046; Folkraft 1160; Imperial 1008**; World of Fun M 101.
	Piano: Fox, Grace, *Folk Dancing in High School and College*, p. 67.
	Herman, Michael, *Folk Dances for All*, p. 56.
Formation	Promenade.
Steps	Double circle, couples facing line of direction.
Position	Polka, schottische, three-step turn, step hop.

DIRECTIONS FOR THE DANCE

Music 2/4   NOTE: Directions are same for both man and lady, except when specially noted.

MEASURES

Figure I. **Heel Toe Polka**

A   1   Beginning left, place left heel forward, touch left toe in front of right toe.

    2   Take one polka step forward (hop on right).

    3–4   Beginning right, repeat action of measures 1–2.

    5–8   Repeat action of measure 1–4. On the last beat of the polka, the lady must touch her right foot in place, keeping the weight on the left foot so the right foot will be free to lead into the chorus.

        Chorus:

B   9   Hands on hips, man beginning left, lady right, take one schottische step moving away from each other diagonally forward.

    10   Take one schottische step diagonally forward toward partner.

    11–12   Shoulder-waist position. Take four step hops, turning clockwise.

    13–16   Repeat action of measures 9–12.
        Interlude*: Single circle, partners face, two hands joined. Man's left arm, lady's right, point down toward center of circle; man's right arm, lady's left, slightly bent, held high.

---

* Interlude: An introductory phrase of two measures played after each chorus. During this time, partners take position for the next Figure.

References in Bibliography: 25 (p. 51), 33 (p. 7), 36 (p. 67), 52 (p. 54).

Dance annotation form © 1948 by the Folk Dance Federation of California.

** Out of print.

MEASURES

Figure II. **Center and Back**

A 1–2   Man beginning left, lady right, repeat action of measures 1–2, Figure I. Take polka step toward center of circle.

3–4   Reverse arm position. Man beginning right, lady left, repeat action of measures 1–2, Figure II, moving away from center of circle.

5–8   Repeat action of measures 1–4, Figure II.

Chorus:

B 9–16   Repeat Action of measures 9–16, Chorus.
Interlude: Promenade position, couples face line of direction.

Figure III. **Step Point**

A 1   Beginning left, step to side (ct. 1), point right toe across left (ct. 2).

2   Beginning right, repeat action of measure 1, Figure III.

3–4   Take two polka steps forward.

5–8   Repeat action of measures 1–4, Figure III.

Chorus:

B 9–16   Repeat action of measures 9–16, Chorus.
Interlude: Partners face, man's back to center, join right hands, elbows bent, forearms touching, and place free hands on hip.

Figure IV. **Step Point**

A 1–8   Beginning left, repeat action of measures 1–8, Figure III. This action turns the couple clockwise in a small circle.

Chorus:

B 9–16   Repeat action of measures 9–16, Chorus.
Interlude: Partners face, man's back to center, inside hands joined, extended at shoulder height toward reverse line of direction, outside hands on hip.

Figure V. **Three Step Turn**

A 1–2   Man beginning left, lady right, take a three-step turn, turning away from partner, both moving forward (cts. 1–2–1). The joined hands swing downward and forward at beginning of turn and are released for turn. Partners join hands, man's left, lady's right, and man bows as lady curtsies (ct. 2).

3–4   Beginning right, repeat action of measures 1–2, Figure V in reverse line of direction.

5–8   Repeat action of measures 1–4, Figure V.

Chorus:

B 9–16   Repeat action of measures 9–16, Chorus.

STYLE:
The movement for the figures has a light quality, while the movement for the chorus is vigorous. The free foot comes up under the body during the hop in the schottische step and should not be swung forward. The free hand is placed on the waist, fist on hip bone with elbows forward. The Swiss often accept the first beat of each measure with a heavier step. This is true of the chorus part of Weggis.

MIXER:
Partner changes may be made after each chorus. Men progress forward to assume new positions with new partner.

VARIATION:
A clever ending to the dance is to have the man lift the lady up into the air on the last two beats of the last chorus. He lifts at her waist. She presses down on his shoulders with her hands. They both bend knees and as he raises her she pushes off into a jump assisting the elevation of her weight upward. She must be careful to land afterwards with a give of the knees and body.

SOCIAL DANCE

HISTORY AND TREND

Ballroom dance had its start with the court dances when during the Renaissance Period all the courts of Europe were trying to out-do the others for the most elaborate ball. Dance masters were hired to dignify and teach many of the peasant dances to the aristocracy. Even the great masters Beethoven, Brahms, Strauss, and others wrote special music for these great court occasions. Exquisite dress and polished manners were the ultimate for any lady and gentleman of the court. These same elements appear in the elaborate cotillions of society today and have been reflected further in the college prom and military ball.

Constantly changing trends in music, bands, entertainment, and entertainers, each striving to appeal to the various levels of society, keep social dance at the top of a long list of popular activities for teenagers and adults. With the reappearance and disappearance of a wide variety of styles and variations in its interesting history, social dance continues to provide pleasure for many people and is gaining more and more attention from the four corners of the world. Even our foreign visitors and students seek out dance instruction because they find the possession of this skill provides an avenue for getting acquainted and mixing with people socially which is seldom equalled in any other way.

Dance changes as people use it. Nearly every dance on our ballroom floor today was ushered in with wild hysteria and daring. People literally threw up their hands in each case but gradually those truckin', rockin', swingin' rhythms won over and people made them fit their more conservative needs. The fads have a place which the dance teachers cannot afford to overlook in keeping up with the times.* They chal-

lenge and they stimulate fresh interest in rhythm, in movement, and in all dance.

Age Group Preferences . . . Style and preference will vary according to the age group, the current music, and the prevailing popularity of dances. The young teen group will find true enjoyment in swing, slow foxtrot, and the fad dances as they come and go. The cha cha cha has been a new favorite with them because of the open positions and the opportunity for individual style and creativity. Even the faster samba has proven to be good fun. A particular hop, drag, twist or line dance can be found in almost every high school across the country. These are the expressions of a need to move and to create. Many of them are tremendously fun to do and have a real charm, although they are seldom seen beyond one particular locality. The older more sophisticated young adult is thrilled with the existing style of the rumba or the tango and even appreciates the smooth beauty of the waltz. They are easily challenged with the more difficult skills in dance.

Adult dancers enjoy the smoother, slower styles of swing, moderate tempos in foxtrot, and a combination of new tunes with sentimental old favorites. Many now are organizing and joining Latin-American dance clubs which offer some regular instruction and a planned party once a month with live music where they can dance what they have learned. The senior adult still prefers the old tunes he recognizes and wants to dance medium foxtrots and waltzes.

The Challenge . . . Dancers in general find pleasure in moving. They are satisfied with the use of a few simple steps, varied by changes in rhythm, direction, style, and tempo. Those who have discovered the art

---

* Refer to page 334.

264

of dancing thrill to the use of fancier patterns and take pride in a high standard of form. It is the function of the dance teacher to expose and inspire those whom they teach to understand what they learn, in order that they may have a desire for good standards of leading and following, careful use of good footwork and position and an appreciation of how to recognize, listen to, and move to the music.* Somewhere at school or recreation center, every boy and girl should have the opportunity to learn to dance.

GROUP LEARNING AS IT RELATES TO SOCIAL DANCE

1. Learning with a group is more fun because the dancer can get lost in the group and work out the steps without worrying about being watched.
2. A group generates a spirit which makes a learning situation more like a social occasion than a class.
3. There is opportunity to make new friends and have many partners for dancing.
4. There is the advantage of watching all types of dancers and of developing the ability to recognize and appreciate good rhythm and style.
5. The opportunity to have questions, answers, and demonstrations before the group is valuable for all.
6. A group situation provides need for and opportunity for practice of good social etiquette such as introductions, invitation and acceptance to dance, partner encouragement and assistance, and social responsibility for others.

Group and Individual Help

1. The leader may see the same problem encountered by several of the group and by stopping to re-explain or re-demonstrate there is a clarification for many in the group.
2. After a brief walk-through, the leader may permit the group to practice freely in normal ballroom style while he moves among them, giving individual help or allowing individuals to come up and ask for help.
3. A leader may give help quickly while the individual keeps right on dancing, by the use of the casual correction of a position, a verbal cue to help with the step, or a rhythm cue (slow quick quick) to help get the dancer in step with the music.*
4. A word cue called over the microphone may be helpful to a class practicing a new step.
5. A few words of encouragement such as "that's right" — "good" — "now you look good" — "that's better" — will go a long way to help build up confidence and security which makes it possible for the learner to relax and enjoy dancing.
6. By dancing with a person who is having difficulty it is often easy to find where the individual needs help. It may be that the man does not have an effective lead. It may be that the girl is leading or leaning heavily on her partner. It may be that special help is needed in getting that person to hear the beat of the music.
7. Extra ideas may be given to those who learn quickly and are ready to think of additional details.
8. A leader can help the group be more at ease if he encourages partners to learn together, laugh at their mistakes, and talk things over from time to time for suggestions.
9. Sometimes a few minutes of assistance after class will help an individual student overcome an embarrassing problem.

Particular consideration need be given to the importance of the individual as a person. The pride an individual can take in the performance of a few lovely patterns in good form, and the ease and relaxation a couple can enjoy together when leading and following is no longer a chore, are two priceless possessions. These reflect the confidence of a person who understands what he is trying to do. Far greater is this type of help from a teacher rather than one who teaches steps and lets the dancers find their own way to use them. Only the very creative find their way. The majority are afraid. Fear of making a mistake and fear of being embarrassed makes them revert to old habits and go on struggling as before.

---

* For music in relation to dance, refer to page 51.

SOCIAL DANCE STYLE

Few dancers realize the importance of good basic posture and footwork to the beauty and style of any dance. An easy upright balanced posture and moving of the feet in line with the body will make the dancer look good regardless of how limited his knowledge of steps. A detailed discussion of correct posture for dance may be found on page 52. Beyond this, the characteristic way of moving, slight changes in position, the expression or impression the dancers give to the interpretation of the music, all make up the specific differences in style from one type of dance to another. These differences may be influenced by the rhythmic peculiarities of the music or by the cultural characteristics of a country which determine the quality of the movement and make it unique.

American ballroom dancing has borrowed steps and dances from many, many countries. Few of these are now done in the authentic style of any country. In most cases it was the rhythmic quality that was fascinating, and not its meaning. Therefore, only a semblance of the original style remains in the Latin-American dances done on our dance floors. It is true also that styles of dances change from time to time with the rising popularity of some new figure or dance team who originated it.

The specific style for each dance has been described in its own section as it is so closely related to the foot patterns and rhythm.

DANCE POSITIONS

Before a dancer begins to learn dance steps, the correct dance position should be considered. Teachers of dance should give more attention to correctness of dance position, as it is so often the determining factor for good balance, comfort, confidence in leading, security in following, and therefore a successful performance. There are five positions generally used in Social Dance. The basic closed position will be discussed in detail here. The others are adaptations of it and are fully described in the glossary.

Closed position

Open or Conversation position

Right Reverse Open position or Left Parallel position

Left Reverse Open position or Right Parallel position

Flirtation position

Closed Position. Each factor in the analysis of this position has a significant reason for its importance. It is not merely a whim for it's important. It is not merely a whim or a formality of dance. Those who are learning dance will tend to form better dance habits if they understand specifically how the position aids the dance rather than being left on their own to discover it or manage as best they can.

1. *Partners should stand facing each other with shoulders parallel.* If almost toe to toe, this generally provides a comfortable distance and allows freedom in leading and following. The body posture is in good alignment.
2. *The feet should be together and pointing straight ahead.* The weight is over the ball of the foot.
3. *The man's right arm* is placed around the lady so that his arm *gives her security* and support. *The right hand is placed in the center of the lady's back* just below the shoulder blade level. The fingers should be closed but not tense. A cupped hand allows the man to lead with the fingers and the heel of the hand. *The man's arm is away from the body* with the elbow pointing slightly out to the side. *A majority of leads are initiated by the man's shoulder, right arm and hand.*
4. *The lady's left arm rests gently but definitely in contact with the man's upper arm* and the hand should lie along the back of the shoulder as is comfortable in relation to each partner. The lady's ability to follow is often determined by her response to the actions of the man's shoulder, arm and hand.

* For music in relation to dance, refer to page 51.

5. *The free hand* is raised sideways and the man holds the lady's right hand in his left approximately between them at just above the lady's shoulder level. The man may let the lady's fingers rest on his upturned palm or he may grasp lightly with his thumb against the fingers of her hand and close his fingers around the back of her hand. *He should not push with this hand.*

6. *Resistance is essential.* A limp body, a limp hand is the surest indication of insecurity, a poor lead, and a slow response in following. Dancers need to feel the difference between *tension* and *relaxation* and the happy medium between the two which may be called *resistance*. This is the difference between a light partner which one cannot control and a tense, rigid partner which one cannot move. The man must provide his ready supporting right arm and a firmness in his hand at her back. The lady must give him just the right amount of resistance against this hand at the back so he knows she is there and will move with his hand. She must also give resistance along his upper right arm — not leaning, but a sure responsiveness to the actions of his arm so that he can turn her to any desired position.

7. Partners may look straight ahead or at each other. *The lady should always assist a return to closed position* from other positions by bringing her head around to look over the man's right shoulder. This tends to bring the shoulders around also and close the position definitely as opposed to leaving position half open.

Common Errors in the Use of Closed Position:

1. Partner standing at an angle in a half open position: causes diagonal motion of the footwork and is uncomfortable.
2. Partner too close or too far away.
3. Lack of support in the man's right arm.
4. Lack of contact of the lady's left arm.
5. Primary use of man's left hand to lead by a pushing or pumping action.
6. Lack of resistance by either man or lady.
7. Man's right hand too high on lady's back, pulling her off balance.
8. Lady's weight back on heels.
9. Man's leaning forward from the waist off balance.
10. Man's pulling back with his left shoulder and hand, causing an awkward angle of motion.

FOOTWORK IN SOCIAL DANCE

Footwork is a term used to discuss the manner of using the feet in the performance of dance steps. With the exception of body posture, it has the most significant bearing on form and style. Far too often the placement of the feet and the action of the legs give a distorted appearance to the dance. The beauty, the continuity, the balance of a figure may be lost entirely due to this comic and, at the same time, tragic caricature given to the motion unintentionally.

Some general principles are involved in the application of good footwork to good dance style.

1. The weight should be carried on the ball of the foot for easy balance and alert transfer of weight from step to step and change of direction.
2. The feet should be pointing straight ahead. When moving from one step to another, they should reach straight forward or back in the direction of the desired action and in line with or parallel to partner's feet.
3. Any action will start with feet together and when moving the feet should pass as closely as possible. With a few exceptions, the feet should always come together before reaching in a new direction.
4. The legs should swing forward or backward from the hip. The action is initiated by stabilizing the trunk and swinging the leg freely.
5. The feet are never dragged along the floor from one step to another, but

picked up and placed in the new position, or they may glide smoothly into place without a scraping sound on the floor.

6. The faster the rhythm the shorter the step. The slower the rhythm the more gliding the step.

7. Changes of direction are more readily on balance and under control if initiated when the feet are close together rather than when apart.

8. For the specific actions of reaching with one foot forward or back, as in a corte or a hesitation step, the arch of the foot should be extended and the toe pointed.

9. Turning and pivoting figures are most effectively executed from a small base of support with the action of the man's and lady's feet dovetailing nicely. This is possible when the action of the foot is a smooth turn on the ball of the foot with the body weight *up*, not pressing into the floor.

10. In accordance with the characteristic cultural style of a dance, the footwork will involve specific and stylized placement of the feet. This styling is described with each dance.

THE DANCE GLIDE

The dance glide is the basic step used in Social Dance. It is unlike the natural walk due to the action on the ball of the foot. The sooner a feeling of security can be achieved in this simple movement, the easier it is to add step combinations, because of the correct body balance and freedom of action. A practice session, first alone and then with a partner, moving forward and backward, will help overcome the early tendencies of insecurity felt by the lady moving backward and the man's fear of stepping on her toes. With this gliding motion the man may bump her toe but never step on it. The following points will describe the mechanics involved in the dance glide:

The Forward Glide

1. The body sways forward from the ankles. The weight is on the ball of the foot.

2. The trunk is stabilized firmly. The leg swings forward from the hip joint. The reach results in a longer step rather than a short choppy step. An exaggerated knee bend will cause bobbing up and down.

3. Swing the foot forward in pendular fashion. The feet do not drag along the floor. The ball of the foot touches the floor and glides forward for about a three-inch glide. The weight is not high on the toes.

4. The heel is then allowed to come down for greater stability and balance.

5. The legs should be kept close together, gliding forward as if along a narrow line, letting the feet pass as closely as possible.

6. The toes are kept in a straight line with the forward motion. One should avoid letting the feet straddle the partner's feet.

The Backward Glide

This is not a natural movement but should be practiced particularly by the lady since she will be using the backward glide a large part of the time. The body weight is forward over the supporting foot.

1. The body sways forward. The weight is on the ball of the foot.

2. The trunk is stabilized firmly. The leg swings backward from the hip joint, pressing with the back of the knee. The reach results in a longer step rather than a short choppy step. Exaggerated bending of the forward knee causes undue bobbing up and down.

3. The foot is placed backward with the weight going onto the ball of the foot and transferred smoothly. The heel comes down as that foot becomes the supporting foot, weight remains over ball of foot.

4. The legs and feet pass as closely as possible and in a straight line. One should avoid toeing out or heeling out.

THE TECHNIQUE OF LEADING AND FOLLOWING

Dancing is like conversation. A person's interest is held through the use of natural, interesting speech. In dancing, a partner's interest must be held through the use of varied, interesting steps. The man sets the rhythm, decides what steps are to be used, and controls their direction and progression around the floor. The lady is completely dependent upon her partner. Through the use of a gentle but definite lead, the man can make dancing a mutually pleasant experience rather than a tugging on the part of one and a hoping and groping on the part of the other.

The Lead . . . Good leading results from five basic understandings:

1. An alert posture which moves as a complete unit.
2. A basic position which gives security and support.
3. Consciousness of various musical tempo and style.
4. Knowledge of the basic steps and a few simple variations.
5. Proper application of pressure timed to indicate in advance the new step.

The use of the body and the arms is the chief technique of leading. If the body dances as well as the feet, then the movement of the shoulder and chest will be a natural lead indication to a partner held in correct dance position.* The man's arms, particularly the right arm, should be held away from the body. The upper arm and shoulder should then act as the guiding force for all dance movement. A limp arm is ineffectual in guiding a partner. The right hand with the palm cupped against the lady's back allows the man to lead with the fingers and the heel of the hand. It is the steering unit which turns her and guides the changes of direction. This arm and hand action should *not* be like a switch that turns off and on when needed and is otherwise idle. On the contrary, the arm and hand working together should act as a continual barometer of action, giving gentle but confident warning of all changes of step or direction.

---
* Common errors in dance position, refer to page 266.
** For music in relation to dance, refer to page 51.

General Rules for Leading:
1. Hold partner firmly, but not tensely.
2. Listen to the music to get the beat before starting. Step out on the accented beat.**
3. Start each new step with a left foot lead.
4. Give the lead for the new step or direction just before stepping out into it.
5. Think ahead so as to be ready to go into the new step.
6. Start with the easy steps. Before going into variations be sure partner can follow.

Specific reminders for learning to lead may be given to the beginner. *On the pages of dance descriptions to follow, a lead reminder, indicated by a check in the margin,* indicates when a lead is given. The dance instructor may refer back to the following list of specific directions for help in teaching leading.

Specific Directions for Leading:
1. *To lead into the first step,* forward motion in the shoulders and chest and a slight raise of the right arm should precede a step off on the left foot.
2. *To lead a forward moving pattern,* forward or turning motion in the shoulders and right arm will direct the lady firmly in the desired direction.
3. *To lead a backward moving pattern,* pressure of the right hand will draw the lady forward in the desired direction.
4. *To lead a box step,* a lift with the right arm and guidance with the right hand will indicate change of direction sideways. Alternate release and pressure at the lady's back with the right hand will indicate change of direction forward and back.
5. *To lead into a box turn,* with slight pressure of the right hand, the right arm and shoulder guides and banks into the turn. The shoulders press forward when stepping forward and release that pressure when stepping backward, plus drawing of the right hand.

6. *To lead into an open position or conversation position*, pressure on the heel of the right hand turns the lady into open position. The right elbow relaxes to side. The left arm relaxes slightly and the arm and hand give lead for steps in open position.

7. *To lead from open to closed position*, pressure of the right hand turns the lady to closed position. At the same time the right arm should be raised to original position away from the body. Left arm returns to position away from body.

8. *To lead into left reverse open position (right parallel position)*, pressure of the right hand tends to turn the lady to open position, so a better lead indication is desirable. The man will find more success if he raises the right arm, rotating to the left, and turns the lady on a slight diagonal so as to be offset from the original position. The lady is still in front of him but slightly to the right of him, and he is facing a diagonal line forward left. The man should avoid turning this position too far so that it brings them side by side as this is uncomfortable and results in poor form and awkward motion.

9. *To lead from left reverse open to right reverse open (left parallel position)*, the man pulls with his right hand, lowering the right arm and pushes slightly with his left hand as he rotates himself to a diagonal line forward right. The lady is in front but the action has turned her to a position slightly to his left side.

10. *To lead into a pivot turn*, the man holds the lady firmly and slightly closer. There is total body resistance exerted outward in order to take advantage of the centrifugal force of the circular motion. The right foot steps between partner's feet and is used as a pivot foot for the turn, while the left foot alternately reaches in close around partner on the curve of the circle.

11. *To lead into a corte (dip)*, there is a slight increased resistance of the body as well as the right arm going into the preparation step. With firm pressure of the right hand, he should draw partner toward him when going into the dip. The foot taking the dip should carry the weight and careful balance of the weight should remain over the standing foot. Pressure is released with the recover step.

12. *To lead a pressure lead*, the man may need to indicate an unusual change of position by exerting firm pressure with his hand or arm. This type of lead is necessary when moving the lady apart to a flirtation position or to change direction when the man and lady will not be traveling in the same direction. It is used also on the hesitation step and magic left turn when the man needs to indicate with pressure of his right hand, on the first beat, that there will be a hold or a direction change. This prepares the lady not to swing her free foot sideward or backward.

NOTE: Directions for leads specific to one particular figure or dance can be found with the description for that dance.

Following . . . The lady's responsibility in dancing is to follow her partner and adapt to any rhythm or style he dances. She should maintain an easy resistance (not rigidity or tension) throughout the body which gives the man an alert movable partner which he can lead. If the lady is too relaxed or too light, leading becomes very difficult as there is no resistance. In other words, it takes cooperation for two people to dance well, the same as it takes both persons for a satisfactory handshake. The lady should always maintain contact with his upper right arm and shoulder and give resistance against his hand at her back, moving with it as it guides her. If the man is a poor leader, then the lady must pay close attention to his body movement, particularly his chest and shoulder movement, in order to follow. Following, when in an open apart position, requires a firm contact arm which responds to a lead by the simultaneous action of the body. A limp arm with no resultant body response makes leading difficult in swing, rumba, and cha cha cha.

The good dancer will aim to dance with beauty of form. The lady can make a poor dancer look good or a good dancer look excellent. She can also "cramp his style" if she takes too small a step, has poor control of balance, dances at an awkward angle, or leans backward. The lady should learn the basic dance steps and practice them carefully so as to be able to respond easily and smoothly to the lead.

General Rules for Following:
1. Keep the man's rhythm.
2. Be alert to partner's leads.

3. Support one's own weight. Learn to keep good balance moving backwards.
4. Step straight backward with reaching motion so as to give him room to reach straight ahead.
5. Pass the feet close together.
6. Try not to anticipate partner's lead but move with the action.
7. Become familiar with the basic steps a partner is likely to lead.
8. Give careful thought to proper body alignment and good posture.

PRACTICE COMBOS

The beginning social dancer needs some practice routines to help learn how to put steps together and to give confidence while learning. However, it should be kept in mind that the learner must have ample opportunity to combine steps in his own way and not be required to dance set routines at all times.

Once the separate basic steps are learned, a routine can be described by speaking in terms of dance patterns instead of foot patterns step by step. In this way the dancer learns to think in terms of phrasing and coordinated sequences of movement rather than beats and counts.

Any combination of steps can be put together in a routine. The authors refer to

this as a "dance combo." It is not necessary to have an even number of measures. Short practice routines of four to eight measures are handy and easy for the learner to repeat over and over for practice. Beginning teachers are also more comfortable using routines with an even number of measures. The experienced dancer learns to get the feeling of the music so that he automatically responds to the phrasing of the music.

The combination of steps is a matter of selection and personal preference. It is largely related to one's skill and understanding of the steps and rhythms. Practice combos are listed with each type of dance and should serve as examples of how steps can be combined for practice.

DISCOTHEQUE

Contemporary dance forms have been generally grouped under the term discotheque which in France is a place where records, *disques*, are stored. The majority of these dance forms come from Europe with the notable exception of the Twist which is American and not generally classified as a Discotheque form. The Frug reins as the basic form to which one adds variations to achieve such other dances as the Swim, Bug, Hitchhiker, Monday, Jerk, Mouse, Bird or whatever term best describes the action. These dances are characterized by (a) lack of foot pattern, *i.e.*, stationary base, (b) response to a steady beat, (c) action in the upper torso, *i.e.*, styling of hands and movement of body above the hips, and (d) not following the lead of a

partner. The Pony departs from these characteristics in that a movement pattern of 1,2,3 - 1,2,3, walk, walk is considered basic. However, even these movements are done largely in place. The trend seems to be back toward more foot patterning as can be noted in the Skate, the basic pattern being step, close, step; step, close, step, walk, walk done to the side right and left with appropriate hand actions and a lift of the lower leg to depict skate-like action.

Perhaps more than in other dance forms, constant change and variation is common in social or ballroom dance. This can be at the same time both frustrating and interesting. Interesting from the standpoint that they are not really new nor do they really depart from the age-old dynamic cycle of infusion and diffusion. These dances reflect and indeed are derived from folk dance forms and variations found in our culture and in time are perpetuated as folk forms. The rhumba and conga are examples of folk forms that have been devised for ballroom use. Social dance forms serve our social needs. Dance literature spells out the historical trek of the social dance as beginning with primitive courtship and tribal dances of a social nature. Evolving then through the folk process to form such early ballroom styles as the gavotte, pavane, and minuet. These forms served, in their time, the social needs of the royal courts of Europe.

Even a cursory look at what the literature tells us about the past leads us to conclude that dance forms are indeed dynamic movements which have moved up the scale, from past to present, to enrich and be enriched by man as an individual, a member of a group, a gregarious animal, an inventor, a borrower, a sharer, and last but not least as an intellectually curious and creatively sensitive human being.

Contemporary forms have not violated this traditional cyclic effect. Havelock Ellis[1] points out that dance as an art has been intimately mixed with all the finest and deepest springs of life and will thus always "assert itself afresh." He further notes that ". . . beyond the manifold practical significance, dancing has always been felt to possess also a symbolic significance." This assertion and symbolism can best be perceived in current forms if they are analyzed vis-a-vis categories which group them according to major characteristics apparent in their movement structure such as imitation, vibration, and patterning.

Imitation. The current version of "man the mimic" is embodied in the Swim, Monkey, and Wheelchair. Each evidences man's age-old and continued response to the thousands of patterned sounds and gestures in his environment. The Wheelchair borrows boldly from American Square Dance by using a caller or prompter. In all three dances one can note that: (a) the action is imitative, (b) communal in nature, (c) individualistic and non-patterned, and (d) culturally relevant, *i.e.*, associated with a current human experience.

Vibration. All the discotheques, especially the Frug, belong in this category because they use a stable to semi-stable base, with movement general throughout the trunk or localized some part of the trunk. The arms are used for balance rhythmic emphasis, or follow through to the trunk movements. Arm action often gives the dance its name. Prominent in this group are the Dog, Jerk, and of course the Frug.

Patterned. The link with other forms may be noted in the Hully Gully. The use of a box pattern for direction and the recognizable grapevine step, three step turn, backward hop, and other movements give evidence of borrowing from folk forms. The breakdown of the traditional couple arrangement for social dance began in the 1930's with the Conga Line and the Big Apple. The Hully Gully and other dances of this type continue this non-partner aspect of modern social dance in America.

Analysis and classification best serves to sharpen our senses to the fact that dance is no mere translation or abstraction from life; indeed, it is life itself. Dance lies at the beginning and end of art and as surely as civilization has produced the fabric from which the dance is made, modern man will continue to weave the maze of the dance.

FOXTROT

The foxtrot, as a present-day form, is of relatively recent origin. The only truly American form of ballroom dance, it has had many steps and variations through the years. The foxtrot gets its name from a musical comedy star of the years 1913-14, Mr. Harry Fox,[2] who danced a fast but simple trotting step to ragtime music in one of the hit Ziegfeld shows of that time. As an additional publicity stunt, the theatre

1 Ellis, Havelock. *The Dance of Life*, New York: Grosset & Dunlap, 1923, p. 62-63.
2 Hostetler, Lawrence, *Walk Your Way to Better Dancing*, New York, N. Y.: A. S. Barnes & Co., 1942, Ellis, Havelock. *The Dance of Life,* New York; Grosset & Dunlap, 1923, p. 62-63.

management requested that a star night club performer, Mr. Oscar Duryea, introduce the step to the public but found that it had to be modified somewhat, since a continuous trotting step could not be maintained for long periods without exhausting effort. He simplified the step so that it became four walking steps alternating with eight quick running steps. This was the first foxtrot.

Since that time under the influence of Vernon and Irene Castle, and a series of professional dancers, the foxtrot has been through a gradual refining process and has developed into a beautifully smooth dance. It claims considerable popularity today as more than seventy-five per cent of the dances on an evening's program will be the foxtrot in one of its forms.

Music from ragtime through the blues on down to modern jazz and swing has had its effect on the foxtrot. The original foxtrot was danced to a lively 2/4 rhythm. Its two parent forms were the one-step and the two-step. Both of these forms are danced today but have given way to a slower, smoother 4/4 time and a more streamlined style. It is danced to three different tempos, slow, medium, and fast. The slow foxtrot is currently more popular due to the style and tempo adapted by the outstanding bands of the nation. The fundamental steps of the foxtrot can easily be adapted to all three tempos of the music.

The basic foxtrot steps can be used together in any combination or sequence. A dancer who knows the basic steps and understands the fundamentals of rhythm can make up his own combinations easily and gradually develop the possibilities for variation in position, direction, and tempo.

Foxtrot Rhythm . . . The modern foxtrot in 4/4 time,* or cut time, has four quarter beats or their equivalent to each measure. Each beat is given the same amount of time but there is an accent on the first and third beats of the measure. When a step is taken on each beat 1-2-3-4, it is a one-step rhythm and these are called *QUICK* beats. When steps are taken only on the two accented

---

* Refer to page 37.

beats 1 and 3, they are twice as long and are called *SLOW* beats.

4/4

quick	quick	quick	quick
1	2	3	4

or 4/4

slow	slow
1-2	3-4

A use of these *quick* and *slow* beats and a combination of them into rhythm patterns form the basis for all of the modern foxtrot steps. For example, any one measure of 4/4 foxtrot time can have all four possible combinations of *slow* and *quick* beats.

one-step 4/4

quick	quick	quick	quick
1	2	3	4

promenade step 4/4

slow	slow
1-2	3-4

two-step 4/4

quick	quick	slow
1	2	3-4

Westchester 4/4

slow	quick	quick
1-2	3	4

There are additional rhythm patterns which take more than one measure of beats.

For example:

magic step 4/4

slow	slow	quick	quick
1-2	3-4	1	2

The magic step pattern represents broken rhythm as it takes a measure and a half of music and may be repeated from the middle of the measure.

The rhythm of the *twinkle step* may be a one, two, or three measure pattern.

Variation I 4/4

single twinkle

slow	quick	quick

Variation II   4/4 —————— ——————

	slow 1-2		slow 3-4
quick 1	quick 2	quick 3	quick 4

double twinkle step

Foxtrot Style . . . Foxtrot style truly reflects its American origin. It is the least affected of any of the ballroom dances. Completely without stylized or eccentric arm, foot, head, or torso movement, the foxtrot is a beautifully smooth dance. The body is held easily erect and follows the foot pattern in a relaxed way with little up-and-down or sideward movement. The good dancer glides normally along the floor and blends the various steps together without bobbing or jerking. This gliding effect* is accomplished by long reaching steps with only as much knee bend as is needed to transfer the weight from step to step smoothly. It gives the foxtrot a streamlined motion and a simple beauty of form which can be enjoyed without strain or fatigue, dance after dance. As one becomes more and more skillful at putting together steps for the foxtrot, there will be increasing joy derived from the tremendous variety of quick and slow combinations.

* Refer to dance glide, page 268.

FUNDAMENTAL FOXTROT STEPS

Introductory or Connecting Steps	Twinkle Step
Box Series	Corte or Dip
Magic Step Series	Fundamental Foxtrot Turns

Directions are for man, facing line of direction;
Lady's part reverse, except as noted.

Introductory or Connection Steps

A large majority of all dance steps are composed from a combination of these introductory steps. Any of them may be used to connect one figure with another or *fill in* at the beginning or end of a phrase of music.

Steps	4/4 Counts	Rhythmic Cue	Lead Indication*
PROMENADE STEP (dance glide)**			
Step L forward	1–2	Slow	√
Step R forward	3–4	Slow	
Step L forward	1–2	Slow	
Step R forward	3–4	Slow	

Style: Step should be long, smooth, forward reaching motion.

SIDE CLOSE (chasse)			
Step L sideward	1	Quick	√
Touch R to L, take weight on R	2	Quick	

Style: Steps should be short, smooth, sideward motion.
Note: Repetition of this step will continue action to the left.

ROCK STEP			
Step L sideward	1	Quick	√
Close R to L, weight remains on L	2	Quick	
Step R sideward	3	Quick	√
Touch L to R, weight remains on R	4	Quick	

Style: Steps should be short.

Box Series

Two styles of the box pattern are presented here: *The westchester box* is based on a slow quick rhythm, and the *two-step* is based on a quick quick slow rhythm.

WESTCHESTER HALF-BOX PROGRESSIVE STEP			
Step L forward	1–2	Slow	√
Step R sideward	3	Quick	
Close L to R, take weight on L	4	Quick	

(Repeat, beginning with right foot)

Step Cue:
a. forward   side   close
b. forward   side   close

    long step   short steps

Floor Pattern:

Start:

Style: The forward step should be a long smooth gliding step.
Note: This may progress either forward or backward.

---

* Check the lead indication, page 269.
** Refer to page 268.

Steps	4/4 Counts	Rhythmic Cue	Lead Indication*

WESTCHESTER BOX STEP, a combination of promenade and side close.

Step L forward	1–2	Slow	√
Slide R alongside of L, no weight change			
Step R sideward	3	Quick	
Close L to R, take weight on L	4	Quick	
Step R backward	1–2	Slow	√
Slide L alongside of R, no weight change			
Step L sideward	3	Quick	
Close R to L, take weight on R	4	Quick	

Step Cue:
a. forward   side   close
b. backward   side   close

{ long steps } { short steps }

Floor Pattern:

[Diagram: square with arrows, labeled a. and b.]

Start:

Style: Forward and backward steps should be long gliding steps.

BOX TURN (left)

Step L forward, toe out, turn ¼ to L	1–2	Slow	√
Step R sideward	3	Quick	
Close L to R, take weight on L	4	Quick	
Step R backward, toe in, turn ¼ to L	1–2	Slow	√
Step L sideward	3	Quick	
Close R to L, take weight on R	4	Quick	
Step L forward, toe out, turn ¼ to L	1–2	Slow	√
Step R sideward	3	Quick	
Close L to R, take weight on L	4	Quick	
Step R backward, toe in, turn ¼ to L	1–2	Slow	√
Step L sideward	3	Quick	
Close R to L, take weight on R	4	Quick	

Step Cue: Turn side close, turn side close, etc.

Style: The lady is taking the reverse of this pattern except that when the lady steps forward with her left foot, instead of toeing out as described for the man, she steps forward between man's feet. This style for the lady greatly facilitates the turn.

CROSS STEP

Step L forward	1–2	Slow	√
Step R sideward, turning to open position	3	Quick	
Close L to R, take weight on L	4	Quick	√ (open)
Cross R over L	1–2	Slow	
Step L sideward, turning to closed position	3	Quick	√ (close)
Close R to L, take weight R	4	Quick	

Step Cue:

a. forward   side   close
b. cross   side   close

    long steps   short steps

Floor Pattern:

b.

Start: a.

Style: Open slightly for the cross step and step into it on the ball of the foot.

Steps	4/4 Counts	Rhythmic Cue	Lead Indication*
TWO-STEP BOX			
Step L sideward	1	Quick	
Close R to L, take weight R	2	Quick	
Step L forward	3–4	Slow	
Step R sideward	1	Quick	
Close L to R, take weight L	2	Quick	
Step R backward	3–4	Slow	

Step Cue:

a. side   close   forward
b. side   close   backward

    short steps   long steps

Note: Any of the Westchester Box Variations may be used with the two-step.

Magic Step Series

The Magic Step was created by Arthur Murray[3]. It is called by this name because it can be varied in a surprising number of ways. The pattern requires a measure and a half for one basic step. This is called broken rhythm.

MAGIC STEP			
Step L forward	1–2	Slow	√
Step R Forward	3–4	Slow	
Step L sideward	1	Quick	√
Close R to L, take weight on R	2	Quick	

Step Cue:

forward   forward   side   close

    long steps   short steps

Floor Pattern:

Start:

Style: The forward steps should be long smooth gliding steps.

VARIATIONS OF THE MAGIC STEP PATTERN

In Closed Position, the man faces forward and progresses forward or on a curve around the floor. By maneuvering on the quick steps the man may lead into a right or left turn on the quick beats in order to go around another couple to the right or left. With a right turn, it is particularly handy in leading a partner out of a crowded situation away from the center of the floor.

In Open Position, the man leads forward with the left (slow), steps through forward with the right (slow), then in place left, right (quick, quick) turning into closed position.

---

* Check lead indication, page 269.

3 Arthur Murray, *"How to Become a Good Dancer."* New York: Simon & Schuster, '54.

When changing from closed to open position or from open to closed position, the transition should always be made on the (quick, quick) steps.* *Note:* This variation provides a directional change which allows a couple to travel toward the center of the floor or go around another couple on the left. However, when a change of direction is not desired, the open variation may be used by the man opening in to the line of direction. To do this the man must step around the lady as he turns her to open position so that they both may travel down the line of direction. To go back to closed position, the man will turn to face the lady on the quick quick beats closing the position and follow this with a magic left turn to return to original line of direction.

MAGIC LEFT TURN (closed position)

Step L forward...........................1–2......Slow......√......
Step R backward, toe in, and
     start turning ¼ L..................3–4......Slow......√......
Step in place L, finishing ¼ turn.......1.......Quick............
Step in place R.........................2.......Quick............

Step Cue:
rock rock step close

Style: The forward and back steps are small and taken like a rocking motion. The quick beats are in place. The figure makes a ¼ turn.

Note: The degree of turn may be increased to a half turn or even to a full turn, remembering to keep the steps and the turning base small. This variation provides a means of turning in place or of turning to maneuver into position for another variation or recovering the original line of direction. Because of this it is often used to tie together all types of foxtrot variations.

In Left and Right Reverse Open Position (Parallel Position), this variation should move the couple in the normal direction around the floor, but it is interesting because the man may dance first on one side of the lady then the other progressing diagonally forward as he changes from left reverse position to right reverse position. The man leads into left reverse position on the quick beats. He must be careful to take these quick beats *in place* as he changes position in order to have a smooth transition from one diagonal position to another. See also note for leading this, page 248.

A more advanced use of this variation is to make a ½ turn clockwise in place on the quick beats as the man changes from left reverse position to right reverse position so that the man would then travel backward in the line of direction and the lady forward. A ½ turn counterclockwise in place would then turn the couple back to left reverse position.

Innumerable combinations of this variation will develop as dancers experiment with changes of direction.

In the Side Rock

Step sideward L, slide R to L, no weight change............Slow
Step sideward R, slide L to R, no weight change...........Slow
Step sideward L, and close R to L, take weight on R.......Quick, Quick

The Side Rock may also be used as a *turning* pattern. The turn may go either to the right or to the left. This is useful for dancing in place on a crowded floor.

In the Conversation Spin, the man leads into open position, and the two *slow* steps are taken left and right . . . then taking closed position, the two *quick* steps make a sharp pivot turn clockwise, once around in place. In order to make this a smooth pattern instead of a jerky one, the man must anticipate the quick turn as he begins the slow steps. There is an increased tension in the man's right arm, holding the lady close as he makes the turn. The quick steps are a pivot turn in place. It is helpful if the man will lead into the turn by bringing his left shoulder in toward his partner and if both man and lady turn their heads to look over the shoulder (man's right, lady's left).

Twinkle Step

This step is so-called because of the quick steps bringing the feet together to cause a quick change of weight. The change of rhythm and the possibilities for variation make it fascinating.

Steps	4/4 Counts	Rhythmic Cue	Lead Indication*
SINGLE TWINKLE STEP			
Step L forward	1–2	Slow	√
Step R in place	3	Quick	√
Close L to R, take weight on L	4	Quick	
Step R backward	1–2	Slow	√
Step L in place	3	Quick	
Close R to L, take weight on R	4	Quick	

Style: The quick steps are very small.

Note: 1. This may be used in closed position or in right or left reverse open position (parallel position).

2. It may be used to progress diagonally down the line of direction changing from right to left reverse positions by taking the slow beat always forward in the diagonal line. The lead for changing position is given on the first quick beat. Innumerable combinations of this variation are possible as dancers experiment with changes of direction.

3. A more advanced use of this variation is a combination of closed, open and left reverse open positions, as follows:

Steps	4/4 Counts	Rhythmic Cue	Lead Indication*
ADVANCED TWINKLE			
Man's Part: starting in closed position			
Step L forward	1–2	Slow	√
Step R sideward, turning to open position	3	Quick	√
Close L to R, taking weight on L	4	Quick	
Step R forward in open position	1–2	Slow	
Step L in place, turning lady to left reverse position	3	Quick	√
Close R to L, taking weight on R	4	Quick	
Step L backward	1–2	Slow	√

* Check lead indication, page 269.

Step R in place, turning lady to
   open position ....3.......Quick......√......
Close L to R, taking weight on L.........4.......Quick............
Step R forward in open position.......1–2.....Slow.............
Step L in place, turning lady to
   closed position ....3.......Quick......√......
Close R to L, taking weight R...........4.......Quick............
Lady's Part: starting in closed position
Step R backward...................1–2.....Slow..............
Step L sideward, turning to
   open position ....3......Quick............
Close R to L, taking weight on R........4......Quick............
Step L forward in open position........1–2.....Slow............
Step R forward, turning to left
   reverse position ....3......Quick............
Close L to R, taking weight on L.........4......Quick............
Step R forward in left reverse position...1–2.....Slow.............
Step L forward, turning to open position..3......Quick............
Close R to L, taking weight on R........4......Quick............
Step L forward in open position........1–2.....Slow............
Step R forward, turning to closed position.3......Quick............
Close L to R, taking weight on L........4......Quick............
<u>Style:</u> Keep weight over the ball of the foot at all times.

THE HOOK STEP (semi-open position) from box step

Man's Part:
Step L sideward.....................1–2......Slow......√......
Cross R over L, take weight on
   both toes, and....................3–4......Slow............
Pirouette on the toes, turning
   ½ turn counterclockwise
   end weight on right...............1–2–3–4....Q Q Q Q..........

Lady's Part:
Step R sideward.....................1–2......Slow.....√......
Cross L over R, take weight on L........3–4......Slow............
Step R, L, R, L.....................1–2–3–4....Q Q Q Q..........

<u>Style:</u> These are small steps moving in a circle around with the man as he takes the pirouette turn. The man turns on a small pivot base. Both man and lady finish facing the opposite direction in closed position. The lady must remain close to the man.

<u>Lead:</u> Man turns lady to semi-open position on his first step and guides her forward around him with his right hand at her back, as he pirouettes counterclockwise. On the last beat he turns her to closed position.

<u>Note:</u> Hook step may be followed by a corte (dip), backward on the left foot for the man and forward on the right for the lady. A detailed description of the corte will be found on page 304.

---

* Check lead indication, page 269.

The Corte
(Dip)

The corte or dip is a figure borrowed from the tango rhythm and is a fascinating trimming or finishing step easily adapted for foxtrot dancing. The corte is described in detail in the tango section, page 304.

.The corte rhythm is described as Quick, Quick, Slow, Slow. The two quick steps here serve as a preparation step for the dip figure. When this figure is used in the foxtrot, the two quick steps may be the two (quick steps) at the end of a box step, a magic step, or a twinkle step.

For example:

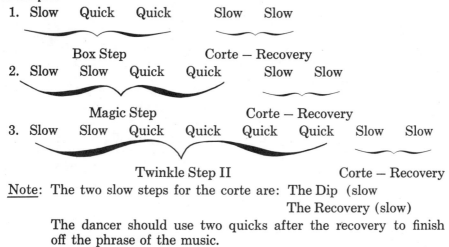

1. Slow   Quick   Quick   Slow   Slow

 Box Step   Corte — Recovery

2. Slow   Slow   Quick   Quick   Slow   Slow

 Magic Step   Corte — Recovery

3. Slow   Slow   Quick   Quick   Quick   Quick   Slow   Slow

 Twinkle Step II   Corte — Recovery

Note: The two slow steps for the corte are: The Dip (slow
                                              The Recovery (slow)

The dancer should use two quicks after the recovery to finish off the phrase of the music.

Fundamental Foxtrot Turns
(in addition to the box turns)

THE PIVOT TURN is a series of steps turning to the right. It begins with a left foot lead but the preceding step must act as a preliminary step in order to go into the pivot turn smoothly.

For Preliminary Step, man's right foot turns out toward his partner and the foot is placed in between her feet. At the same time, there is an increase in tension of the man's right arm and hand, holding the lady closer and bracing against the circular movement of the turn. This step may be either a slow or a quick beat.

Diagram: Preliminary step with right foot is shown in black.

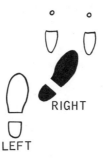

RIGHT

LEFT

Steps	4/4 Counts	Rhythmic Cue	Lead Indication*

PIVOT TURN:

Step L forward on the curve,
turning right .... 1 .... Quick ....
hold tension thruout turn

Step R, turning foot in place, and
moving forward between partner's feet .. 2 .... Quick ....

Step L forward on the curve,
still turning R .... 3 .... Quick ....

Step R, turning foot in place, and forward
between partner's feet .... 4 .... Quick ....

Style: While pivoting on his right foot, the man leads into the turn by bringing his left shoulder in toward his partner and stepping forward around with his left foot into the curve of the turn. The right foot moves forward coming in between the lady's feet each time in a small step on the ball of the feet. The lady's feet move in the same manner, the right foot in between man's feet each time and the left moving on the outside curve. In addition to the placing of the feet in the circular pattern, the dancer actually rolls on the ball of the foot. This action makes it possible to maneuver the pivot smoothly either fast or slow.

Diagram: Preliminary step shown in black.

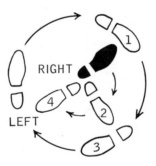

The pivot turn may be taken in a variety of different tempos, and may be any number in length. For example:

1. Slow Slow Slow Slow
2. Quick Quick Quick Quick
3. Slow Slow Quick Quick
4. Slow Slow Quick Quick Quick Quick

---

* Check lead indication, page 269.

Foxtrot Combos*

A number of foxtrot routines are listed here merely as examples to show how the various steps can be used in combination for practice routines. They are listed from simple to complex.

Closed position unless otherwise indicated.

1. *Promenade Box*
   4 promenade steps
   1 box step
2. *Two-Step —*
   Promenade
   two-step L
   2 promenade steps
   two-step R
   2 promenade steps
3. *Box Step*
   2 westchester prog.
      fwd.
   1 box step
   add: box turn
4. *Rock Step — Box*
   4 balances (LRLR)
   1 box step
5. *Magic Step*
   1 magic step, R ¼
      turn
   magic left turn
6. *Magic Step*
   1 magic step (open
      to line of direction)
   2 magic steps (open)
   1 magic left turn
7. *Magic Step — Box*
   2 magic steps
   1 box step
   2 magic steps
      (open)
8. *Side Rock —*
   Box Turn
   2 magic steps
      (side rock)
   1 box turn
9. *Reverse Magic Step*
   2 magic steps
   4 magic steps
   (L & R reverse
      position)
   2 magic steps
      (side rock)
   1 box turn

10. *Magic Step — Corte*
    1 magic (open or
       closed)
    corte (recover)
    1 side close
    1 box turn
    corte (recover)
11. *Cross Step — Turn*
    2 cross steps
    1 box turn
12. *Cross Step — Corte*
    2 magic steps
    2 cross steps
    corte (recover)
13. *Advanced Combo*
    1 magic step
    1 single twinkle to
       open
    1 single twinkle to
       L reverse
    1 single twinkle
       to open
    1 single twinkle
       to close
14. *Advanced Combo*
    1 box step
    4 twinkle steps (R
       and L reverse po-
       sition) pivot turn,
       (S QQQQ)
    2 promenade steps
       (open)
    2 side close steps
15. *Advanced Combo*
    1 box turn
    1 magic step
    1 magic step (open)
    1 conversation spin
       (underarm turn)
    1 conversation pivot
    1 hook step
    corte (recover)

---

* Refer to notes on Practice Combos, page 271.

SWING
(Jitterbug)

Jitterbug is a modern expression of the old ragtime. It is said to be Negroid in origin. It went through a fad period of being an extremely eccentric dance with its wild acrobatics inspired by the rising popularity of boogie woogie. In its present form, it may be a lively though smooth dance, or it may be a slow sophisticated style. More currently referred to as "Swing," it is the delightful answer to a large number who enjoy the syncopated quality. The livelier tunes, the more open and informal positions, and the lesser demand on the man to be a good leader have all made swing appealing. There are steps and variations as broad in scope as the dancer's imagination. They vary in routine and style in practically every section of the country, but all routines and styles have a similarity in rhythm which makes it possible to find a common step which is basic to many variations. While the shag and single lindy represented the earlier popular basics, they gave way to the double lindy when the rock and roll beat was introduced following World War II, and this was joined by the smooth sophisticated triple rhythm a short time later. Both of these can still hold their own with the modern rhythms.

Swing Rhythm

Swing is written in foxtrot time 4/4*, or cut-time, and can be danced to any foxtrot tempo; however, the more syncopated tunes are more desirable. The shag was actually the first dance to be called jitterbug and its *slow slow quick quick* rhythm has set the basic pattern for all the others. The *single lindy* has the same rhythm pattern.

4/4	step	step	rock	step	Single Lindy
	1–2	3–4	1	2	

The double lindy is very adaptable to slow or fast rhythm and has proven to feel good with modern swing tunes even though "rock and roll" has gone the way of all fads.
In 4/4, or cut time, the action is an even six pattern. All are quick beats. The accent in the movement falls on beats 2, 4, 2.

4/4	touch	step	touch	step	rock	step	Double Lindy
	1	2	3	4	1	2	

The triple rhythm is most often danced to slow sophisticated tempos. The quick beat may be divided into two counts, *one and*.

4/4	step	close	step	step	close	step	rock	step	Triple Lindy
	1	and	2	3	and	4	1	2	

When combined with single rhythm it appears as follows:

4/4	step	touch	step	close	step	rock	step	Single Lindy
	1	2	3	and	4	1	2	

---

* Refer to page 37.

Swing Style

The important difference between the foxtrot and swing is the syncopated quality which varies with the individual dancer and is a matter of style. A 1-2 beat may be taken as a step hop, as a kick step, as a touch step (dip step), or merely as a step bend. It is essential that the basic rhythm pattern be maintained by both man and lady, in open or closed position. The step should be small and under the body as a narrow moving base. The body should be free from tension but not saggy. Good swing requires a magnificent alertness to maneuver the open jitterbug variations. This must be reflected by a firm body and a calculated resistance in the arm and hand which will respond to a lead of the man's hand in any direction. Swing steps do not carry the dancers around and around the floor, but appear as a series of rolling and turning figures covering a circular space in one area. A subtle smoothness of movement is a joy to see as two dancers swirl and roll through an elaborate combination of open steps to the off-beat rhythm.

Fundamental Swing Steps

Shag
Single Lindy
Double Lindy
Triple Rhythm
Variations on the Lindy

Directions are for man, facing line of direction: lady's part reverse, except as noted.

Steps	4/4 Counts	Rhythmic Cue	Lead Indication*
SHAG			
Step L and hop in place, lifting R foot up in back, heel up	1–2	Slow	√
Step R and hop R in place, lifting L foot up in back, heel up	3–4	Slow	
Step L in place	1	Quick	
Step R in place	2	Quick	

<u>Step Cue:</u> Step Hop Step Hop Rock Step

<u>Style:</u> Closed position. The shag is a sideward rocking motion in place. It can be varied by turning around slowly or quickly while the step is in motion.

Steps	4/4 Counts	Rhythmic Cue	Lead Indication*
SINGLE LINDY			
Step L sideward	1–2	Slow	√
Step R sideward	3–4	Slow	
Rock Step:			
Step L backward, a little behind R heel	1	Quick	√
Step R in place	2	Quick	

<u>Step Cue:</u> Side Side Rock Step

<u>Lead:</u> The man relaxes his right arm to a position at the lady's waist. He uses both right hand and left hand to guide the lady out to open position.

<u>Style:</u> Semi-open position is used on the slow steps. When stepping back on the rock, roll outward quickly to position side by side, and roll immediately back on the second quick step. This should be a smooth roll. The knees should bend easily on each step.

---

* Check lead indication, page 269.

Step	4/4 Counts	Rhythmic Cue	Lead Indication*

DOUBLE LINDY

Touch L to instep of R.................1......Quick.....✓......
Step L forward........................2......Quick............
Touch R to instep of L................3......Quick............
Step R backward.......................4......Quick............
Step L backward, a little behind R heel...1......Quick.....✓....
Step R forward........................2......Quick............

Step Cue: Dig   Step   Dig   Step   Rock   Step

Style: The position is semi-open and easily upright. The hand grasp position (man's left, lady's right) is low with a straight elbow and held in close to the body. The "dig" is a touching of the toe lightly to instep of other foot. It should not be a tap step making a slapping noise on the floor. The feet are close together for this beat. The weight is carried on the ball of the foot and the steps are small throughout the step. The amount of knee bend depends on individual preference as to style; however, the action is smooth and rolling rather than bouncy.

Lead: The man leads the starting motion by bending his left elbow to bring his hand in to waist level on the first dig. This cues the lady. She is waiting with her right foot in dig position and with the lead she can step with him into the second beat.

TRIPLE RHYTHM is three little steps to each *slow* beat. These are similar to a fast two-step.

Step L sideward................
Close R to L, take weight R.......⎫ 1 and 2......Slow......✓......
Step L sideward................⎭
Step R sideward................
Close L to R, take weight L.......⎫ 3 and 4......Slow......✓......
Step R sideward................⎭

Rock Step:
Step L backward, a little behind R heel...1.......Quick.....✓......
Step R in place.......................2.......Quick............

Step Cue: Shuf-fle   Step,   Shuf-fle   Step,   Rock   Step

Style: The triple rhythm should be small shuffling steps, keeping the feet close to the floor. Weight is on the ball of the foot. The style is similar to double lindy.

Lead: The man cues the lady for the triple steps by increasing the tension in his right hand as he starts the shuffle step forward. Other leads are the same as for the single lindy.

VARIATIONS ON THE LINDY can be used with either the shag, single lindy, double lindy, or triple rhythm. The description will be given for the double lindy rhythm. Easy adaptations can be made for other rhythms.

BASIC TURN

The basic step is used in semi-open position as described above. When repeated over and over, it should be done turning the couple around in place clockwise. The man makes the motion turn by taking his second beat

* Check lead indication, page 269.

step forward toward the lady, pivoting clockwise a quarter turn, and finish the rest of the step with no change in rhythm. As the dancers become skillful at this turn they will find they can turn a half turn or more each time by pivoting a greater degree on the stepping beats.

SINGLE UNDERARM BREAK

This turns the lady out clockwise under the man's left arm to *swing out position* facing him.

Lead: The man moves his left hand which has been extended low to a position in close at waist level. This acts as a "cock" position and occurs on the "dig" beat or count 1. Then he immediately raises his left arm above her head and turns her under the arm as they both take the second beat or the step forward.

Man: The man takes the entire pattern in the same position as for basic, just being sure to give the "cock-lift" lead.

Lady: The lady takes the dig step in place with her right foot. Having received the lead, she spins clockwise a half turn on her right foot as she takes a small step forward on the second beat. The second dig step (ct. 3) comes as she finishes the half turn. She is now facing the man but in close. Count 4 is a short step backward on the left foot and the rock step follows back right, forward left (cts. 1, 2).

Style: The lady turns smoothly without going out too far. Both man and lady should keep the connecting arm firm, the elbow down, and slightly flexed. If the arm is permitted to extend freely, the dancers are too far apart, and may lose the control which permits the "uncoil and recoil" for repeated turns.

BREAK TO CLOSE POSITION from swing out position.

The man and lady are facing in swing out position. They execute one basic step, coming together to the original starting position.

On the first dig step they step forward toward each other to closed position, the man's right arm going around the lady (cts. 1, 2). On the second dig step they face semi-open and take the step backward (cts. 3, 4). Then they take the rock as in the original basic step because they are back to the original position.

Lead: The man leads by pulling down with his left hand to the original starting position as he steps forward toward the girl.

CONTINUOUS UNDERARM TURNS from swing out position.

The man and lady exchange places as he turns her counterclockwise across to his position and he steps around her to her position.

Lead: Man increases pressure on her hand on dig (ct. 1) and lifts his arm turning her on the step (ct. 2).

Man: Makes a half turn clockwise on his left foot on the first dig step (cts. 1, 2) as he turns her counterclockwise under his left arm. The second dig step he steps back away from the lady on the right foot (cts. 3, 4) and the rock step follows back, forward (cts. 1, 2).

Lady: The lady takes the dig (ct. 1) in place and turns counterclockwise on her right foot half way around (ct. 2) under his left arm. The second dig (ct. 3) helps her finish the half turn and the next step is backward away from partner (ct. 4). The rock step follows back, forward (cts. 1, 2). They have exactly exchanged places by this maneuver since both have turned a half turn.

Style: Both man and lady should take small steps and keep the figure in close so that there will be room after the two dig steps for them to rock step without getting too far apart. The lady must maintain a firm arm.

Note: As this turn may be repeated continuously over and over, it is necessary for the man to hold a firm pivot hand above her head as she is turning, so that she can let her fingers slip around his fingers. This prevents an awkward twisting of the wrist.

Variation: This underarm turn may be done in reverse with the man turning counterclockwise and the lady clockwise. The only difference is on the lead as the man indicates a different direction as he raises the lead arm.

COLLEGIATE (formerly called Row Step).

The step begins in swing out position. The man takes both of the lady's hands. Stepping in close to each other, they take the two dig steps turning clockwise on an inner circle and then as they take the rock step they are turning still clockwise but on the rim of an outer circle. In order to maneuver this, the man's and lady's parts differ as follows:

Man: Stepping forward toward the lady, he takes the first dig step on the left. The foot is placed just to the left of the lady. He pivots on this foot, turning the couple clockwise. Resistance in the arms and fingers holds the couple in a tight facing position on this pivot. The second dig step is a short step sideward with the right foot again pivoting clockwise and then is followed by the rock step when he pushes the girl away and back, still turning clockwise.

Lady: With the right foot she takes the dig step in place and steps right foot across the left into the direction of the turn and pivots on that foot clockwise with him. The second dig step is sideward (not backward) to the left around him again pivoting clockwise and is followed by the rock step when they step apart and together, still turning clockwise.

Lead: The man leads this starting with his two hands close together in front of him on the first dig (ct. 1). On the step (ct. 2) he reaches out to the side to butterfly position* as they pivot clockwise. On the second dig step he brings the hands back into a close position. On the rock step he pushes her back by extending his arms momentarily and pulls her back again. A slight lean forward with his left shoulder will guide this figure into a clockwise turn.

Style: The collegiate step should be a turning step. It is a popular variation because, when repeated over and over, the effect is that of the couple whirling on two concentric circles. They turn on the rim of the inner circle when they take the slow steps, and they turn on the rim of the outer circle while doing the rock step. The turn is clockwise.

Note: To come out of the collegiate step, the man drops his right hand grasp and leads into either the underarm break, brush off or break to closed position.

* Refer to page 49.

BRUSH OFF

This step also begins with the lady in swing out position. The man shifts the lady's right hand to *his* right while he turns quarter counterclockwise around in place, with his back to her on the *first dig step.* Bringing both his hands behind him, he shifts the lady's hand into his left hand and continues around another quarter turn counterclockwise, to face her on the *second dig step.* Meanwhile, the lady takes two dig steps in exactly the same manner as in the collegiate above, coming around him clockwise as he turns. They now take the rock step away and together.

Lead: This is the man's turn, so the transfer of hands is the only lead. It is especially fun if the brush off step is followed by the underarm break, so the man should be prepared to lead into it immediately after he takes the rock step.

Style: A smooth transition of steps is needed to retain the continuity and the rhythm pattern.

TUCK SPIN from swing out position.

As in the collegiate, the man and lady are facing close and with both hands joined. The man takes one basic in place as he spins the lady clockwise and around in place on the two dig steps and they finish off with the rock step in swing out position.

Lead: There must be good arm and finger control in order for the girl to respond to the lead with the proper timing. On the first dig (ct. 1) the man takes a "cock" of the hands in the reverse direction, then he will spin her. That is, he "cocks" to the right — spins her clockwise. On the step (ct. 2) he releases the hands with a quick flip, spinning the lady clockwise. She spins about half way around on her right foot (ct. 2) and finishes the turn on the next dig step, so that she is facing him for the rock step. The man will take either one or both of her hands on the rock step depending upon whether he wishes to repeat the motion or go into an underarm turn.

Style: The lady should keep her spin in close.

Note: This tuck spin may be used in either direction. The man may also spin once around at the same time if desired. If she spins clockwise, he will spin counterclockwise.

WRAP from swing out position.

As in the tuck spin, the man and lady are facing with both hands joined. Without releasing hands, the man will raise his left hand across in front of her and up over her head, turning her at the same time into a position close to him on his right side. His right arm is around her waist, and her arms are crossed in front as they finish in this wrap position. The wrap is executed while dancing the two dig steps. Then they finish off the rock step side by side.

Lead: The lead is given by the raise of the man's left hand on the first dig (ct. 1) so that the lady may respond by rolling in counterclockwise as she steps on ct. 2.

Style: The man may enhance the smoothness of the movement by moving forward around her slightly as she rolls in.

UNWRAP from wrap position.

The man may lead an unwrap by merely initiating a reverse roll, turning the lady clockwise. This should be taken on the two dig steps and they finish off with the rock step in swing out position.

<u>Lead</u>: The man will initiate a "cock" position by turning her slightly counterclockwise on the first dig step (ct. 1) and then raising his left arm to let her roll under clockwise, assisting with a gentle right arm push.

Another variation on the unwrap is for the man to release with his left hand grasp and pull with the right hand, rolling the lady out to his right. Again this should be taken on the two dig steps and they finish off with the rock in side by side position.

<u>Note</u>: Either variation of unwrap may be followed by a tuck spin, rolling the lady in the opposite direction.

Swing Combos*

The swing routines listed here are merely examples to show how the various steps can be used in combination for practice routines. They are listed from simple to complex. They may be used for either shag, single lindy, double lindy, or triple rhythm.

Closed position unless otherwise indicated

1. <u>Basic Swing Out and Close</u>
   1 basic
   single underarm break
   break to close position
2. <u>Basic — Swing Out — Underarm Turn Close</u>
   1 basic
   single underarm break
   underarm turn
   break to close position
3. <u>Basic Continuous — Underarm Turn</u>
   1 basic
   single underarm turns
   continuous underarm turns
   break to close position
4. <u>Swing Out and Collegiate</u>
   2 basic
   single underarm break
   3 collegiate steps
   underarm turn
   close
5. <u>Swing Out and Brush Off</u>
   2 basics
   single underarm break
   brush off

   underarm turn
   close
6. <u>Collegiate — Brush Off</u>
   2 basic
   single underarm break
   underarm turn
   3 collegiate steps
   underarm turn
   brush off
   underarm turn
   close
7. <u>Collegiate — Tuck — Spin</u>
   2 collegiate steps
   tuck spin
   underarm turn
8. <u>Collegiate — Wrap</u>
   2 collegiate steps
   wrap
   unwrap
9. <u>Wrap — Unwrap Spin</u>
   2 collegiate steps
   wrap
   unwrap
   tuck spin
   underarm turn

---

* Refer to notes on Practice Combos, page 271.

WALTZ

Although a majority of the Middle European countries lay some claim to the origin of the waltz, the world looks to Germany and Austria where the great waltz was made traditional by the beautiful music of Johann Strauss. It has a pulsating, swinging rhythm which has been enjoyed by dancers everywhere, even by those who dance it only in its simplest pattern, the waltz turn. Its immediate popularity or its temporary obscurity is not unlike other fine inheritances of the past which come and go with the ebb and flow of popular accord and discord. Early use of the waltz in America was at the elegant social balls and cotillions. Its outstanding contribution to present day dancing is the "waltz position." It was quite some time even in its early stages before this position was socially acceptable. Now the closed position is universally the basic position for ballroom dancing.

The waltz music is played in three different tempos, slow, medium, and fast. The slow or medium waltz is preferred by most people. However, the fast waltz is a favorite of those who know the Viennese style. The slower American style is danced for the most part in a box pattern, but the use of other variations has added a new interest.

Waltz Rhythm

The waltz is played in 3/4 time.* It has three beats per measure of music, with an accent on the first beat. The three beats of waltz time are very *even*, each beat receiving the same amount of time. The three movements of the waltz step pattern blend perfectly with the musical tempo or beat of each measure.

3/4 /___ ____ ____
     slow slow slow
      1   2   3

Canter rhythm in waltz time is a means of holding the first and second beats together so the resultant pattern is as follows:

3/4 /_____ ____
     step   step
     1–2   3

Waltz Style

The waltz is a smooth dance with a gliding quality that weaves an even pattern of swinging and turning movement. The first accented beat of the music is accented in the motion also. The first step of the waltz pattern is the reaching step forward, backward, sideward, or turning. Since it is the first beat that gives the dance its new impetus, its new direction, or a change of step, there evolves a pulsating feeling which can be seen rather markedly and is the chief characteristic of the beauty of the waltz. This should not be interpreted as a rocking or bobbing motion of the body. The footwork is most effective when the foot taking the second beat glides past the standing foot as it moves into the sideward step. The feet should never be heard to scrape the floor but should seem to float in a "silent" pattern. The weight is forward over the ball of the foot.

* Refer to page 37.

Fundamental Waltz Steps

Box Steps
Balance and Hesitation Steps
Weaving and Scissors Steps
Waltz Turns
Waltz Corte

Directions are for man, facing line of direction; lady's part reverse, except as noted.

Box Steps

Steps	3/4 Counts	Rhythmic Cues	Lead Indication*
FORWARD WALTZ			
Step L forward	1	Slow	√
Step R forward	2	Slow	
Close L to R, take weight L	3	Slow	
Step R forward	1	Slow	√
Step L forward	2	Slow	
Close R to L, take weight R	3	Slow	

Step Cue:
a. forward   forward   close
b. forward   forward   close

Style: Man turns alternately left and right on the first beat, making a slight diagonal pattern down the floor.

Note: The pattern may go either forward or backward.

Floor Pattern:

Steps	3/4 Counts	Rhythmic Cues	Lead Indication*
BOX WALTZ			
Step L forward	1	Slow	√
Step R sideward	2	Slow	
Close L to R, take weight L	3	Slow	
Step R backward	1	Slow	√
Step L sideward	2	Slow	
Close R to L, take weight R	3	Slow	

Step Cue:
a. forward   side   close
b. backward   side   close

Style: Allow sideward stepping foot to glide past the standing foot as it moves to place, thus preventing a straddling effect.

Floor Pattern:

Start: a.

Steps	3/4 Counts	Rhythmic Cues	Lead Indication*
WALTZ BOX TURN (LEFT)			
Step L forward, toe out, turn ¼ L	1	Slow	√
Step R sideward	2	Slow	
Close L to R, take weight L	3	Slow	
Step R backward, toe in, turn ¼ L	1	Slow	√
Step L sideward	2	Slow	
Close R to L, take weight R	3	Slow	

* Check lead indication, page 269.

Steps	3/4 Counts	Rhythmic Cue	Lead Indication*
Step L forward, toe out, turn ¼ L	1	Slow	✓
Step R sideward	2	Slow	
Close L to R, take weight L	3	Slow	
Step R backward, toe in, turn ¼ L	1	Slow	✓
Step L sideward	2	Slow	
Close R to L, take weight R	3	Slow	

Step Cue: turn side close, turn side close, etc.

Lady: The lady is taking the reverse of this pattern except that when the lady steps forward with the left foot, instead of toeing out as described for the man, she steps forward between man's feet. This style for the lady greatly facilitates the turn.

Style: Accent the first step by reaching into the turn with a longer step. However, the man must be careful not to over-reach his partner.

Note: For the right turn, start with the right foot and reverse the pattern.

CROSS STEP (closed position)

Steps	3/4 Counts	Rhythmic Cue	Lead Indication*
Step L forward	1	Slow	✓
Step R sideward	2	Slow	✓
Close L to R, take weight L	3	Slow	(open)
Cross R over L, take weight R	1	Slow	
Step L sideward	2	Slow	✓ ✓
Close R to L, take weight R	3	Slow	(close)

Step Cue:
a. forward   side   close
b. cross   side   close

Floor Pattern:

Style: Turn into open position momentarily for the cross step. Step into the crossing beat on the ball of the foot.

Start:

Balance and Hesitation Steps

WALTZ BALANCE

Forward

Steps	3/4 Counts	Rhythmic Cue	Lead Indication*
Step L forward	1	Slow	✓
Close R to L, raise on both toes, take weight on R	2	Slow	
Take weight on L	3	Slow	

Backward

Steps	3/4 Counts	Rhythmic Cue	Lead Indication*
Step R backward	1	Slow	✓
Close L to R, raise on both toes, take weight on L	2	Slow	
Take weight on R	3	Slow	

Sideward

Steps	3/4 Counts	Rhythmic Cue	Lead Indication*
Step L sideward	1	Slow	✓
Close R to L, raise on both toes, take weight on R	2	Slow	
Take weight on R	3	Slow	

Style: Balance step should be small with weight on ball of foot.

* Check lead indication, page 269.

Steps	3/4 Counts	Rhythmic Cue	Lead Indication*

WALTZ HESITATION

Steps	3/4 Counts	Rhythmic Cue	Lead Indication*
Step L forward	1	Slow	√
Swing R leg forward past L	2	Slow	
Touch R toe lightly to floor, forward	3	Slow	
Step R backward	1	Slow	√
Swing L leg backward past R	2	Slow	
Touch L toe lightly to floor, backward	3	Slow	

<u>Style</u>: Swing the leg smoothly and reach to an extended leg and toe.

<u>Variation</u>: The hesitation step may also be done by omitting the swing and merely touching the free toe to the instep of the standing foot for counts 2 and 3.

Weaving and Scissors Steps

WEAVING STEP (closed position)

Steps	3/4 Counts	Rhythmic Cue	Lead Indication*
Step L forward	1	Slow	√
Step R sideward, turning to open position	2	Slow	√ (open)
Close L to R, take weight on L	3	Slow	
Cross R over L, take weight on R	1	Slow	√
Step L sideward, turning to reverse open	2	Slow	(reverse open)
Close R to L, take weight on R	3	Slow	
Cross L over R, take weight on L	1	Slow	√
Step R sideward, turning to open position	2	Slow	√ (open)
Close L to R, take weight on L	3	Slow	
Cross R over L, take weight on R	1	Slow	√
Step L sideward, turning to closed position	2	Slow	√ (closed)
Close R to L, take weight on R	3	Slow	

Step Cue:

a. forward side close
b. cross side close
c. cross side close
d. cross side close

Floor Pattern:

```
        ←——— d.
        ———→ c.
        ←——— b.
             ┐
Start: │ a.
```

<u>Lead</u>: Turn into open position for first cross step, man drops right arm and leads through with his left hand on the second cross step, then returns to open position for the third cross step.

<u>Style</u>: Keep weight on ball of foot for all crossing steps.

SCISSORS OR TWINKLE STEP (right reverse open position)

<u>Man's Part:</u>

Steps	3/4 Counts	Rhythmic Cue	Lead Indication*
Step L diagonally forward of R	1	Slow	√
Step R sideward, pivoting to left reverse open position	2	Slow	(left reverse)
Close L to R, take weight on L	3	Slow	
Step R diagonally forward	1	Slow	√
Step L sideward L, pivoting to right reverse open position	2	Slow	√ (right reverse)
Close R to L, take weight on R	3	Slow	

* Check lead indication, page 269.

Steps	3/4 Counts	Rhythmic Cue	Lead Indication*

Lady's Part:

Step R diagonally backward . . . . 1 . . . . . . Slow . . . .

Step L sideward, pivoting to
   left reverse position . . . . 2 . . . . . . Slow . . . .

Close R to L, take weight R . . . . 3 . . . . . . Slow . . . .

Step L diagonally backward . . . . 1 . . . . . . Slow . . . .

Step R sideward, pivoting to
   right reverse position . . . . 2 . . . . . . Slow . . . .

Close L to R, take weight L . . . . 3 . . . . . . Slow . . . .

Step Cue: **Floor Pattern:**

a. cross   side   pivot

b. cross   side   pivot

Lead: The man leads into right reverse
        open position from the back of a   **Start:**
        normal box step and is therefore
        ready to begin this pattern. He leads into each change of direction
        on the second beat of the measure.

Style: The second step should be short. Weight is on ball of foot through-
       out.

HOOK STEP (semi-open position)

Man's Part:

Step L sideward . . . . 1 . . . . . . Slow . . . . (open)

Cross R over L, take weight on both
   toes and . . . . 2 . . . . . . Slow . . . . . . ✓ . . . . . .

Pirouette on the toes, turning
   counterclockwise . . . . 3–1–2–3 . All Slows . . (Close on 3)

Lady's Part:

Step R sideward . . . . 1 . . . . . . Slow . . . .

Cross L over R, take weight on L . . . . 2 . . . . . . Slow . . . .

Step R, L, R, L, following man as
   he pirouettes counterclockwise . . . . . . 3–1–2–3 . . All Slows . . ., ...

Lead: Man turns lady to semi-open on his first sideward step and guides
       her forward around him with his right hand at her back, as he
       pirouettes. On the last beat, he turns her to closed position.

Style: The man turns on a small pivot base and the lady moves with small
       smooth steps in close to him as he turns. They will finish facing
       the opposite direction.

Note: This pattern is an adaptation of the hook step in the foxtrot. The
       man may follow the hook step with a regular box or with a corte.
       Refer to pages 280, 281.

Waltz Turns
(In addition to box turn)

HALF-TURNS (Refer to page 35)

THREE STEP TURN (LEFT), canter rhythm.

Step L sideward, toe out . . . . 1–2 . . . . . . Slow-hold . ✓ . . . . . .

Step R across in front of L, toe in,
   turn ½ to L . . . . 3 . . . . Slow . . . .

---

* Check lead indication, page 269.

Steps	3/4 Counts	Rhythmic Cue	Lead Indication*

Swing L behind R, turn ½ to L,
  take weight on L, bring R up to
  L but no change of weight . . . . 1–2–3 . . . . . Slow-hold-hold . . . . .
  Style: This is an individual turn usually taken by the lady. Refer to the
      Floor Pattern below.
  Note: To make right turn, start with right foot and reverse position.

BALANCE AND TURN

Balance L . . . .   1–2–3 . . . Refer to page 268
Balance R   1–2–3
Lady: Three step turn in canter
      rhythm as described above   1–2–3, 1–2–3
Man: Cross over, canter rhythm
Step L sideward   1–2   . . . . Slow-hold . . . √ . . . .
Step R across in front of L . . . . 3 . . . . . . Slow . . . .
Step L sideward, bring R to L,
  but no change of weight . . . . 1–2–3 . . . Slow-hold . . . .
Balance R . . . . 1–2–3 . . . as above
Balance L 1–2–3
Lady: Three steps turn to her L 1–2–3, 1–2–3
Man: Cross over step to his R 1–2–3, 1–2–3

Step Cue: Floor Pattern:
a. balance   balance   a. Lady
    step   turn   step   Man
b. balance   balance   b. Lady
    step   turn   step   Man
  Note: This three-step turn may be used for both man and lady to turn
      simultaneously. See diagram b, above.

PIVOT TURN, a series of steps turning right. It begins with a left foot lead
    but the preceding step *must* act as a preliminary step in order to go into
    the pivot turn smoothly. This foot action is diagrammed in the descrip-
    tion of the foxtrot pivot turn, page 258. For the waltz pivot turn, the
    footwork is the same. Only the rhythm is different and is shown below.
  Preliminary Step, man's right toe turns out toward partner and between
  her feet. This is the third beat of a forward waltz.
  Pivot turn
Step L forward on the curve,
    turning R . . . . 1 . . . . . . Slow . . . . . . √ . . . . . .
Step R turning foot in place, and moving
    forward between partner's feet . . . . 2 . . . . . Slow . . . .
Step L forward on the curve,
    turning R . . . . 3 . . . . . . Slow . . . .
Step R turning foot in place, and moving
    forward between partner's feet . . . . 1 . . . . . . Slow . . . . . . √ . . . . . .
Step L forward on the curve,
    turning R . . . . 2 . . . . . . Slow . . . .
Step R turning foot in place, and moving
    forward between partner's feet . . . . 3 . . . . Slow . . . .

* Check lead indication, page 269.

<u>Style</u>: It is usually a six beat turn. The right foot moves forward coming in between partner's feet each time in a small step on the ball of the foot. The left foot steps around on the outside curve.

<u>Lead</u>: There is total body resistance backward in order to take advantage of the force of the turn.

Waltz Corte

The corte or dip is a figure borrowed from the tango rhythm and is a fascinating step easily adapted to waltz time. The corte is described in detail in the tango section, page 304.

The corte rhythm is described as quick, quick, slow, slow. The two quick beats serve as a preparation step for the dip figure. In waltz time, the second and third beats of the waltz measure serve as the preparatory motion.

WALTZ CORTE

Starting L, take two forward waltz steps, 1–2–3, 1–2–3. On the second waltz, as the man is taking the side close motion on the second and third beats, he lifts his shoulders to prepare the lady for the corté. Then he steps backward (lady forward) into the corté holding it one full measure (1–2–3) and recovers into a forward waltz on his R foot (forward side close).

Pursuit Waltz

This is a traveling waltz pattern. It requires a small step on each beat with the first beat accented as before. The difference is that there is no closing step. All three steps progress. There are endless possibilities for originality of pattern, direction, and design through the use of the pursuit waltz.

VARIATIONS:

Closed Position, forward or backward
Open Position, forward, circular
Left or Right Reverse Open Position (parallel position), forward, backward, circle.

Waltz Combos**

A number of waltz routines are listed here merely as examples to show how the various waltz steps can be used in combination for practice routines. They are listed from simple to complex.

Closed position unless otherwise indicated

1. <u>Balance and Box</u>
   2 balance steps
      (forward, backward)
   1 box step
2. <u>Balance and Box</u>
   2 balance steps
      (forward, backward)
   1 box step turning
   Repeat all
3. <u>Waltz Box</u>
   1 box step
   2 forward waltz steps
   1 box turn

4. <u>Cross Box and Turn</u>
   2 cross steps
   1 box turn
5. <u>Hesitation and Box Turn</u>
   2 hesitation steps
      (forward, backward)
   1 box turn
6. <u>Three Step Turn</u>
   2 balance steps (L, R)
   1 three-step turn
   2 balance steps
   1 three-step turn

---

* Check the lead indication, page 269.
** Refer to notes on Practice Combos, page 271.

7. <u>Box and Pivot Turn</u>
   1 box step
   1 pivot turn (6 beats)
   corté recovery (6 beats)
8. <u>Cross Step and Weaving</u>
   2 cross steps
   1 weaving step
9. <u>Cross Step and Corté</u>
   2 cross steps
   corté (3 beats)
   1 forward waltz step
10. <u>Box and Scissors Waltz</u>
    1 box step
    2 scissors steps (L R L R)
    box turn
11. <u>Hesitation and Scissors</u>
    2 hesitation steps
      (forward, back)
    4 scissors steps (L R L R)
    corté (3 beats)
    1 forward waltz step

12. <u>Advanced Combo</u>
    1 box turn
    4 scissors steps
    2 hesitation steps
    2 pursuit waltz steps
    1 corté
    1 forward waltz step
13. <u>Advanced Combo</u>
    2 cross steps
    4 pursuit waltz steps
      (left reverse open)
    4 pursuit waltz steps
      (right reverse open)
    2 balance steps
    1 hook step
    corté (3 beats)
    1 forward waltz step

TANGO

The Argentine cowboy or gaucho dance known as the tango has won itself an accepted place in our modern-day social dance. Like all dance forms, the tango has been through much evolution and adaptation from its earlier and more sensuous form as a gaucho dance. The American version of the tango comes to us via Paris, and it is entirely possible that the Argentine gaucho would have a difficult time recognizing this creation as it is performed today.

The tango has undergone more changes than any of the ballroom dances. Each change has resulted in gradual loss of many of the tango's Latin characteristics. However, in losing some of its original features, it has gained a thrilling smoothness and is one of the most beautiful dances on the ballroom floor today. The tango has a sophistication and suave style that cannot be matched. Its slow accented glide and the contrasting excitement of the tango close are enhanced by the unusually beautiful musical accompaniment and its unique variations including the corté, the fans, the flares, and the rock steps.

Tango Rhythm

The modern tango is written in 2/4 or 4/4 time.* For this chapter it will be described in 2/4 time. It is slower than many 2/4 rhythms. The two quarter beats in each measure have a deliberate accent and represent the slow beats of the rhythm pattern.

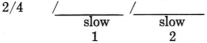

```
2/4      /_____ /_____
              slow         slow
               1            2
```

The tango close and other tango variations are built as a one measure pattern with an uneven rhythm as follows:

```
2/4   /_____ _____/_____      tango close
       quick  quick    slow
         1     and      2
```

The promenade and tango close together represent the basic tango rhythm.

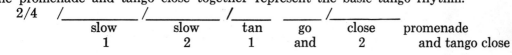

```
2/4     /_____ /_____ /_____ _____/_____
            slow         slow       tan    go    close     promenade
             1            2          1     and     2        and tango close
```

The tango box rhythm is based on the same rhythm as the box foxtrot.

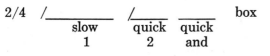

```
2/4    /_____  /_____ _____     box
            slow       quick  quick
             1          2     and
```

Tango Style

The tango is characterized by a deliberate glide, more like the natural walk than the other dance forms, but still not a heel toe weight change. It is rather the full foot on the floor and the weight on the ball of the foot. Although the deep knee bend has been replaced by the straight knee, the tango step is still distinctive with its long reaching glide and its subtle quickness emphasized by the draw step at the end of the pattern. Restraint is achieved by the use of continuous flow of movements and controlled stylized break.

The dancer should strive to eliminate a reflection of rhythm in the upper body and effect the idea of floating. Care should be taken to avoid the look of stiffness. The closed position should be maintained in most variations and the dance is close. All action should be kept in the legs and feet. Since the long reaching glide is used, the feet should pass each other close together.

---

* Refer to page 37.

The draw in the tango close is executed slowly, taking the full length of the slow beat to bring the feet together, and then sweeping quickly into the beginning of the basic rhythm again. The lady should synchronize the action of her drawing step with that of the man. The twinkle and box step variations of the foxtrot are often used with the tango.

Teaching the tango is one of the greater thrills in teaching ballroom dance. The tango style is appealing and the feeling of the unique figures is exciting. A dancer has a sense of real accomplishment in being able to dance the tango. Students will take a great pride in learning it, and amazingly enough, a considerable amount of poise or smoothness rubs off on the foxtrot after a class has danced the tango.

Fundamental Tango Steps
Tango Promenade
Tango Close
Basic Tango Rhythm and Variations
Rock Steps
Corté
Fan Steps

Directions are for man, facing line of direction: lady's part reverse, except as noted.

Steps	2/4 Counts	Rhythmic Cue	Lead Indication*
TANGO PROMENADE			
Step L forward	1	Slow	√
Step R forward	2	Slow	
Step L forward	1	Slow	
Step R forward	2	Slow	
Style: Steps long, smooth, and gliding.			
TANGO CLOSE			
Step L in place	1	Quick	√
Step R sideward, taking weight on R but leaving left toe still touching out to the L	and	Quick	
Draw the L foot in slowly to the R arch, weight remains on R	2	Slow	
Step Cue: Tango Close			
Style: Steps short, with slow drawing step. Avoid tendency to make this step waddle from left to right. Take first quick beat short and in place or slightly forward.			
BASIC TANGO RHYTHM (combination of tango walk and tango break).			
Step L forward	1	Slow	√
Step R forward	2	Slow	
Step L in place	1	Quick	√
Step R sideward	and	Quick	
Draw L to R, weight remains on R	2	Slow	
Note: Repeats over and over with L foot lead.			

* Check lead indication, page 269.

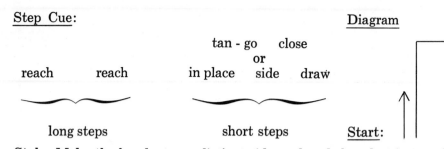

Step Cue: Diagram

tan - go   close
or
reach   reach   in place   side   draw

long steps   short steps   Start:

Style: Make the break step a distinct sideward and slow drawing motion. The forward step on the first quick beat in place or slightly forward.

Variations on the Basic Tango Rhythm

FIRST PROMENADE: This is the basic tango rhythm forward in closed position. Due to the draw to the right, when the forward step is repeated several times it moves the couple toward the outer edge of the dance floor. The man may use a 1/4 turn left in the tango close as follows:

SECOND PROMENADE: This is the promenade step taken in left reverse open position (right parallel). The man leads into it with an abrupt lift of the right arm on the first promenade beat. The second promenade beat is an exaggerated reaching step forward. Then the man turns to face his partner for the Tango close.

THIRD PROMENADE: In this the two promenade steps are taken in open position. The man leads into open position abruptly as he steps out on his left foot. The second promenade step is a short step forward in open position. At the same time the man pivots on his right foot to make a ¼ turn counterclockwise, bringing up his right arm which turns the girl into a closed position. She is pivoting on her left foot, making a ¾ turn as the man brings her around to closed position. Then they do a Tango close. The lady should be prepared to pivot easily around into closed position on the left foot as she takes the second promenade step.

FOURTH PROMENADE: This pattern also starts with the two promenade steps in open position. The man leads into open position abruptly as he steps on his left foot, then on the right, and this time the man pivots on his right foot turning clockwise to come around to face the lady in closed position. Then they both take the Tango close.

Steps	2/4 Counts	Rhythmic Cue	Lead Indication*
TANGO CLOSE (¼ turn left)			
Step L forward, toe out, turn ¼ L	1	Quick	✓
Step R sideward	and	Quick	
Draw L to R, no change of weight	2	Slow	

Lead: The man must give a sharp bank of the arm to turn the girl to a ¼ left turn on the Tango close rhythm.

CROSS STEP AND TANGO CLOSE TURN. The crossing step is in closed position.			
Step L sideward	1	Slow	✓
Step R across in front of L, take weight R	2	Slow	✓
Step L sideward, turn toe out, turn ¼ to L	1	Quick	

* Check lead indication, page 269.

Steps	2/4 Counts	Rhythmic Cue	Lead Indication*
Step R sideward	and	Quick	
Draw L to R, no change of weight	2	Slow	

Step Cue: Floor Pattern:

side   cross   turn   side   draw

‿‿‿‿   ‿‿‿‿‿‿‿‿

long steps   short steps   Start:

Style: There is a slight pivot on the standing foot and a turn of the hips when stepping with the crossing foot. The shoulders remain facing in closed position throughout the pattern.

DOUBLE CROSS (Twinkle Variation)

Steps	2/4 Counts	Rhythmic Cue	Lead Indication*
Step L sideways	1	Slow	✓
Step R across in front of L	2	Slow	
Point L sideways, take weight slightly	1	Quick	✓
Pivot hips to R with a slight push on L, take weight of R	and	Quick	
Swing L across in front of R, take weight L	2	Slow	
Point R to side	1	Quick	
Pivot hips to L with slight push on R, take weight L	and	Quick	✓
Swing R across in front of L, take weight R	2	Slow	

LADY'S HALF TURN

Note: Man's step is the same as for the double cross.

Steps	2/4 Counts	Rhythmic Cue	Lead Indication*
Step R sideways	1	Slow	✓
Step L across in front of R	2	Slow	
Point R sideways, take weight slightly	1	Quick	
Pivot hips to R with slight push on R, take weight L	and	Quick	
Swing R across in back of L, take weight R	2	Slow	✓
Point L to side	1	Quick	
Pivot hips to L with slight push on L, take weight R	and	Quick	✓
Swing L across in back of R, take weight L	2	Slow	

Lead: On the quick beats the man turns the lady to right reverse open position (left parallel) for the next slow and then turns to left reverse open position (right parallel) on the second set of quick beats for the last slow. They may finish with Tango close in closed position.

Note: This may be done with both man and lady turning.

* Check lead indication, page 269.

Rock Steps

The rhythm of the rock step is quick quick slow. The style is a deliberate rocking motion with a controlled bend of the knee and an accompanying follow through with the body in opposition. Sometimes a flare of the free foot is used to add to the cunningness of the style. It may be danced in any combination of direction or position and should be used more often in the tango to relieve the overworked basic tango rhythm. The quick quick beats of the rock step may be used as a delightful preparation step for any tango variation.

FORWARD AND BACKWARD ROCK (closed position)

Step L forward............................1.......Quick.....√......

Step R backward.....................and.......Quick............

Step L forward............................2......Slow.......√......

Step R forward............................1......Quick............

Step L backward.....................and......Quick............

Step R forward............................2.......Slow......√......

Lead: The body is rotated slightly in opposition to the stepping foot. That is, the right shoulder rotates forward as the left foot steps forward. This position is maintained throughout the quick quick slow movement. At the end of the slow beat as the right foot prepares to step forward into the next rock the body rotates so that the left shoulder is slightly forward.

Style: Care should be taken so the steps are straight forward or back, not stepping wide to throw the motion off balance. The rock is subtle and controlled, not bouncy.

Note: This motion may be taken in reverse with action moving backward. It may be taken forward in open position with less emphasis in body rotation.

ALTERNATE FORWARD, OPEN ROCK

Step L forward............................1......Quick.....√......

Step R backward.....................and......Quick............

Step L forward, pivoting to
open position ....2.......Slow.......√......

Step R forward in open position.·........1.......Quick............

Step L backward in open position.......and......Quick............

Step R forward, turning to
closed position ....2.......Slow......√......

Style: In this a flare of the foot may be used going from closed to open position. Actually the motion is taken on the end of the slow beat as the inside foot swings through. It may be slightly lifted off the floor by bending the knee and arching the foot, the toe pointing toward the floor. This is repeated again with the other foot when going from open to closed position.

Note: To come out of this step finish with a tango close.

Corté

The corté is a dip, most often taken backward on the man's left or right foot. It is a type of break step used to finish off almost any tango variation or is used as an ending to the dance. The skilled dancer will learn to use the corté in relationship to the music of the tango so that the feeling of the corté will correspond to the climax or phrase of the musical accompaniment.

The left corté will be described here. A right corté may be taken by starting on the right foot and reversing the pattern. There is nearly always a preliminary step used as preparation for going into the dip. It is described here as a part of the rhythm of the corté (quick, quick, slow, slow).

Steps	2/4 Counts	Rhythmic Cue	Lead Indication*
VARIATION I (PREPARATION STEP)			
Step forward L	1	Quick	√
Shift weight back on the R	and	Quick	
CORTE:			
Swing L back past R, take weight bending L knee slightly	2	Slow	√
Recover forward, taking weight on R	1	Slow	√
VARIATION II (PREPARATION STEP)			
Step forward L	1	Quick	√
Close R to L, take weight R	and	Quick	
CORTE:			
Step backward on L, take weight, bending L knee slightly, keep R leg straight	2 and	Slow	√
Recover forward, taking weight on R	1	Slow	√

Step Cue:

a. rock and dip recover

or

b. step close dip recover

Diagram:

Lead: The left shoulder leads forward as the man goes into the preparation step. There is an increase of tension of the man's right arm and hand plus general increased resistance throughout the upper body. The man will draw the lady with his right arm when stepping into the dip and release on the recovery step. The lead is essential for the corte as the pattern cannot be executed correctly unless both man and lady are completely on balance, and ready for it.

Style: As *the man* steps backward into the corte, the weight is all taken on the standing foot with a bent knee. His back should remain straight. He should avoid leaning either backward or forward. His right foot is only touching the floor and the arch should be extended so that the toe is down on the floor. The man should turn his bent knee slightly outward so that the lady's knee will not bump his as they go into the dip.

The lady should step forward on the right, arch her back and place all of her weight over the forward right foot. The right knee

---

* Check lead indication, page 269.

should be bent. The left leg is extended behind her and should be straight. A bent leg behind makes the whole figure sag. The left arch of the foot should be extended so that the toe is pointed and remains in contact with the floor. If the lady steps forward too far or does not bend the forward knee, she will be forced to bend at the waist, which destroys the form of the figure.

The execution of the dip should be as smooth as any slow backward step. The man should avoid leaping or falling back into the dip. The recovery forward on the right foot may be followed by the tango close, a quick in place, or a basic tango step.

Fan Steps

The fan is a term used to describe a manner of executing a leg motion, in which the leg swings in a whip-like movement around a small pivoting base. This should not be a large sweeping movement in a wide arc, but rather a small subtle action initiated in the hip and executed with the legs close together. The balance is carefully poised over the pivoting foot at all times. When the man and lady both take the fan motion, the action is taken parallel to partner. The leg generally fans out from front to back (or the reverse) and is accompanied by a half turn of the pivoting foot (on the toe of the foot) with the hip lead turning the body and giving the impetus for a lift of the body. This lift permits the free leg to swing through gracefully extended and close in a beautiful floating style.

Steps	2/4 Counts	Rhythmic Cue	Lead Indication*
SWING STEP (also called a "fan" step)			
Step L sideward	1	Slow	√
Step R across in front of L, take weight R	2	Slow	
Step L sideward	1	Quick	
Close R to L, take weight R	and	Quick	
Step L sideward	2	Quick	
Swing R across L	and	Quick	√
Swing R back to R	1	Quick	
Step R behind L, take weight R	and	Quick	
Step L sideward (short step) to L	2	Quick	
Close R to L, take weight R	and	Quick	

Style: The swinging foot goes across the standing foot as a preparation action for the swing or "fan." The foot swings out sideways and in behind taking the weight as it steps behind the other foot. This is a continuous smooth swing done forward with one quick beat, out and in behind with two quick beats. If the first beat is too long, there will not be time for the "fan" action.

Note: This may be followed by a tango close or any other step.

PARALLEL FAN (A fan step in left reverse open position)

Man's Part: Starts and ends in closed position, an 8 measure pattern:
Starting L, take 1 basic tango step, 1 2 1 and 2 Slow Slow Quick Quick Slow

	2/4 Counts	Rhythmic Cue	Lead Indication*
Step L forward	1	Slow	
Step R forward	2	Slow	
Step L forward	1	Quick	

---

* Check lead indication, page 269.

Steps	2/4 Counts	Rhythmic Cue	Lead Indication*
Step R sideward, turning lady to left reverse open position	and	Quick	
Step L backward	2	Slow	
Step R beside L, turning lady to open position	1	Quick	
Step L in place	and	Quick	
Step R forward, turning lady to left reverse open position	2	Slow	
Rock backward onto L, turning lady to open position	1	Slow	
Rock forward onto R, turning lady to left reverse open position	2	Slow	
Rock back onto L, turning lady to open position	1	Slow	
Step R forward, turning to closed position	2	Slow	
Take tango close	1 and 2	Quick, Quick, Slow	

Lady's Part:

Starting R, take 1 basic tango step, 1 2 1 and 2 Slow Slow Quick Quick Slow

Steps	2/4 Counts	Rhythmic Cue	Lead Indication*
Step R backward	1	Slow	
Step L backward	2	Slow	
Step R backward	1	Quick	
Step L sideward, pivoting counter-clockwise to left reverse open position	and	Quick	
Step R forward	2	Slow	
Step L beside R, pivoting to open position	1	Quick	
Step R in place	and	Quick	
Step L forward (fan), pivoting to left reverse open position	2	Slow	
Step R forward (fan), pivoting to open position	1	Slow	
Step L forward (fan), pivoting to left reverse open position	2	Slow	
Step R forward (fan), pivoting to open position	1	Slow	
Step L forward, turning to closed position	2	Slow	
Take tango close	1 and 2	Quick, Quick, Slow	

Lead: Man's first lead will be a lift of right arm into left reverse open position as he steps sideward on his right foot and then guides her forward on the next step as he steps back. Then he turns her half around to open position on the two quick steps and from there with his right hand moving her alternately from left reverse open to open until the end of the step when he leads to closed position for the tango close.

* Check lead indication, page 269.

Style: The man in the fan part of the step rocks forward, back, forward, back, in place as he turns the lady. The lady takes her fan, pivoting alternately on the left, right, left, right, swinging the free leg forward a short distance until the toe just clears the floor, then turning the hip with her pivot to the new direction and reaches through for the next step. The rhythm of the fan is step, swing forward, pivot, and reach through, which is all done on each slow beat. The lady should rise slightly on her toe as she pivots. This smooths out the turn and makes one of the most beautiful movements in tango.

Steps	2/4 Counts	Rhythmic Cue	Lead Indication*

OPEN FAN

Step L forward.........................1.......Slow.............

Step R forward.........................2.......Slow.............

Taking the Tango Close, QQS, in place, the man releases his right arm around the lady and turns ¼ clockwise, the lady turns ¼ counterclockwise, so that they end up in a side by side position, the man's left still holding the lady's right hand.

The man: from side by side position

Step forward L and swing the R leg forward, pivoting (fan) on left foot toward partner and around to open position....1.......Slow.............

Step forward R in open position, pivoting toward lady into closed position.....2.......Slow.............

Tango Close ....1 and 2....Quick, Quick, Slow..

The lady: from side by side position

Step forward R and swing the L leg forward, pivoting (fan) on right foot toward partner and around to open position....1.......Slow.............

Step forward L in open position, pivoting toward man to closed position......2.......Slow.............

Tango Close ....1 and 2....Quick, Quick, Slow..

Style: The fan is a forward swing of the leg from the hip as the body pivots to open position, the hip turning over so the knee faces down. The foot is kept close to the floor and the leg then swings forward in open position. It is a smooth rolling motion forward and through — but not an arc.

Lead: The man drops his right arm and pulls away from the lady to side by side position. Then with his left hand he pulls in as he fans through to open position and from there lifts his right arm into closed position for tango close.

GRAPEVINE AND SINGLE FAN

Man's Part: starts in open position.

Step L forward..........................1.......Slow.............

Step R forward..........................2.......Quick.....√......

Step L backward....................and......Quick.............

Step R backward, swinging left leg backward (fan) ....1.......Slow......√......

Step L backward, turning to face partner..2.......Quick.....√......

---

* Check lead indication, page 269.

Steps	2/4 Counts	Rhythmic Cue	Lead Indication*
Step R sidewards, turning to face reverse open position	and	Quick	√
Step L forward in reverse open position and turn to open position, fanning right foot sideways and through	1	Slow	√
Step R forward in open position, turning partner to closed position	2	Slow	√
Finish with tango close break	1 and 2	QQS	

Lady's Part: starts in open position.

Steps	2/4 Counts	Rhythmic Cue	Lead Indication*
Step R forward	1	Slow	
Step L forward	2	Quick	
Step R backward	and	Quick	
Step L backward, swinging right leg backward (fan)	1	Slow	
Step R backward, turning to face partner	2	Quick	
Step L sideward, turning to face reverse open position	and	Quick	
Step R forward in reverse open position, and turn to open position, swinging left leg sideward and through	1	Slow	
Step L forward in open position, turning to closed position	2	Slow	
Finish with tango close	1 and 2	QQS	

Style: The couple should not get too far apart or lean forward to maneuver this grapevine pattern. They should stand upright and keep carefully balanced over standing foot. The fanning leg swings in line with the traveling and facing action, not in a wide arc. The legs are kept close together.

---

* Check lead indication, page 269.

Tango Combos*

A number of tango routines are listed here merely as examples to show how the various steps can be used in combination for practice routines. They are listed from simple to complex.

Closed position unless otherwise indicated

1. <u>Basic</u>
   2 basic steps forward
   1 basic step with closed turn
2. <u>Basic and Cross Step</u>
   2 basic steps forward
   2 cross steps with tango close turn
3. <u>Basic Four Promenade Steps</u>
   Closed position — 1st promenade step
   Left reverse closed position —
   2nd promenade step
   Closed position — 1st promenade step
   Open with clockwise and counterclockwise turns — 3rd and 4th
   promenade steps
4. <u>Basic and Corte</u>
   1 basic step (forward)
   1 corte I or II
5. <u>Basic — Cross — Corte</u>
   1 basic forward
   1 cross step (without tango close)
   1 corte I or II
6. <u>Basic — Rock Step — Corte</u>
   1 basic forward
   2 rock steps forward
   corte
   tango close

7. <u>Cross Step — Swing Step</u>
   1 cross step and tango
   close turn
   1 swing step (fan)
   tango close
8. <u>Advanced Combo</u>
   2 basics: fourth promenade
   4 rock steps
   grapevine and single fan
9. <u>Advanced Combo</u>
   4 alternate closed and
   open rock steps
   parallel fan
   corte
   open fan
10. <u>Advanced Combo</u>
    1 basic forward
    1 cross step and tango
    close turn
    1 swing step (fan)
    tango close
    1 swing step (fan)
    tango close

---

* Refer to notes on Practice Combos, page 271.

RUMBA

The Latin-American dances are to American dancing what garlic is to the good cook. Used sparingly, they can add a tangy interest to our dancing. The rumba is a Cuban dance, along with the mambo, bolero, and the cha cha cha, but has enjoyed greater popularity than any of the others, probably because of its slower, more relaxed, smooth style. The music is usually identified by the tantalizing rhythms of the percussion instruments known as the maracas, which carry the continuous quick beat and the sticks or bongo drum, which beats out the accented rhythm of the dance.

Rumba Rhythm

The rumba is written in 4/4 time* and is played both fast and slow. Many Americans prefer the slower bolero type tempo, but actually in the Latin countries the rumba is danced considerably faster. It is thought that originally the rumba rhythm was a quick-quick-slow combination, and it was danced that way in America for many years. Gradually, however, more and more teachers have changed over to the slow-quick-quick rhythm. This change may possibly have occurred because of the accents in the rhythm which come on the first and third beats of the measure.

4/4 /_____   /___ ____
     slow   quick quick
     1–2   3   4

Learning the rumba does not necessitate learning a new group of dance steps. The actual difference between the rumba and the foxtrot is not in step pattern, but in the style of the body movement. Synchronizing of the step with the beat occurs simultaneously with the placing of the foot, the transfer of weight being delayed or between beats.

Rumba Style

Rumba movement is a subtle continuous quick and slow rolling motion of the weight from foot to foot. The action occurs in the feet and the knees, and the secret lies in the delayed shift of weight which makes it the reverse action of a normal walking step. The upper body is held upright and quiet, giving this dance a most sophisticated air. The step itself is comparatively short and flat footed, with the knee leading, although the weight is carried over the ball of the foot for easy balance and directional control.

The Cuban rumba movement is a spring-like action resulting from a placing of the left foot on the floor first without taking weight but with a bent knee. This is followed by a pressing of the weight into the floor and a straightening of the left knee. Accompanying this press into the floor there is a smooth roll of the weight being shifted to that left foot. The right knee begins to bend and leads the right foot, now free of weight, into its new position. The roll is completed as the weight is transferred gradually to the newly placed right foot, keeping the knee bent. Now the entire action is repeated by a pressing of the weight into the right foot and a straightening of the right knee rolling smoothly. As the left foot is freed of weight, the knee leads, shifting the left foot to its new position with the weight coming over it, completing the roll.

The knees should bent directly over the foot, and the feet should be placed with the toes pointing straight ahead. A pigeon-toed effect should be avoided. As the feet pass each other, the steps are small, close together, with toes pointed straight ahead in line of direction. The movement of the hips is merely the subtle result of the specific action of the feet and the knees. There should be no intentional swinging of the hip from side to side. There needs to be a stabilization of the upper trunk at the waist, in order to keep easily upright and the shoulders straight.

The head is held with the focus constantly on one's partner. The arm and hand, when free from partner, is held in a bent elbow position, waist level, palm down. The man does not hold his partner close. There is seldom any body contact.

The rumba, with its open and encircling patterns, is generally danced within a small space and reflects a dignified, although flirtatious, quality.

* Refer to page 37.

TEACHING SUGGESTIONS FOR RUMBA STYLE:

First, practice the motion described above, moving forward in a slow, slow rhythm, working to achieve the feeling of the roll. Practice in front of a mirror is usually helpful.

Second, practice the same motion forward in a slow quick quick rhythm.

Third, practice the motion as in the box step.

Finally, practice with partner in closed dance position.

Fundamental Rumba Steps
Cuban Walk
Box Step
Variations of the Rumba
    Bolero Break
    Flirtation Break
    Varsouvianna Break
    Back Cross and Turn
    Spot Turn

Directions are for man, facing line of direction: lady's part reverse, except as noted.

Steps	4/4 Counts	Rhythmic Cue	Lead Indication*
CUBAN WALK			
Place L forward — roll weight slowly onto L	1–2	Slow	√
Place R forward — roll weight quickly onto R	3	Quick	
Place L forward — roll weight quickly onto L	4	Quick	

Step Cue: place – roll   roll   roll
              1–2   3   4

Style: The roll is the spring-like action of pressing into the floor. The knee of the free foot bends and leads the foot into its new position, followed by the transfer of weight to that foot.

Note: The Cuban walk step is used for all moving variations when not in closed dance position. It may move forward, backward, or in a circle.

Steps	4/4 Counts	Rhythmic Cue	Lead Indication*
BOX STEP (closed dance position)			
Place L forward — roll weight slowly onto L	1–2	Slow	√
Place R sideward — roll weight quickly onto R	3	Quick	
Place L close to R — roll weight quickly to L	4	Quick	
Place R backward — roll weight slowly onto R	1–2	Slow	√
Place L sideward — roll weight quickly onto L	3	Quick	
Place R close to L — roll weight quickly onto R	4	Quick	

---

* Check lead indication, page 269.

Step Cue: forward   side   close   Floor Pattern:
             back   side   close

Style: Movement as above. The feet are placed flat on the floor, in a small box pattern.

Start: a.

Note: The rumba box step is the same foot pattern as the Westchester box step in the foxtrot. The box turn will follow the same pattern then as the foxtrot box turn described on page 276. The style is different. Other foxtrot variations useable in the rumba are the chasse, page 275; the cross step, page 276; and the single twinkle, page 279.

Variations of the Rumba

BOLERO BREAK. Starting in closed dance position, the man executes the rumba box step in place, turning the lady under his own left arm. After she goes under, she circles clockwise in a wide arc until she faces him again at arm's distance; he will then draw her forward to closed dance position.

Lead: The man gives the lead for bolero break just before he steps back on his right foot into the back half of the box step. This will allow the lady to start turning when she steps on her right foot. She turns clockwise under the man's left arm and dances in a wide arc until she is facing the man again at arm's distance.

Style: The lady will use the Cuban walk when moving around in a wide arc. This is a slow turn. Any number of steps may be taken so long as she keeps his rhythm. She should keep body upright, arm up and focus on her partner.

Diagram:

VARIATIONS (of bolero break)

1. WALK AROUND. As the lady comes around from bolero break, instead of going into closed position, the man, with his left hand in contact with the lady, will lead her toward his right side and past his right shoulder bringing her around behind him and toward his left side. He then turns ½ turn left to face her and they move into closed dance position.

Lead: The man should raise his left arm high enough so that he does not have to duck his head as she goes around. He will move slightly forward under his own left arm before he turns left to meet the lady.

Style: The lady will use Cuban walk and keep her circle in close to the man. The man will keep the box step going until she passes his right side, then he will go into the Cuban walk for his forward and turning movement. Both should focus on each other.

Diagram

2. PARALLEL TURN. As the lady comes around in her wide arc at arm's distance, the man will move in toward her coming into left reverse open position (right parallel) and they will turn clockwise as far as desired. The man may then lead lady to closed position or into right reverse open position (left parallel) and turn her counterclockwise. He may return to the left reverse open position, turn clockwise and then twirl the lady clockwise once around in place to finish in closed position. The lead for the twirl should come as the man steps forward into a box step with the left foot so that the lady may turn on one basic step starting with her right foot. They finish together in the back part of the box step in closed position. Style: They use the Cuban walk. Focus is on partner.

Diagram:

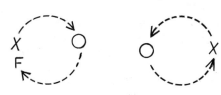

3. CIRCULAR TURN. Immediately after the man turns the lady under his left arm to start bolero break, he brings his left arm down to a pressure position against her right elbow and turns ¼ right to be in a side position. Then the man moves backward, the lady forward, turning in place clockwise. To get out of this turn, the man leads ¼ turn to face partner and brings lady forward into closed dance position.

Lead: Firmness in the arm is necessary by man and response to this firm pressure is needed by lady.

Style: They must be in a tight side by side position. They will use the Cuban walk. Focus should be on partner, outside arm up.

FLIRTATION BREAK (from closed dance position)

The man guides the lady away from him by a pressure lead to a position apart from him at arm's distance, but facing partner. From this position they may travel forward or backward depending upon the directional lead given in the man's left hand. The man must maneuver the changes so as to move into the free spaces on the floor and not work against the traffic.

Lead: The pressure lead is a firmness in the hand. The lady will feel this and respond to it effectively if her contact arm has a firmness which responds to his lead and follows with body action. A limp arm makes following very difficult. The lead may be given on the quick steps of the Cuban walk rhythm.

VARIATIONS (from flirtation position)

1. The man may turn the lady ¼ left and himself ¼ right so as to travel side by side down the floor.

2. From this side by side position the man may give a pressure lead against her elbow and reverse his direction to travel backwards, pulling her forward so that they move clockwise in a circular turn. He acts as the pivot for the turn.

3. From facing position the man may lead her into the walk around or the parallel turn as described under bolero break.

VARSOUVIANNA BREAK (from closed dance position)

Turn into the varsouvianna position: The man releases the lady's right hand and reaches across in front of his right shoulder to take her left hand, pulling it across in front of him, causing the lady to turn clockwise a half turn until she is by his right side facing in the same direction. The man now holds the lady's left hand in his left and has his right around her waist to take her right hand at her right side. They circle clockwise one complete turn. To do this effectively the man moves forward, the lady backward to turn in place.

Turn into reverse varsouvianna position: The man releases the lady's right hand and turns to his own right, bringing their joined left hands across in front of lady as she turns left until she is by his left side and slightly behind him, facing in the same direction. She reaches around behind him with her right hand to take his right hand at his right side. They continue to circle clockwise another complete turn, the man now moving backward, the lady forward.

Return to varsouvianna position: The man releases the lady's right hand and leads her with his left hand from behind him into the original varsouvianna position. As the lady moves from behind the man into this position, she must turn clockwise a full turn to end in front of and to the right of the man. If the man turns ¼ to the left as she moves he will assist and shorten her turn and smooth out the figure. They will continue turning clockwise, the man again moving forward and the lady backward for this turn.

Turn back to closed position: The man releases the lady's left hand and by leading with the right, turns her clockwise to closed dance position. The man starts the box step in closed position, but as soon as he begins the figure, they go into Cuban walk for the entire pattern.

Style: Although this is described in four parts, the transitions into each part should be smooth so as to make the entire maneuver blend into one figure rather than four disconnected parts. There is no set number of Cuban walk steps to be taken for each part. The couple should turn continuously clockwise throughout the figure. Dancers should be careful to maintain good rumba style throughout.

Variation: A beautiful combination of figures is the circular turn and the varsouvianna break. The man turns left in a half turn out of the circular turn, changing hands and ending up in the reverse varsouvianna position as above. Finish the varsouvianna figure to closed position.

Steps	4/4 Counts	Rhythmic Cue	Lead Indication*
BACK CROSS			
Step L sideward L	1–2	Slow	√
Step R directly behind L heel	3	Quick	
Step L in place	4	Quick	
Step R sideward R	1–2	Slow	√
Step L directly behind R heel	3	Quick	
Step R in place	4	Quick	
BACK CROSS WITH TURN			
Man's Part: Take back cross as above, then add:			
Step L sideward, toeing out and turn counterclockwise about ¼ turn	1–2	Slow	
			Release L hand Lower R arm toward floor

---
* Check lead indication, page 269.

Steps	4/4 Counts	Rhythmic Cue	Lead Indication
Step R, close to L, pivoting on R counterclockwise about ½ turn	3	Quick	
Step L, coming on around to face partner	4	Quick	
Step R, across in front of L in line of direction	1–2	Slow	(Take closed position)
Step L sidewards	3	Quick	
Close R to L	4	Quick	
Lady's Part: Take back cross as above (reverse for lady)			
Step R sideward, toeing out and turn clockwise about ¼ turn	1–2	Slow	
Step L, close to R, pivoting on L clockwise about ½ turn	3	Quick	
Step R, coming on around to face partner	4	Quick	
Step L, cross in front of R in line of direction	1–2	Slow	
Step R sideward	3	Quick	
Close L to R	4	Quick	

Lead: The man releases closed position and lets his right arm reach low to his side, keeping in close to lady as he turns. Her left arm will reach to her left side, keeping in close to him.

Note: Back cross may be used with the turn going in the opposite direction by leading into it after the first half of the back cross step above. The left arm will reach low and guide the motion.

---

* Check lead indication, page 269.

Rumba Combos*

The routines given here are merely examples to show how the various steps can be used in combination for practice routines. They are listed from simple to complex.

Closed position unless otherwise indicated

1. Cuban Walk and Box
   4 Cuban walks
   2 box steps
2. Box and Bolero Break
   2 box steps
   bolero break
3. Box and Flirtation Break
   2 box steps
   flirtation break —
     forward and back
4. Flirtation Break Variations
   flirtation break
   progress side by side
   open turn
5. Bolero Break and Walk Around
   2 box steps
   bolero break
   bolero break and walk around
6. Bolero Break and Reverse Turn
   2 box steps
   bolero break
   left reverse turn
7. Bolero Break and Open Turn
   2 box steps
   bolero break
   open turn

8. Flirtation Break and Reverse Turn
   2 box steps
   flirtation break
   left reverse turn
   right reverse turn
9. Back Cross with Turn
   2 box steps
   back cross with turn
     (in either direction)
10. Advanced Combo
   2 box steps
   bolero break
   open turn
   varsouvianna series
11. Advanced Combo
   2 box steps
   bolero break
   bolero break and walk around
   varsouvianna series
   2 box steps
   flirtation break
   open turn

* Refer to notes on Practice Combos, page 271.

SAMBA

The samba, from Brazil, is the most active of the Latin American dances, except perhaps its newer more sensuous cousin, the bossa nova. It is interesting to discover how similar they are to some of the native dance rhythms in Africa. The samba is sensitive and smooth. The music is fiery, yet lyrical, and the dance is characterized by the tiny light footwork, the rise and fall of the body, always turning and at the same time swaying back and forth at an almost impossible pendular angle.

Samba Rhythm

Samba is written in 4/4 cut time* and may be found both slow and fast, although it is generally preferred at the faster tempo. The rhythm is quick quick slow. It has a double accent on each of the two major beats and these downbeats are represented by the down movements of the dance. It will be counted as 1 and 2 of the cut-time beat.

¢   quick quick   slow   rhythm pattern

         1   and   2   counts

¢   /   /   accent

    up down   up down   cue

The execution of the up down up down weight change is the secret to the smooth springing rhythm. There is a change of weight, from one foot to the other, on each of the three beats, down-up-down, but a preliminary "up" lift of the body on the upbeat of the music sets the rhythmical swing in motion.

Samba Style . . . In contrast to the rumba, which is a lower body movement, the samba has a total body action. The easy springing motion comes from the ball of the foot, the flexible ankle, and the easy relaxed knees. The upper body is held firmly poised, never sagging, and seeming to sway forward and back about an axis which centers in the diaphragm. The arm position when not in contact with partner is held out from the body, a little above waist level, bent at the elbow, parallel to the floor, palm down.

Fundamental Samba Steps
Basic Step
Slow Side Close
Sideward Steps
Open Progressive Step

Directions are for man, facing line of direction: lady's part reverse, except as noted.

Steps	¢ Counts	Rhythmic Cue	Lead Indication**
BASIC STEP (forward and back)			
Step L forward......................	1	Quick	/
Step R forward next to L..............	and	Quick	
Step L in place.......................	2	Slow	
Step R backward......................	1	Quick	/
Step L backward beside R.............	and	Quick	
Step R in place.......................	2	Slow	

Step Cue:			Floor Pattern:
a. forward	change	weight	
b. back	change	weight	

---
* Refer to page 37.
** Check the lead indication, page 269.

Lead: With increased tension of his right hand at her back, the man leans backward slightly after stepping forward with his left foot and rocks forward after stepping backward with his right foot. The lady's movement is in reverse.

Style: The steps are small. Feet are close together on change step. The rise and fall of the body begins on the upbeat with a rise of body. This is the preparatory motion for each step. With the first step the down motion is executed on the first quick beat followed by an up motion on the second quick beat and down again on the slow beat. The body is firm.

Basic Turn: By leading out to the left with his left foot as he steps forward, the man can turn the couple in a left turn much the same as any box turn. By leading to the right, he can make a right turn. By leading into left reverse open position, he can turn the couple counterclockwise in a circle.

Steps	¢ Counts	Rhythmic Cue	Lead Indication*
SLOW SIDE CLOSE			
Step L sideward	1	Slow	√
Close R to L, take weight R	2	Slow	

Repeat three times moving left. The last time, do not take weight right but be ready to go back the other direction. Take four side close steps to the right.

Lead: Man pulls to the stepping side. The rock is discontinued as is the down up motion. The rhythm is even.

Note: Many beginners find the samba basic step very tiring, so this step may be used to permit the dancers a resting variation and also a moving step.

SIDEWARD STEPS

Steps	¢ Counts	Rhythmic Cue	Lead Indication*
SIDEWARD BASIC			
Step L sideward	1	Quick	√
Step R behind L heel	and	Quick	
Step L in place	2	Slow	
Step R sideward	1	Quick	
Step L behind R heel	and	Quick	
Step R in place	2	Slow	

Step Cue: Floor Pattern:
a. side   change   weight   b. ————————→
b. side   change   weight   ←———————— a.

Lead: The man turns the lady ¼ counterclockwise as he steps to the left side, so that she turns her back on the direction they are traveling. As he repeats the step to the right, he turns her ½ turn clockwise.

Style: This figure may be done without the lady turning from side to side, but it is an interesting variation and provides a good lead for getting into the open steps.

Steps	¢ Counts	Rhythmic Cue	Lead Indication*
CHASE LEFT, closed position			
Step L sideward	1	Quick	√
Step R behind L heel	and	Quick	

Note: When repeated, it will cause travel to left side. It may be done to right side, starting with right foot.

* Check lead indication, page 269.

SIDE BASIC AND CHASSE
One side basic L
One side basic R
Four chasse steps L
One side basic R
One side basic L
Four chasse steps R

Lead: Head lead as style indicates below. Man guides L or R and increases body tension.

Style: Couple remains in closed position. Both turn head to look over shoulder to the side (man's left and lady's right) when taking chasse left (to the opposite side for chasse right).

OPEN PROGRESSIVE STEPS

Steps	¢ Counts	Rhythmic Cue	Lead Indication*

THE FORWARD PROGRESSIVE BASIC (side by side position, hands joined, man's right, lady's left)

Step L forward, toe out, ¼ turn L, turning back on partner	1	Quick	√
Step R sideward in line of direction	and	Quick	
Draw L to R taking weight on L	2	Slow	
Step R forward, toe turned in toward partner, ¼ turn to face partner	1	Quick	√
Step L sideward in line of direction	and	Quick	
Draw R to L, taking weight on R	2	Slow	

Note: When repeated, action will travel forward in line of direction turning alternately back to back and face to face. It may also travel in reverse line of direction by opening in the other direction.

Lead: Man leads into side by side position from the back half of the basic samba step, at the same time releasing his right arm around her and taking her left hand in his right. On the following measure he will turn out with the left and begin the progressive basic as above. He controls the back to back and face to face turn with his right hand. He will lead back to closed position as he turns face to face. Take one basic forward and back to finish.

Style: Read under samba style the action of the free arm. The arm moves with the body as it turns. Avoid any swinging of the arm.

COPA STEP (open position)

Step forward L	1	Quick	√
Step back in place on R toe	and	Quick	
Drag L foot back, take weight L	2	Slow	
Step forward R	1	Quick	
Step back in place on L toe	and	Quick	√
Drag R foot back, take weight R	2	Slow	

---

* Check lead indication, page 269.

Step Cue:
a. forward   and   pull
b. forward   and   pull

Lead: The man leads into open position from the back half of the basic samba step. Copa step will then begin on left foot. When repeated any number of times the copa step will travel forward in open position. The man leads back to closed position when his step begins on the inside or right foot and he may go back to basic samba step.

Floor Pattern:

Style: The knee bends as the foot steps forward and the body rocks backward. On the second step and the pull, the body rises and rocks forward.

Note: One may lead into copa step from the closed, open, right and left reverse position or reverse copa step.

REVERSE COPA (side by side position facing in reverse line of direction, man on right, lady on left)

The copa step is used as above. A slight turning motion of the body occurs when the left foot is leading, the body turn is left and when the right foot is leading, the body turn is right, thus causing alternate facing diagonally out and in. General direction of travel is forward.

Lead: The man leads into the position for reverse copa on the forward half of the basic samba so that the first reverse copa is taken with the outside foot and the body turns away slightly from partner. The man may lead back to closed position with a left foot lead, and finish with the back half of a basic samba step.

Style: Read arm style as described for samba and for copa step.

Note: One may lead into the copa step from the reverse copa step by taking a turn toward partner and into open position on the left foot lead, starting the copa pattern on the inside foot.

Samba Combos*

A number of routines are listed here merely as examples to show how the various steps can be used in combination for practice routines. They are listed from simple to complex.

Closed position unless otherwise indicated

1. Basic Slow Side Close
   8 basic (forward and backward)
   8 side close (4 left, 4 right)
2. Basic Step and Turn
   4 basic steps
   4 turning left
   8 side close (4 left, 4 right)
3. Basic: Forward and Sideward
   8 basic (forward and backward)
   4 sideward steps
4. Side Basic — Chasse
   4 basic
   side basic and chasse
5. Turn — Sideward Step — Open
   4 basic
   4 turning
   side basic — chasse
   8 open steps

6. Reverse Copa — Copa
   4 basic
   4 reverse copa
   4 copa
7. Advanced Combo
   4 basic
   4 sideward
   8 open steps
     (reverse open)
   8 copa steps (open)
8. Advanced Combo
   4 basic
   side basic and chasse
   4 reverse copa
   4 copa steps

* Refer to notes on Practice Combos, page 271.

CHA CHA CHA

A Cuban innovation of the old basic Latin form, danson, the cha cha cha is said to be a combination of the mambo and American swing. A close look shows its rhythm to be that of a triple mambo, its style that of the rumba, and its open swingy variations that of the triple lindy. It is not as heavy in quality or as large a foot pattern as the mambo; nor has it the smooth sophistication or the conservative figures of the rumba. It reflects a light breezy mood, a care-free gaiety, and a trend, in the challenge steps, for dancers to ad-lib variations to their heart's content. Consequently, one sees variations in almost every known position.

Cha Cha Cha Rhythm

In 4/4 time,* the catchy rhythm and delightful music of cha cha cha has brought dancers and musicians alike a new treat in the undeniable Latin flavor. Like the mambo, this dance was originally done starting on the offbeat of the measure, but there is widespread acceptance of the onbeat rhythm as an easier way to learn. It will be described here as starting on the first beat of the measure with the accents on one and three.

4/4   /_____   _____   /_____   __   _____
           1   2   3   and   4

cha cha cha

The first two counts represent the *break* beats and counts 3 and 4 represent the familiar "cha cha cha" triple.

Cha Cha Cha Style

The cha cha cha may be danced in either a closed position or an open position facing partner with one or both hands joined. The man reaches over the top of the girl's fingers to grasp for the cha cha cha. His knuckles are on top and fingers over hers. The challenge position is apart from partner completely. The cha cha cha with its light bouncy quality is delightfully Latin as it carries with it some of the subtleness of the rumba movement. The foot should be placed nearly flat on the floor and the knees are easy and lead forward with the step. The back step is (instead of a flat step which tends to give the appearance of a sag) a toe step, holding the body firmly so as to avoid the sag. The cha cha cha triple is taken with very small steps in place or travelling, but kept very close to the floor.

The upper body is held comfortably upright and the head focuses on the partner in a somewhat flirtatious manner. The arm and hand when free are held up parallel to the floor in bent arm position, palm down. The arms turn with the body and are in relatively the same position throughout the dance.

Fundamental Cha Cha Cha Steps

Forward Basic
Back Basic
Side (H) Basic
Open Break
Crossover and Turn
Freeze
Chase (half turn and full turn)
Jody Break and Variations
Kick Swivel
Kick Freeze
Challenge Steps

---

* Refer to page 37.

Directions are for man, facing line of direction: lady's part reverse, except as noted.

Steps	4/4 Counts	Rhythmic Cue	Lead Indication*

FORWARD BASIC

Step L forward...........................1......Slow......✓.....

Step R backward in place................2......Slow......

Step L in place.........................3......Quick (cha) ......

Step R in place......................and.....Quick (cha) ......

Step L in place.........................4......Slow (cha) ....

BACK BASIC

Step R backward.........................1......Slow......✓.....

Step L forward in place.................2......Slow......

Step R in place.........................3......Quick (cha) ......

Step L in place......................and.....Quick (cha) ......

Step R in place.........................4......Slow (cha) ....

Step <u>Cue</u>: forward step cha cha cha
        back step cha cha

<u>Note</u>: This is the basic step of cha cha cha. The forward half is also called the "forward break"; the back half is the "back break." They may be used with *either* foot leading when a preparatory step is needed to get into the next variation. Sometimes the cha cha cha part of the step is used to travel rather than being in place.

<u>Position</u>: Dancers may use either closed position or face each other two hands joined. The latter is recommended for beginners.

SIDE (H) BASIC (closed position or face with two hands joined)

Step L, diagonally forward to R..........1......Slow......✓......

Step R, back in place...................2......Slow......

Step L, sideward to L...................3.......Quick (cha) ✓......

Step R, closing R to L...............and.....Quick (cha) ......

Step L, sideward to L...................4......Slow (cha) ....

Step R, diagonally behind to L..........1......Slow......✓.....

Step L, back in place...................2......Slow.

Step R, sideward to R...................3.......Quick (cha) ✓......

Step L, closing L to R...............and.....Quick (cha) ....

Step R, sideward to R...................4......Slow (cha) ....

<u>Step Cue</u>:   Diagram:
a. forward step side close side
b. back step side close side

<u>Lead</u>: If the lady responds well to a lead, the man may lead the H basic into a turn clockwise by increasing the angle of the diagonal step each time.

<u>Style</u>: The diagonal styling makes a beautiful pattern on the floor. It requires more room so the man must watch carefully so as not to interfere with other dancers. The lady must keep a firm arm and let the body move with the arm.

<u>Note</u>: The side basic is sometimes called the H basic because of the

⟋ shape of the pattern.

---

* Check lead indication, page 269.

OPEN BREAK (closed position or two hands joined). Take regular forward basic, then step right backward, the man dropping his right hand, step left in place turning ¼ to man's right, man leads through with his left hand so they are side by side. Take cha cha cha moving slightly forward in this side by side position. This is right crossover position.

Cue: break open cha cha cha

Style: As the couple turns to right crossover position the free arm remains up waist level so it is ready for future leads.

Note: The man may take the open break to the left side by turning open on the forward basic ¼ to his left. This would be left crossover position.

CROSSOVER (take right open break to right crossover position). Starting with the inside foot (man's left, lady's right), step left forward in right crossover position, step back right in place turning to face partner and change hands. On the cha cha cha steps (left, right, left), the man's right hand now leads through to complete the turn to left crossover position. The three cha cha cha steps are in place, turning to new position.

Repeat from left crossover position.

Starting with the inside foot (man's right, lady's left), step right forward in left crossover position, step back left in place turning to face partners and change hands. On the cha cha cha, the man's left hand now leads through to complete the turn to right crossover position.

Step Cue: forward face turn about

1   2   cha cha cha

Lead: The man's hand lead can assist this to be a smooth beautiful figure. If the arm of both man and lady remains up in place when they turn to the new position, it is ready to give or receive the lead in changing from right or left crossover position.

Style: The body position remains easily upright and focus is on partner. Avoid leaning forward and looking at the floor. The feet should toe straight ahead on the forward step in right or left crossover position. Avoid a toeing out or crossover toward the outside line.

Note: This crossover may be repeated from side to side any number of times.

Return to basic from left crossover position.
Starting with the inside foot, step left forward in right crossover position, step back right in place turning to face partner and take both of her hands. The cha cha cha is in place (left, right, left) facing partner. With the right foot now free take a back basic.

Return to basic from left crossover position.
Starting with the inside foot, step right forward in left crossover position, step back left in place turning to face partner and take both hands. The cha cha cha is in place (right, left, right) facing partner. With the left foot now free take a forward basic.

Note: This detailed description is given here, opening to either side because such a maneuver is basic to all cha cha cha variations and will be referred to often.

CROSSOVER TURN (right crossover position)

Starting with the inside foot (man's left), step left forward pivoting away from partner clockwise a litle more than a ¼ turn. Step right, back in place continuing to pivot until facing partner. The cha cha cha is in place facing partner. Take both hands and return to basic on the free foot which at this time is a right back basic.

Diagram:

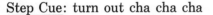

Lady
Man

Step Cue: turn out cha cha cha

Lead: The man knowing he is going to take the crossover turn instead of a simple crossover will *not take* hold of the lady's hand as he comes through but pushes the hand lightly to indicate the turn.

Style: Keep the arm up. Stay in close to partner.

Note: The crossover turn may be done from left crossover position starting with the right foot and turning counterclockwise. Return to basic on the left forward basic.

FREEZE (right crossover position)

Starting with the inside foot (man's left), step forward left, step back in place right, step forward again left, step back in place right turning to face partner and take cha cha cha turning around to left crossover position.

Step Cue: The man reaches with his contact hand forward and down toward the floor as he goes into the freeze, holding this straight elbow position for the counts 1, 2, 1.

Style: This lead holds the body position firm so that it is a small change of weight and not a big sway back and forth in place. Focus on partner.

Note: There are two extra counts added to this pattern. It is best to repeat the pattern to left crossover position in order to make it fit rhythmically with the music. *Start and Return to Basic,* from either side as described for the crossover.

CHASE — Half Turn

The chase is taken from facing position, two hands joined. It is a turning figure in which the man is always one basic step ahead of the lady. He will start the turn while she takes a back basic. On her next forward basic she starts the turn. After the desired number of turns he will finish with a forward basic while she completes her last turn to face him. The *forward break* is used for *all* turns.

Half Turn, man's part

Step left forward, pivoting clockwise toward the right foot ½ turn, step right in place and take cha cha cha in place (man has his back to partner). Step right forward, pivoting counterclockwise toward the left foot ½ turn, step left in place and take cha cha cha in place. (Man has now turned back to original spot but lady took her turn and has her back to man). This may continue over and over until the man decides to change. He then must take a forward basic while she completes her last turn, then he takes her hands for a basic together (man's R, Lady's L).

Half Turn, lady's part

Lady will take a back basic and start turn on left as described for man's part. She will continue turning as long as he does.

Full Turn

Step left forward, pivoting clockwise ½ turn. Step right in place again pivoting clockwise ½ turn. Take cha cha cha in place facing partner.

Lead: The lead is given by the mere letting go of hands to start the turn and the taking of the hands to finish it.

Style: The manner is a bit cocky as they look over the shoulder at partner. The pivoting steps are narrow and on the ball of the foot for good balance.

Note: The man will make a complete turn while she does a back basic, then she follows with a complete turn while he does a back basic.

JODY BREAK (partners face, two hands joined)

Man's Part: Starting on *left* foot into back break.

Step left backward, and at the same time changing hands from a two hand grasp to a right hand grasp.

Step right forward, and at the same time pull with the right hand to guide the lady into a counterclockwise turn.

Take cha cha cha (left, right, left) in place, guiding the lady into varsouvianna position beside the man.

Step right backward, in varsouvianna position.

Step left forward in place, and at the same time guide the lady with the left hand to turn clockwise.

Take cha cha cha (right, left, right) in place, guiding the lady out to original position to face man completing ½ turn clockwise.

Note: This may be repeated over and over without changing the right hand grasp. When the man desires to go back to regular basic, he will change to two hand grasp and forward basic.

Lady's Part: Starting right foot into regular back break.

Step right backward, allowing man to change from two hand grasp to a right hand grasp.

Step left forward, toeing out and pivoting on left counterclockwise, being guided by man's lead toward varsouvianna position.

Take cha cha cha (right, left, right) finishing the turn into varsouvianna position, beside man.

Step left backward in varsouvianna position.

Step right forward, toeing out and pivoting on the right clockwise, being guided by the man's lead towards the original facing position.

Take cha cha cha (left, right, left) in place finishing the turn to face partner.

Style: Both man and lady should keep steps small and not get too far apart. Large steps and big movement spoil the beauty of this lovely figure and make it awkward to maneuver.

Lead: Arm tension control makes it possible for the man's lead to guide the lady smoothly and provide a good feeling to the movement.

VARIATIONS FROM THE JODY POSITION (varsouvianna)

1. DOUBLE JODY. While in varsouvianna position, both break back on the inside foot, the man maintaining the varsouvianna grasp, step forward and begin to turn clockwise. Take cha cha cha completing a half

turn clockwise to a position with the lady on the left side of the man.

Note: Repeat starting with the inside foot and turn counterclockwise to end up in original varsouvianna position. This may be repeated any number of times.

2. SHADOW. While in varsouvianna position, both break back on the inside foot, then releasing the varsouvianna grasp, step forward, the man guiding the lady across in front of him. Take the cha cha cha finishing the crossover and catch inside hands. Lady is to left of man.

Note: Repeat starting with the inside foot and crossing the lady always in front of the man to a hand grasp position on his right. This may be repeated any number of times. *Return to varsouvianna position* with the lady on the right when ready to break out to a facing position and back to a regular basic.

Style: Dancers must keep steps small and not get too far apart in the crossover. Keep a controlled semi-bent arm. Focus on partner.

KICK-SWIVEL (partners face, two hands joined)

Step left sideward, man guiding both of his hands with firm pressure toward the left direction.

Kick right across in front of left (lady's left across in front of right).

Put both feet together and swivel both toes to the right, swivel both toes to the left.

Note: Repeat starting to the right and kick left across right, then swivel left, the right. The two swivel steps take the place of the three cha cha cha steps and are even rhythm being the equivalent of counts 3, 4. *Return to basic* from either side by using the free foot, if left to lead a forward basic, if right to lead a back basic.

Style: Dancers should take small steps. Keep the kick low and take the swivel steps with the feet and knees close together. One may bend the knees slightly.

KICK-FREEZE (partners face, two hands joined)

Step left sideward, man guiding both of her hands with firm pressure toward the left direction.

Kick right across in front of left as in the kick-swivel.

Touch right sideward to the right in a stride position and hold for counts 3, 4. The posture straightens to be extra firm and holds still. Arms come to butterfly position.

Take cha cha cha (right, left, right) moving to the right without releasing hands. The body may turn slightly to the right during the cha cha cha, but should end up facing partner.

Repeat the pattern starting on the same foot.

Note: The freeze is on counts 3, 4. These are two extra counts added to the regular pattern. It is best to take the kick freeze twice in order to make it fit rhythmically with the music. *Return to basic* by leading forward with a left basic.

CHALLENGE STEPS

These are started when partners are slightly apart from each other, facing, no grasp. The man may lead from basic forward and back steps into a fancy variation while the lady continues in the basic until he is finished. Then without a break in the rhythm she tries to do the variation exactly as he did it, while he keeps the basic step going. Either man or lady may lead a challenge step. Dancers are encouraged to create their own varia-

tions. These should correspond in rhythm to one or two measures of cha cha music and should be able to pick up the regular forward or back basic without a break in the rhythm. The following variations are used as examples.

1. <u>Cross-Hop</u>, follows a regular basic right.
 Step left across in front of right, pivoting sharply on left to the left.
  Lift the free knee sharply in preparation for the next step.
 Step right across in front of left, pivoting sharply on right to the right.
 Hop backwards on right quickly and
  Take cha cha cha (left, right, left) in place or backward.
 Finish off with back basic starting right, recovering space forward on the cha cha cha.

 <u>Step Cue</u>: cross, cross, hop cha cha cha
  back step cha cha cha
  1 2 and 1 and 2

 <u>Style</u>: Take small pivoting steps letting the lady twist with the motion. The hop is a quick beat, small and low to the floor.

2. <u>Jump Turn</u>, follows the 1, 2 counts of a regular forward basic and takes two measures.

	Count
Step left forward	1
Step right back in place	2
Jump apart into stride position	3
Jump, right foot crossed in front of left	4
Pirouette on the toes, turning counterclockwise a full turn around, ending with weight on left foot	1–2
Take cha cha cha (right, left, right) travelling slightly forward	3 and 4

 <u>Step Cue</u>: forward step jump cross turn cha cha cha
  1 2 3 4 1–2 3 and 4

 <u>Style</u>: To be fitted together as smoothly as possible with careful balance and perfect synchronization of the cha cha cha at the end. The knees may bend on the cross jump and straighten on the pirouette turn.

Cha Cha Cha Combos*

The routines given here are merely examples to show how the various steps can be used in combination for practice routines. They are listed from simple to complex.

Closed position unless otherwise indicated

1. <u>Forward Back Side and Turn</u>
 2 forward and back basics
 2 side (H) basics
 4 side (H) basics turning
2. <u>Open break and Cross Over</u>
 2 forward and back basics with open break
 4 cross overs
3. <u>Cross Over with Turn</u>
 2 basics with open break
 3 cross overs and turn
 repeat
4. <u>Cross Over and Freeze</u>
 2 basics with open break
 2 cross overs
 2 freeze
 1 cross over and turn

* Refer to notes on Practice Combos, page 271.

5. <u>Basic and Chase</u>
   2 basics
   4 half turns
   2 full turns
6. <u>Basic and Jody</u>
   2 basics
   4 jody breaks
7. <u>Jody Variations</u>
   2 basics
   jody break
   2 double jody
   2 shadow
8. <u>Cross Over and Kick Swivel</u>
   2 basics
   cross over and turn
   4 kick swivels

9. <u>Basic and Kick Freeze</u>
   2 basics in closed position
   2 kick freeze
10. <u>Challenge Steps</u>
    2 basics
    cross over and turn
       (to apart position)
    2 basics
    jump turn
11. <u>Challenge and Chase</u>
    2 basics
    cross over and turn
       (to apart position)
    jump turn
    cross hop
    full turn (chase)

MAMBO

The mambo is a Cuban dance which was introduced in America right after World War II and enjoyed rather widespread popularity as a jazzy offbeat rhythm. It was a very free dance allowing for individual interpretation. Probably due to its difficult rhythm, the mambo gave way to the easier cha cha cha in the fifties. The mambo has survived for the advanced dancer and has become more sophisticated and conservative, being done most often in closed position.

Mambo Rhythm

Probably more controversy has existed over this dance than any other as to whether the rhythm is offbeat or onbeat, quick quick slow or slow quick quick. Because of its highly syncopated beat, it has been a difficult rhythm to learn. For this text it will be described as 4/4 time*, quick quick slow.

| 4/4 | 4 | 1 | 2 | hold |

A preparation step on the first two beats of the measure is helpful in getting started with the mambo beat.

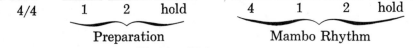

| 4/4 | 1 | 2 | hold | 4 | 1 | 2 | hold |

Preparation   Mambo Rhythm

Mambo Style

The sultry rhythm and oddly accented beat gives the dance a heavy jerky quality which may be interestingly thought of as a "charge." Basically the style is rumba movement, but as one steps forward on the accented 4th beat, it is with the suddenness of a quick lunge, but immediately pulling back for the second quick beat, giving the jerky quality to the dance. The "charge" is further accented by a slightly heavier step and the action of the shoulders which move forward alternately in opposition to the stepping foot. The arms and hands are carried in a bent elbow position parallel to the floor, palm down. The arm moves with the shoulders and thus the mambo presents a more dynamic body movement than any of the other Cuban dances.

Fundamental Mambo Steps

The mambo will be given rather brief treatment in this text due to the fact that all variations may be taken from the cha cha cha. Therefore, only the basic step and the relationship between mambo and cha cha cha rhythm will be described. (See cha cha cha, page 322.)

Directions are for man, facing line of direction: lady's part reverse, except as noted.

Steps	4/4 Counts	Rhythmic Cue	Lead Indication**
PREPARATION STEP (is used *only* at the beginning of the dance to get started on mambo beat.			
Step L in place	1	Quick	√
Step R in place	2	Quick	
Hold	3		
THE H BASIC (see note below)			
Step L, diagonally forward to R	4	Quick	√
Step R, back in place	1	Quick	
Step L, sideward L	2	Slow	
Hold, closing R toward L, no weight change	3		

* Refer to page 37.

Steps	4/4 Counts	Rhythmic Cue	Lead Indication*
Step R, diagonally backward to L	4	Quick	√
Step L, back in place	1	Quick	
Step R, sideward R	2	Slow	
Hold, closing L in toward R, no weight change	3		

Step Cue: cross back side, cross back side

Lead: The man's lead is a sharp shoulder action as his shoulder moves forward in opposition to the stepping foot. The lady should merely follow the action of his leading shoulder and not try to figure out what shoulder she should move.

Style: Dancers should avoid taking too large a step. The sideward step tends to increase the size of the total pattern and may look very awkward if taken too wide. The quality is sultry.

Note: The first half of this step is referred to as the forward break and the back half as the back break and may be used as in cha cha cha, page 292.

VARIATIONS AS DESCRIBED IN CHA CHA CHA (See also cha cha cha combos, pages 328, 329).

1. Open Break
2. Cross over and cross over turn
3. Chasse
4. Jody Break and Double Jody
5. Shadow

Note: In making the transition from cha cha cha to mambo one must keep in mind the relationship between the two rhythms.

		Mambo					Cha Cha Cha		
4/4	/				.4/4	/		/	
	4	1	2	hold		1	2	cha cha / cha

* Check lead indication, page 269.

MERENGUE

This clever little dance from the Caribbean could very well be a favorite with the young adult set if they really had a chance to explore it. The music is a peppy, pert, march-like rhythm and the dance patterns are the most simple of all the Latin dances. There are two styles: The original "limp step" from the Dominican Republic and the more even, smooth Haitian style. The latter will be described here.

Merengue Rhythm

In 4/4 cut-time,* there is an accent on each beat of the rhythm and the tempo is lively. The dance pattern follows the even beat, with a definite step on each beat of the measure, which in cut time would be the slow beats of the rhythm. It feels more like a 2/4 beat.

slow	slow
1	2

Merengue Style

Perhaps merengue style could be described as a combination between the rumba movement and a majorette swagger step. The feet are placed flat, but the weight is on the ball of the foot for easy balance. It is a controlled hip movement resulting from the bent knee action with each step as in the rumba, but it has the almost sassy quality and breezy manner of the majorette. A slight rock sideways with the shoulders to accompany the foot pattern is optional. It is not meant to be an exaggerated body movement, but the lively music and the character of the step give this dance a delightful touch of humor.

Fundamental Merengue Steps
Basic Side Step
Box Step and Box Turn
Cross Step
Ladder
Side Close and Back Break

Directions are for man, facing line of direction: lady's part reverse, except as noted.

Steps	4/4 Cut Time	Rhythmic Cue	Lead Indication**
BASIC SIDE STEP (closed position)			
Step L sideward	1	Slow	√
Close R to L, take weight on R	2	Slow	
Step Cue: Side, close			
Style: Steps are small, head high, focus on partner.			
BOX STEP (closed position)			
Step L forward	1	Slow	√
Close R to L, take weight on R	2	Slow	
Step L backward	1	Slow	√
Close R to L, take weight on R	2	Slow	
Step Cue: Forward together, back together.			
BOX TURN (closed position)			
Step L, toeing out to L a ¼ turn counterclockwise	1	Slow	√
Close R to L, take weight on R	2	Slow	
Step L backward	1	Slow	√
Close R to L, take weight on R	2	Slow	

* Refer to page 37.
** Check lead indication, page 269.

Steps	4/4 Cut Time	Rhythmic Cue	Lead Indication*

Step Cue: turn, close, back, close.
Note: Repeat 3 times to make one full turn counterclockwise.
Style: A shoulder rock on the turn makes it very easy to lead and also adds interest.

CROSS STEP (closed position)
Step L sideward, turning to open position. . 1 . . . . . . Slow . . . . . . √ . . . . . .
Step R forward in open position . . . . 2 . . . . . . Slow . . . . . .
Step L sideward, turning to closed position . 1 . . . . . . Slow . . . . . . √ . . . . . .
Close R to L, take weight on R . . . . 2 . . . . . . Slow . . . . . .

LADDER (closed position)
Step L sideward . . . . 1 . . . . . . Slow . . . . √ . . .
Close R to L, take weight on R . . . . 2 . . . . . . Slow . . . . .
Step L forward . . . . 1 . . . . . . Slow . . . . √ . . .
Close R to L, take weight on R . . . . 2 . . . . . . Slow . . . . .

SIDE CLOSE AND BACK BREAK (closed position)
Step L sideward . . . . 1 . . . . . . Slow . . . . √ . . .
Close R to L, take weight on R . . . . 2 . . . . . . Slow . . . . .
Step L sideward . . . . 1 . . . . . . Slow . . . . √ . . .
Close R to L, take weight on R . . . . 2 . . . . . . Slow . . . . .
Step L sideward . . . . 1 . . . . . . Slow . . . . √ . . .
Step R, in place, turning to open position . . 2 . . . . . . Slow . . . . √ . . .
Step L, backward, in open position . . . . 1 . . . . . . Slow . . . . .
Step R, in place, turning to closed position . 2 . . . . . . Slow . . . . √ . . .

Merengue Combos

These simple variations may be added to the other in any order. The teacher is encouraged to let the students with this much background use their own creative efforts to work out variations. Refer to page 271.

---

* Check the lead indication, page 269.

FAD AND NOVELTY DANCES

Any collection of ballroom dances is hardly complete without recognizing the fads and novelties that come and go with the general public, yet which do not last long enough to earn a place in the standard repertory of ballroom dances. They are like many popular songs. They fill the need at the moment for something different but soon become tiresome. The twist, for example, gave a lot of fun to millions of people because it was easy and individual. One might lose himself in the dance and being less self-conscious or inhibited may enjoy variations of their own. There is of course less demand upon the man to lead a partner. The bop, the twist, the hully gully, the mashed potato, the watusi, the twirl, and others fill this restless need currently as did the charleston, the black bottom, and the big apple in the early 20th century. The urge to move and be individual in dance is as human as raccoon coats, souped up old cars, above-the-knee hemlines, and beehive hairdos.

Another category of novelty dances is the *line* dance which we knew earlier as the congo line or the lambeth walk. Teenagers have shaken the dust out of many a rafter with the bunny hop while the stroll was a more quiet variation. In the sixties almost every part of the country could find young people in lines of 3 to 10 swingin' in unison to the garfield or the bristol stomp or a local variation of some kind.

The novelties have left a mark on the dancing of America. They are not an unhealthy trend. Dance teachers cannot, even in the public schools, turn their backs on them. They should, in fact, keep their eyes on what is coming and going. The philosophy which encompasses these fads and novelties is based on the following opinions:

1. Teachers who encourage students to bring these new novelties into class win the respect of the young people just as parents who encourage their children to discuss ideas at home. Here they can be evaluated and, if worthy of the time, can be taught correctly to all of the youngsters.

2. Students who know that their novelty and fad dances may be given a place at a school dance will tend to come to school dances where the atmosphere is supervised and wholesome rather than escape to some less desirable place.

3. Students who feel that their teachers know what is going on and are open minded will in turn be more receptive to learning the more standard ballroom dances.

4. These novelty and fad dances down through the years are open position dances. They have been and will continue to be popular because there is less demand upon a dancer for standardized skill or the ability to lead and follow. There is an opportunity for more individuality and tremendous possibilities for those who are creative. This is a wholesome basic need.

5. The novelty line dance is a perfect mixer type activity which does not require asking a partner to dance. Everyone may participate. One may get lost in the group activity and have fun dancing without the fear of self-consciousness and social pressure.

6. Students participate in groups. All can take part and do not have to pair off, as these dances accommodate odd numbers of boys and girls.

7. The far-away look on the faces is a sign of complete concentration. And the devotion to a single physical activity for long periods is far less wasteful than lying on the floor listening to pop records, or talking on the telephone for hours, or riding around town in cars.

8. They lead to healthy expenditure of energy. Even though they seem a bit "far out" at times, they provide good exercise and good fun.

9. These dances lend themselves to casual school dress. More students will attend dances when they do not have to dress up because they feel more relaxed and at ease. This encourages more students to take part in school dances.

The schools can help encourage the wholesome participation in the dance and can make school dances a lot more fun by recognizing the interests of students. They can have a powerful influence in shaping the trend of these fads and novelties by encouraging them within the bounds of acceptable standards and good taste.

It is part of our responsibility in physical education to help develop a sense of value by discussing fad materials and seeing them in their proper relationship as fleeting items of interest in comparison with the more lasting needs for skill in standard ballroom styles.

It is not the purpose of this manuscript to describe those dances which have made fad history. They are now behind us. But in writing this material for beginners, it seems appropriate to encourage dance teachers to lend an ear to developing trends and seek a way to use some of these novel ideas to stimulate and promote interest in dance at its highest level.

MIXERS AND ICEBREAKERS XI

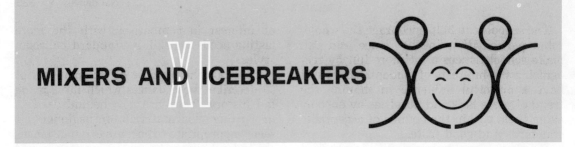

The term "play party game" evolved in America at a time and in sections of the country where dancing was frowned upon as a device of the devil. During this period dancing in public became almost extinct, but flourished in social groups and in the home under the label "games." In executing such favorites as Skip to My Lou, Brown Eyed Mary, and Shoo Fly, instrumental musical accompaniment was abandoned in favor of response to such rhythmic accompaniment as clapping, stamping, singing, and chanting. As is true of other aspects of our culture, these activities are part of our European heritage, few are indigenous.

Play party games are still popular in many sections of the country, particularly where religious or philosophical beliefs do not permit dancing, *per se*. However, their greatest appeal lies in the fact that they are particularly suitable activities for large numbers and, therefore, are ideal as mixers and icebreakers.

DEFINITION AND PURPOSE

Mixers and similar activities are ones in which new partners are acquired through exchange, cutting in, "cheating," or "stealing." Icebreaker refers to simple line and circle dances that do not involve partners. The social purposes of any dance party are greatly enriched and served by including mixers and icebreakers. These activities serve to add variety, provide automatic change of partners, and an opportunity for all to participate. A particularized list of purposes may include: (a) provide fun and maximum participation, (b) tend to make the occasion more informal, (c) assure simple, quick and easy accomplishment, thus enhancement of fun and fellowship, (d) add variety to the program, (e) include stags or extras in groups where both are permitted, and (f) are valuable as pre-party warm-up activities for the early arrivals.

HOW TO USE MIXERS

The success of these activities depends upon the choice of materials, adaptability to the group, and the manner of presentation. Information upon which to base preplanning may range from very little to a great deal; very little in the case of the "one night session," to a great deal in the case of a class, club, or church group.

Selection . . . Select materials suitable for the group and the occasion. Avoid activities that make anyone appear foolish, or become embarrassed. Begin with mixers and icebreakers that involve all participants en masse or in accumulative fashion. After general participation and enthusiasm have been generated, move to activities which involve participants in smaller units of two, three, or four. Varying the selections in this manner allows progression from mass to small group and back to mass activity, thus beginning and ending with all participating yet allowing for more personal exchange during the central portion of the program. In selecting and planning, keep clearly in mind whether the occasion is one in which mixers and icebreakers are used for change of pace and temporary partner exchange, or whether it is an occasion which depends completely upon these activities for acquiring partners throughout the evening.

Adaptability . . . The theme, skill ability, and age level of a group should be considered in adapting activities otherwise suitable for other ages, occasions, and themes.

At a carnival dance, for example, instead of using a lemon for a tag dance, stuff a clown costume as a dummy and let it be passed about from couple to couple. In like manner, activities traditionally associated with an early age group may be adapted for use with an adult group. Hokey Pokey is an example of an activity formerly traditionally associated with early elementary activities, now adapted in music and action to adult use.

Presentation . . . The most important admonition to remember is to make the activity sound lively and fun. Additional pointers to observe include: (a) present the activity in an interesting and clever manner, (b) create opportunities for participants to regain partners of their choice, (c) be alert and sensitive to the changing desires of the group, (d) encourage courtesy whenever possible; that is, stress social graces, (e) if the group is large, have a pre-dance meeting with a group of selected leaders and teach them the activities to assure greater fun and success.

CLASSIFIED INDEX OF MIXERS AND ICEBREAKERS

NUMBER OF PEOPLE INVOLVED

MIXERS FOR SPECIAL OCCASIONS

Although the mixers and icebreakers are adaptable to all situations, some are more suitable than others for special occasions. The following index is merely a *suggested* list (not complete) classified for Social Dances, Recreation Events, and Folk and Square Dances. The simplicity of presentation governed the choice of mixers for Recreation Events.

---

* A caller or leader is involved as the dance progresses or the dancers sing.

DANCES FROM OTHER SECTIONS

Many of the dances from the Western Square Dance, Round Dance, and International Folk Dance sections are excellent mixers, icebreakers, or may be adaptable for that purpose. The dances are listed according to the number of people involved.

---

* A caller or leader is involved as the dance progresses or the dancers sing.

ALL AMERICAN PROMENADE

This dance was originated by Doc and Winnie Alambaugh, Alhambra, Calif.

Music　　　Record: Western Jubilee 721; Windsor 4605, A754; Folkraft
　　　　　　　1061, 1482.

Position　　Couple.

Formation　Double circle, couples facing line of direction.

DIRECTIONS FOR MIXER

Music 4/4　　　NOTE: Directions are for man; lady's part reverse.

MEASURES

I. Walk Step

1–2　　Beginning left, walk four steps forward, turn toward partner on fourth step to face reverse line of direction, join inside hands. Back up four steps in line of direction.

3–4　　Repeat action of measures 1–2 in reverse line of direction.

II. Balance, Exchange Places

5　　Beginning left, balance away from partner (cts. 1-2), balance toward partner (cts. 3-4). Face line of direction during balance.

6　　Beginning left, man walks four steps behind lady to opposite side. Beginning right, lady takes one four step turn counterclockwise in front of man to opposite side. Man assists turn with right hand, releases during turn and catches inside hand at end of turn.

7　　Beginning left, balance toward partner (cts. 1-2), balance away from partner (cts. 3-4).

8　　Beginning left, man walks four steps, crossing behind lady, and moves forward to meet a new partner. Beginning right, lady takes one four step turn to original side and moves back to meet a new partner.

VARIATION:

Measure 8. Beginning left, man takes four steps diagonally forward to inside of circle to meet a new partner. Beginning right, lady tkaes one four step turn, moving behind man to outside of circle to meet new partner.

Reference in Bibliography: 23 (p. 9).
Dance annotation form © 1948 by the Folk Dance Federation of California.

BUNNY HOP

Music Record: Capitol 6026; Old Timer 8161; MacGregor 6995; or any schottische.

Formation Single file (conga line), hands placed on waist or shoulders of person ahead.

DIRECTIONS FOR MIXER

Music 4/4 NOTE: Directions are same for both lady and man.

MEASURES

1 Hop right, touch left heel out to side. Hop right, touch left toe near right. Repeat.

2 Beginning with hop on left, repeat action of measure 1.

3–4 Jump forward (slow), jump backward (slow), take three jumps forward (quick, quick, quick).

NOTE:

Leader leads in line in any direction around room.

TEN PRETTY GIRLS

Music Record: *Ten Pretty Girls*, Blue Star 1670; MacGregor 604; Old Timer 8004; Folkraft 1036X45.

Formation Groups of three, four, six or as many as desired, arms around waist, facing line of direction.

DIRECTIONS FOR MIXER

Music 4/4 NOTE: Directions are same for both lady and man.

MEASURES

1 Beginning left, tap left to side twice, grapevine to right stepping left behind right, right to side, cross left in front of right.

2 Beginning right, tap right to side twice, grapevine to left stepping right behind left, step left to side, and cross right in front of left.

3 Beginning left, walk forward four steps.

4 Swing left forward, swing left backward, stamp three times in place. Body leans backward and forward with action of leg swing.
  Repeat dance beginning right.

Dance annotation form © 1948 by the Folk Dance Federation of California.

BUZZ'S MIXER

This mixer was originated by Henry "Buzz" Glass, Oakland, California.

Music	Record: Windsor 4637 or any lively two-step.
	Piano: *Pretty Girl Dressed in Blue.*
Position	Partners face, two hands joined.
Formation	Double circle, man's back to center.

DIRECTIONS FOR MIXER

CALL: **SHUFFLE IN AND SHUFFLE OUT**
Partners shuffle or two-step toward each other and shuffle or two-step away from each other.

TURN THAT LADY ALL ABOUT
Partners change sides, lady turning under man's right arm, taking four steps.

SHUFFLE IN AND SHUFFLE OUT
Partners shuffle or two-step toward each other and shuffle or two-step away from each other.

TURN THAT LADY
Partners change sides, lady turning under man's right arm, taking four steps.

SWING, SWING, EVERYBODY SWING

PROMENADE, GO 'ROUND THAT RING
Promenade position. Promenade.

FLIP 'EM IN, THE PRETTY SIDE IN

COME ON, BOYS, YOU'RE GONE AGAIN
As promenade continues, lady crosses over from outside of circle to inside. Do not drop hands.

BOYS, STEP OUT ON THE OUTSIDE TRACK

YOU'LL MEET A LADY COMING BACK
Ladies continue promenading in line of direction as men turn back and promenade in reverse line of direction.

SWING, SWING, EVERYBODY SWING
Swing nearest lady. Those without partners go to center and find one.

PROMENADE, GO TWO BY TWO

PROMENADE, LIKE I TELL YOU TO

ONE FOOT, TWO FOOT, THREE FOOT, FOUR

GET READY NOW
This is the cue for repeat of pattern.

WE'LL DANCE SOME MORE.

Dance annotation form © 1948 by the Folk Dance Federation of California.

CIRCLE TWO-STEP

Music   Record: Any lively two-step or square dance tune.
Formation   Single circle, couples facing center, lady to right of partner, hands joined.

DIRECTIONS FOR MIXER

THE CIRCLE TWO-STEP CONSISTS OF THREE PARTS:

1. Figure of figures
2. A change of partners
3. Partners two-step in closed position.

Leadership

The leader calls out any of the following figures or others that lend themselves to this type mixer. The commands may be given simply or accompanied by patter. For example, "Promenade" or "Promenade two by two." The leader should vary the calls so as to include several figures, a change of partners and a two-step in closed position.

Figures

Honor — partner or corners
Circle — left or right
Swing — partner, corner, or right hand lady
Allemande left and grand right and left

Move to center and back
Promenade
Promenade in fours
  Circle four. Call Right and Left Through, Ladies Chain, any trims for circle of four (see page 65), or any simple visiting couple figures.

Method of Changing Partners

Promenade corner
Swing corner — promenade
Swing girl across the hall — promenade
Grand right and left — promenade.

References in Bibliography: 94 (p. 42), 78 (p. 398).
Dance annotation form © 1948 by the Folk Dance Federation of California.

IRISH WASHERWOMAN MIXER

Music   Record: Folkraft K 1240; Folkraft 1155; RCA-Victor 45-5017; RCA-Victor LPM 1623; World of Fun M 103; Mac-Gregor 008-3.

Formation   Single circle, couples facing center, lady to right of partner, hands joined.

DIRECTIONS FOR MIXER

CALL: ALL JOIN HANDS AND GO TO THE MIDDLE
          Beginning left, take four steps to center.

          AND WITH YOUR BIG FOOT

          KEEP TIME WITH THE FIDDLE
          Stamp four times in place.

          AND WHEN YOU GET BACK REMEMBER MY CALL
          Take four steps backward to place.

          SWING YOUR CORNER LADY AND PROMENADE ALL
          Swing corner lady and promenade in line of direction.

ALABAMA GAL

This mixer was taught by Jane Farwell at the Oglebay Folk Dance Camp, Wheeling, West Virginia, 1948.

Music   Record: World of Fun M 112.

Formation   Longway sets, men on left, ladies on right, partners facing. Large groups should be divided into sets of sixteen couples or less.

DIRECTIONS FOR MIXER

SINGING CALL:

Verse 1   Comin' through in a hurry
          Comin' through in a hurry
          Comin' through in a hurry
          Alabama Gal.

Verse 2   You don't know how how
          You don't know how how
          You don't know how how
          Alabama Gal.

Verse 3   I'll show you how how
          I'll show you how how
          I'll show you how how
          Alabama Gal.

Verse 4   Ain't I rock candy
          Ain't I rock candy
          Ain't I rock candy
          Alabama Gal.

INSTRUCTIONS:

1. Head couple join two hands, extending arms shoulder height. Slide down and back between two lines.

2. Head couple reels down the set by starting with a right hand swing, once and a half. When the active couples reach the foot of the set, they join the lines.

3. As soon as all four verses have been sung, next couple starts to slide down center and back and reel. Therefore each time the first verse is sung, a new couple starts "comin' through in a hurry." The fun comes when a new couple begins to slide through the set while the reeling continues!

References in Bibliography for Alabama Gal: 32 (p. 37), 91 (Kit R, p. 2).
Dance annotation form © 1948 by the Folk Dance Federation of California.

SHOO FLY SWING

This dance was taught by Jane Farwell at Oglebay Folk Dance Camp, Wheeling, West Virginia, 1948. It is believed to come from the Ozarks. It is an excellent dance for active teen-agers!

Music   Record: Folkraft F 1102; Folk Dancer MH 1108, Windsor A 7S1; MacGregor 803, 804, or any lively two-step.

Formation   Single circle, couples facing center, lady to right of partner, hands joined. Large groups may be arranged in several single circles of twenty couples or less.

DIRECTIONS FOR MIXER

Select one couple to start the mixer. The man of that couple faces his partner (man's back to center of circle). He swings his partner by the right hand, she swings the man of the next couple (to lady's right) by the left hand, back to own partner with the right, left to the next man (second couple to right around circle) and so on around the circle. Her partner follows on the inside of the circle. After the first couple has passed three couples, the next couple starts the same pattern. Everyone claps as the action continues.

RANGE RIDER MIXER
(Brown Eyed Mary)

Brown Eyed Mary is one of the oldest Early American play part mixers. The Range Riders of Amarillo, Texas, have been dancing this mixer for many years. It is commonly referred to as Range Rider Mixer in the Amarillo, Texas, area.

Music   Record: *Brown Eyed Mary*, Old Timer 8005, 8051; Western Jubilee 703; *Pennsylvania Polka* Golden Square 6007*; or any lively polka.

Position   Promenade
Formation   Circle, couples facing counterclockwise.

DIRECTIONS FOR MIXER

MEASURES	CALL
1–8	PROMENADE THE RING
	Couples promenade counterclockwise.
9–12	GENTS SWING IN AND THE LADIES SWING OUT
	Partners face, join right hands. Couples should separate slightly as they join hands.
13–16	PARTNER WITH THE RIGHT AND ALL THE WAY AROUND
	Man turns partner once around clockwise.
1–4	LADY IN FRONT WITH THE LEFT AND ALL THE WAY AROUND
	Man turns lady in front once around counterclockwise.
5–8	PARTNER WITH THE RIGHT AND ALL THE WAY AROUND
	Man turns partner once around clockwise.
9–16	AND PROMENADE YOUR CORNER AS SHE COMES DOWN
	Man promenades lady of couple immediately behind.

References in Bibliography for Range Rider Mixer: 91 (Kit P, p. 10), 117 (Vol. II, No. 5, March 1948, p. 10).
* Out of print.

FIVE FOOT TWO MIXER

Music	Record: Folkraft 1420; Lloyd Shaw 122; Windsor 4619. Honor Your Partner Album 6 Side 8.
Position	Promenade.
Formation	Double circle, couples facing line of direction.

DIRECTIONS FOR MIXER

Music ₵ *   NOTE: Directions are for man; lady's part reverse.

MEASURES

I. Promenade

1–2   Beginning left, take two two-steps forward in line of direction.

3–4   Walk four steps forward in line of direction.

5–6   Repeat action of measures 1–2.

7–8   Drop left hands (keep right hands joined). Man walks four steps forward turning to face out of circle on last two steps. Lady walks four steps backward turning to face inside of circle. All join hands in one large single circle.

II. Balance and Walk Around

9–10   Beginning left, balance forward, balance back.

11–12   Drop left hands (partners keep right hands joined). Walk four steps around partner moving clockwise to change places. Ladies now face out of circle and men face in. All join hands in single circle.

13–14   Repeat action of measures 9–10.

15–16   Drop partner's hand. Each man takes lady on his left for a new partner and both walk four steps to face in line of direction in promenade position.

---

* Cut time is 4/4 time changed to 2/2 time which is a faster tempo than the average 4/4 time. There are two strong beats in each measure.
References in Bibliography: 15 (p. 18), 23 (p. 26).
Dance annotation form © 1948 by the Folk Dance Federation of California.

GRAND MARCH

Music   Record: Any lively march, two-step or square dance tune.
Position   Escort.
Formation Double circle, couples facing line of direction, or two single files, men in one and ladies in the other.

DIRECTIONS FOR THE GRAND MARCH

A grand march is an excellent activity to begin a dance program, to insert in a program for variety, or to use after an intermission to start activity again. It may be used as an end in itself, since it is impressive and stimulates group feeling, or it may be used as a means for organizing a group quickly for another activity. A grand march is most effective when many people participate. Since guests do not always arrive punctually, this fact should always be considered in scheduling a grand march.

LEADERSHIP ... The leader stands at either the front or rear of the room. A change in pattern is indicated as the group nears the leader. It is helpful if the first two or three couples are familiar with the various figures to be used in the grand march. Experienced couples will follow the leader's cues more easily and set the pattern for the others to follow.

BEGINNING ... A grand march may be started either in couples or from two single files of individuals. The latter is particularly suited for groups not already acquainted.

A. *Two Single Files*. Men line up on one side of the room and the ladies on the other. Both files face either the front or rear of the room as indicated by the leader. NOTE: The leader must be careful to indicate the proper direction for the two files to face so that the ladies will be on the right side of the men when couples are formed. Each line marches toward the end of the room, turns, and marches toward the opposite line. The files meet, forming couples in escort position, ladies to the right of the men, and march down the center of the room.

B. *Couples in a Double Circle*. Couples in escort position form a double circle, and march counterclockwise. One couple is selected as the leader and that couple, followed by the others, moves down the center of the room.

FIGURES ... These figures may be used in any order, as long as they flow from one to the other.

A. *Single Files*
   1. Inner and Outer Circle. When each couple reaches the front of the room, partners separate, men left and ladies right, and travel down the side of the room until they meet at the opposite end. Then the lines pass each other. The ladies traveling on the inside, men on the outside, and down the side of the room until they meet again at the front of the room. They pass again, the men traveling on the inside, ladies on the outside, and down the sides of the room.
   2. The Cross (X). When each file reaches the rear corner, the leader of each file makes an abrupt turn and travels diagonally toward the front corner on the opposite side. Both files cross in the center of the room, lady crossing in front of partner. The files travel down the side of the room toward the rear corners. The diagonal cross is repeated, the man crossing in front of his partner.

Reference in Bibliography: 49.

3. Virginia Reel. Couples move down the center in double file. When each couple reaches the front of the room, partners separate, man left, ladies right, and travel down the sides of the room to form two files about ten to fifteen feet apart. Both lines face each other. The head lady and the foot man meet in the middle and dance away. Then the head man and foot lady meet in the middle in like manner and dance away. This process is repeated until all have partners and are dancing.

B. *Couples*

1. Four, Eight, or Sixteen Abreast. When the couples marching down the center arrive at the front of the room, the lead couple turns to the right, marches to the side of the room, and back toward the rear of the room. The second couple turns left, the third right, etc., and march to the side and back to the rear of the room. When they meet at the rear of the room, the two approaching couples march down the center of the room together, thus forming a group of four abreast. At the front of the room each group of four marches alternately to the right and left, down the sides and at the rear of the room they form a line eight abreast. The same procedure is followed to form lines of sixteen or more abreast. After the group has formed lines of sixteen abreast they may be instructed to mark time in place.

2. "Ring Up" for Squares. If groups of eight are desired for the next activity, for example, a square dance, the couples mark time when they are eight abreast. Each line of eight then "rings up" or makes a circle.

3. Over and Under. When the couples are four abreast, the two couples separate at the front of the room, one turning right, the other left. When the couples meet at the rear of the room, the first couple of the double file on the right side of the room makes an arch. The first couple of the other double file goes under the arch and quickly makes an arch for the second couple they meet. All couples in both double files are alternately making an arch or traveling under an arch.

4. Snake Out. When the couples are eight or sixteen abreast, the person on the right end of the front line leads that line in single file to the right of the column of dancers and in between lines two and three. As the person on the left end of the first line passes the person on the right end of the second line, they join hands and line two then follows line one. The leader then leads the line between line three and four and again as the last person in the moving line passes the right end of the third line, they join hands and line three joins with line one and two. The moving line weaves in and out of the remaining lines and each time the person on the end of the moving line passes the right end of the next line they join hands and continue weaving in and out. After all lines have been "snaked out" the leader may lead the line in serpentine fashion around the room and eventually circles the room clockwise in a single circle, all facing the center.

5. Bridge
   a. Couples march down the center double file. As the first couple nears the end of the room partners face, join hands, and form an arch under which the other couples march as the lead couple moves in reverse direction over the double file of couples. As each couple passes under the arch, they face and form an arch, and follow the lead couple.

b. Or when the couples are four abreast the two couples separate at the front of the room, one turning right, the other left. When the couples meet at the rear of the room, the couples on the right travel through a tunnel of arches formed by the other group. When the couples meet at the front of the room the process is reversed.

6. <u>Danish March</u>. When couples are in a double circle or double file, partners face and stand about four feet apart. The first couple joins hands holding arms out shoulder height and slides the length of the formation used. The second couple follows, etc. When couples reach the end, they join the group. This may be repeated with partners standing back to back as they slide.

7. <u>Grand Right and Left</u>. When couples are in a single circle, partners face and start a grand right and left. This may continue until partners meet or until the leader signals for new partners to be taken for a promenade or other figure.

8. <u>Paul Jones</u>. When couples are in a single circle, any of the figures for a Paul Jones* may be used.

ENDING ... There is no set ending for a grand march. However, the ending should be definite so that there is a feeling of completion and satisfaction. It may end with people in groups for the next activity or in a circle with everyone joining in a song or dancers may swing into a waltz, polka or some other planned activity.

PISTOL PACKIN' MAMA
(Glowworm Mixer)

Music	Record: *Pistol Packin' Mama*, Imperial 1106*, Old Timer 8055, Windsor 4427, 4613, Top 25130, MacGregor 445-3, 004-2.
Position	Couple.
Formation	Double circle, couples facing line of direction.

DIRECTIONS FOR MIXER

Music 4/4   NOTE: Directions are same for both lady and man.
MEASURES

I. **Forward**
1   Beginning left, walk four steps forward in line of direction.

II. **Away**
2   Partners face, beginning left, man walks backward into center of circle four steps as lady walks backwards away from center of circle four steps.

III. **Diagonal Left**
3   Both man and lady face diagonally to their own left. Beginning left, walk four steps forward to new partner.

IV. **Turn Four**
4   Beginning left, hook right arms with new partner and turn around in four steps, ending in couple position.

NOTE: During the Christmas Season the pattern may be danced to *Jingle Bells*.

---

* Refer to Paul Jones Your Lady, page 353.
 Dance annotation form © 1948 by the Folk Dance Federation of California.
* Out of print.

HITCH HIKER MIXER

This dance was originated by Jane A. Harris, Pullman, Washington.

Music   Record: *Five Foot Two*, Folkraft 1420X45, Lloyd Shaw 122, Windsor 4619. *Buzz's Mixer*, Windsor 4637; any lively two-step, preferably in rag time.

           Piano: *Five Foot Two* or *Pretty Girl Dressed in Blue*.

Formation   Double circle, partners facing, man's back to center of circle.

DIRECTIONS FOR MIXER

Music 4/4   NOTE: Directions are for man; lady's part reversed.
MEASURES

Jump and Hitch

1–2	Moving away from partner, take two small jumps backward.
3–4	Man wags left thumb, lady right, twice as if thumbing and turn left toe, lady right, out twice toward line of direction.
5–8	Repeat action of measures 1–4, thumbing and toeing out toward reverse line of direction with other thumb and toe.
9–10	Repeat action of measure 1–2.
11–12	Wag both thumbs, turning out both toes twice.

Do-Sa-Dos

13–16	Strut 8 steps around partner doing a do-sa-do, passing right shoulders back to place facing forward and holding partner's inside hand.

Promenade

1–2	Beginning left, take 4 steps moving forward in line of direction.
3–4	Strut four steps turning in place (man L, lady R).
5–6	Repeat action of measures 1–2.
7–8	Man turning left, take four struts and move back to lady behind for a new partner. Lady turning right, takes four struts in place.

HOKEY POKEY

The Hokey Pokey is a modern adaptation of Looby Lou. The dance became very popular in England during World War II and since that time has enjoyed wide popularity in this form in the United States. The action sequence on several records with calls varies slightly from the one given here. The tune is simple and may be easily done without musical accompaniment. The leader may sing the call for the group or have them sing and perform the action.

Music   Record: Capitol 6026; Old Timer 8086, 8163. MacGregor 699, 6995.

Formation   Single circle, individuals face center, or single circle couples facing center, lady to right of partner.

DIRECTIONS FOR MIXER

CALL   YOU PUT YOUR RIGHT FOOT IN
          Place foot forward into circle.

          YOU PUT YOUR RIGHT FOOT OUT
          Place foot back away from circle.

          YOU PUT YOUR RIGHT FOOT IN

          AND YOU SHAKE IT ALL ABOUT
          Shake foot toward center of circle.

          YOU DO THE HOKEY POKEY
          Place palms together above head and rumba hips.

          AND YOU TURN YOURSELF AROUND
          Individuals shake arms above head and turn around. If couples, man turns lady on left once and a half with right elbow and progresses one position clockwise.

          THAT'S WHAT IT'S ALL ABOUT
          Clap hands four times.

Repeat the above call substituting the following parts of the body: left foot, right arm, left arm, right elbow, head, right hip, whole self, back side.

Ending: YOU DO THE HOKEY POKEY
          YOU DO THE HOKEY POKEY
          Raise the arms above head and lower arms and head in a bowing motion.

          YOU DO THE HOKEY POKEY
          Kneel on both knees and raise arms above head and lower arms and head in a bowing motion.

          THAT'S WHAT IT'S ALL ABOUT
          Slap the floor six times.

Dance annotation form © 1948 by the Folk Dance Federation of California.

PATTY CAKE POLKA

Music   Record: Honor Your Partner 401; Lloyd Shaw 149/50; Old
               Timer 8162; Windsor 4624; *Buffalo Gal*, Folk Dancer
               MH 1501; World of Fun M 107; Folkraft 1124, 1018,
               1260, 1167.

Position   Partners face, two hands joined.

Formation   Double circle, man's back to center.

DIRECTIONS FOR MIXER

Music 2/4   NOTE: Directions are for man; lady's part reverse.

MEASURES

I. Heel Toe Polka and Slide

1–2   Beginning left, place left heel to left, place left toe to
           right instep. Repeat.

3–4   Take four slides in line of direction.

5–8   Beginning right, repeat the action of measures 1–4, mov-
           ing in reverse line of direction.

II. Claps

9   Clap own hands, clap partner's right hand.

10   Clap own hands, clap partner's left hand.

11   Clap own hands, clap partner's hands (both).

12   Clap own hands, slap own knees.

13–14   Hook right elbows and walk around partner and back to
           place.

15–16   Man moves forward in line of direction to new partner.
           Lady spins clockwise twice, as she moves in reverse line of
           direction to new partner.

VARIATION:

9   Clap partner's right hand three times.

10   Clap partner's left hand three times.

11   Clap partner's hands (both) three times.

12   Slap own knees three times.

References in Bibliography: 15 (p. 26), 32 (p. 23), 51 (p. 5).

PAUL JONES YOUR LADY

Music   Record: Blue Star 3-1547, Old Timer 8160, or any lively two-step.

Position   Promenade.

Formation   Double circle, couples facing line of direction.

DIRECTIONS FOR MIXER

The leader calls out each figure and signals clearly. Each figure is danced briefly as it is merely a method of changing partners.

I. **Paul Jones Your Lady or Promenade**
Couples promenade around room in one large circle.

II. **Figures**

A. Single Circle. Couples form a single circle, hands joined. Slide left, right, and/or shuffle to center and back. Each man takes his corner lady for a new partner.

B. The Basket. Ladies form an inner circle, hands joined and slide left. Men form an outer circle, hands joined, and slide right. Both circles stop. Men raise joined hands. Ladies move backward through arches made by men and stand beside a man. Men lower arms. Everyone slides left then right. Each man takes lady on right for a new partner.

C. Across the Circle. Couples form a single circle, hands joined. Slide left, right and shuffle to center, back, and center. Each man takes lady across the circle as a new partner.

D. Grand Right and Left. Couples form a single circle, hands joined. Slide left, right and shuffle to center and back. Face partner and grand right and left around the circle. Each man takes lady facing him or lady whose hand he holds when leader signals for new partners.

E. Gentlemen Kneel. Couples form single circle, and face partner. Men kneel, ladies move in reverse line of direction, weaving in and out between kneeling men. Each man takes lady facing him when leader signals for new partners.

F. Count Off. Double circle, couples facing counterclockwise. Ladies stand still and men move forward, counting off as many ladies as indicated by leader. Men may stand still while ladies move forward and count off in like manner.

III. **Two-Step**

Couples in closed position, two-step about the room. Upon signal "Paul Jones Your Lady," they again fall into a double circle and promenade counterclockwise around room until the signal for a new figure action is given.

Reference in Bibliography: 92 (p. 176), 96 (p. 398).
Dance annotation form © 1948 by the Folk Dance Federation of California.

Plain and Novelty Mixers

GAIN OR EXCHANGE PARTNERS

1. Upset the Cherry Basket. When the music stops, the leader requests that everyone change partners. If couples are asked to change with the couple nearest them, everyone is involved, and no one walks to the side for the lack of a partner.

2. Paul Jones. Use any figure or figures from Paul Jones Your Lady, page 319.

3. Snowball, Whistle Dance, Pony Express, or Multiplication Dance. One to three couples start to dance. When the music stops, each couple separates and goes to the sidelines and gets a new partner. This is repeated until everyone is dancing.

4. Line Up. The men line up on one side of the room facing the wall; the ladies on the other side facing the wall. When the signal is given each line backs up until they gain a new partner.

5. Dance Bids. The custom of signing for dances on the dance bid is seldom used today. The dance bids still exist for many dances as a ticket and token of the dance.

    a. The dance committee may easily reactivate this custom and therefore effect a change of partners in this manner.

    b. Each lady is given a bid with four dances marked red, green, yellow, or blue. There are four tickets attached, one each of these colors. As ladies move clockwise, men counterclockwise around the circle, they are signalled to stop before a partner. The lady requests this partner to sign her bid for the red dance; she gives the man a red ticket with her name on it. They march around again until signalled to stop. This process is repeated for the remaining three dances. At some time during the evening, color dances are named, and the man finds the lady whose name is on his corresponding tag.

    c. Bids may add to the atmosphere at a dance where people have come alone or at a class party. Each gentleman requests a lady to dance and they form a circle. The gentleman signs his name on the first and last dances of his partner's bid. Then the leader moves the men around the circle. Each time they stop in front of a lady, they sign for the next dance in that lady's bid. Eventually all of the dances are signed and a change of partners is arranged for the whole party.

6. Arches. All the dancers form a single circle and walk counterclockwise around the circle. Two couples form arches on opposite sides of the circle. When the music stops the arch is lowered. Those caught in the arch go to the center of the circle, gain a partner, and go back to the circle to form new arches. Eventually just a few dancers will be walking through the tunnel of arches. When all have partners the dancing proceeds.

7. Star by the Right. Six men form a right hand star in the center of a single circle formed by the group. The star moves clockwise, and the circle counterclockwise. As the leader gives the signal, six ladies hook onto the star; alternate sexes are called out until all have hooked onto the star. A little spice is added if the last person on each spoke winks or beckons a specific person from the ring to join his or her spoke. When the star is completed the lady dances with the man on her right.

8. Matching. Advertising slogans (Ivory Soap – 99.9 per cent pure, it floats), split proverbs (a rolling stone—gathers no moss), famous couples (Romeo-Juliet), pairs of words that belong together (ham-eggs), playing

cards (spades match with hearts for each number, clubs with diamonds), pictures cut in half (cartoons), or songs may be used for this mixer. Half of the slips of paper are given to the men, and the corresponding half are distributed to the ladies. As the people circulate they try to find the person with the corresponding half of their slogan, proverb, cartoon, or whatever has been selected to be matched. When everyone has found his partner, the dancing proceeds. If songs are used, each person sings his song until he finds the person singing the same song.

9. Musical Chairs. Set up a double row of chairs, back to back, almost the length of the room. Leave space between every group of four chairs so that partners can get together. The group marches around the chairs. When the music stops, each person tries to gain a seat. A man must sit back to back with a lady. These two become partners and proceed to dance while all the others continue to play the game until all have partners. When all are dancing, the next signal is given and partners separate and rush for a chair, thus providing a change of partners. *Musical knees:* played like musical chairs except that on a signal, the men get down on one knee and the girls rush to sit on a knee. Those left out go to the side.

10. Gimme. The men form a circle and the ladies form a circle on the inside. Each person takes a partner. Upon the signal from the leader they exchange names and the lady requests a small token (finger nail file, comb, nickel, shoe) from her partner. The leader then asks all ladies to move forward to the third man. Names are exchanged and another small token is requested. The leader instructs the group to continue this process four or five times. When the leader calls out, "Jiggers the cops!" the ladies rush to return all articles to the proper person. *The articles must be handed to the owner, not thrown.* If the game is played a second time, the men are on the inside circle.

11. Popularity Mixer. The men form a large single circle, facing the line of direction, the ladies stand in the center of the circle. The men walk around the circle with their left hands on their hips. At the signal from the leader, all ladies take a partner by taking a man's left arm. The extra ladies remain in the center. Partners walk round the circle. At the next signal, the men continue to walk in the line of direction and the ladies walk in the reverse line of direction. The extras join the ladies' circle. At the next signal, all take partners and walk in the line of direction. The extra ladies remain in the center. Walking with partners and in opposite directions is repeated alternately.

TRADE DANCES

1. Are You on the Beam? While everyone is dancing, a spotlight is suddenly focused on a specific area. Those people standing in the rays of the light are requested to give a yell, sing a song, or trade partners.

2. Hats Off! Four hats are distributed among four couples. Each couple with a hat places it on one member of another couple. When the music stops, the couples with the hats must change partners.

TAGS

1. Ladies' Tag or Men's Tag. Certain dances may be designed as Ladies' Tag or Men's Tag.

2. Similarity Tag. Either a man or a lady may tag, but the person tagging can only tag someone who has a similar color of hair, eyes, shirt, shoe, etc.

3. "You Take the Lemon, I'll Take the Peach." A few lemons or other designated articles are distributed among the men or ladies. Anyone

who holds the article may tag. Additional fun may be had by stopping the music periodically and anyone holding the article pays a forfeit. Later the forfeits are redeemed by performing a humorous stunt.

ELIMINATION DANCES

1. <u>Number Please</u>? Each couple is given a number. Each time the music stops a number is called out and the couple or couples having the numbers called sit down. Numbers are called out until only one couple remains.

2. <u>Lemon Dance</u>. An object, for example, a lemon, is passed from couple to couple. When the music stops, the couple with the object sits down. Eventually one couple is left.

3. <u>Dance Contest</u>. Determine the type of dancing for the contest, for example, waltz or jitterbug. It should be conducted in a casual manner with qualified judges. Gradually the contestants are eliminated until one or two couples remain. Choosing two couples, instead of one, for the winners keeps competition from becoming too keen.

PROGRESSIVE SCHOTTISCHE

This dance was arranged from notes taken at the National Folk Festival in 1947. This dance was taught by Bud Brown of Phoenix, Arizona.

Music	Record: *American Mixer*, Folkraft 1186; *Military Schottische*, MacGregor 4005; *Starlight Schottische*, Western Jubilee 700, or any medium tempo schottische.
Position	Varsouvianna.
Formation	Double circle, couples facing line of direction.

DIRECTIONS FOR MIXER

Music 4/4   NOTE: Directions are same for both lady and man.

MEASURES

    I. **Heel and Toe, Walk Forward**

1–2   Beginning left, place heel forward, place left toe backward, walk forward three steps.

3–4   Beginning right, repeat action of measures 1–2.

    II. **Swing Lady to Center**

5–6   Beginning left, place heel forward, place left toe backward. Man releases lady's right hand (keep left hands joined). Take three steps, man moving to right (stepping back left, right to side, forward left), and lady moving across in front of man to center of circle. Lady now faces reverse line of direction.

    III. **Meet New Partner**

7–8   Beginning right, place heel forward, place right toe backward. Lady takes three steps forward in reverse line of direction, extending her right hand to new partner who turns her into original position as man moves forward in line of direction three steps.

References in Bibliography: 15 (p. 25), 49; 117 (Vol. II, No. 1, Nov. '47).
Dance annotation form © 1948 by the Folk Dance Federation of California.

RED RIVER VALLEY

Music	Record: Folkraft 1056, 1269; Old Timer 8001, 8037, 8162; World of Fun M 104; Windsor A 753.
Position	Set of three, man between two ladies, arms linked.
Formation	Two sets of three, facing each other in large circle. Each set alternately faces line of direction and reverse line of direction.

DIRECTIONS FOR MIXER

SINGING CALL:

Verse 1   NOW YOU LEAD RIGHT DOWN TO THE VALLEY
Walk diagonally forward to right and pass opposite set to meet new set.

CIRCLE TO THE LEFT THEN TO THE RIGHT
All join hands and circle left, then right.

NOW YOU SWING WITH THE GAL IN THE VALLEY
Man swings (elbow or waist swing) right hand lady.

AND YOU SWING WITH YOUR RED RIVER GAL.
Man swings left hand lady.

Verse 2   NOW YOU LEAD RIGHT ON DOWN THE VALLEY
Each set links arms. Walk diagonally forward to right and pass opposite set to meet new set.

CIRCLE TO THE LEFT THEN TO THE RIGHT
All join hands and circle left, then right.

NOW THE GIRLS MAKE A WHEEL IN THE VALLEY
Four ladies make right hand star, walking clockwise once around and return to place.

AND THE BOYS DOS-A-DOS (DO-SA-DO) SO POLITE.
Two men dos-a-dos (do-sa-do), passing right shoulders.

Verse 3   NOW YOU LEAD RIGHT ON DOWN THE VALLEY
Each set links arms and passes opposite set as before to meet new set.

CIRCLE TO THE LEFT THEN TO THE RIGHT
All join hands and circle left, then right.

NOW YOU LOSE YOUR GAL IN THE VALLEY
Two right hand ladies change places crossing diagonally.

AND YOU LOSE YOUR RED RIVER GAL.
Two left hand ladies change places in same manner.
Each man now has two new partners for repeat of dance.

Reference in Bibliography: 32 (p. 44).

SKATER'S DELIGHT WALTZ

This dance was originated by Art and Metha Gibbs of Portland, Oregon.

Music	Record: *Skater's Waltz*, Lloyd Shaw 102, Old Timer 8050, Western Jubilee 719.
Position	Partners face, two hands joined.
Formation	Double circle, man's back to center.

DIRECTIONS FOR MIXER

Music 3/4   NOTE: Directions are for man; lady's part reverse.

MEASURE

1–4   Beginning left, step to side in line of direction (ct. 1), hold (ct. 2), close right to left (ct. 3). Step left to side in line of direction (ct. 1), and swing right forward dropping left hand grasp, pivoting a half turn counterclockwise (ct. 2), hold (ct. 3). Partners are now in a back position. Step right to side in line of direction (ct. 1), hold (ct. 2), close left to right (ct. 3). Step right in line of direction (ct. 1), hold (cts. 2–3).

5–8   Drop hands. Man takes lady's right in his left. Beginning left, repeat action of measures 1–4 in reverse line of direction. On last step man pivots a quarter turn counterclockwise with back to line of direction and takes partner in closed position.

9–12   Beginning left, step backwards waltzing four, turning clockwise, progressing in line of direction. On fourth waltz, twirl lady under man's left arm and end facing each other, two hands joined.

13–14   Step left, swing right over left. Step right, swing left over right. Drop hands.

15–16   Partners turn away from each other (man left, lady right) taking two waltz steps (or six steps in waltz rhythm) in solo turns. Man progresses in reverse line of direction as lady progresses in line of direction to receive new partners. End facing new partner, two hands joined. NOTE: On the solo turns the man and lady may come back to their partner instead of progressing to a new partner.

VARIATION:

To simplify the dance, omit the action described in last step of measures 5–8 and change action of measures 9–12 as follows: balance backward on left (cts. 1, 2, 3) and then three waltz steps turning clockwise, progressing in line of direction.

Reference in Bibliography: 124 (Je. '54, p. 34).
Dance annotation form © 1948 by the Folk Dance Federation of California.

SQUARE DANCE MIXERS

METHODS FOR SQUARING UP

1. Grand March. The grand march is a traditional way of squaring sets. It serves chiefly as a mixer of couples rather than individuals. It is a particularly good and efficient way of organizing a large crowd into sets. Refer to page 313 for detailed description of the procedure.

2. Paul Jones. This procedure will enable a group to get partners for forming sets. Ladies form a single circle facing out, circle to the left. Men form a single circle around the ladies, facing in, circle to the left. The larger group usually forms the outside circle. When the music stops the men take the lady directly opposite or nearest him for a partner. Refer to Paul Jones Your Lady, page 319, for additional variations.

3. Circle Two-step. Once partners are secured the leader may call out "circle four," "circle six," "circle ten," or any even number so that partners are not separated. Eventually "circle eight," may be called and sets arranged for dancing. Younger groups may enjoy this procedure: the leader blows a whistle or claps hands indicating the number of couples he wishes to have form a circle.

4. Grand Promenade. After partners are secured, the leader may use the following call to organize the group into sets.

> Promenade go two by two
> Now promenade a little bit more
> Pick up two and make it four
> Promenade and don't be late
> Grab a four and make it eight
> Line up now and keep it straight
> Spread that line way out wide
> And circle up eight on all four sides.

5. Promenade Around the Hall. This call may be used at the beginning of the dance or at the end of any one call during the dance to arrange couples in different sets for the next call.

> Promenade one and promenade all
> Promenade around the great big hall
> Circle up four with any old two
> Go 'round and 'round like you used to do
> Now break that four and circle up eight
> Find your place right in that set
> Stand right there, we ain't through yet.

Variation: The following variation of the preceding call may be used to break up the sets and arrange the dancers in formation for a round dance.

> Break up your sets and promenade all
> Promenade, go around the hall
> Around the great big beautiful hall
> Now stand right there upon the floor
> Stand right there, we'll dance some more.

6. <u>Promenade Out of the Square</u>. During a call, usually where a trim or break is in order, the caller may change a couple or couples from one set to another and finish the call with new couples in every set. The following call indicates how this may be done.

> One and three — promenade
> Right out of that square
> And find yourself a brand new square
> Promenade, go anywhere
> Just find yourself a brand new square
> Look for hands around the floor
> Fill in there — they need two more
> There's a spot — go over there
> They need two more to make a square
> One for the money, two for the show
> All get set — 'cause here we go!

<u>Variation</u>: While the promenading couples are relocating, the caller may keep the other couples dancing by calling a ladies chain, right and left through or do-si-do. The following call indicates how this may be done:

> One and three — promenade
> Right out of that square
> And find yourself a brand new square
> Now two and four — while they are gone
> Circle up four and carry on
> Do-si-do in the middle of the set
> 'Cause one and three ain't ready yet
> Two and four go home to your places
> And take a look at the brand new faces.

7. <u>New Partner Calls</u>. The following calls may be used to secure new partners at the end of a call.

> Honor your partner and thank her too
> Now swing the gal to the left of you
> Swing your corner, that pretty little maid
> Keep this gal and all promenade
> Honor your partner, corners too
> Swing that gal across from you
> Swing that gal but not too hard
> Stand right there with a brand new pard!

8. <u>Directed Changes</u>. The leader may simply direct dancers to change places in one of the following ways:
   a. All ladies move one position to the right in the set.
   b. Each gentleman takes his opposite, corner, or right hand lady for a new partner.
   c. All the ladies or gentlemen move to the adjacent square and take the same positions in the new set.

9. <u>Scoot and Scat</u>. Scoot is the cue for the man and scat is the cue for the ladies. In general, the leader must explain the action to the group so that they will respond in the desired manner. The ladies or men may be directed to form a star in the center of the set; while the star is revolving the leader calls "scoot" and the men leave the square and go to another one to form a star. If ladies are directed into a star figure, on the call "scat" the ladies leave the square and get into another to form a star.

Scoot and Scat may also be called as a part of Texas Star. If the men are on the outside spokes of the star, "scoot" is called. The ladies continue to star and the men hook onto the spoke of the ladies' star in another set. When all squares have eight people, the caller continues the Texas Star. New partners promenade to the home position of the lady.

10. <u>Birdies in the Cage</u>. The following variation of the regular Birdie in the Cage and "7" Hands Around (refer to page 70) may be used as a mixer.

> All four gents swing your right hand lady
> With a right hand around
> Partner left with a left hand around
> Corner lady with a right hand around
> Now swing your partner with two hands around
> And cage those birds as you come around
> Now four hands up and away we go
> The birds fly away through that open door!

All four ladies are placed in the center of the set back to back. The men join hands and circle left around the ladies (birds). The men hold their hands up high forming arches through which the ladies (birds) fly on the call "The birds fly away through that open door." The call may be repeated with the "crows," the men, in the center and the ladies circling around with joined hands raised high. The "crows" fly away on the call "The crows fly away through that open door." The "birds" or "crows" simply go to any new set and take a new partner for a repeat of the call.

TETON MOUNTAIN STOMP

This dance was originated by Doc Alumbaugh, Arcadia, California. It was adapted from the old Buffalo Glide.

Music   Record: Western Jubilee 725; Windsor 4753, 4615; Folkraft 1482X45; Old Timer 8207.

Position   Closed.

Formation Single circle, men facing in line of direction.

DIRECTIONS FOR MIXER

Music 4/4   NOTE: Directions are for man; lady's part reverse.

MEASURES

I. Side Step and Stamp

1–2   Beginning left, step toward center, close right to left, step left toward center, and stamp right next to left.

3–4   Beginning right, repeat action of measures 1–2, moving away from center of circle.

5–6   Step left to side, stamp right beside left. Step right to side, stamp left beside right.

II. Walk

7–8   Left reverse open position. Walk four steps in line of direction (lady moves backward).

9–10   Right reverse open position. Walk four steps backward in line of direction (lady moves forward).

11–12   Man takes half turn to face line of direction and walks four steps forward to meet the second lady for new partner. Lady walks four steps forward in reverse line of direction to meet second man for new partner.

III. Two-step, Pivot

13–16   Closed position. Take two two-steps, turning clockwise, and four pivot steps. End with man facing line of direction.

TENNESSEE WIG-WALK MIXER

Music   Record: Decca 28846.*

Formation Single circle, partners facing, men face counterclockwise, ladies face clockwise, right hands joined.

DIRECTIONS FOR MIXER

Music 2/4   NOTE: Directions are the same for both lady and man.

MEASURES

Touch Cross, Touch Out, and Grapevine

1–2   Beginning left, touch left toe in front of right, touch left toe to the side left, step left behind right, step right to the side right, bring left to right and take weight on left.

3–4   Repeat measures 1 and 2, beginning right.

Turn, Walk, Walk, Brush

5–6   Partners join right hands (forearm grasp preferred), turn one full turn, beginning left, walk, walk, walk, brush, walk, walk, walk, brush.

Men Progress CCW, Ladies CW

7–8   Beginning left, shuffle three small quick steps and hold slightly on fourth count, and repeat to new partner. Men progress forward in line of direction, ladies progress forward in reverse line of direction to meet new partner.

VERBAL CUES:

Meas. 1–2   Touch - and - touch - and grapevine step.
            (1)   and   (2)   - and (1 - 2 - 3 - hold)

3–4   Touch - and - touch - and grapevine step.
            (1)   and   (2)   - and (1 - 2 - 3 - hold)

5–6   Turn - 2 - 3 - brush; Turn - 2 - 3 - brush.
            (Quick-quick-quick-brush) (repeat)

7–8   Shuffle - 2 - 3 - hold; Shuffle - 2 - 3 - hold.

NOTE:
A different mixer to this same music appears in File O'Fun by Jane Harris.

Reference in Bibliography: 49.
Dance annotation form © 1948 by the Folk Dance Federation of California.
* Out of print.

TURKEY IN THE STRAW

This dance was arranged as a mixer by the authors.

Music   Record: Folk Dancer MH 10066; Folkraft 1067, 1312; Mac-
               Gregor 656, 668; Old Timer 8027; RCA-Victor 45-
               5017.

Position   Couple.

Formation   Single circle, couples facing center, lady to the right of partner,
               hands joined.

DIRECTIONS FOR MIXER

Music 4/4   NOTE: Directions are same for both lady and man.
MEASURES

      I. **Slides**

1–2   Beginning left, take eight slides to left.

3–4   Beginning right, take eight slides to right.

      II. **To the Center**

5   Beginning left, walk two steps to center and stamp three
                 times.

6   Beginning right, walk two steps backward to place and
                 stamp three times.

      III. **Right and Left Arm Swings**

7–8   Hook right arms with partner and turn in place with four
                 skipping or walking steps; men progress forward in line
                 of direction with four skipping or walking steps to meet
                 a new partner.

TUCKERS WALTZ

Music   Record: Lloyd Shaw 121, or any lively two-step or march and
               a good waltz.

Position   Promenade.

Formation   Double circle, couples facing line of direction.

DIRECTIONS FOR MIXER

One or more extra men stand in the center of the circle. Couples promenade around the circle to a lively two-step or march. The extra men cut in the
circle, taking the place of some man who has a partner. The man who is then
without a partner turns quickly to his left and in effect "rolls" back, taking
the lady behind him as his partner before the music changes to a waltz.

When the waltz music begins, all extra men without partners are left in
the center as the other couples waltz gayly around the room. When the music
changes again to a two-step or march, then all couples assume the promenade
position and again two-step or march.

When using records, this may be facilitated by placing a ten inch record
on top of a twelve inch record (one a two-step, the other a waltz). The change
of tempo may be made quickly by picking up the needle (arm on manual)
from the two-step record and moving it on the waltz record without having
to change records.

References in Bibliography for Tuckers Waltz: 41 (p. 68), 96 (p. 391).

WHITE SILVER SANDS

Music   Record: Decca 9-30363*; Grenn 14028.

Formation   Double circle, couples in promenade position, inside hands joined, facing counterclockwise.

DIRECTIONS FOR MIXER

Music 4/4   Directions for man; lady's part reversed.

MEASURES

Walk Four Turn Back Four

1–2   Beginning man's left, walk forward four steps in line of direction. Turn individually, rejoin inside hands. Continue in same direction, walking backwards four steps.

Walk Four Turn Back Four

3–4   Beginning man's left, walk forward four steps in reverse line of direction. Turn individually, rejoin inside hands. Continue in same direction, walking backwards four steps.

Balance Away — Together

5   Beginning man's left, balance away from partner, balance toward (together) partner.

6   Repeat — balance away, balance together.

Turn Four — To New Partner

7   Beginning left, take four walking steps, the man turning left to meet girl behind; the lady turns to right around in place and meets new man.

Balance Down the Line and Up the Line

8   Join both hands in butterfly position with new partner. Balance in line of direction, then balance in reverse line of direction and turn to face original line of direction side by side.

Reference in Bibliography: 84 (Sets In Order Yearbook #6, p. 89).

Dance annotation form © 1948 by the Folk Dance Federation of California.

* Out of print.

GLOSSARY

ACTIVE COUPLE. Relating to square dance, refer to Lead Couple. Relating to contra dances, any of the following terms are used to mean the same thing: Active Couples, First Couples, Head Couples, Top Couples. Active Couples are every other couple (1, 3, 5, etc.) or every third couple (1, 4, 7, 10).

ALL AROUND YOUR LEFT HAND LADY. Square dance term. Corners move around each other, the man moving around behind the lady and back to place, the lady moving in front of the man and back to place, both always facing the center of the set.

SEE SAW YOUR PRETTY LITTLE TAW. Partners move around each other in the same manner. The entire action makes a figure eight pattern.

ALL EIGHT. Square dance term. Refers to all eight members in the set.

ALL GET STRAIGHT. Square dance term. All couples are in their home position in set.

ALL JUMP UP AND NEVER COME DOWN. Square dance term. All jump into the air, usually followed by partner swing.

ALLEMANDE A. Square dance term. "A" is the key word. Men allemande left corner, give partner a right, pass partner and half sashay with right hand lady. Resashay right hand lady and men star right in center of set to opposite lady (original opposite), turn her with left hand once to face original corner, right to corner, pull her past and swing original partners. Refer to call on page 70.

ALLEMANDE LEFT. Square dance term. Corners join left hands, turn around each other and go back to place.

ALLEMANDE O. Square dance term. "O" is the key word. Men allemande left corners, give right to partner, pass by, left to right hand lady, and with her begin do paso, e.g., left to right hand lady, back to partner with the right and back to right hand lady with a left. Progress to next lady with a right, the next with a left and begin one full do paso, e.g., corner left, opposite right, corner left. Move on to partner or as caller directs. Refer to call on page 69.

ALLEMANDE RIGHT. Square dance term. Man joins right hands with the lady indicated by the call, turns her once around and goes back to place.

ALLEMANDE THAR. Square dance term. "Thar" is the key word. Men turn corners with left allemande, give right to partner, pass to right hand lady with a left, men hold on with left forearm grasp and walk counterclockwise into center to form a right hand star. Ladies are facing counterclockwise, gents clockwise. Star revolves counterclockwise. Men back up and ladies move forward. At caller's direction, men release right hand star, walk counterclockwise around lady to progress around set counterclockwise to the next lady with a right, the next

with a left, and again men hold on and walk into the center to form a right hand star. Men move back, ladies forward. Men break star and move out at caller's directions. Refer to call on page 69.

ALLEMANDE X. Square dance term. "X" is the keyword. Allemande left corners, give right hand to partner, pass by and swing the next or right hand lady.

BACK CROSS POSITION. Man and lady stand side by side, the lady on the right. Arms are crossed behind them so that the lady's left arm is behind him and her left hand holds his left hand at his left side; his right arm is behind her and his right hand holds her right hand at her right side. Refer to page 49.

BACK TO BACK. Refer to Face to Face.

BACK TRACK. Square dance term. This call usually comes during a grand right and left. Dancers meet their partners opposite home positions, grasp right hands and turn half around to face reverse direction. Dancers then repeat grand right and left in reverse direction. Refer also to Double Back Track and Turn Back. Refer to call on page 69.

BALANCE.

Contra	There are actually many kinds of balances used. The only contra balance used in this text is same as described for Folk Dance Balance, 2/4 time.
Folk Dance	The balance may be done forward, backward or to the side.
3/4 time	Step left (ct. 1), touch right to left, rising on balls of both feet (ct. 2), lower heels in place (ct. 3). Repeat same movement, beginning right.
2/4 time	a. Step left (ct. 1), touch right to left, rising on balls of both feet (ct. and), lower heels (ct. 2), and hold (ct. and). Repeat, beginning right.
	b. Or, step left (ct. 1), touch right to left (ct. 2). Repeat same movement, beginning right. Omit the pronounced lift of the heel in this analysis. However, there should be a slight lift of the body as the movement is executed.
Square Dance	Partners face, join inside hands or man may hold lady's left hand in his right.
	a. Each takes two steps backward, dipping back on second step, then two steps forward to original position.
	b. Or, man rocks back on left, taking weight on left, pointing

367

right in front (cts. 1, 2), then steps forward right to original position (cts. 1, 2). Lady's part reverse.

Social Dance. Refer to page 293.

BALANCE HOME. Man takes lady to his home place, and then balances and swings.

BALANCE AND SWING. Refer to Square Dance Balance above. Balance, then step forward into swing position (waist swing) and swing once around.

BANJO POSITION. Refer to Left Reverse Open Position. Refer to diagram on page 49.

BEND THE LINE. Square dance term. From any line of even numbers (four usually) the line breaks in the middle, the ends move forward, the centers back up, so that one half of line now faces the other half.

BLEKING — 2/4 time. Hop right, extending left foot forward, heel touching floor (ct. 1 and), hop left, extending right foot forward, heel touching floor (ct. 2 and), hop right, extending left foot forward (ct. 1), hop left, extending right foot forward (ct. and), hop right, extending left foot forward (ct. 2), and hold (ct. and), or hop left, extending right foot forward (ct. and).

BOX THE FLEA (Swat the Flea). Square dance term. Partners face, join left hands, exchange places, lady turning right, face under man's raised left arm, man moves half left, face to lady's position.

BOX THE GNAT. Square dance term. Partners face, join right hands, exchange places, lady turning left face under man's raised right arm, man makes half right face to lady's original position, end facing partner. Refer to call on page 66.

BREAK. Drop clasped hands.

BREAK AND SWING. Drop clasped hands and partners swing with a waist swing.

BREAK AND TRAIL ALONG THAT LINE. Square dance term. Drop hands, turn and face in opposite direction, move in single file to home position; the lady leads, the man follows.

BROKEN CIRCLE. Refer to page 47.

BUTTERFLY POSITION. Couple faces, arms extended shoulder high and out to the sides, hands joined. In this position couple may dance forward and back, to the right or to the left sideways, and in the line of direction and reverse line of direction. Refer to diagram, page 49.

BUZZ STEP. A step used in folk, square or social dance. It may be done alone or with a partner in the same position as for a waist swing. When done alone the buzz step may go sideways or revolve clockwise or counterclockwise. When done as a couple, the dancers turn clockwise. Step right pivoting clockwise on ball of foot ct. 1), push with left, which is slightly behind, and close to right (ct. and). Repeat as many times as desirable. The body weight remains on the right, the pivot foot, while the impetus for the pivot is by the slight push of the left foot. If to the side, the turning action of the pivot foot is omitted.

BUZZ STEP SWING. Refer to Swing.

CALIFORNIA TWIRL. Used by couples to change or reverse facing without changing relative relation of couple position. Lady's left in man's right, man walks around lady clockwise as lady executes a left face turn, moving under

raised right arm of man. If partners begin movement side by side facing center of set, they now are side by side facing away from center of set. A repeat of the movement puts dancers in original position.

CANTER RHYTHM — 3/4 time. It is an uneven pattern resulting from a long beat (cts. 1-2) followed by a short beat (ct. 3). A step is taken on (ct. 1), holding over (ct. 2), and a step on (ct. 3). The three-step-turn in canter rhythm is step left (ct. 1), pivot on left half counterclockwise (ct. 2), step right (ct. 3), pivoting almost half counterclockwise, step left (ct. 1), completing the turn and hold (cts. 2-3). Close right to left on (ct. 3) but keep weight on left. It may be done clockwise by starting with the right foot.

CAST OFF. Primary method of progression in contra dances. The active couples continue to move down the set, while inactive couples move up. There are many methods of casting off.

CATCH ALL EIGHT. Square dance term. Partners face, take right forearm grasp, move forward half way around (clockwise), face and release forearm grasp and take left forearm grasp, move one full turn (counterclockwise). Wait for caller's directions. Refer to call on page 69.

CCW. Symbols referring to counterclockwise. Refer to Counterclockwise.

CENTER. The space in the middle of the square (set) or circle formed by dancers.

CHA CHA CHA. Refer to page 322.

CHAIN. Refer to Ladies Chain for square dancing. Also refers to Grand Right and Left in European folk dancing.

CHALLENGE POSITION. A term used in social dance to refer to position of man facing lady, approximately arm distance. Hands are not joined.

CHUG STEP. Refer to Push Step.

CIRCLE. Four, six, eight, or more dancers join hands in a circle and move left or right as directions of the call or dance indicate. In a square dance call, if the direction is not indicated, circle left. Refer to page 47 for descriptions and diagrams of different types of circles.

CIRCLE WIDE. Dancers join hands and circle left. In a square dance call it may also mean for dancers to enlarge circle as they circle left.

CLOCKWISE. Refers to the movement of dancers around a circle in the same direction as the hands of a clock move. or turning action of one dancer or couple as they progress around the floor. In directional terms, clockwise is to the left, e.g., "circle to the left."

CLOSED POSITION. Partners should stand facing each other, shoulders parallel and toes pointed directly forward. Man's right arm is around the lady and the hand is placed just below her left shoulder blade. The lady's left hand and arm rests on the man's upper arm and shoulder. Man's left arm is raised sideward to the left and he holds her right hand in his palm. For detail description, refer to page 266. Refer to diagram, page 49.

CONTRA DANCE FORMATION. Refer to diagram, page 47.

CONVERSATION POSITION. As described for open position but with the forward hand released, and arm (man's left, lady's right) hanging at the side. Refer to diagram, page 49.

CORNER. The lady on the man's left — also called left hand lady. The lady's corner is the man on her right.

CORNER SWING. A waist swing with left hand lady.

CORTE. Refer to Dip. Also Tange Corte, page 304.

COUNTERCLOCKWISE. Refers to the movement of dancers around a circle in opposite direction from the movement of the hands on a clock, or turning action of one dancer or couple as they progress around the floor. In directional terms, counterclockwise is movement to the right, e.g., "circle to the right."

COUPLE. A man and a lady. The lady stands at the man's right.

COUPLE POSITION. Partners stand side by side, lady on man's right, inside hands joined, both face in same direction. Also referred to as: strolling, side by side, open position, or inside hands joined. Refer to diagram, page 49.

COURTESY TURN. A movement in which partners turn as a unit in place. Used to finish a Do Paso, Right and Left Thru, or Ladies Chain. The man takes partner's left hand in his left, places his right arm around lady's waist (in her right hand) and they turn around once counterclockwise to starting position. The man backs up to make the turn possible and guiding the lady forward.

CROSS OVER. Change place to other line across the set. Also variation in cha cha cha, refer to page 324.

CROSS TRAIL THRU. Square dance term. Active couples meet, pass right shoulder to right shoulder; lady then crosses in front of partner to her left, man crosses behind lady to his right. Wait for caller's direction.

CUT STEP. Quick change of weight from one foot to the other, displacing the supporting foot. May be done forward, backward, or to the side.

CUT TIME. Refer to page 37.

CW. Symbols referring to clockwise. Refer to Clockwise.

DAL STEP. A Swedish step in 3/4 time. Step left (ct. 1), swing right across in front of left (ct. 2), raise left heel from floor as weight rolls to ball of left foot and complete swing of right across left (ct. 3). Repeat movement, beginning right.

DANCE GLIDE. Refer to page 268.

DANCE WALK. Refer to Dance Glide.

DIP (CORTE). Step back on foot indicated, taking full weight, bending the knee. The other leg remains extended at knee and ankle forming a straight line from the hip. The toe remains in contact with the floor.

DIVE THRU. Square dance term. Active couple will duck under an arch made by the couple they are facing. If the arching couple then faces the outside of the square, they turn a California Twirl to reverse direction and end facing in. Note use with Square Thru, page 104.

DIXIE CHAIN. Square dance term. Two couples meet in single file, move past each other as in a grand right and left; the first two to meet use right hands, the second two to meet use left hands, remain in single file, wait for caller's directions.

DOCEY DOE. Square dance term. Refer to Do-Si-Do #2 Shaw style.

DO-PASO. Square dance term. Refer to Do-Si-Do #3 Do-Paso.

DO-SA-DO The man and lady face, pass each other right shoulder to right shoulder, move around each other back to back and return to original position. This movement is also executed in certain regions to the call Dos-A-Dos and Do-Si-Do.

DO-SI-DO.
1. Texas-Southwest Style (for two or more couples in a circle). Square dance term. Partners face, join left hands, turn once around to face corner; corners join right hands. Dancers describe a figure eight pattern as they execute the figure. The Texas-Southwest Style Do-Si-Do is generally repeated until the caller calls "one more change and promenade." And the last time the man turns his partner, the man puts his right arm around the lady's waist and turns her counterclockwise into place to promenade.
2. Shaw Style (for two couples in a circle). Square dance term. Form a circle of four, release hands, ladies pass left shoulders, turn left, give left hand to partner. As the ladies move around behind partner, the men do a. or b.
   a. Always facing each other and moving forward and backward to minimize the amount of space that the ladies must travel, release partner's hand, give right to opposite lady who moves around behind him once.
   b. Pass back to back, releasing partner's hand; give right to opposite lady and turn once around until the men again pass back to back. Then man takes partner's left hand and turns lady with a courtesy turn.
3. Do Paso. Square dance term. Partners face and take left forearm grasp. Turn partner with left arm around; turn corner with right forearm and then partners turn with a courtesy turn. This may be for two or more couples in a circle.
4. Contra Dances. The call do-si-do in contra dances is the same as defined by do-sa-do.

DRAW STEP — 2/4 time. Step sidewards on left (ct. 1), draw right to left, transferring weight to right (ct. 2). To draw, the foot is dragged along the floor. 3/4 time, step sidewards on left (cts. 1-2), draw right to left (ct. 3).

DOUBLE BACK TRACK. Square dance term. Dancers meet partner on grand right and left, take forearm grasp, turn half way around, facing reverse direction. Go grand right and left in reverse direction to meet partner for the second time, turn half way around to face original direction. Go grand right and left in original direction to meet partner for the third time. A promenade usually follows. Also called TURN BACK. Refer to call on page 69.

DOUBLE FILE. A type of formation. Couples stand in a column one behind the other, all facing in the same direction. Refer to page 47 for additional information and diagram.

DROP THE GATE. Square dance term. Called to form one circle of eight from two circles of four. Men of active couples release hands with corner lady in circle of four and join hands with original corner ladies to form a circle of eight.

EIGHT ROLL AWAY (with a half sashay). Square dance term. From an Allemande Thar movement, men roll left, face to outside, ladies roll left, face to inside, to exchange places. Men may assist roll by taking lady's right forearm in his right on the left face roll.

ELBOW SWING. Hook right elbows (or left) with person indicated and turn once around. Sometimes a forearm grasp is used in place of hooked elbows. The elbow swing is often used in the trim, once and a half.

ENDS TURN IN (Ends Turn Out). Square dance term. In any line of four, all facing same direction, the center two form an arch by raising joined hands; the end two in the line move forward and together duck under arch formed by center two. Center two execute a California Twirl to face in same direction with the end two. Line will end facing center of set if movement started when line faced out. The reverse is true if line began facing in.

ENGLISH RUNNING STEP. A light, bouncy, dignified, half walk, half run step.

ESCORT POSITION. Couple face line of direction, lady to man's right. The lady slips her left arm through the man's right arm which is bent at the elbow so that her left hand may rest on his right forearm. Free arm hangs to side. Refer to diagram on page 49.

FACE TO FACE, BACK TO BACK. A pattern of movement used by a couple moving in line of direction or reverse line of direction. Partners face, inside hands joined. The basic steps most generally used to effect this movement are: two-step, polka, or waltz. For example, the two-step: man beginning left, lady right, take first two-step in line of direction, turning toward each other as inside joined hands are swung back, arms extended; take second two-step in line of direction, turning away from each other, inside joined hands swing forward, arms extended. Repeat pattern.

FAN. Refer to Social Dance, page 305.

FILE. A type of formation. Dancers stand one behind the other, all facing the same direction. Refer to page 47 for additional information and diagram.

FIRST FOUR. Refers to the first and third couples in the set. Also called Head Couples, First Two Couples, or Heads.

FIRST TWO COUPLES. Refers to the first and third couples in the set. Also called Head Couples, First Four, or Heads.

FLARE. An exaggerated lift of the foot from the floor accompanying a knee bend. It is often used in the Tango.

FLIRTATION POSITION. Partners are facing, mans left hand and lady's right hand are joined. The arm is bent and used with control throughout the arm and hand so as to indicate or receive a lead. Refer to diagram on page 49. Also referred to as Swing Out Position.

FOOT FOUR. In longway sets, the Foot Four refers to the last two couples. Refer to page 47 for additional information and diagrams.

FOOT OF SET. In longways (contra) sets, the end of the set farthest from the caller and musicians. Refer to page 47 for diagram.

FOREARM GRASP. Partners grasp each other by the forearm just below the elbow with either right or left hand as directions indicate. This grasp is commonly used in Western Square

Dance for: Allemande Left, Back Track, Do Paso, Do-Si-Do, and Allemande Thar.

FORM A RING. Join hands and circle left.

FORWARD AND BACK. Move forward four steps and back up four steps into place.

FOUR SIDES. All four couples in the set.

FOX TROT. Refer to page 275.

FOUR STEP TURN. One complete turn is made in four steps. The turn may be made to the left (counterclockwise) or to the right (clockwise). To right (clockwise): Step right to side (ct. 1), pivot clockwise on right and step left to face opposite direction (ct. 2), pivot clockwise on left and step right to side to face original direction (ct. 3), step left across right in line of direction (ct. 4).

GALLOP. Refer to page 40.

GRAND CHAIN THE LADIES. Refer to Ladies Chain for Four.

GRAND RIGHT AND LEFT. Partners face, grasp right hands, move forward to the next person grasping left hands, move to the next grasping right hands and so on around the circle until partners meet. Ladies move clockwise, men counterclockwise around the circle. The grand right and left is also referred to as a "right and left grand" or a "right and left eight." In Western Square Dancing when partners meet on the opposite side of the set from home position, the caller usually directs them to "promenade home"; however, if directed by the caller, they may be allowed to continue the grand right and left until they meet in home position. In European folk dancing the term "chain" refers to Grand Right and Left.

GRAPEVINE. Step left to side (ct. 1), step right behind left (ct. 2), step left to side (ct. 3), step right in front of left (ct. 4). Bend knees, let hips turn naturally and keep weight on balls of feet.

HALF SASHAY. Refer to Sashay Half Way Around.

HALF WAY AROUND. Move in one direction left or right, half way around the circle (180 degrees). In a circle of four couples move left or right until they are on the opposite side of circle from original position.

HEADS. Refers to couples one and three in the set. Also called Head Four.

HEAD COUPLE. In square dancing the Head Couple is couple number one or the couple with their back to the music.

HEAD COUPLES. Refers to couples one and three in a set of four couples. In longway sets, head couples refer to first two couples. Refer to page 47 for additional information and diagrams.

HEAD FOUR. Refers to couples one and three in a square or head couples in longway sets.

HEAD OF SET. In longway (contra) sets, the end of the set closest to the caller and musicians. Refer to page 47 for diagrams.

HEEL AND TOE POLKA. Moving to the left, hop right (ct. and), place left heel close to right instep (ct. 1), hop right (ct. and), place left toe close to right instep (ct. 2), take one polka step to the left (cts. and 1 and 2). Repeat beginning hop on left, moving to the right.

HEEL AND TOE SCHOTTISCHE. Moving to the left, place left heel close to right instep (cts. 1, 2), place left toe close to right instep (cts. 3, 4), take one Schottische step to the left (cts. 1, 2, 3, 4). Repeat beginning right.

HESITATION. Refer to page 293.

HOME POSITION. Original position of each dancer or couple in the set.

HONEY. Partner.

HONOR PARTNER OR CORNER. Man bows to lady, lady curtsies to man. "Honors Right" means bow to partner, "Honors Left" means bow to corner.

HOP. A transfer of weight, by a springing action, from one foot to the same foot. Push off from the ball of one foot and land on ball of same foot. Refer to page 39 for additional analysis and musical notations.

HUNGARIAN BREAK STEP (Cross Apart Together). Hop left, touching right toe in front of left (ct. 1), hop left in place, touching right toe to right side (ct. 2), draw right foot to left, clicking heels together (ct. 3). Hold (ct. 4).

INDIAN STYLE. Square dance term. Refer to Promenade in Indian Style.

JITTERBUG. Refer to page 285.

JODY POSITION. Refer to Varsouvianna Position.

JUMP. One or both feet leave the floor, knees bending, and both return to the floor together landing toe-heel with an easy body. Spring off the floor on the upbeat of the music and land on the beat. Refer to page 39.

KOLO STEP. Moving right, hop on left foot, leap onto right foot, step on left foot behind right, step on right in place, hop on right foot.

LADIES CHAIN. Two Ladies Chain: Ladies meet in center, clasp right hands, pass right shoulders and give left hand to opposite man. Man puts his right arm around lady's waist and turns her with a courtesy turn. Ladies return to partner in the same manner.
Four Ladies Chain: All four ladies place right hands in the center, forming a star as they catch hands, and move to the left around circle to opposite man. He turns lady with a courtesy turn. Ladies return to partner in the same manner.

LADY BY YOUR SIDE. Square dance term. Left hand lady, corner or lady on man's left.

LADY GO GEE, GENT GO HAW. Square dance term. Lady goes to right, man goes to left.

LEAD COUPLE. In square dancing refers to the couple indicated by the caller to move (lead out) and progress through a figure with another couple, as in a visiting couple dance. If two couples are requested to lead out, there are two lead couples. Also called Active Couple.

LEAP. A transfer of weight from one foot to the other foot. Push off with a spring and land on the ball of the other foot, letting the heel come down, and bend the knee to absorb the shock. Refer to page 39.

LEFT FACE TURN. Dancer turns individually one full turn to the left or counterclockwise.

LEFT REVERSE OPEN POSITION. A variation of the closed position in which the lady is turned counterclockwise to a position in front of but off center to the right of the man. Man leads forward on the left foot. Also referred to as Banjo or Swing position in Round Dance. Same as right parallel position in Social Dance. Refer to diagram on page 49.

LEFT SQUARE THROUGH. Square dance term. Same as square through (full), except begun with left hand grasp instead of right.

LINDY. Refer to pages 285, 286.

LINE. A type of formation. Dancers stand side by side, all facing in the same direction. Refer to page 47 for additional information and diagram.

LINE OF DIRECTION. Refers to the direction of movement of dancers around the circle. counterclockwise.

LOD. Symbols for Line of Direction. Refer to Line of Direction.

LONGWAY SET. Couples stand in a double line (file or parallel lines), men in one line and ladies in opposite line. Partners face in a double line or partners face head of set in a double file. This is also known as a Contra Formation. Refer to page 47 for additional information and diagram of a longway set.

MAGIC STEP. Arthur Murray Magic Step. Refer to Magic Step Series, page 277.

MAMBO. Refer to page 330.

MAZURKA. Step left (slight stamp), bring right up to left with a cut step displacing left, hop right while bending knee so that left foot approaches right ankle. Refer to page 41 for additional analysis and musical notations.

MEASURE. Refer to page 38.

MERENGUE. Refer to page 332.

METER. Refers to time in music or group of beats to form the underlying rhythms within a measure. Refer to page 37.

NOTE VALUES. Refer to page 37.

NOVELTY DANCES. Twist, Watusi, and others. Refer to page 334.

OCEAN WAVE. Square dance term. A line of dancers, usually four, facing in alternate directions, join hands and balance, e.g., step or rock, forward and back. Counts 1, 2 for forward movement, 2, 3 for backward movement.

ONCE AND A HALF. Square dance term. Executed during a grand right and left. Beginning with partner, in position opposite home, men take a right forearm grasp with partner, turns her one full time clockwise and pass by her, in regular grand right and left direction, to the next lady. Turn her in same manner with a left forearm grasp. Continue turning ladies with a forearm grasp until caller directs dancers otherwise.

ONE MORE CHANGE. Square dance term. Patter at the end of a Do-Si-Do No. 1 which indicates that the dancers shall make one more complete cycle and end with partner.

ONE STEP. Refer to Shuffle, page 40.

OPEN POSITION. Partners stand side by side, lady on man's right facing in the same direction. Man's right arm is around lady's waist. Lady's left hand rests on man's right shoulder. Man holds lady's right hand in his left, arms extend easily forward. In social dance also called conversation position. Refer to diagram on page 49.

OPPOSITE. The person standing in opposite position across the set.

PARALLEL POSITION. Refers to right or left Parallel position. Right Parallel is the same as Left Reverse Open Position. Left Parallel is the same as Right Reverse Open Position.

PARTNER. Lady to immediate right of man and man to immediate left of lady. Also called Taw, Honey, etc.

PAS-DE-BASQUE.
3/4 time. Leap to side on left foot (ct. 1), leap right across left (ct. 2), leap left in place (ct. 3).
2/4 time. Leap to side on left (ct. 1), leap right across left (ct. and), leap left in place (ct. 2), hold (ct. and).

PASS THROUGH. Two couples face. They move toward each other, each passing his opposite by the right shoulder and then wait for the next call.

PASS RIGHT THROUGH. See Pass Through.

PHRASE. Refer to page 38.

PICK UP TWO. Square dance term. Lead off couple adds a couple as they visit each home position progressing to the right around the set. Couple is always added between the lead off man and his left hand lady.

PIVOT. Turning clockwise or counterclockwise on balls of one or both feet.

PIVOT TURN. Step left pivoting clockwise (ct. 1), continuing in same direction, step right (ct. 2), step left (ct. 3), step right (ct. 4). Make one complete turn and finish in original direction. May also be done counterclockwise. Refer to Pivot Turn, pages 281, 282 for additional analysis and diagrams.

PIVOT TURN DIP. Step left, turn clockwise (ct. 1), step back on right continuing turn (ct. 2), step left facing forward (ct. 3), dip back on right foot, still facing forward (ct. 4).

POLKA. Hop right, step left forward, close right to left, step forward left. Repeat beginning hop left. Refer to page 40 for additional analysis and musical notations.

POSTURE. Refer to page 52.

PRESSURE LEAD. A lead in which extra pressure is exerted by the fingers, arm, or body in order to lead the lady into a particular position or step.

PROMENADE. Couples move counterclockwise around the set or large circle in promenade position (refer to Promenade Position for description). In Square Dance the man may give his partner a finishing whirl, bow and/or swing before resuming ready position facing the center of the set. Refer to Twirl.

PROMENADE BUT DON'T SLOW DOWN. Square dance term. Couples continue promenading until caller gives the next call. They do not stop in home position.

PROMENADE EIGHT. Square dance term. All four couples promenade once around the set and return to home position.

PROMENADE INDIAN STYLE. Square dance term. Promenade one behind the other in single file back to place — lady in front, man behind. The call "promenade in Indian style" is usually followed by the call "Turn right back

and swing the girl behind you," the men turn around and swing the girl immediately behind. Refer to page 63 for the full call. Refer also to Turn Back.

PROMENADE INSIDE RING. Square dance term. Promenade counterclockwise around the inside of the square.

PROMENADE OUTSIDE RING. Square dance term. Promenade counterclockwise around the outside of the square.

PROMENADE POSITION. Partners stand side by side facing line of direction. The lady stands to the right of the man. The man holds the lady's right hand in his right and her left in his left. The man's right arm is crossed above the lady's left arm. In some sections of the country it is customary for the man to cross his right arm underneath the lady's left arm. The promenade position is also referred to as the skater's position. Refer to diagram on page 49.

PROMENADE RED HOT. Square dance term. Refer to Red Hot.

PURSUIT WALTZ. Refer to page 297.

PUSH STEP. Moving to the left, beginning left, step (chug) to the side (ct 1), bring right toe close to left instep and push right foot away from body (ct. and). Repeat pattern. The push step is similar to a buzz step except that the action is taken to the side instead of in a turning or circling movement.

RED HOT. Square dance term. Executed during a promenade by all four couples. Men release lady's right, walk partner to center with left forearm grasp, men move forward to meet right hand lady with right forearm, turn once around clockwise to meet partner, turn partner with left once and a half counterclockwise, face corner, turn corner with the right once clockwise. move back to partner with a left, turn once around counterclockwise. Wait for caller's directions.

REEL. A figure used in longway dances. Head couple meets in middle of set and hook right elbows, turn once and a half around. Man faces ladies' line, lady faces men's line. Couple separates and the head man hooks left elbows with second lady in line, head lady hooks left elbow with second man in line and turn once around. Head couple returns to middle of set and hook right elbows, turn once and return to respective lines to swing third dancer. Repeat the "reeling action" until head couple reaches the foot of the set.

RE-SASHAY. After having done a Half Sashay (refer to Half Sashay for description) dancers retrace steps to original positions. Often the call " go all the way around" is given following a re-sashay. To "go all the way around" dancers, beginning in original positions, encircle each other once and back to position. Men generally move in front of partner first. Dancers usually face center of set while traveling on any variation of a sashay.

REVERSE LINE OF DIRECTION. Refers to the direction of movement of dancers around the circle clockwise. Dancers move in the opposite direction from the line of direction.

REVERSE OPEN POSITION. From an open social dance position, facing line of direction, partners turn in toward each other to face reverse line of direction, but to not change arm or hand positions. Refer to diagram on page 50.

REVERSE VARSOUVIANNA POSITION.
From varsouvianna position, facing the line of
direction, release left hands, still holding right
hands the lady moves out to the right and
around the man clockwise until she comes to a
position a little behind him and to his left side.
Her right arm is around his shoulders and she
takes his left hand in front. For social dance the
right arm is sometimes extended behind partner
at waist level and takes partner's right hand at
the right side. Refer to diagram, page 50.

RHYTHMIC PATTERN. Refer to page 37.

RIGHT AND LEFT EIGHT. Same as Right
and Left Grand.

RIGHT AND LEFT FOUR. Refer to Right and
Left Through.

RIGHT AND LEFT THROUGH. Two couples
face, extend right hands to opposite, pass opposite's right side to exchange positions, courtesy
turn in opposite position. Repeat back to place
only if called.

RIGHT FACE TURN. Dancer turns individually one full turn to the right or clockwise.

RIGHT HANDS ACROSS. Men or ladies join
right hands in center, and turn clockwise. Usually followed by the call "Back with the left"
which means break with the right, join left
hands in the center and turn counterclockwise.

RIGHT HAND LADY. Square dance term. The
lady in the couple on the right, not partner.

RIGHT REVERSE OPEN POSITION. A variation of the closed position in which the lady
is turned clockwise to a position in front of but
off center to the left of the man. Man leads
forward on the left foot. This position is also
referred to as the side car position in round
dance and to left parallel position in social
dance. Refer to diagram on page 50.

RING. Circle formed by two or more dancers
joining hands, usually moving left unless otherwise indicated.

RIP AND SNORT. Square dance term. The
couple indicated leads down the center and goes
under the arch formed by the opposite couple.
The lead couple only, drops inside hands and
leads the entire circle under the arch, the man
going to the left, lady right. The couple forming
the arch rings the dishrag and the circle is back
in its original position. All hands remain joined
throughout movement except as indicated above
for the lead couple.

RLOD. Symbols for Reverse Line of Direction.
Refer to Reverse Line of Direction.

ROCK STEP. Step (rock) forward left (ct. 1),
step (rock) backward (ct. 2). For social dance
see foxtrot, page 275, and Lindy, page 285.

RUMBA. Refer to page 310.

RUN. Refer to page 39.

RUNNING STEP. Refer to RUN, page 39.

RUSSIAN POLKA. The customary polka hop is
omitted. Step left (ct. 1), close right to left (ct.
and), step left (ct. 2), hold (ct. and). Repeat
beginning right.

SAMBA. Refer to page 317.

SASHAY. Dancers move once around each other.
The man moves sideways to the right and behind the lady and the lady moves sideways to
the left and in front of the man. Dancers face
the center of the circle throughout the Sashay.

SASHAY HALF WAY AROUND. The man
moves sideways to the right and behind the lady

as the lady moves left and sideways in front of
the man to exchange places. Dancers do not
encircle each other. This call is often followed
by "Re-Sashay," which means for dancers to
simply retrace their steps to original places.

SCHOTTISCHE. Step left (ct. 1), step right
(ct. 2), step left (ct. 3), hop left (ct. 4). Repeat
beginning right. Refer to page 34 for additional
directions and musical notations.

SCISSOR KICK. Kick the left leg (stiff legged)
forward (ct. 1), exchange by kicking the right
leg forward and left back to place (ct. and).
Continue action.

SEE SAW. Square dance term. Man moves to
his right around behind, then in front of partner
and back to home position.

SEMI OPEN POSITION. A term referring to a
position half way between open and closed
position.

SET. Refers to a group formation. In square
dancing it is used to refer to the arrangement
of the four couples in a "square" formation.
The terms "Set" and "Square" are used interchangeably in referring to this formation. Set
is also used to describe other formations. For
example, set of three, longway set, etc. Refer
to page 48 for additional information and
diagram.

SHOULDER WAIST POSITION. Partners
face. Man places his hands at the lady's waist
far enough around to be able to support her
firmly. Lady places her hands around the sides
of the man's shoulders. They make the arms
bow out so as to provide a controlled form. Both
should lean back slightly. This is also called
Peasant Position. Refer to diagram on page 50.

SHUFFLE. An easy light one step keeping feet
lightly in contact with the floor as they move.
Principal step used in square dancing. Refer to
page 40 for additional description.

SICILIAN CIRCLE. A double circle couples
facing, lady is to man's right. Couples may be
numbered one, two, three, etc. All even numbered couples face line of direction while all odd
numbered couples face reverse line of direction.

SIDE BY SIDE POSITION. Refer to couple
position.

SIDES. Refers to couples two and four.

SIDE STEP. Refer to Step Close.

SIDE CAR POSITION. Refer to Right Reverse
Open Position.

SIDE COUPLES. Refer to couples two and four
in a set of four couples. Refer to page 48 for
additional information and diagram.

SIDE FOUR. Refer to couples two and four.

SIDE TWO COUPLES. Refers to couples two
and four in the set. Also called side four.

SKATER POSITION. Refer to Promenade Position, page 50.

SKIP. Refer to page 39.

SLIDE. Refer to page 39.

SPLIT THE RING. Square dance term. The
lead off couple goes down the center of the
square and divides the opposite couple. The
lady goes to her right, the man to the left, and
move around the outside of the set to original
position.

SQUARE. The formation for square dancing. A
square is composed of four couples, each standing on the imaginary sides of a square, facing
the center. Each couple stand with their backs

to one side of the room. Also called a set. For further information, refer to page 62.

SQUARE DANCE SET. Refer to Set.

SQUARE THROUGH (Full). Square dance term. The Square Through is executed when two couples are facing. Couples move forward, take opposite's right hand, pull by, quarter turn to face partner, join left hands, pull by, quarter turn to face original opposite again, join right hands, pull by, make quarter turn to face partner, join left hands, pull by, wait for caller's directions.

SQUARE THROUGH (Half). Square dance term. The Half Square Through is executed when two couples are facing. Couples move forward, take opposite right hand, pull by, quarter turn to face partner, join left hands, pull by and wait for caller's directions. Note: This is one half of a full square through.

SQUARE THROUGH (Three quarters). Square dance term. The Three Quarters Square Through is executed when two couples are facing. Couples move forward, take opposite's right hand, pull by, quarter turn to face partner, join left hands, pull by, quarter turn to face original opposite again, join right hands, pull by and wait for caller's directions. Note: This is three quarter of a full Square Through.

STAMP. Place the ball of one foot firmly on the floor, accenting the placement. The weight is not usually transferred to the foot taking the stamp, however, in some instances it does take the weight.

STAR PROMENADE. Square dance term. Formed with men in a star in the center, free arm around partner's waist, partners face same direction. Ladies may place arm around partner's waist, on near shoulder, or hook elbows as the call may indicate. Couples move in same direction.

STAR THROUGH. Square dance term. Executed when two couples are facing. Man takes opposite lady's left in his right and walks forward to exchange places with her as she walks under man's raised right arm. The person with whom you star becomes your partner. Couples end with new partner on the man's right and facing the other couple which is made up of your original partners.

STEP CLOSE. Step sideward left (ct. 1), close right to left, transferring weight to right (ct. 2). Note: The right foot does not draw along the floor but moves freely into place beside left.

STEP HOP. Step on the left foot (ct. 1) and hop on the same foot (ct. and).

STEP SWING. Step left (ct. 1), swing right across in front of left (ct. 2). Repeat movement beginning right.

STRIDE POSITION. Legs straight, feet apart.

SWAP AND TRADE. Swing the left hand lady.

SWING. Right or left hand swing: The lady and man clasp right (or left) hands and swing around clockwise. Forearm grasp may be used. Two hand swing: The lady and man face each other, join both hands and one step or shuffle once around clockwise. The elbows are held in close to the body. Waist swing: Couples take swing position (left reverse open position) and turn clockwise with a shuffle step, two-step, or buzz step. A waist swing is generally twice around. When they stop swinging, the man should steady the girl with his right hand at her back until their momentum has stopped. Both should lean back slightly for the swing. Buzz Step Swing: Couples take swing position. Outer borders of right feet side by side, move clockwise using a buzz step. Refer to Buzz Step for analysis of this movement. The action of the feet, in the buzz step, is like pushing a scooter. The lady leans back against the man's right hand to help gain momentum in the swing. Forearm swing: Refer to Forearm Grasp.

SWING POSITION. Modified left reverse open position except dancers tend to face each other. Refer to diagram of left reverse open position, page 49.

SWING OUT POSITION. Refer to Flirtation Position.

SWING THROUGH. From a four hand ocean wave formation, the end dancers hook right elbows with the dancer next to them and turn half around, next the center two dancers hook left elbows and turn half around. The entire sequence, e.g., ends half turn, then center half turns on single call "swing through."

TANGO. Refer to page 299.

TAW. Partner.

TEMPO. Refer to page 38.

THREE QUARTER CHAIN. Square dance term. Ladies, as indicated by call, form a right hand star, in the center of the set, move clockwise past two positions in the set, extend left hand to next man, man courtesy turns lady or as directed by call.

THREE STEP TURN. One complete turn made in three steps. The turn may be made to the left (counterclockwise) or to the right (clockwise). To turn right, (clockwise); step right to side (ct. 1), pivot clockwise on right and step left to face opposite direction (ct. 2), pivot clockwise on left, and step right to side to face original direction (ct. 2). Hold the last count of 2/4 or 4/4 music. For 3/4 time, refer to Canter Rhythm, page 291.

THROW IN THE CLUTCH. Square dance term. Executed from an allemande thar or wrong way thar movement. On the call "throw in the clutch," dancers in the center retain hold on the star, but release hand with outside dancers. The star changes direction and moves forward while the dancers on the outside (ones released) continue in same direction, e.g., forward. Dancers then follow the next call.

TIP. Square dance term. One completed square dance call (sequence) is considered a "tip."

TRIPLE ALLEMANDE. Square dance term. Men turn corner lady with a left allemande and send her to the center. Ladies form a right hand star, move star clockwise, while men walk counterclockwise around star. Men again turn corner with left allemande one full turn, men move to center and form a right hand star. Star moves clockwise, as ladies walk counterclockwise around men star. Men again, third time, turn corner (original always) with left allemande one full turn and move into a grand right and left or wait for caller's directions. Refer to call on page 70.

TSCHERKESSIA. Cross left in front of right (ct. 1), step right to side (ct. 2), cross left behind right (ct. 3), step right to side (ct. 4). May also be done beginning "cross right in front of left."

TURN BACK. Square dance term.
1. Sometimes used as "Gents turn back and swing the girl behind you."
2. Other times used as "Gents step out and turn right back and go the other way." In this case the men step out of a single file circle turn around and move in an outside circle of their own clockwise. The ladies will keep moving counterclockwise. Refer to call Back Track, page 67.
3. Refer to Double Back Track.

TWINKLE STEP. Refer to page 279.

TWIRL. A term used to turn the lady. It is used in all types of dances. In square dance the lady always twirls clockwise but in other types of dance she may be twirled in either direction. The man may twirl the lady with either arm depending upon the figure preceding it. In 2/4 time the lady will take two steps or four to make the turn. In 3/4 time, she will take three. The couple may make the twirl in place or progressing forward in the line of direction.

TWO HAND SWING. Refer to Swings.

TWO STEP. Step left (ct. 1), close right to left (ct. 2), step left (ct. 3), hold (ct. 4). Refer to page 40 for further analysis and musical notations on the two-step as a folk or square dance fundamental.

TYROLIAN WALTZ. A series of waltz steps taken in line of direction. Beginning left, step diagonally forward to the left on the first waltz step; step diagonally forward to the right on the second waltz step. Repeat pattern. Partners tend to face away and toward each other, with alternate steps, as they glide forward.

VARSOUVIANNA POSITION. Couple face in line of direction. Lady in front and slightly to the right of the man. Man holds lady's left hand in his left at shoulder level. Man's right arm extends back of lady's shoulders and holds lady's raised right hand in his right. In social dance is sometimes called Jody Position. Refer to diagram on page 50.

WAGON WHEEL BREAK. Square dance term. Men turn corner with allemande left, give right to partner, use forearm grasp, turn once clockwise. Men star left in center as they spin turn partners once clockwise. Ladies hook left hand in men's right elbow. Couples move counterclockwise, in star promenade. Men break the star, couples back out, turning counterclockwise once and a quarter face partners in a single circle formation. Men give right to partners, left to next, and right to next (opposite lady). Execute one and a half turn plus spinning lady and form a star promenade. Continue as called.

WALK. Refer to page 38.

WALTZ. Refer to pages 41 and 291.

WALTZ BALANCE. Refer to balance, 3/4 time.

WEAVE THE RING. Same as grand right and left except that dancers do not touch hands in passing each other.

WHEEL AROUND. Square dance term. From the promenade position, couples wheel around as a unit to face in opposite direction. Men back up, lady moves forward around man. Dancers retain the promenade position hand hold.

WHEEL AND DEAL. Square dance term. From a line of four, e.g., two couples both facing the same direction, the left couple moves forward as the right hand couple turns counterclockwise, man as pivot point, to face in opposite direction, left hand couple immediately turns in behind the right hand couple. End in double file or column formation, with left hand couple behind right hand couple. Couple both face same direction.

WHIRL. Term used for waist-swing in Square Dance. Also refers to several, rather rapid, individual right or left face turns.

WHIRLAWAY (With a Half Sashay). Square dance term. Lady's left, in man's right, man whirls lady across in front. Lady executes a full left face turn as she moves from the man's right to his left side, dancers exchange places.

WRAP POSITION. The lady is at the right of the man. His right arm is around her waist and his hand holds her left hand. His left hand is holding her right hand in front. Refer to diagram on page 50.

BIBLIOGRAPHY

BOOKS

1. Alford, Violet, *Dances of France, III. The Pyrenees.* New York: Crwo Publishers, 1963.
2. Alford, Violet, *The Traditional Dance.* 36 Essex Street W. C. 2, London: Methven and Co. Lts., 1935.
3. American Association for Health, Physical Education and Recreation, *Materials for Teaching Dance, Volume II: Folk, Square, and Social Dance.* 1201 16th Street, N. W., Washington, D. C. 20036.
4. Ballwebber, Edith, *Group Instruction in Social Dance.* New York: A. S. Barnes and Co., 1938. (Out of Print).
5. Bauer, Lois and Barbara Reed, *Dance and Play Activities for the Elementary Grades.* New York: Chartwell House, Inc., 1953. Volume I for grades one to three; and Volume II for grades four to six.
6. Beliajus, V. F., *Dance and Be Merry.* Volume I and II. Evanston, Illinois; Summy-Birchard Co., 1940.
7. Bergquist, Nils W., *Swedish Folk Dances.* New York: A. S. Barnes and Co., 1928.
8. Bossing, Ed and Elsie Bossing, *Handbook of Favorite Dances.* Chicago: H. T. Fitz-simmons Co., 1955.
9. Briggs, Dudley T., *Thirty Contras from New England.* Burlington, Massachusetts: Dudley T. Briggs.
10. Burchenal, Elizabeth, *Folk Dances and Singing Games.* New York: G. Schirmer, 1922.
11. _____ *Folk Dances of Germany.* New York: G. Schirmer, 1938.
12. _____ *Folk Dances of Denmark.* New York: G. Schirmer, 1940.
13. _____ *Folk Dances from Old Homelands.* New York: G. Schirmer, 1922.
14. California Folk Dance Federation, *Folk Dances from Near and Far.* San Francisco: Folk Dance Federation of California. International Series; Volumes I-VII, 1946-1952; Volume A1 (30 basic dances); Volume A2 (33 beginner dances) 1962; Volume B1 (25 intermediate dances) 1959; Volume C1 (16 advanced dances) 1960.
15. _____ *Dances from Near and Far, International Folk Dance Series.* San Francisco: Folk Dance Federation of California. Beginner Dances, Volume A-1; Beginner Dances, Volume A-2; Intermediate Dances, Volume B-1; Advance Dances, Volume C-1.
16. Chochem, Corinne and Muriel Roth, *Palestine Dances.* New York: Behrman's Jewish Book House, 1941.
17. Chujoy, Anatole, *The Dance Encyclopedia.* New York: Thomas Yoseloff, Inc.
18. Clossin, Jimmy and Carl Hertzog, *West Texas Square Dances.* El Paso, Texas: 1949. (Note: This is a revised and enlarged edition of *Honor Your Partner* by Buck Stinson, 1948.)
19. Cole, *One Thousand Fiddle Tunes.* Chicago: M. M. Cole, 1940.
20. Covarrubias, Luis, *Regional Dances of Mexico.* Isabel La Catolica 30, Mexico, D. F.: Eugenio Fischgrund.
21. Czarnowski, Lucille and Jack McKay, *How to Teach Folk and Square Dancing.* 1965 Tenth Avenue, San Francisco, California: 1954.
22. Dannett, Sylvia and Frank Rachel, *Down Memory Lane.* New York: Greenberg Publisher, 1954.
23. Day, Mel, *Blue Book of Rounds.* Santa Barbara, California: Sets in order.

24. Duggan, Anne and Jeannette Schlotman and Abbie Rutledge, *Folk Dances of the British Isles*. New York: Ronald Press, 1948.

25. _____ *Folk Dances of European Countries*. New York: Ronald Press, 1948.

26. _____ *Folk Dances of Scandinavia*. New York: Ronald Press, 1948.

27. _____ *Folk Dances of the United States and Mexico*. New York: Ronald Press, 1948.

28. _____ *The Teaching of Folk Dance*. New York: Ronald Press, 1948.

29. Dunsing, Gretel and Paul Dunsing, *Dance Lightly*. Delaware, Ohio: Cooperative Recreation Service, 1946.

30. _____ *German Folk Dances*, Volume 1, Verlag Friedrich Hofmeister, Leipzig: 1936.

31. Durlacher, Ed., *Honor Your Partner*. New York: Devin, 1949.

32. Eisenberg, Helen and Larry Eisenberg, *And Promenade All*. 2403 Branch Street, Nashville, Tennessee.

33. _____ *The World of Fun Series of Recreational Recordings*. 810 Broadway, Nashville, Tennessee: The Methodist Publishing House, 1951.

34. Farwell, Jane, *Folk Dances for Fun*. Delaware, Ohio: Cooperative Recreation Service, Inc.

35. Ford, Henry, Mr. and Mrs., *Good Morning*. Dearborn, Michigan: Dept. R, Box 100.

36. Fox, Grace I. and Kathleen G. Merrill, *Folk Dancing in High School and College*. New York: Ronald Press, 1957.

37. Gadd, May, *Country Dances of Today*, Book 2. New York: 31 Union Square W., Country Dance Society of America, May 1951.

38. Gotcher, Les, *Hash 'n Breaks*. 14641 East Palm Avenue, La Puente, California: Les Gotcher Enterprises, 1961.

39. _____ *Caller's Material*. A monthly publication of "Tips to Callers." 14641 East Palm Avenue, La Puente, California: Les Gotcher Enterprises.

40. _____ *Textbook of American Square Dancing*. 14641 East Palm Avenue, Les Gotcher Enterprises, 1961.

41. Greggerson, Herbert F., *Herb's Blue Bonnet Calls*. Carrizo Lodge, Ruidoso, New Mexico: 1946.

42. Grim and Michaelis, *The Student Teacher in the Secondary School*. New York: Prentice Hall, Inc., 1953.

43. Haire, Frances H., *The Costume Book*, New York: A. S. Barnes, 1937.

44. Hall, J. Tillman, *Dance! A Complete Guide to Social, Folk and Square Dancing*. Belmont, California: Wadsworth Publishing Company, Inc., 1963.

45. Hamilton, Frank, *American Round Dancing*. 462 No. Robertson Blvd., Los Angeles, California: Sets in order, 1956.

46. _____ *Introduction to American Round Dances*. 462 No. Robertson Blvd., Los Angeles, California: Sets in order.

47. _____ *Round Dance Manual* for callers, teachers, club committees, and dancers. 462 No. Robertson Blvd., Los Angeles, California: Sets in order.

48. Harbin, E. O., *The Fun Encyclopedia*. New York and Nashville: Abingdon-Cokesbury Press. (Out of print.)

49. Harris, Jane A., *File O' Fun*. Mixers, games and social recreation. Minneapolis, Minnesota: Burgess Publishing Co., 1962.

50. Heaton, Alma and Israel Heaton, *Ballroom Dance Rhythms*. Dubuque, Iowa: William C. Brown Company, 1961.

51. Herman, Michael, *Folk Dance Syllabus No. 1*. 108 West 16th Street, New York 11, New York: A. S. Barnes, 1930. (Out of print.)

52. Herman, Michael, *Folk Dances For All*. New York: Barnes and Noble, Inc. 1947.

53. Hinman, Mary Wood, *Group Dances, Gymnastics and Folk Dances*, Volume IV, New York: A. S. Barnes, 1930. (Out of Print.)

54. Hipps, R. Harold and Wallace Chappell, *A World of Fun.* P.O. Box 871, Nashville, Tennessee: General Board of Education, Methodist Church, Division of the Local Church, 1959.

55. Holden, Rickey, *The Contra Dance Book.* Newark, New Jersey: American Squares, 1956.

56. _____ *The Square Dance Caller*, Newark, New Jersey: 1951.

57. _____ and Mary Vouras, *Greek Folk Dance.* Newark, New Jersey: Folkcraft Press, 1965.

58. Horst, Louis, *Pre-Classic Dance Forms.* New York: Dover Publications, 1940.

59. Hostetler, L. A., *Walk Your Way to Better Dancing.* New York: Revised 1952.

60. Hunt, Paul, and Charlotte Underwood, *Calico Rounds.* New York: Harper and Bros., 1955.

61. Jankovic, Ljubica and Danica Jankovic, *Dances of Yugoslavia.* New York: Crown Publishers, 1952.

62. Joukowsky, Anatol M., *The Teaching of Ethnic Dance.* New York: J. Lowell Pratt and Company, 1965.

63. Klausmeier, Herbert J., *Principles and Practices of Secondary School Teaching.* New York: Harper and Bros., 1953. Revised as: *Teaching in the Secondary School.* 1958.

64. Kozman, H. C., R. Cassidy, and O. Jackson Co., *Methods in Physical Education.* 551 Market Street, San Francisco, California: T. W. Stacey, Inc., 1967.

65. Kraus, Richard G., *Folk Dancing.* A guide for schools and colleges and recreation groups. New York: The MacMillan Company, 1962.

66. _____ and Lola Sadle, *Beginning Social Dance.* Belmont, California: Wadsworth Publishing Company, Inc., 1964.

67. Kulbitsky, Olga and Frank Kaltman, *Teacher's Dance Handbook. Number One: Kindergarten to Sixth Year.* Newark, New Jersey: Bhiebird Publishing Company, 1959.

68. Lapson, Dvora, *Dances of the Jewish People.* New York: The Jewish Education Committee of New York, 1954.

69. LaSalle, Dorothy, *Rhythms and Dances for Elementary Schools.* New York: Ronald Press, 1951.

70. Lawson, Joan, *European Folk Dances — Its National and Musical Characteristics.* 2 West 45th Street, New York 36, New York: Pitman Publishing Co., 1953.

71. Leeming, Joseph, *The Costume Book for Parties and Plays.* Philadelphia, New York: J. B. Lipincott Co., 1938.

72. Lidster, Miriam D. and Dorothy H. Tamburini, *Folk Dance Progressions.* Belmont, California: Wadsworth Publishing Company, Inc., 1965.

73. Lobsenz, Norman M. *is anybody happy.* Garden City, New York: Doubleday & Company, Inc., 1962.

74. *Materials for Teaching Dance Volum II, for Folk, Square and Social Dance.* Published for National Section on Dance by the American Association for Health, Physical Education and Recreation. 1201 Sixteenth Street N. W., Washington 6, D. C.

75. McIntosh, David Seneff, *Singing Games and Dances.* New York: Association Press, 1957.

76. McNair, Ralph J., *Western Square Dance.* Denver, Colorado: Oran V. Siller Co., 1941.

77. Mooney, Gertrude X., *Mexican Folk Dances for American Schools.* Coral Gables, Florida: University of Miami Press, 1957.

78. Morton, Virgil L., *The Teaching of Popular Dance.* New York: J. Lowell Pratt & Company, 1966.

79. Murray, Ruth Lovell, *Dance in Elementary Education.* New York: Harper and Row, Revised edition, 1963.

80. Murray, Arthur, *How to Become a Good Dancer*. New York: Simon and Schuster. Revised edition, 1959.

81. National Recreation Association, 8 West Eighth Street, New York 11, New York. Yearly catalog of selected publications (musical mixers, simple squares and social recreation materials.)

82. Neilson, N. P. and Winnifred Van Hagen, *Physical Education for Elementary Schools*. Ronald Press. Third edition, 1966.

83. O'Keefe, J. G., *A Handbook of Irish Dances*. Dublin: M. H. Gill and Sons, 1944.

84. Osgood, Bob, *Square Dancing for Beginners, Square Dancing for Intermediates, Square Dancing the Newer and Advanced, A Collection of Square Dance Breaks and Fillers, Square Dance Coordinates (Breads and Fillers), American Round Dancing* (a text), *Yearbooks of Square Dancing No. 1–8,* (includes calls and round dances since 1953). 462 No. Robertson Blvd., Los Angeles, California: Square Dance Publishers.

84. Osgood, Ginger, *Round Dances Up-to-date, Round 'N' Round, Dancing a Round, Today's Round Dances*. 462 No. Robertson Blvd., Los Angeles, California: Square Dance Publishers.

85. Owen, Lee, *American Square Dances of the West and Southwest*. Palo Alto, California: Pacific Books, 1949.

86. ———— and Viola Ruth, *Advanced Square Dances*. Palo Alto, California: Pacific Books, 1950.

87. Petrides, Theodore and Elfleida Petrides, *Folk Dances of the Greeks*. New York: Exposition Press, 1961.

88. Pinon, Roger and Henri Jamar, *Dances of Belgium*. London: Max Parrish and Company, 1953.

89. Riel, Fran and Beulah Davis, *Happy Dancing: Handbook of Dance Mixers*. 426 South Sixth Street, Minneapolis, Minnesota: Burgess Publishing Company, 1966.

90. Roberts, Henry M., *Roberts Rules of Order*. New York: Scott Foresman & Co., 1956.

91. Rohrbough, Lynn, *Handy II, Kit T, Kit R, Kit P*. Delaware, Ohio: Cooperative Recreation Service.

92. Ryan, Grace, *Dances of Our Pioneers*. New York: Ronald Press, 1939.

93. Sedillo, Mela (Brewster), *Mexican and New Mexican Folk Dances*. Albuquerque, New Mexico: University of New Mexico Press, 1938.

94. Shaw, Lloyd, *Cowboy Dances*. Caldwell, Idaho: The Caxton Printers, Ltd., 1939.

95. ———— *Cowboy Tunes*. Caldwell, Idaho: The Caxton Printers, Ltd., 1939.

96. ———— *The Round Dance Book*, Caldwell, Idaho: The Caxton Printers, Ltd., 1948.

97. Smith, Raymond, *Square Dance Handbook*, Volume I. Dallas, Texas: 1947.

98. ———— *Collection of Square Dances and Mixers, Supplement to Square Dance Handbook*. Dallas, Texas: 2nd edition, 1950.

99. Spicer, Dorothy Gladys. *The Book of Festivals*, New York: The Woman's Press, 1937.

100. Sumrall, Bob, *Do-Si-Do*. Abilene, Texas: 1948.

101. Tolman, Beth and Ralph Page, *The Country Dance Book*. Weston, Vermont: The Countryman Press, 1937.

102. Turner, Margery J., *Dance Handbook*. Englewood Cliffs, New Jersey: Prentice-Hall, 1959.

103. Valley of the Sun, *Arizona Style of Square Dancing*. Phoenix, Arizona: Square Dance Organization, Inc.

104. Vannier, Maryhelen, *Methods and Materials in Recreation Leadership*. Philadelphia: W. B. Saunders Company, 1956. (Chapter 6). Revised edition, 1966.

105. ———— and Mildred Foster, *Teaching Physical Education in Elementary Schools*. Philadelphia: W. B. Saunders Company, 1958. Second edition (Chapter 10). Third edition, 1963.

106. Veloz and Yolanda, *Tango and Rumba*. New York: Harper and Bros., 1938.

107. Wakefield, Eleanor Ely. *Folk Dancing in America*. New York: J. Lowell Pratt & Company, 1966.

108. White, Betty, *Ballroom Dancebook for Teachers*. New York: David McKay Company, Inc., 1962.
109. _____ *Latin American Dance Book*. New York: David McKay Company, Inc., 1958.
110. _____ *Teen Age Dance Book*. New York: David McKay Company, Inc., 1952. Revised edition, 1963.
111. _____ *Teen Age Etiquette*. New York: David McKay Company, Inc., 1956.
112. Witzig, Louise, *Dances of Switzerland*. New York: Chanticleer Press, 1949.
113. Wright, A. P. and Wester Wright, *How to Dance*. New York: Doubleday & Company, 1958.
114. Zielinski, Stefan J., *Dances of Poland*. Chicago: W. H. Safewski Music and Publishing Company, 1953.

MAGAZINES

115. *American Squares*, Arvid Olson, editor, 6400 N. Leoti Avenue, Chicago 46, Illinois.
116. *Country Dancer*, The Country Dance Society of America, 31 Union Square West, New York, New York.
117. *Folk Dancer, The*, Michael Herman, editor, 108 W. 16th Street, New York City, New York. Back issues available. Not currently published.
118. *Foot Notes*, Folk Dance Federation of Washington, P.O. 455, Mercer Island, Washington.
119. *Journal of American Association of Health, Physical Education & Recreation*, 1201 Sixteenth Street N. W., Washington, D.C.
120. *Let's Dance*, Folk Dance Federation of California, Inc., Room 213, 1095 Market Street, San Francisco, California 94103.
121. *New England Caller*, Charles Baldwin, editor. 1621 Hancock Street, Quincy 69, Massachusetts.
122. *Northern Junket*, Ralph Page, editor, 117 Washington Street, Keene, New Hampshire.
123. *Recreation Magazine*, National Recreation Association, 8 West Eighth Street, New York 11, New York.
124. *Rosin the Bow*, Rod LaFarge, editor. 115 Cliff Street, Halidon, New Jersey. No longer published.
125. *Sets In Order*, the official magazine of Square Dancing. 462 No. Robertson Blvd., Los Angeles, California 90048.
126. *Square 'n Round Magazine*, Les Gotcher, editor. Les Gotcher Enterprises, 14641 East Palm Avenue, La Puente, California.
127. *Viltis*, Box 1226, Denver 1, Colorado, 80201.

RECORDS

I. **Suggested Sources for Records**

Try your local dealer first. Some of the listed Record Companies also sell dance records other than their own label.

A. **Record Companies**

1. Aqua Record Co.*, 960 Westlake Avenue, Seattle 9, Washington.
2. Burns Record Company, 755 Chicadee Lane, Stratford, Connecticut.
3. Capitol Records, Arthur Murray Ballroom Dance Series, Hollywood, California.
4. Columbia Records, 1473 Barnum Avenue, Bridgeport, Connecticut.
5. Educational Activities, Inc., P.O. Box 392, Freeport, New York 11520.
6. Educational Dance Recordings, Inc., P.O. Box 6062, Bridgeport, Connecticut.
7. Electro Vox, 5546 Melrose Avenue, Hollywood, California.
8. Evans Records, Chartwell House, Inc., 280 Madison Avenue, New York 16, New York.
9. Folk Dancer Record Service, P. O. Box 201, Flushing, Long Island, New York.
10. Folkraft Records, 1159 Broad Street, Newark, New Jersey.
11. Folkways Records, 117 West 46 h Street, New York City, New York.

12. Grenn Records, Inc., P.O. Box 16, Bath, Ohio.
13. Hoctor Records, Waldwich, New Jersey.
14. Imperial Records, 137 No. Western Avenue, Los Angeles, California.
15. Lloyd Shaw Records, Inc., Box 203, Colorado Springs, Colorado.
16. MacGregor, 729 South Western Avenue, Hollywood, California.
17. Merrbach Record Service, 323 West 14th Street, Houston, Texas.
18. Methodist Publishing House, 150 Fifth Avenue, New York, New York.
19. Old Timer Record Co., Inc., 708 E. Weldon Avenue, Phoenix, Arizona.
20. Pioneer Records, 2005 Labranch, Houston, Texas.
21. Roper Records, The Specialists in Dance Music, 43–48 48th Street, Long Island City, New York 11104.
22. Russell Records, Educational Series, Ventura, California.
23. Scandinavian Music Co., Berkeley 2, California.
24. Sets in Order Records*, 462 No. Robertson Blvd., Los Angeles, California.
25. Victor Records Radio Corp. of America, Camden, New Jersey.
26. Western Jubilee Master Record Service*, 1210 E. Indian School Road, Phoenix, Arizona.
27. Windsor Records, 5528 No. Rosemead Blvd., Temple City, California.
* Serves as an outlet for other dance records, also.

B. **Record Shops Specializing in Dance Records**
    1. Dance Craft, 1406 West Broadway, Vancouver, B.C., Canada.
    2. Berliner Music Shop, 154 Fourth Avenue, New York, New York.
    3. Canadian F.D.S. Audio Vision Aids, 605 King St. W., Toronto 28, Ontario, Canada.
       Folklore Imports, 4220 9th Avenue N. E., Seattle, Washington.
    4. Festival Folkshop, 161 Turk Street, San Francisco 2, California.
    5. Hall's Record Roundup, 2323 E. Evans Avenue, Denver 10, Colorado.
    6. The Hitchin' Post, 11736 95th Street, Edmonton, Alberta, Canada.
    7. Merrbach Record Service, 323 W. 14th Street, Houston, Texas.
    8. P. A. Kennedy Co., Ltd., Box 816, Brandon, Manitoba, Canada.
    9. The Record Center, 1614 North Pulaski, Chicago, Illinois.
    10. The Record Groove, 11952 S. E. Division, Portland, Oregon.
    11. Record Land, Thomas Mall, East Thomas Road, Phoenix, Arizona.
    12. Square Dance Distributors, 1815 Douglas Street, Omaha 2, Nebraska.

II. **Selected Records for Square Dance (with calls)**
Records *with calls* are excellent supplementary teaching aids. They should never, however, be considered a substitute for active instruction and calling by the teacher. Records with calls act as supplementary teaching aids in three ways: (1) for drills on basic techniques, (2) for grading and evaluation, and (3) as "assists" in learning to call. *Note:* Recommending a selected group of records with calls is possible but somewhat impractical since any such group becomes obsolete rather rapidly due to technical advances and current demands in musical style and taste. The best approach is to *first* check your local outlet for current and available records, *second*, write directly to one or several record companies for current catalogues to obtain the latest available listings.

The following suggested recordings are examples of the type of material available:
1. *Basic Square Dancing No. 1 First Steps in Square Dancing*, Caller – Bob Ruff, Sets in Order LP 4012. For the Beginning Teacher.
2. *Student Dancer No. 1*, Caller – Bob Ruff, Sets in Order LP 4002. Written instructions including description of basic figures. It is excellent material for beginner groups. Birdie in Cage, Seven Hands Around, Texas Star, The Route, Inside Out Outside In, Alabama Jubilee, Four Gents Star, Arkansas Traveler.
3. *Square Dancing for the Student Dancer No. 2*, Caller – Bob Ruff. Sets in Order LP 4005. Written instructions including description of basic figures. Box the Gnat, Back Track, Pass Thru, Allemande Thar, Allemande A, Allemande O, Cross Trail Thru, Pull Away With Half Sashay, Ends Turn In, Wheel Around, Box the Flea,

Red Hot, Throw in the Clutch, Dixie Chain, Bend the Line, Square Thru, Back Track, California Twirl.

4. *Square Dancing in Hi-Fi*. Caller—Arnie Kronenberger. Warner Bros. Records W 1301. Singing calls and pattern calls at intermediate level.
5. *Requested Square Dances*. Caller — Bob Van Antwerp. MacGregor 1206.
6. *Bill Castner Square Dancing*. Caller — Bill Castner.
7. *Dance-A-Tape Co.*, Less Gotcher Enterprises, 14641 E. Palm Avenue, La Puente, California. Square Dance Programs on tape.
8. *Andy Andrews Calls 'em Wild*. Caller — Andy Andrews. Blue Star LP 1003.

III. Selected Records for Square Dance (without calls)

Recommending a selected group of records *without calls* is possible but somewhat impractical since any such group becomes obsolete rather rapidly due to technical advances and current demands in musical style and taste. The best approach is to *first* check your local outlet for current and available records; *second*, write directly to one or several record companies for current catalogues to obtain the latest available listings.

The following selected titles are square dance tunes that have become traditionally associated with square dancing in America:

Tom and Jerry	Leather Britches	Boil Them Cabbage Down
Devil's Dream	Eighth of January	Hell Amongst the Yearlings
Earl's Hoedown	Old Joe Clark	Orange Blossom Special
Jerry's Hoedown	Chinese Breakdown	Black Mountain Rag

IV. Selected Records for Folk Dancing

Folk Dance Funfest, F.D.1, Educational Dance Recordings Inc., Kinderpolka, Greensleeves, La Raspa, Chimes of Dunkirk, Carrousel, Circassian Circle, Norwegian Mountain March, Gustaf's Skoal, Noriu Miego, Come Let Us Be Joyful, Cshebogar, I See You.

Dancing 'Round the World, F.D.2, Educational Dance Recordings Inc., Jessie Polka, To Ting, Napolean, Seven Steps, Maitelitz, Cumberland Square Eight, Masquerade, Hora, Doudlebska Polka, Troika, Seljancica Kolo, Road to the Isles.

Folk Dance Festival, F.D.3, Educational Dance Recordings Inc., St. Bernard's Waltz, Miserlou, Oklahoma Mixer, Cotton Eyed Joe, Sellenger's Round, Eide Ratas, Portland Fancy, Cherkassiya, Kalvelis, Mexican Waltz, Korobushka, Puttjenter.

V. Selected Records for Social Dance

Recordings* for social dances are perhaps the most unstable of all records in terms of tempo, musical style, and "current sound." It is essential that the teacher check with local record outlets for appropriate musical selections in this area of dance.

Although an unstable area, "standards" or records that are recognized by musicians and public alike as "favorites" continue through several generations. These are often combined and published specifically for teaching purposes. The following are suggested as a point of departure.

Dance Along With Mitch. Hector LP 3083.
    Cha Cha, Merengue, Tango, Rumba, Bossa Nova, Mambo, Samba.
Let's Dance. Hector LP 3067.
    Fox Trot, Waltz, Lindy, Rumba, Tango, Cha Cha.
Arthur Murray's Music for Dancing. RCA-Victor LPM 1909.
    Fox Trot, Merengue, Tango, Mambo, Samba, Rumba, Cha Cha, Rock 'n' Roll, Waltz.
Your Guy Lombardo Medley. Capitol T739.
    Fox Trot, Waltz, etc.
Spotlight on Dancing. Windsor WLP 310.
    Albums 1 thru 4. Contain music for all areas of social dance.
The Standard Thirteen for Dancing. Roper RLP 1007A.
    Waltz, Fox Trot, Swing, Peabody, Polka.

---

* Refer to page 381 for record sources.

INDEX